PRAIRIE DIRECTORY OF NORTH AMERICA
THE UNITED STATES AND CANADA
by
Charlotte Adelman
&
Bernard L Schwartz

FIRST EDITION

A LAWNDALE ENTERPRISE BOOK

Prairie Directory of North America
The United States and Canada
Copyright © 2001
by
Charlotte Adelman
All Rights Reserved

ISBN 0-9715096-0-3

Library of Congress Catalog Card Number: 2001098353

Manufactured in Canada by Kromar Printing Ltd, 725 Portage Rd, Winnipeg, MB R3G0M8

Lawndale Enterprises ·P.O. Box 561 · Wilmette, Illinois 60091-0561 · USA

On the internet: http://www.lawndaleenterprises.com

Publisher's Cataloging-in-Publication

Adelman, Charlotte, 1937-
   Prairie directory of North America : the United
States and Canada / Charlotte Adelman & Bernard L.
Schwartz. -- 1 st ed.
   p. cm.
   Includes bibliographical references and index.
   LCCN 2001098353
   ISBN 0-9715096-0-3

   1. Prairies--United States--Directories. 2. Prairies
--Canada--Directories. 3. Savannas--United States--
Directories. 4. Savannas--Canada--Directories.
I. Schwartz, Bernard L., 1933- II. Title.

QH104.A34 2001   577.4'4'0257
                         QBI01-201462

ABBREVIATIONS USED

ANHC	Arkansas Natural Heritage Commission
BCSWCD	Bureau County Soil and Water Conservation Dept
BLM	Bureau of land Management
CDOW	Colorado Dept of Wildlife
DNP	Division of Nature Preserves
DNR	Department of Natural Resources
DOT	Department of Transportation
DU	Ducks Unlimited
EPA	Environmental Protection Agency
IDNR	Indiana Department of Natural Resources
IDOT	Illinois Department of Transportation
INHF	Iowa Natural Heritage Foundation
KDOT	Kansas Department of Transportation
KDWP	Kansas Dept of Wildlife and Parks
MFWP	Montana Fish Wildlife and Parks
MNA	Michigan Nature Association
NA	Natural Area
NDGF	North Dakota Game and Fish Dept
NDPR	North Dakota Parks and Recreation
NGPC	Nebraska Game and Park Commission
NPAT	Native Prairie Assoc of Texas
NPS	National Park System
NWA	National Wildlife Area
NWR	National Wildlife Refuge
ODWC	Oklahoma Dept of Wildlife Conservation
OTRD	Oklahoma Tourism and Recreation Dept
PFRA	Prairie Farm Rehabilitation Administration
PPRI	Prairie Plains Resource Institute
SIU	Southern Illinois University
SNA	Scientific and Natural Areas
TNC	The Nature Conservancy
TPE	The Prairie Enthusiasts
TPWD	Texas Parks and Wildlife Dept
USFS	United States Forest Service
USFWS	United States Fish & Wildlife Service
USCE	United States Corp of Engineers
WA	Wildlife Area
WDOT	Wisconsin Department of Transportation
WGFD	Wyoming Game and Fish Dept
WMD	Wetland Management District
WSPHS	Wyoming State Parks and Historical Sites

STATE ABBREVIATIONS

AZ	Arizona
AK	Arkansas
AL	Alabama
CO	Colorado
CA	California
GA	Georgia
FL	Florida
IA	Iowa
IL	Illinois
IN	Indiana
KS	Kansas
KY	Kentucky
LS	Louisiana
MA	Massachuettes
MN	Minnesota
MO	Missouri
MS	Mississippi
MT	Montana
ND	North Dakota
NE	Nebraska
NM	New Mexico
NY	New York
OH	Ohio
OR	Oregon
PA	Pennsylvania
SD	South Dakota
TN	Tennessee
TX	Texas
WI	Wisconsin
WY	Wyoming

PROVINCE ABBREVIATIONS

AB	Alberta
MB	Manitoba
ON	Ontario
SK	Saskatchewan

HOW TO USE THIS BOOK

This book is intended as a reference for people interested in seeing a prairie, including nature lovers, family and friends, schoolteachers, photographers, artists, hikers, bikers and tourists. We have attempted to include every public prairie and savanna that exists in the prairie bioregion, the geological area that consists of the Great Plains and the tallgrass prairies. Also, we included prairies that lie outside of this bioregion. Ironically, although the prehistoric prairie is almost gone, we found the numbers of individual prairie remnants or restorations so numerous that we could not achieve our goal. However, we believe that this book presents a very good start in this kind of definitive listing.

Space limitations and sometimes difficulties in obtaining information, prevented us from listing each prairie's complete facilities and the fascinating background data regarding the flora and fauna and naturalistic and historical aspects. For more in-depth information about a site, please refer to the contacts listed. As a further caveat, we note that changes may have occurred regarding our information, including visitation policies and who to contact and how. To facilitate obtaining new or corrected telephone numbers, we have attempted to connect each prairie to its nearest city, as is usually required by telephone information.

Many directories list sites by alphabetical order, leaving it up to the reader to figure out their location in any given state or province. Because the states are broken up into counties or parishes, we assisted US prairie visitors by listing the prairies alphabetically under each county or parish.

We have tried our best to provide accurate information about the sites in this book. However, it is inevitable that some of the information has either changed or was incorrect to begin with or that we left out some prairies. Please inform us of inaccuracies or prairies we overlooked at the publisher PO Box or our website (see copyright page) or at e-mail address blschw@aol.com.

For more information about prairies and how to grow them, contact native plant societies, prairie organizations, environmental organizations, Departments of Natural Resources and Transportation, and libraries and bookstores for the many excellent books and magazine articles on the subject. Also, please see this book's bibliography.

Acknowledgements

We appreciate all the help that was given to us from all the Departments of Natural Resources, The Nature Conservancy (TNC), (National and States), Ducks Unlimited, the State and Province Department's of Transportation, and the many Conservation and Nature Organizations that are working to restore and preserve prairie and savanna areas. Without these organizations and the many individuals working to conserve the environment, and the help provided by those associated with the prairies listed it would have been impossible to complete this book.

Table of Contents

Illustrations

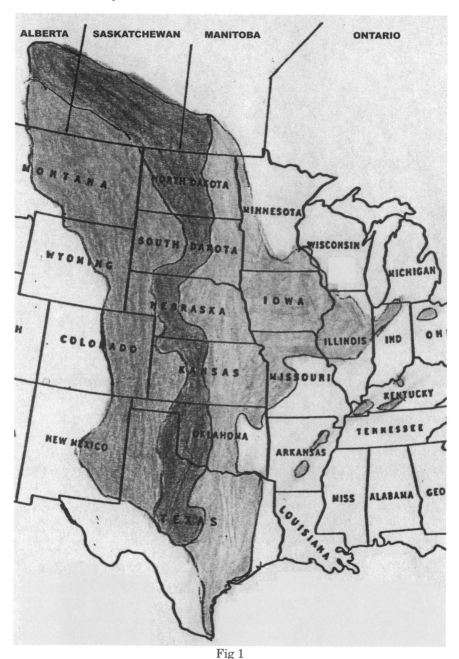

Fig 1

Map of North America showing the pre-settlement prairie bio-regions, with short-grass prairie to the west, tallgrass prairie to the east and mixed-grass prairie in between (See Section 1 introduction for a fuller explanation).

Map by Bernard L Schwartz

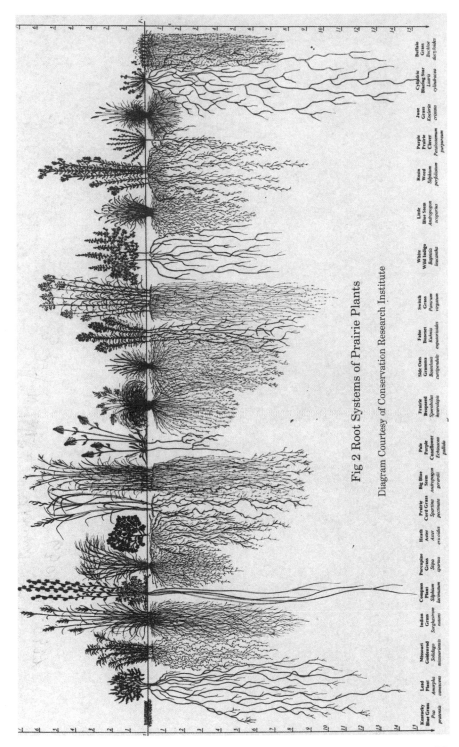

Fig 2 Root Systems of Prairie Plants

Diagram Courtesy of Conservation Research Institute

Fig 3
The Authors' backyard prairie/savanna. (Also see this book's cover)

Photo by Bernard L Schwartz

Section 1

UNITED STATES PRAIRIES & SAVANNAS

Between some 75 and 50 million years ago,[1] the uplift of the Rocky Mountains blocked humid east-blowing winds and created the Rocky Mountain "rain shadow." The region's aridity decimated any plants that required high moisture, but provided opportunities for plants with low moisture requirements to evolve and expand in the interior of North America. This brought about what we now call prairie plants, which had evolved deep roots (see Fig 2) and could survive for long periods of time on very little rainfall. The short grass prairie grasses appeared about 22 million years ago and became what we know as the Great Plains. Tallgrass prairie appeared about 7 million years ago[2].

Famed 1900s American ecologist, John T Curtis wrote: "The prairie is a plant community dominated by grasses rather than by trees as in a forest. Growing with the grasses are many other species of non-grassy herbs, which are known by the collective name 'forbs.' Many woody shrubs are present in the prairie as well, and, under certain circumstances, tree seedlings may also be found" and "less than one mature tree per acre."[3] Early 1800s prairie so dominated the United States that John Bradbury, an English botanist, wrote it covered "an extent of territory, which probably equals in area the whole empire of China."[4]

The almost seamless grassland was divided into three major grassy belts. Two belts, the short-grass prairie belt and the mid-grass prairie belt are considered the Great Plains. This prairie region covers 3.2 million square km, or 1.2 million square miles. Of this, 1.8 million square km, or 700,000 square miles lie in Canada and 1.4 million square km, or 500,000 square miles lie in the United States. The Great Plains constitutes about 18 percent of Canada and about 15 percent of the United States. The third belt, tallgrass prairie consists of 573,511 square km, or 221,436 square miles. The boundaries separating the belts change with climatic episodes of dryness and wetness. Because of the fluidity of each belt of prairie, any map is merely an approximation. (See Fig 1)

The oldest of the three belts of prairie is the short-grass prairie bordered on the west by the Rocky Mountains, although some prairie exists in the lower elevations and also west of the mountains. This belt occupies much of Montana, eastern Wyoming, eastern Colorado, western Kansas, the Oklahoma panhandle, northern Texas and eastern New Mexico and sometimes the Nebraska panhandle. It does not rely on fire, and flourishes under intensive grazing. Its unpredictable rainfall sometimes measures less than an annual 10 inches. "True" grassland animals live here, including Prairie Dog and Pronghorn and Swift

Fox and Blacktailed Jack Rabbit and Desert Cottontail.

The mid-grass or mixed-grass prairie belt, which lies between the short-grass and the tallgrass prairie, is an ever-shifting area due to climatic variation. Its irregular eastern border runs from north central Texas through Oklahoma, Kansas and Nebraska, northwest into west central North Dakota and South Dakota. Holding plant species from the other two belts, it forms the eastern boundary for "true" grassland animals and was the bison's major habitat.

The youngest belt, but the first to be exploited by the white settlers is tallgrass prairie with flowers that tower 12 feet. Before European settlement, prairie fire enabled this kind of prairie to hold its own against encroaching forest. It is uniquely home to the Plains Pocket Gopher and Franklin's Ground Squirrel and it once held wolf, buffalo and cougar and abundant elk. This wettest of all prairie belts is nonetheless classified as semi-arid. Tallgrass prairie runs from the bluestem prairie of southern Manitoba through eastern North Dakota and western Minnesota south to eastern Oklahoma and east central North and South Dakotas to southern Nebraska. Historically, prairie also occurred in parts of Iowa and the eastern edge of Kansas as well as outliers or fingers occurring in the interior of Texas and along the Gulf Coast in Texas and Louisiana.

The last major geological event in the area occurred between 12,000 and 25,000 years ago. A huge ice sheet covered the Great Plains in Canada and in parts of the northern United States. When the ice retreated it left behind glacial deposits, which vary in depth from a few meters to over 30 meters, cover the older sedimentary rocks, and created the areas of rolling topography in the plains. As the last glacier melted, the prairie expanded easterly into areas previously covered by ice.

The prairie is a huge part of our North American natural heritage. However, only 30 percent remains of the Great Plains' short-grass and mid-grass prairies, and Manitoba, Canada has lost 99.9 percent of its mixed grass prairie. Today only 1 percent of the tallgrass prairie survives, and in some individual states, such as Illinois, it is as little as 1/10 of 1 percent. Even states actively trying to conserve their remaining prairies, such as Minnesota and Missouri, work with less than 9 percent of their pre-settlement prairie. Amazingly, despite the huge losses – and virtual extinction - of this unique-to-North America native ecosystem, we continue building over, plowing up and degrading its few remaining remnants. Preserved prairies suffer a new threat: the invasion of "exotic" or non-native plants introduced accidentally and purposely for reasons ranging from erosion control to landscaping, which then require millions to be spent trying to eradicate them.

The destruction of this ecosystem is a real loss to modern man, as the prairie sod served as a "carbon sink" that absorbed large quantities of carbon dioxide.[2] Also, prairie, from its cottonwood trees to its forbs such as sunflower have a giant ability to collect toxins, lead, pesticides, explosives, and radioactive particles from the environment. [5 & 6] In the long term, the restoration and preservation of prairie and all the other native ecosystems in their native regions will be good for human health.

[1]Telephone conversations with Professor Gene Humpreys, University of Oregon Department of Geological Science.
[2]Various papers by Professor Gregory J. Retallack, University of Oregon Department of Geological Science.
[3] *The Vegetation of Wisconsin, An Ordination of Plant Communities* by John T. Curtis, University of Wisconsin Press. 1959
[4]*Travels in the Interior of America in the Years 1809, 1810, and 1811* by John Bradbury. Forward by Donald Jackson. 1986. See page 56 (footnote 27) and page 239.
[5] Cleanup-Flower Power by William Speed Weed. Audubon Nov/Dec 2000.
[6] Shaggy Grass Country by James H. Locklear. NEBRASKALand June 1997.

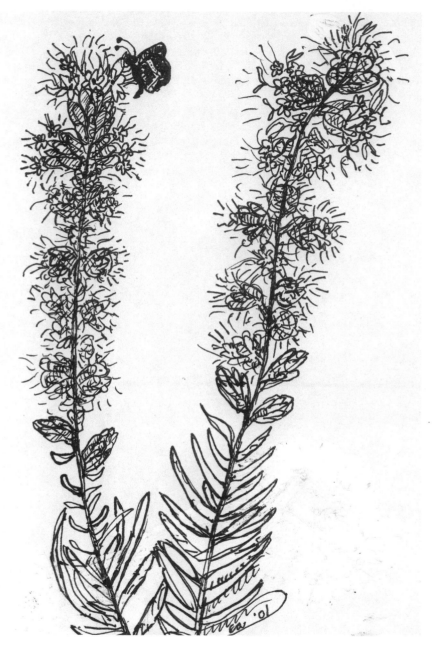

Fig 4
Prairie Blazing Star (with butterfly). See Fig 2 for root structure.

Illustration by Charlotte Adelman

ALABAMA

When Columbus discovered America, a mosaic of savanna and grass-land extended along North America's Coastal Plain from southeastern Virginia to Texas and south Florida. The prairie vegetation that covered about 1,000-square miles of Alabama was mostly in what in Alabama and Mississippi is called the Black Belt. Agriculture has consumed most of this landscape. A virgin prairie exists on the state line between Alabama and Mississippi, but it is not protected.

Although Alabama is not considered a prairie state, prairies can still be seen in the following Alabama locations:

Autauga County:
JONES BLUFF: 539-acre mosaic of tallgrass prairie and forested ravines that support deer and turkey. The Bluff is located between Montgomery and Selman in central Alabama. Call the US Corp of Engineers (USCE) at 334/872-9554.

Lawrence County:
PRAIRIE GROVE GLADES PRESERVE: 191-acres that support tall grasses such as little bluestem and prairie species unique to Alabama, Kentucky and Tennessee. The Preserve is north of Needmore, AL on a dirt road. Call TNC, AL in Birmingham, AL at 205/251-1155.

Sumter County:
OLD BLUFF PORT: 32-acres at an old steamboat cotton shipping port support a high quality remnant of Black Belt tallgrass prairie plus plants rare to Alabama. Call Richard Holland, University of West Alabama in Livingston, AL at 205/652-3415.

ARIZONA

Although Arizona is not considered a prairie state, throughout parts of Arizona, but generally above 3,500 feet, one may find broad areas dominated by three types of grasslands: Great Basin, Plains, and semi-desert grasslands. The first two grasslands are southwestern extensions of prairies found in the Great Basin and High Plains respectively. Semi-desert grasslands occur in central and southern Arizona and here grasses are often mixed in with succulent plants such as prickly-pear cactus, and yucca, or century plant. In other areas, small shrubs or desert "trees" such as mesquite grow with the grasses.

Below are some areas where grasslands and prairies can be found in Arizona.

Cochise County:

SAN BERNADINO/LESLIE CANYON NATIONAL WILDLIFE REFUGE: 2,309-acres in San Bernadino, 1,240-acres in Leslie Canyon. The San Bernadino Refuge has uplands of Chihuahuan desert scrub and desert grassland, while bottomlands are primarily mesquite bosque and fallow fields. The Leslie Canyon Refuge is dominated by shrubs and desert grasses such as sideoats grama, sandpaper bush, ocotillo and beargrass. The NWR is north of Douglas, AZ off Hwy 191. Call the NWR at 520/364-2104.

Coconio County:

HART PRAIRIE PRESERVE AND HOMESTEAD: 245-acre preserve containing short-grass prairie, surrounded by thousands of acres of forest and meadows, uncommon wildflowers, old growth ponderosa pine, a rare grove of willows, and crisp mountain air at an elevation of 8400-9000 feet. Good for bird watching, exploring ecological interactions between bats, birds, butterflies and bugs, and views of elk herds, black-tailed prairie dogs, and eagles. TNC, AZ manages the preserve, but is looking for financial help to permanently protect this site. The preserve is 14-miles form Flagstaff, AZ. Call TNC, AZ at 520/774-8892 (Flagstaff) or 602/220-0490 (Phoenix).

Pima County:

BUENOS AIRES NATIONAL WILDLIFE REFUGE: 115,000-acres of grasslands, cienegas (wetlands), riparian stream, and desert mountains. The US Fish and Wildlife Service (USFWS) is in the process of restoring the grasslands to their native condition. Overgrazing had left the ground bare and an alien grass (Lehmann's grass) was planted to protect against erosion, but it was a poor substitute for the diverse native grasses it replaced. When the native grasses disappeared so did some of the native animals. The USFWS is re-introducing the masked bobwhite quail and the pronghorn antelope. Many other birds and animals are found in the Refuge. The NWR is 38-miles south of Three

Points, AZ off Hwy 286. Call the USFWS at 520/823-4251.

EMPIRE-CIENEGA RESOURCE CONSERVATION AREA: 45,000-acres of public land in southeastern Pima County and northeastern Santa Cruz County. Tall, lush grass, six feet high in some locations, is the dominant feature here. Its high desert basin setting is ideally suited by elevation (4,500 feet) and rainfall (15 inches annually) to support some of the best examples of native grasslands in Arizona. The Area is south of Hwy 10 off Hwy 82. Call the Bureau of Land Management, Tucson, AZ at 520/722-4289.

Pinal County:
ORACLE STATE PARK, CENTER FOR ENVIRONMENTAL EDUCATION: 4,000-acre park located in the northeastern foothills of the Santa Catalina Mountains near the town of Oracle, AZ. Ranging from 3,500 to 4,500 feet in elevation, the park consists of oak grassland, riparian woodland, and mesquite scrub habitats, which contain a diversity of wildlife and plant species. This park's primary functions are to serve as an environmental education center and a wildlife refuge. Access to the Park is limited to groups by reservation only. Call the Park at 520/896-2425.

Santa Cruz County:
APPLETON-WHITTELL RESEARCH RANCH: 8,000-acre refuge has a broad diversity of native plant and animal species. It encompasses a mix of habitats including semi-desert grasslands, oak savanna, and oak woodland ribboned with riparian ecosystems. The Ranch is the largest, best remaining example of southwestern semi-desert grassland. Here they are studying the effects of grazing and non-grazing on grasslands. The Ranch is located in Elgin, AZ. Access is restricted For details call 520/455-5522.

EMPIRE-CIENEGA RESOURCE CONSERVATION AREA: (See Pima County above).

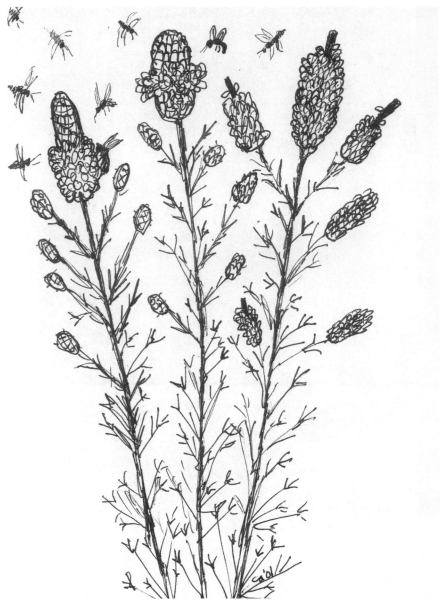

Fig 6

Purple prairie clover (with bees). See Fig 2 for root structure.

Illustration by Charlotte Adelman

ARKANSAS

Arkansas is the name of an Indian tribe. The French Jesuits learned of a tribe probably called Quapaw, or Oo-gaq-pa, which the Algonquins pronounced Oo-ka-na-sa, which Marquette wrote Arkansoa; LaSalle wrote Arkensa; DeTonti, Arkancas; and LaHarpe, Arkansas. When the state was admitted to the Union in 1836, it was spelled Arkansas. The 1881 legislature appointed a committee to ascertain the rightful pronunciation of the last syllable, and the result was a resolution declaring the pronunciation to be Ark-an-saw.

The state's first human occupants were probably mound builders.

Three natural divisions characterize Arkansas prairies: The alluvial plains, Arkansas Valley prairie, and Ozark Plateau. The original almost 1-million eastern Mississippi alluvial plain acres are now down to 600. The almost 150,000 Arkansas Valley acres now number 2,200, and the almost 500,000 northwest Ozark Plateau acres are reduced to 160. TNC, AR (501/663-6699) and the Arkansas Natural Heritage Commission (ANHC)(501/324-9619), among others, are attempting to preserve the remaining prairies in Arkansas.

The following are some Arkansas prairies to visit:

Arkansas County:
ROTH PRAIRIE NATURAL AREA: 41-acres of tallgrass prairie on strongly acidic soil that formerly grew hay. Dotted by conspicuous "Pimple Mounds," its rare plants include tuberous grass-pink, prairie evening primrose and prairie dropseed. Arkansas State University holds title. The NA is south of Stuttgart, AR off Hwy 11. Call the Arkansas Natural Heritage Commission (ANHC) at 501/324-9619.

Ashley County:
BERYL ANTHONY/LOWER OUACHITA WILDLIFE MANAGEMENT AREA: 7,500-acres of mostly seasonally flooded bottomland hardwood. A few pine ridges and prairie remnants (see Coffee Prairie below) occur in the area. The WMA extends into Union County. The WMA is 15-miles west of Crossett, AR. Call the Arkansas Game & Fish Commission (AGFC), at 877/836-4612.

COFFEE PRAIRIE: 56-acres of rare lowland prairie. This site is the best of the very few known examples of a type of grassland classified as Lowland Sand Prairie. The Prairie is 6-miles southwest of Crossett, AR and a part of the Lower Ouachita Wildlife Management Area (see above). Call the ANHC at 501/324-9619.

Benton County:
SEARLES PRAIRIE NATURAL AREA: 10-acres of original Osage tallgrass prairie whose "Pimple Mounds" and natural seep support a high diversity of prairie plants. The NA is located 1½-miles west of the intersection of Hwys 102 & 94, at the northern limits of the city of Rodgers,

AR. Call the ANHC at 501/324-9619.

Boone County:
BAKER PRAIRIE NATURAL AREA: 30-acres in the town of Harrison, AR constitutes the largest remnant tract of Arkansas Ozark prairie growing on soil lying over a substance called chert. Spring brings blooming Indian paintbrush and nesting grasshopper sparrows. One can park in the Harrison High School parking lot on Goblin Dr. The prairie is managed jointly with TNC, AR's adjunct tract of 40-acres. Call TNC, AR at 501/663-6699 or the ANHC at 501/324-9619.

Bradley County:
WARREN PRAIRIE NATURAL AREA: 875-acres of savanna and prairie plants. The site is made up of a group of grassy openings marked with mounds that support woody plants. The NA extends into Drew County and is southeast of Warren, AR off of Hwy 172. Call the AHNC at 501/324-9619.

Clark County:
TERRE NOIRE NATURAL AREA: 80-acres of now-rare blackland tall-grass prairie constitutes one of the state's best remaining sites. Part of 5,000-acres remaining of 12,000,000-original U. S. acres, its thick black soil, high in organic matter, is considered an extension of the tallgrass prairie. These sites show much erosion. The goal is to restore them to their natural state, and to restore the mosaic of prairie openings within oak/pine forest and to rid the prairies of woody vegetation and to boost populations of native prairie plants. This site is 5-miles west of Arkadelphia, AR on Hwy 51. For more information on this mosaic of native herbaceous and woody vegetation, punctuated by prairie openings separated by small waterways bordered by dense tangles of small trees, shrubs and vines, call the AHNC at 501/324-9619 or TNC, AR in Little Rock, AR at 501/663-6699.

Drew County:
WARREN PRAIRIE NATURAL AREA: (See Bradley County above).

Franklin County:
CHEROKEE PRAIRIE NATURAL AREA: The largest remnant of prairie in Arkansas is located 2-miles north of the City of Charleston, AR at the intersection of Hwys 217 & 60. It consists of 566-acres of never plowed, virgin tallgrass prairie containing a full compliment of native prairie grasses and flowers. For more information on this tract, call the AHNC at 501/324-9619.

H. E. FLANAGAN PRAIRIE NATURAL AREA: 258-acres representing a fine example of the tallgrass prairies that formed an important component of the pre-settlement vegetation of Arkansas. This acreage is a remnant of what was originally known as the Cherokee Prairies.

The NA is located 1-mile north of Charleston, AR. Call the AHNC at 501/324-9619.

PRESSON-OGLESBY PRESERVE: 155-acres of high quality tallgrass prairie. This tract is representative of the once extensive Cherokee prairies that originally covered tens of thousands of acres within the Arkansas River valley of west central Arkansas. Acquired by the TNC, AR, this preserve connects the above two prairies managed by the Arkansas Natural Heritage Commission. It will be managed as a nature preserve for its 150 species of plants and animals, such as the Henslow's sparrow and LeConte's sparrow. This preserve will be open to the public. Call the TNC, AR in Little Rock, AR at 501/663-6699.

Hempstead County:
COLUMBUS PRAIRE: 80-acres of high quality blackland prairie, blackland savanna, and blackland woodland. Blackland soils are characterized by a deep mantle of black soil high in organic matter that is found over a substrate of chalk or marl formed from shellfish beds that existed when the Gulf of Mexico covered the area during the Cretaceous period, 150 million years ago. The Prairie consists of 3-4 feet tall grasses, and is a sea of flowers. Call TNC, AR in Little Rock, AR at 501/663-6699 for more information as to when it will open to the public, and where it is located.

RICK EVANS/GRANDVIEW PRAIRIE WILDLIFE MANAGEMENT AREA: 4,885-acre multi-use area. This prairie represents the largest, contiguous tract of blackland prairie in public ownership in the USA. The area consists of improved pasture, woodlands, wooded draws, bottomland habitats, and native grasslands comprised of blackland prairie communities. It is managed by the Arkansas Game & Fish Commission (AGFC) for, among other things, the protection, enhancement and restoration of the blackland prairie found here. The WMA is 2-miles north of Columbus, AR. Bird watching, and wildlife viewing is encouraged. A white-tailed deer herd is managed here. Call the AGFC at 877/777-5580.

Howard County:
STONE ROAD GLADE NATURAL AREA: 107-acre preserve with approximately 30-acres of glade openings within a mixed pine/hardwood forest. Little Bluestem is the dominant grass and the common forbs are purple prairie clover and black-eyed Susan. This is the largest and least disturbed example of the Coastal Plain Limestone Glade community in southwest Arkansas. The NA is northeast of Center Point, AR off Hwy 369. Call TNC, AR in Little Rock, AR at 501/663-6699 or the ANHC at 501/324-9619.

Lonoke County:
RAILROAD PRAIRIE STATE NATURAL AREA: 257-acres of tallgrass prairie occupying portions of abandoned railroad rights-of-way off US 70 in Lonoke and Prairie Counties between the towns of Carlisle and DeValls Bluff, AR. A complete transect of the Grande Prairie, this prairie remnant has great importance for providing an understanding of the Grand Prairie's soils and the pre-settlement vegetation that is intimately associated with those soils. Its location is ideal for purposes of visitation and interpretation. The plant communities on parts of the right-of-way strip are especially vigorous, complete, and weed-free. Call the AHNC at 501/324-9619.

Miller County:
MILLER COUNTY SANDHILLS: 35-acres with some of the area open and supporting a sandhill prairie; the remainder is hardwood forest. The Nature Conservancy and The Natural Heritage Commission share an interest, with each owning an adjoining tract. The site is 15-miles south of Texarkana, AR on Hwy 237. Call TNC, AR in Little Rock, AR at 501/663-6699 or the AHNC at 501/324-9619.

Montgomery County:
HANKEWICH NATURAL AREA: 80-acres that features prairie wildflowers alongside wetland plants. Permission required for visiting. Call TNC, AR in Little Rock, AR at 501/663-6699.

Prairie County:
KONECNY GROVE NATURAL AREA: 22-acre example of the prairie slash vegetational community. The thicket includes a four-acre wet opening dominated by cattail, bordered by black willow, which is locally reported to have been a buffalo wallow in early days. The NA is southwest of Hazen, AR. Call the AHNC at 501/324-9619.

KONECNY PRAIRIE NATURAL AREA: 50-acres, which is the largest block of tallgrass prairie in the Grand Prairie of eastern Arkansas. This NA is near the above Konecny Grove NA. Call the AHNC at 501/324-9619.

RAILROAD PRAIRIE STATE NATURAL AREA: (See Lonoke County, above).

Saline County:
DRY LOST CREEK GLADES: 80-acres containing nepheline syenite rock outcrops, glades, and woodlands. Grasses such as little bluestem, and forbs such as fameflower, and the fragrant calamint occur in areas of shallow soil. Call TNC, AR in Little Rock, AR at 501/663-6699 for when the glades will be open to the public and its exact location.

CALIFORNIA

California is not a prairie state but some of its landscape resembles a prairie. See below:

Solano County:

JEPSON PRAIRIE PRESERVE: The Preserve has native bunchgrass prairie and spring wildflowers. Call the Preserve at 707/421-1351 or TNC, CA in San Franncisco, CA at 415/777-0487.

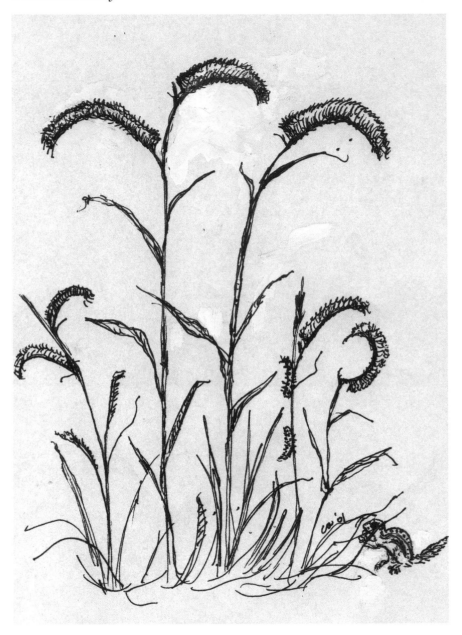

Fig 6
Blue Grama, a short-grass prairie species (with caterpillars and a thirteen line ground squirrel). See Fig. 2 for typical root structures of prairie plants.
This is the state grass of Colorado and New Mexico.

Illustration by Charlotte Adelman

COLORADO
"The prairie provides a unique opportunity for solitude and open spaces. Take the time to appreciate a soaring hawk, a gentle breeze caressing a carpet of flowers and grasses, and the cloud shadows creating a mosaic on the horizontal landscape. Observe the power of a thunderstorm and enjoy the coolness and clean smell after it passes. There is much to see on the Grassland if you take the time to look," states a USDA Forest Service Pawnee National Grassland brochure. For information and brochures on the Pawnee National Grassland call 970/353-5004.

Colorado prairies are mostly in the eastern part of the state. The grasslands in the western part of the state are usually not associated with the prairie, but may still have some plants in common with the Great Plains prairie plants. Blue grama is the state grass.

Some of the places to view prairie in Colorado are listed below:

Adams County:
ROCKY MOUNTAIN ARSENAL NATURAL WILDLIFE REFUGE: 27-square miles (17,000-acres) of formerly short-grass prairie near Denver support the doe-eyed Ord's kangaroo rat, badger, black-tailed prairie dog -that shares its burrows with burrowing owl and rattlesnake- and American white pelican, turkey vulture and bald eagle. The Refuge is a designated superfund cleanup area because of past weapons testing and later its use as a pesticide-manufacturing site. The U.S. Fish and Wildlife Service is restoring 8,000-acres to native prairie by using different major seed mixes for particular soils. The short-grass mix includes blue grama, buffalo grass, and western wheatgrass, plus wildflowers and some shrubs. Sandhills prairie includes prairie sandreed, sand bluestem, blue grama, and sand sage. The Refuge is currently closed to the public, but was scheduled to open, on weekends, in October 2001. It was designated a wildlife refuge in 1992, but that will not take effect until the cleanup is completed. This is a wonderful place to view animals and birds. TheRefuge is located approximately 10 miles northeast of downtown Denver, CO. Call the NWR at 303/289-0232 for its status.

BARR LAKE STATE PARK: 1,918-acre lake and surrounding 691-acres of state park lands along with a 125-acre buffer zone (Bergman Acquisition) at the north end of the lake. The lake, wetland and prairie make the Park an exceptional wildlife habitat. Bird watchers can spot over 300 species of birds at the Park, which is home to the Rocky Mountain Bird Observatory, formerly known as the Colorado Bird Observatory. The Park is northeast of Brighton, CO off US 76. Call the Park in Brighton, CO at 303/659-6005.

Alamosa County:
MEDANO-ZAPATA RANCH PRESERVE (Formerly the Rocky Mountain Bison Ranch): 100,000-acre ranch is the biggest preserve protected by the Nature Conservancy in Colorado. Plans have not been finalized, but one plan is to seed a large portion of the Ranch with native grasses and to either hay the grasses or use them as a source for future seeding of other preservation projects. Another possibility is the acquisition of the Baca Ranch nearby and with the help of the Federal Government, to make the Preserve the core of a 400-sq mile national park. The Preserve is near Mosca, Co. Call TNC, CO in Boulder, CO at 303/444-2950.

SAN LUIS STATE PARK AND WILDLIFE AREA: 2,054-acres of land and 890 surface-acres of water in two lakes with San Luis Lake being the bigger. Nestled among low sand dunes in this unique desert are wildlife-laden wetlands and approximately nine miles of easy, level hiking and biking trails. The Park also harbors some prairie plants. Bison can be found nearby at the Medano-Zapata Ranch Preserve (see above). The Park is northeast of Mosca, CO. Call the Park there at 719/378-2020.

Arapahoe County:
CHERRY CREEK STATE PARK: 3,900-acre park with an extensive short-grass prairie remnant. The Park is in Aurora, CO with the entrance to the Park on S. Parker Rd. Call the Park at 303/699-3860.

PLAINS CONSERVATION CENTER 2,000-acre short-grass private prairie preserve in eastern Aurora, CO with the entrance on Hampden Ave. Call the Center office at 303/693-3621.

Baca County:
COMANCHE NATIONAL GRASSLAND: 435,000-acres (203,393 acres in Baca County) of federally owned short-grass prairie featuring lesser prairie chickens, black-tailed prairie dogs, and pronghorn. This site is located in the southeast quarter of Colorado near the towns of Springfield and Campo, CO and is managed by U.S. Forest Service. It has hiking trails, picnic areas and toilet facilities. Bird watchers are welcome. Visitors can also learn about the history and environment of the prairie. Another popular site is Picket Wire Canyonland, a stretch of the Purgatoire Valley that is home to one of the world's longest sets of dinosaur tracks preserved in mud millions of years ago. Now they sit in a layer of rock next to the river. The canyon is about 25 miles south of La Junta, CO. This grassland, a product of the 1960 formation of the "National Grasslands" program, extends into Los Animas and Otero Counties. Call the Comanche National Grassland office, which is 1-mile south of Springfield, CO at 719/523-6591 for information or a map.

TWO BUTTES STATE WILDLIFE AREA: 4,962-acres of short-grass prairie and agricultural field surround a reservoir that is sometimes dry. Prairie dogs and other animals can be seen here. The WA is north of Spingfield, CO off US 385/287 and is also in Prowers County. Call the Colorado Department of Wildlife (CDOW) at 719/336-6600.

Bent County:
ADOBE CREEK RESERVOIR STATE WILDLIFE AREA: 5,147-acres of short-grass prairie around the reservoir with stands of tamarack and cottonwood. The WA extends into Kiowa County and is southeast of Arlington, CO. Call the CDOW at 719/336-6600.

(JOHN) MARTIN RESERVOIR STATE WILDLIFE AREA: 22,000-acres with the north shore of the reservoir a rolling short-grass prairie. The WA is 5-miles east of Las Animas, CO. Call the CDOW at 719/336-6600.

PURGATOIRE RIVER STATE WILDLIFE AREA: 950-acres of sagebrush sandhills, interspersed with grasslands. The WA is 3½-miles south of Las Animas, CO. Call CDOW at 719/336-6600.

Boulder County:
COLORADO TALLGRASS PRAIRIE NATURAL AREA: 269-acres of tallgrass prairie in 8 parcels. This is a remnant of a once-extensive area of tallgrass prairie occupying the South Boulder Creek floodplain and much of the glacial outwash plateaus of the Front Range. These tallgrass prairie remnants support flora similar to the prairies of South Dakota, Kansas, and the Midwest, including big bluestem, switchgrass, and Indiangrass. This site is in the City of Boulder, CO, and the City owns and manages it. Call the Colorado Natural Areas Program at 303/866-3437.

MESA TRAIL: 6.7-mile trail with short-grass and tallgrass prairie at the south end. The south end begins at South Boulder Creek with the north end, ending in Chautauqua Park in Boulder, CO. Call Boulder County Open Spaces at 303/441-4142.

SOUTH BOULDER CREEK NATURAL AREA: 1,193-acres of high quality wetlands, wet meadows, and mesic grasslands, including plains riparian forests and tallgrass prairie ecosystems. The floodplain in the area includes habitat for several species of concern: the Preble's meadow jumping mouse, and bobolink, a locally rare bird on the edge of its range. In addition, the area serves as a research site for on-going floristic and wildlife investigations. This NA is in the southern portion of Boulder, CO. Call the Colorado Natural Areas Program at 303/866-3437.

Denver County:
COMMONS PARK: 20-acre park between 15th and 19th Sts, just east

of the Platte River in Denver, CO. The Park's west border reflects the open prairie with native grasses. Call the Denver Parks and Recreation Dept at 303/964-2500.

BLUFF LAKE NATURAL AREA: 123-acre area with Bluff Lake and remnant short-grass and mid-grass prairies on the bluffs and wetlands at the lake. The NA is in Denver, CO on Havana Way. Call the Friends of Bluff Lake at 303/764-3643.

RIVERSIDE CEMETERY: 88-acre cemetery in Denver, CO off US 25. The Cemetery has open grassy lawns with cattails, willows, and ponds with native grasses on their borders. The Cemetery is privately owned. Call the Cemetery at 303/293-2466.

Douglas County:
CASTLEWOOD CANYON NATURAL AREA in CASTLEWOOD CANYON STATE PARK: 800-acre NA that has one of the best remnants of northern Black Forest plant communities, including unlogged forests of ponderosa pine and Douglas-fir, Gambel oak thickets, and grasslands of mixed prairie and foothill species. The Park and NA is east of Castle Rock, CO. Call the Colorado Natural Areas Program at 303/866-3437.

CHATFIELD STATE PARK: 1,450-acre lake, along with 5,600-acres of parkland with many hiking, biking and horse trails. The prairie grasses and reservoir support many animals, including beaver, muskrat, whitetail and mule deer, coyotes, rabbits and foxes. The Park extends into Jefferson County. The Park is in an urban setting south of Denver off Hwy 121. Call the Park in Littleton, CO at 303/791-7275.

DANIELS PARK: 1,040-acre park with most of the Park a bison preserve and natural area where visitors can view the animals in a high-plains habitat of shrubland and short-grass prairie. The Park is 21-miles south of Denver, CO. off US 25 on Daniels Park Rd. Call Denver Mountain Parks at 303/697-4545.

ROXBOROUGH STATE PARK AND NATURAL AREA: 3,299-acres located in a transition zone between mountains and plains. The area's geological structure has resulted in microclimates that have produced seven distinct plant communities in a unique mixture of prairie and mountain species. The vegetation in the NA is representative of the foothills region. Mixed-grass prairie is characteristic of the areas between hogbacks where landslide debris has accumulated. The NA is home to abundant wildlife, including black bear, mountain lion and elk. The Park and NA is southwest of Denver, CO. Call the Park at 303/973-3959 or the Colorado Natural Areas Program at 303/866-3437.

El Paso County:
AIKEN CANYON NATURAL AREA: 1,621-acre canyon has two plant communities considered extremely rare. One is a woodland combination of pinyon pine, one-seeded juniper, and Scribner needlegrass, and the other is a gamble oak and mountain mahogany shrubland. These communities are valuable because they each support particular combinations of plants and animals living in balance. The canyon also supports tall grasses, such as big bluestem, that have declined to a fraction of their original range in Colorado. The NA is 15-miles southwest of Colorado Springs, Call TNC, CO in Boulder, CO at 303/444-2950.

CHICO BASIN: 151,000-acres (see Bohart Ranch and Chico Basin Ranch below and Pueblo Chemical Depot in Pueblo County).

CHICO BASIN RANCH: 86,000-acres of sand sage prairie, 7 lakes, and perched wetlands on mesa tops. The Ranch is located southeast of Colorado Springs and northeast of Pueblo, CO. The Ranch is also in Pueblo County. Call the Colorado State Land Board in Denver, CO at 303/866-3454.

BEAR CREEK REGIONAL PARK: 1,235-acre park has foothill terrain with open meadows of native grasses. The Park is west of Colorado Springs, CO on 26th Ave. Call El Paso County at 719/520-6387.

BOHART RANCH: 42,000-acres of sand sage and short-grass prairie in the Chico Basin area that was saved from development and supports a host of grassland birds (a group in serious decline), and animals such as swift fox and the black-tailed prairie dog. The Ranch is southeast of Colorado Springs, CO. Hiking is permitted by pre-arrangement. Call TNC, CO in Boulder, CO at 303/444-2950.

Fermont County:
HIGH MESA GRASSLAND RESEARCH NATURAL AREA: 1,100-acres of grassland, and although it is strictly speaking not prairie, the grassland does contain some species of plants associated with prairie, such as blue grama. The NA is located near Canon City CO. Call the Colorado Natural Areas Program at 303/866-3437.

Huerfano County:
LATHROP STATE PARK: 1,734-acre park with marsh, wetlands, and prairie grasslands located southwest of Walsenburg, CO on Hwy 160. Call the Park at 719/738-2376.

Jefferson County:
BEAR CREEK LAKE STATE PARK: 2,600-acre park in the southwest corner of Lakewood, CO, a suburb of Denver, contains a variety of short-grass prairie along with a man-made lake and a golf course. Call the City of Lakewood at 303/697-6159.

CHATFIELD STATE PARK: (See Douglas County above).

GENESEE PARK: 2,341-acres of upland with Ponderosa Pine and some native grasses. One can see a herd of bison here. The Park is 20-miles west of Denver, CO off US 70. Call Denver Mountain Parks at 303/697-4545.

KEN-CARYL RANCH NATURAL AREA: 876-acres containing a textbook example of the geologic formation known as a "hogback." It is vegetated with a mosaic of plant communities representative of the rocky scarps and shallow valleys of hogbacks along the east face of the Front Range. It has examples of foothills mixed-grass prairie, one seed juniper woodland, and Gambel oak thicket. The NA is southeast of Denver, CO. Call the Colorado Natural Areas Program at 303/866-3437.

RED ROCKS PARK: 639-acre park known for its natural amphitheater, has mixed-grass, short-grass prairie, and some tallgrass species. The Park is located on the eastern slope of the Rocky Mountains. Call Denver Mountain Parks at 303/697-4545.

TWO PONDS NATION WILDLIFE REFUGE: 63-acre NWR that borders the Denver suburb of Arvada, CO and has some native grasses. The NWR is on 80th Ave in Arvada, CO. Call the USFWS at 303/289-0232, ext 0.

Kiowa County:
ADOBE CREEK RESERVOIR STATE WILDLIFE AREA: (See Bent County above).

QUEENS STATE WILDLIFE AREA: 4,426-acres that encompasses the Neenoshe, Neegronda, Neesopah, and Upper and Lower Queens, Reservoirs which are surrounded by short-grass prairie and agricultural fields. The WA is southeast of Eads, CO. Call the CDOW at 719/336-6600.

Larimer County:
BIG BEND CAMPGROUND: 120-acres where prescribed burns have reduced shrubs and promoted the growth of grasses and forbs in otherwise bitterbrush and sagebrush uplands. The campground is west of Rustic, CO on Hwy 14. Call the USFS at 970/498-2770.

(CATHY) FROMME PRAIRIE NATURAL AREA: 1,003-acres of rolling terrain with a remnant short-grass prairie on Harmony Rd in Fort Collins, CO. Call the City of Fort Collins at 970/224-6118.

HAMILTON RESERVOIR/RAWHIDE ENERGY STATION: 500-acres with short-grass prairie surrounding the reservoir. Visitation is only by advance reservation. The reservoir is north of Fort Collins, CO. Call the Platte River Power Authority in Fort Collins, CO at 970/226-4000.

LORY STATE PARK: 2,400-acre park in the transition zone between plains and foothills that has some grassland. The Park is west of Fort Collins, CO. Call the Park at 970/493-1623.

PHANTOM CANYON PRESERVE: 1,700-acres where the short-grass prairie meets the shrub land of the Rocky Mountain foothills, constituting a transition zone to the forest ecosystems west of the Preserve. The Canyon is home for black bear, mountain lions, bobcat, redtail hawk, bald and golden eagle. Hiking is permitted by pre-arrangement. The preserve is located 30-miles northwest of Fort Collins. For information about when the Preserve is open, call TNC, CO in Fort Collins, CO at 970/498-0180.

Las Animas County:
APISHAPA STATE WILDLIFE AREA: 7,935-acres containing uplands of short-grass prairie and juniper woodlands. The WA is northeast of Walsenburg, CO. Call CDOW at 719/561-4909.

COMANCHE NATIONAL GRASSLAND: (See Baca County, above).

FORT CARSON-PINON CANYON MILITARY RESERVATION: 236,000-acre military reservation that has mixed habitats including short-grass prairie. A herd of about 1,000 pronghorn live here along with some 400 or so mule deer. The headquarters office is on Hwy 70 southwest of Thatcher, CO. Call the US Army at 719/846-2806.

TRINIDAD LAKE STATE PARK: 2,300-acre park has pygmy conifer, native grassland, with several small riparian areas and includes the 700-acre lake. The Park is nestled in the foothills of southern Colorado, and bordered by the historic Santa Fe Trail and the scenic Highway of Legends. The Park is west of Trinidad, CO on Hwy 12. Call the Park at 719/846-6951.

Lincoln County:
HUGO STATE WILDLIFE AREA: 2,240-acres of rolling terrain that is mostly short-grass prairie. The WA is about 13½-miles south of Hugo, CO off Hwy 2G. Call CDOW at 719/227-5200.

Logan County:
NORTH STERLING STATE PARK: 1,565-acres of short-grass prairie. The Park is located 12-miles outside of Sterling, CO. Call the Park at 970/522-3657.

RED LION/JUMBO RESERVOIR STATE WILDLIFE AREA: 1,498-acres with a reservoir surrounded by short-grass prairie, mud flats, lowland marsh area, and cottonwood riparian zones. This WA is northeast of Crook, CO and extends into Sedgwick County. Call the CDOW at 970/842-6300.

PREWITT RESERVOIR STATE WILDLIFE AREA: 2,900-acres of grassland and old cultivated fields surround the reservoir. The WA extends into Washington County and is south of Merino, CO. Call CDOW at 970/842-6300.

TAMARACK RANCH NATURAL AREA: 470-acres that includes excellent examples of plains cottonwood riparian forest and sandhill prairie. The NA is south of Crook, CO. Call the Colorado Natural Areas Program at 303/866-3437.

Morgan County:
JACKSON LAKE STATE PARK: 2,540-acres of reservoir and wetland prairie featuring a nature trail. The Park is north of Goodrich, CO and supports a nesting colony of white pelicans. Call Colorado State Parks (CSP) at 970/645-2551.

Otero County:
COMANCHE NATIONAL GRASSLAND: (See Baca County, above).

ROCKY FORD STATE WILDLIFE AREA: 550-acres of mixed woodlands and shrubs with open areas of grasses and forbs. The WA is 2-miles east of Rocky Ford, CO. Call CDOW at 719/336-6600.

Prowers County:
TWO BUTTES STATE WILDLIFE AREA: (See Baca County above).

Pueblo County:
CHICO BASIN RANCH: (See El Paso County above).

PUEBLO RESERVOIR STATE WILDLIFE AREA: 4,600-acres that lies amid short-grass prairie. The WA is west of Pueblo, CO. Call CDOW at 719/336-6600.

PUEBLO CHEMICAL DEPOT: 23,000-acres of short-grass prairie, rabbitbush, yucca and cholla. This is the easiest to visit of the three sites that make up the Chico Basin, although prior arrangements are required. It is located northeast of Pueblo, CO and owned by the US Army. The Army stores mustard gas underground here. Call the depot at 719/549-4135 to make arrangements in advance.

Sedgwick County:
RED LION/JUMBO RESERVOIR STATE WILDLIFE AREA: (See Logan County above).

Ray County:
FOX RANCH: 14,070-acres on the Arikaree River support wet tallgrass prairie. Here meet the western and eastern plant and animal species. Greater prairie chickens perform their elaborate mating rituals. The site is home to several other grassland bird species whose population

numbers are declining. Visitation is by field trip. Call TNC, CO in Boulder CO at 303/444-2950.

Washington County:
PREWITT RESERVOIR STATE WILDLIFE AREA: (See Logan County above).

Weld County:
PAWNEE NATIONAL GRASSLAND AND PAWNEE BUTTES: 693,000-acres of short-grass prairie in two units in northeast Colorado. Of the total acreage of the grassland, 193,060-acres are federally owned. The rest is privately owned. Annual rainfall here is only 12 to 13 inches. The dominant grasses are blue grama and buffalo grass, which rarely reach one's boot tops. The site lies about 13-miles south of the WY/CO border, approximately 30-miles east of Fort Collins, CO. The Pawnee Buttes, a critical breeding site for birds of prey such as hawks, eagles and falcons is in the east unit north of New Raymer, CO. Fossils of 3-toed horse, rhinoceros, ancient swine, camel, and a hippopotamus-like animal have been found here.

When Lt Zebulon Pike explored this area in 1806 and Major Stephen Long in 1819, the human population consisted of Indians and a few French fur trappers. Buffalo, as well as deer, antelope and elk were abundant then. The 1862 Homestead Act provided white settlers with 160-acres of land, and brought Texas longhorn cattle. After 1866, building the Union Pacific Railroad across southwestern Nebraska saw the buffalo hunted for hides and to feed construction crews. After 1874, barbed wire fenced in the prairie for agriculture. The Native American population was forcibly removed in 1875. By 1884, the buffalo were exterminated in this region.

The cattle industry and agriculture were devastated by the region's harsh winters, hail, drought, and dry winds carrying off topsoil. The return of the rain cycle saw grassland 60% plowed up by 1930. Then came the dry cycle called the "Dust Bowl." After relocating farm families, the United States began reclaiming the area. Unfortunately, they mostly planted crested wheatgrass[1] on the damaged lands. This introduced species is well adapted to our climate and became an invasive pest. Efforts are being made to replace it with native grasses.

Today, Pawnee National Grassland supports privately owned cattle along with native grassland pronghorn antelope and mule deer. Swift and red fox and coyote co-exist with black tailed prairie dog and burrowing owl. Prairie voles frolic, as do pocket gophers, kangaroo rats,

---

[1] CRESTED WHEATGRASS (**Agropyron desertorum; Agropyron cristatum**) is a cool-season perennial wheatgrass that was introduced into the Great Plains from eastern Europe and Asia in 1898.

pocket mice, western harvest mice, northern grasshopper mice and 13-lined squirrel.

To distinguish private from public land in this internationally known bird-watching site, obtain a grassland map by calling the USFS at 970/353-5004. Also, see the web site at www.fs.fed.us/r2/arnf/png.

Yuma County:
BONNY PRAIRIE NATURAL AREA: 50-acres of loess prairie in BONNY RESERVOIR STATE PARK A 1,300-acre park located east of US 385 on Co Rd 2 or 3. The roads are bumpy and dusty. The NA is a very good example of the high plains loess prairie that once covered millions of acres. There are self-guiding nature trails here. The NA is a good place for bird watching and viewing mule and whitetail deer. The NA is southeast of Idalia, CO. Call the Park at 970/354-7306.

FOX RANCH: 14,070-acres of riparian forest and tallgrass wet prairie including 8-miles of the Arickaree River. A meeting ground of western and eastern species, the Arickaree River supports a rich array of plants and animals, including such rare species as the orange-throated darter, plains leopard frog, brassy minnow, white pelican and the upland sandpiper. Greater prairie chickens perform their elaborate mating rituals here, and the Ranch is home to several bird species whose population numbers are declining, such as the curve-billed thrasher and Cassin's sparrow. Hiking is permitted by pre-arrangement in groups or on field trips arranged by TNC. The Ranch is south of Wray, CO. Call TNC, CO at 303/444-2950.

GREATER PRAIRIE CHICKEN LEKS: Privately held prairie grasslands north of Wray, CO are used by the prairie chickens during spring courtship. These areas can only be visited on private tours, but it is possible to drive some country roads north of Wray, CO and see both the prairie and the prairie chickens. For information call CDOW at 303/291-7227.

SOUTH REPUBLICAN STATE WILDLIFE AREA: 13,140-acres including Bonny Lake State Park (see above) and private land. The area has grassland, a 1,900-acre reservoir, agricultural land, and riparian cottonwood lowlands. The WA is southeast of Idalia, CO. Call CDOW at 970/354-7306.

FLORIDA

The Pleistocene Ice Age, between 2,000,000 to 10,000 years ago, saw prairie extend along the Gulf Coast continuously from Florida to Texas. The melting Wisconsin Glacier caused the sea to rise, isolating these prairies. Today, these prairies graze cattle, or were plowed under. "Marl" prairie is in south Florida's Everglades National Park and Big Cypress National Preserve. Tens of thousands of small, oval prairies lie in central and northern Florida.

Florida is not a prairie state and was not known as a prairie state, but below are some prairies that can be seen in the state:

Aluchua County:
PAYNES PRAIRIE PRESERVE STATE PARK: 21,000-acre preserve contains wet prairie, pine flatwoods, hammocks, swamp and ponds, that provide a rich array of habitats for animal life. The Park is located 10-miles south of Gainesville, FL on US 441 at Micanopy, FL. Call the Park in Micanopy, FL at 352/466-3397.

Escambia County:
PERDIDO PITCHER PLANT PRAIRIE PROJECT: 7,000-acres of wet, grassy prairie dotted with pitcher plants located in southwestern Escambia County along the shores of Tarkiln Bayou. Call the Florida Department of Environmental Protection in Tallahassee, FL at 850/488-2427.

Nassau County:
OKEFENOKEE SWAMP AND NATIONAL WILDLIFE AREA: (See Georgia below).

Okeechobee County:
ORDWAY-WHITTELL KISSIMMEE PRAIRIE SANCTUARY: 7,500-acre dry prairie located in north central Okeechobee County, which is a small remnant of the 3,000,000-acres of dry prairies the once were in Florida. Contact Lake Okeechobee Sanctuaries, in Lorida, Fl at 941/467-8497.

Putnam County:
PUTNAM SAND HILLS PRAIRIE: 1,200-acre prairie. Call TNC, FL in Altamonte, FL at 407/682-3664 about this and their other prairie preserves.

Fig 7
Lead Plant. See Fig 2 for root structure.

Illustration by Charlotte Adelman

GEORGIA

Once Georgia's prairies supported herds of large herbivores, such as the wood bison. This landscape attained its greatest extent during the hot, dry period that existed between about 8,000 to 25,000 years ago, according to pollen studies. With the arrival of cooler weather, the prairie declined. However, according to early European settlers, Native Americans used fire to maintain habitat for grazing wild animals. Today, prairie species can mostly be found in unprotected privately owned sites located in Catoosa County, Dade County and Floyd County. Informally named Wet Prairie, Dry Prairie, Grand Prairie, Sunnybell Prairie, and Ladies-tresses or Bird-foot Prairie. These sites support eastern prairie species that possibly migrated east during the Pleistocene era. For information about Georgia's progress in the protection of prairies, call the DNR Natural Heritage Program at 706/557-3032 or TNC, Georgia in Atlanta, GA at 404/873-6946.

Charlton County:

OKEFENOKEE SWAMP AND NATIONAL WILDLIFE AREA: 396,000-acre NWR in the 490,000-acre swamp with 60,000-acres of prairie. One entrance to the NWR is 11-miles southwest of Folkston,GA off Hwy 121/23. The NWR extends into Brantley, Ware and possibly Camden County Georgia, while the swamp continues into Florida. Call the NWR at 912/496-7836 or visit their website at http://okefenokee.fws.gov/

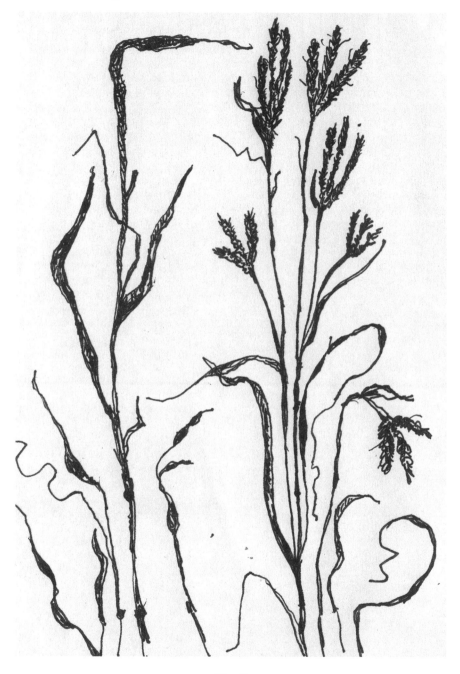

Fig 8
Big Bluestem -the state grass of Illinois. See Fig 2 for root structure.

Illustration by Charlotte Adelman

ILLINOIS

Prairie flowers and grasses blanketed Illinois when Native Americans hunted its 22,000,000-acres of prairie for buffalo and other game. Pioneers, emerging from the dark eastern forests, called it the "Prairie State." "A vast prairie stretched from horizon to horizon. Wildflower formed a seamless carpet of color. One observer commented that for every color of wildflower there was a butterfly to match. Today, the state's prairies are so rare that most people have never seen one. Approximately 99.9% of Illinois' original prairie has been destroyed," a TNC Illinois publication notes. Pioneer cemeteries preserving remnants of the now-rare native prairie landscape exist in Adams County, Bureau County, Carroll County, Ford County, Henry County, Lee County, McHenry County, McLean County, Montgomery County, Ogle County, Putnam County, Vermilion County, and Warren County. Obtain *Prairie Establishment and Landscaping* by William E. McClain, posters, general information on the prairie, or the telephone number of the natural heritage biologist assigned to a specific prairie managed by the Illinois Department of Natural Resources (DNR) by calling the Natural Heritage Division Main Office in Springfield at 217/785-8774.

The DNR, IL and TNC, IL as well as other organizations, such as Grand Prairie Friends, North Branch Restoration Project, Save the Prairie Society, Illinois Nature Preservation Commission, Open Lands, Natural Land Institute, Illinois Audubon, and others, are attempting to protect existing prairie and, where possible, to restore prairie.

The Illinois Department of Transportation (IDOT) has a policy of planting prairie plants (grasses and forbs), on the back slopes along the State Highways, and also at the rest areas, cloverleaves, and intersections. IDOT has initiated a program called "Corridors for Tomorrow" that intends to plant 700-acres of prairie plants annually in the interchange areas of interstates and expressways. In 1993, the IDOT planted 41 interchanges along I-55 (US 55), I-80 (US 80), I-474 (US 474), I-72 (US 72), I-57 (US 57), I-24 (US 24) and I-64 (US 64). One of the visible prairie restorations (Operation Wildflower) can be seen along I-57 between Bloomington and Raymond, IL. Another restoration with a great variety of wildflowers can be observed in Knox County at the Spoon River rest area (see Knox County below). The written policy is also to mow these areas only along the highway to the ditch line or 15 feet, which ever is less, and not to mow further until after grassland birds have finished nesting.

Further, the "Corridors for Tomorrow" program intends to plant, overall, 135,000-acres of the interstate right-of-way with native plants and a more comprehensive prairie development is planned for the 370 interchanges. In addition, 48 rest areas will provide re-constructed prairie settings with possible educational interpretations. "Corridors for Tomorrow" is a joint effort of the (IDOT), the Illinois Natural History Survey, state universities, and other interested groups.

Operation Wildflower, a program with the National Council of State Garden Clubs, has for the past ten years purchased $1,000 in wildflower seeds per year for planting along highways, and 3,000-acres have already been planted along the roadways.

Prairie Planting Programs have during the last 15-years planted over 2,800-acres of right-of-way during construction of various sections of highway.

The state grass of Illinois is big bluestem.

Below are some prairies, savannas or restorations of prairies or savannas that can be seen today in Illinois:

Adams County:
BYLER CEMETERY SAVANNA NATURE PRESERVE: 1-acre of savanna and prairie flowers and grasses perched on a gentle slope interspersed with 1847-1849 settlers' tombstones. Call DNR, IL at 217/785-8774.

SILOAM SPRINGS STATE PARK: 3,323-acres with 450 open acres some of which is prairie. A trail from the dam provides good looks at summer prairie flowers. The park is southeast of Quincy, IL and is also in Brown County. Call DNR, IL at 217/785-8774 or 217/782-9175.

Alexander County:
OZARK HILL PRAIRIES RESEARCH NATURAL AREA: 216-hectare tract of the Shawnee National Forest managed by the US Forest Service. Part of the Ozark Hills Natural Division contains relatively undisturbed natural communities, mostly white oak- black oak- northern red oak forest (117-ha), including a number of scattered hill prairie remnants. The hill prairie remnants are on and beneath the crest of south, and west-facing loess-capped ridges throughout the area. Much of these have almost disappeared in recent years because of encroachment from woody vegetation, especially sassafras. Nevertheless, the openings that remain are dominated by big bluestem, little bluestem, Indian grass, rosinweed, prairie dock, and slender bush clover. Call the USFS at 800/699-6637 or the Southern Illinois University, College of Science, at 618/536-2331.

Boone County:
Originally, Boone County was heavy forest, and groves, and the sparsely treed areas we call "Oak Savannas." The settlers called these "Barrens" and settled here to be close to wood and water. Farmers avoided the "worthless" prairies that covered more than half of the county until John Deere's steel plow enabled them to plow the deep-rooted grasslands.

BOONE COUNTY HISTORIC TRAIL: The trail is composed of four routes each about 30-miles long. Each is the distance that would have been covered in a very hard day's travel by covered wagons during the early 1830s. The Trail mirrors the history of the Illinois prairie beginning with pre-settlement days. Below are the four routes:

1.The South Prairie Route begins in Belvidere, IL at Spencer Park. It was once a Native American market and meeting ground, and close to the prairie/woods transitional zone. Moving through what was once over 50-square miles of prairie grassland early settlers called "South Prairie," the route passes historical sites including South Prairie Quarry.

2.The Belvidere/Caledonia Route begins in Belvidere, IL at Cline's Ford, a permanent gathering place for the native Potawatomi Indians. The route follows former stagecoach and railroad routes.

3.The Piscasaw Route begins in Belvidere, IL at Spencer Park; the route passes through the gently rolling countryside once the northern reaches of the county's large prairie areas. One can pause at prairie-related sites such as the Norwegian Long Prairie Cemetery, the Garden Prairie Road, Long Prairie Settlement and Piscasaw Valley. The word "Piscasaw" is believed to be a corrupted form of a Potawatomi word for "buffalo." One can also overlook a prairie hilltop.

4.The Blain/State Line Route begins 5 miles north of Caledonia, IL at Kinnikinnick Creek Conservation Area. The route moves through a once heavily timbered area dotted with small prairie openings, pauses at Long Prairie, and continues through stretches believed once frequented by buffalo whose wallows may still exist, to the Illinois/Wisconsin border.

For a detailed map of all four routes, call the Boone County Conservation District at 815/547-7935.

FLORA PRAIRIE NATURE PRESERVE: 10-acres of relatively undisturbed dry dolomite prairie, in the southwest corner of the county. It lies on the north side of Poole Rd, and ½-mile west of Wheeler Rd, southwest of the City of Belvidere, IL. Call the Boone County Conservation District at 815/547-7935 or DNR, IL at 217/785-8774.

KINNIKINNICK CREEK CONSERVATION AREA: Small remnant prairie in front of a heavily wooded 120-acre site 13-miles north of Belvidere, IL on Caledonia Rd off Hwy 173. Call the Boone County Conservation District at 815/547-7935.

KISHWAUKEE BOTTOMS: 547 plus-acres of wild land including 7.6-miles of trails which wind through prairies, woodlands and wetlands west of Belvidere, IL along the Kishwaukee River where, for thousands of years, Native Americans transported goods. Call the Boone County Conservation District at 815/547-7935.

LONG PRAIRIE TRAIL: 14.2-miles of paved trail for biking or hiking that runs from the Boone/McHenry County Line through the villages of Capron, Poplar Creek and Caledonia to McMichael Rd in Winnebago County. To access the Trail, parking lots are provided in all three villages and at the Trails' intersection with the Boone/McHenry County Line Road and the way is dotted with interpretive signs and prairie patch remnants of the oak savanna prairies that once blanketed northern Illinois. Its location along a now abandoned rail line preserved the vegetation from plowing, and sparks from the train ignited the dry grasses, killing woody plants and encouraging the prairie. Call the Boone County Conservation District at 815/547-7935.

SPENCER CONSERVATION AREA: 10-15 acres of restored tallgrass prairie in Spencer Park (see below).

SPENCER PARK: Located on the banks of the Kishwaukee River in the City of Belvidere, IL between N State St and W Lincoln Ave on Appleton Rd, with the main entrance located by St. James Cemetery. The park offers educational programs, an interpretive trail, an autumn pioneer festival and several ecosystems including a prairie. Call the Boone County Conservation District at 815/547-7935.

Brown County:
SILOAM SPRING STATE PARK: (See Adams County above).

Bureau County:
The Bureau County Soil and Water Conservation District (BCSWCD) has a program to acquire land for conservation and nature study. For more information call the BCSWCD at 815/879-5251.

CENTER PRAIRIE: 14-acre restored tallgrass prairie between Princeton and Wyanet, IL on Old US 6 where parking is available. Hiking and wildflower observation are encouraged. Call the BCSWCD at 815/879-5251 or 815/875-8732.

HETZLER CEMETERY PRAIRIE NATURE PRESERVE: 1-acre of mesic or medium soil native prairie dominated by prairie grasses like big bluestem, little bluestem and Indian grass interspersed with prairie flowers. Managed under an agreement with the Greenfield Cemetery Association. The oldest grave is dated 1843. The site is a dedicated Illinois Nature Preserve. Call the BCSWCD at 815/879-5251 or DNR, IL at 217/785-8774.

McCUNE SAND PRAIRIE PRESERVE: 200-acre site of virgin prairie is located 5½-miles north of Mineral, IL on Co Rd AA. This preserve once grazed by cattle includes sandy prairie with prickly pear cactus. Call the BCSWCD at 815/879-5251.

MILLER-ANDERSON WOODS NATURE PRESERVE: 268.7-acres plus 71.4-acres of buffer includes a seep spring and hill prairie. The

Preserve extends into Putnam County and is 5-miles north of Putnam, IL on Hwy 29. Call DNR, IL at 217/785-8774 or Site Superintendent, Donnelley State Fish and Wildlife Area at 815/447-2353.

ROSS WILDLIFE REFUGE: 50-acres of reclaimed gravel pits with a mix of ponds, native prairie grasses and forbs, restored prairie areas, and upland woodlot patches serves as a wildlife refuge. There is no public access without permission from the District Office. Call the BCSW-CD at 815/875-8732.

OLD INDIAN BOUNDARY LINE PRAIRIE: 7-acres of restored prairie 2-miles south of Ohio, IL. The Old Indian Boundary Line that required Native Americans to move beyond it was established in accordance with a treaty made at St. Louis in 1816 between the Federal Government and the United Tribes of Indians. The line ran from the south end of Lake Michigan to the Mississippi River at the mouth of the Rock River. Call the BCSWCD at 815/879-5251 or 815/875-8732.

WITNESS TREE: 1-acre site that includes a small restored prairie. The Tree is located about 3-miles south of Mineral, IL on Co Rd 10. Visitors are prohibited from walking beneath the huge 200-year old Burr Oak that served as a chief point of survey for the Rock Island Railroad. In pre-settlement days, the Sac and Fox nations held council meetings at the site. Call the BCSWD at 815/875-8732.

Calhoun County:
JENNINGS FAMILY HILL PRAIRIE NATURE PRESERVE: 29.06-acre natural area that has been family owned for more than 150 years. The site contains hill prairie, a limestone cliff community and mesic and dry-mesic upland forest. The state-threatened timber rattlesnake has also been known to inhabit the property. For information regarding this preserve, contact Debbie Newman at 618/758-3803.

Carroll County:
AYERS SAND PRAIRIE NATURE PRESERVE: 109-acre preserve features dry sand prairie and, although Illinois is in the tallgrass prairie belt, high quality short-grass prairie. The Preserve is 3-miles southeast of Savanna, IL and ½-mile east of Hwy 84 on Airport Rd. Call the DNR, IL at 217/785-8774.

BROOKVILLE LUTHERAN CEMETERY PRAIRIE NATURE PRE-SERVE: ¾-acre remnant of blacksoil prairie located northwest of Brookville, IL. The prairie lies on Ogle Till that was deposited during the Illinoisan stage of the Pleistocene Glaciation. Call the Brookville Cemetery Association at 815/493-6335 or the DNR, IL at 217/785-8774.

SAVANNA ARMY DEPOT: 13,062-acres that were saved from becoming a State prison and now 9,000-acres will be the Lost Mounds

National Wildlife Refuge. The rest will be commercially developed. This was the most extensive remaining remnant of sand prairies and sand savannas in the state. Also in Jo Davis County. The depot is located 7-miles north of Savanna, IL. Call USFWS at 612/713-5360.

SENTINEL NATURE PRESERVE: 48.4-acre site on the Sentinel Trail System located on Hwy 84 along the Mississippi River north of Savanna, IL. This is in the Mississippi Palisades State Park and includes a loess hill prairie. Call the DNR, IL at 217/785-8774.

Cass County:
CHANDLERVILLE-SNYDER HILL PRAIRIE NATURAL AREA: ½-acre of grade A loess hill prairie with a smaller brushy area of former grade B hill prairie. The non-active part of the Chandlerville cemetery is a part of this NA. The NA is east of Chandlerville, IL. Call the Illinois Nature Preserve Commission Field Office at 309/543-2744.

COX CREEK HILL PRAIRIE NATURAL AREA: 175-acre site, located within the 26-sq mile Jim Edgar Panther Creek State Fish & Wildlife Area (JEPC). The NA encompasses remnants of scattered hill prairies composed of loess, which occur within forest openings on steep terrain where soils are droughty and well drained. The JEPC is 10-mile north-east of Virginia, IL off Hwy 78, 25-miles northwest of Springfield, IL off Hwy 125, 10-miles west of Petersburg, IL, and 10-miles northwest of Ashland, IL. Call the JEPC at 217/452-7741.

PANTHER CREEK HILL PRAIRIE: Located within the 26-sq mile Jim Edgar Panther Creek State Fish & Wildlife Area (JEPC, see Cox Creek above). This site is located off Hwy 125. Call the JEPC at 217/452-7741.

Champaign County:
MEADOWBROOK PRAIRIE RESTORATION: 60-acres of restored prairie at Meadowbrook Park in southeast Urbana, IL. The restoration is a project of the Champaign County Audubon Society and the Urbana Park District. Call the Urbana Park District at 217/367-1536 or the Champaign County Audubon Society at 217/367-6788.

SHORTLINE RAILROAD PRAIRIE: 6-acre prairie along a 0.7-mile long 66 foot wide section of track of the abandoned narrow gauge Rantoul to Potomac, IL (Shortline) Railroad. The areas bordering the old railroad bed support a variety of native prairie plants. Since removal of the rails in 1984, the 11 foot wide rail bed is becoming colonized by a variety of disturbance tolerant species such as prairie dock, monarda, and some non-native plants. Contact the Grand Prairie Friends at their web site www.prairienet.org/gpf.

TOMILSON PIONEER CEMETERY PRAIRIE NATURE PRESERVE: 1-acre of dry-mesic savanna supporting typical prairie and savanna plants. Permission to visit is required. Call Champaign County Forest Preserve District at 217/586-2612 or DNR, IL at 217/785-8774.

WINDSOR ROAD PRAIRIE RESTORATION: This restoration is in Champaign on Windsor Rd off 1st St and owned by the City of Champaign, IL. Contact the Grand Prairie Friends at their web site www.prairienet.org/gpf.

Christian County:
ANDERSON PRAIRIE PARK (railroad prairie): This site in Pana Illinois is owned by Pana Unit School District No. 8 and contains some high quality prairie remnants with over 300 plant species and over 65 bird species and 56 butterfly species. For information, contact Dave Nance at nance@mail.christian.k12.il.us.

Cook County:
AIR STATION PRAIRIE: 31-acres including buffer of pre-settlement tallgrass prairie located in the 1,121-acre former naval air base in Glenview, IL off Lake Ave. Dedicated citizens were unable to preserve sufficient land (100-acres) for continued occupancy by upland sand-pipers and short-eared owls. Invasive Eurasian purple loosestrife, intentionally imported to enhance American gardens, is present in the prairie and an attempt to control the plant is being done by the state by releasing an imported beetle. The affects of the beetle have not been determined yet. Call the Glenview Development Department at 847/998-9500 or contact the Glenview Prairie Preservation Project at hauschott@aol.com.

ASHBURN PRAIRIE: 1½-acres of tallgrass prairie in Marquette Park in the City of Chicago. The prairie was created by transplanting plugs of original prairie dug up with spades by volunteers to save the plants from destruction by developers. The park is located just north of 71st & Kedzie Ave. Call the Chicago Park District at 312/747-0700 or 312/747-0692 or 773/434-1415.

BAKERS LAKE PRAIRIE: 20-acre prairie within a 209-acre preserve located south of Hillside Ave and west of Bakers Lake near Barrington, IL in northwest Cook County. The preserve has a heron rookery. Call the Cook County Forest Preserve at 708/771-1330 or the Citizens for Conservation at 847/382-7283.

BARTEL GRASSLANDS: A relatively large grassland area found in a stretch of Cook County Forest Preserve along Flossmoor Road in the southern part of the county. Thorn Creek Audubon has been instru-mental in preserving this area, monitoring the grassland birds, and maintenance of the area. Work will begin to remove invasive shrubs and the interior Osage Orange hedge rows. The project is co-sponsored by the Cook County Forest Preserve Project, Chicago Wilderness, the

Bird Conservation Network, and the National Audubon Society. Call Thorn Creek Audubon for more information at 708/798-3115 or the Cook County Forest Preserve at 708/771-1330.

BLUFF SPRING FEN NATURE PRESERVE: 91-acres near the City of Elgin, IL includes dry gravel and mesic black soil prairie that support a variety of prairie plant species and breeding birds. Call TNC, IL in Chicago, IL at 312/346-8166.

BURNHAM PRAIRIE: 1-acre of wet prairie located at the Burnham Golf Course on the north side of the Grand Calumet river in southeast Cook County. Call the Cook County Forest Preserve District Conservation Department, Land Management Section at 630/257-2045.

BUNKER HILL PRAIRIE: 16-acres of diverse prairie located on the west side of Caldwell Ave north of Devon Ave at the 100-acre Bunker Hill Forest Preserve in northwest Cook County. This is part of the North Branch Prairie Project (see below). There is a parking lot on Caldwell Ave. Call North Branch Restoration Project at 847/679-4289 or the Cook County Forest Preserve at 312/261-8400.

CALUMET CITY PRAIRIE: A privately owned prairie located on the south side of State St just west of Burnham Ave in Calumet City, IL. This prairie is carried on the Illinois DNR's "Gap List" as one of the most important natural areas in Illinois. It is a Grade A category prairie and marsh. Call the DNR, IL at 217/785-8774.

CAMP SAGAWA PRAIRIE: 8-acres of restored prairie in the City of Lemont, IL. Access is by permission only. Call the Cook County Forest Preserve District Conservation Department, Land Management Section at 630/257-2045.

CAP SAUERS HOLDINGS NATURE PRESERVE: 1,520-acres in southern Cook County includes oak savanna and prairie communities that are disturbed due to post-settlement suppression of fire. The Preserve is north of McCarthy Rd and bounded by 104th Ave and Calumet Sag Rd. The Forest Preserve District and The Nature Conservancy have a project to restore much of the site to its pre-settlement condition. Trails and parking are available. Call TNC, IL at 312/346-8166 or Cook County Forest Preserve District at 312/261-8400.

CATHERINE CHEVALIER WOODS PRAIRIE: 2-acres of black soil prairie located on the west side of East River Rd north of Lawrence Ave in northwest Cook County. Call River Trail Nature Center at 847/824-8360 or Forest Preserve District of Cook County, Conservation Department, Land Management Section at 630/257-2045.

CHICAGO BOTANIC GARDENS: 15-acres of re-created tallgrass, gravel hill, sand, and wet prairie occupy part of this site in the Village of Glencoe, IL. The Botanic Gardens is located off US 94 on Lake Cook Rd. Call the Garden at 847/835-5440.

CHICAGO RIDGE PRAIRIE NATURE PRESERVE: 12.9-acres that encompasses 7.9-acres of high quality mesic gravel prairie and wet prairie communities and about 5.0-acres of wetland fill. The Preserve is located at 105th St and Menard Ave in Oak Lawn, IL. Call the Oak Lawn Parks Foundation at 708/857-2225.

CHICAGO WILDFLOWER WORKS: Almost a prairie, this mixture of native and exotic wildflowers designed by artist Chapman Kelley is presented in large circles and covers the roof of the Monroe Parking Garage in Grant Park in downtown Chicago. Call the Chicago Park District Landscape Manager at 312/747-0700 or the Chicago Park District Naturalist at 312/747-0692.

COOK COUNTY FOREST PRESERVE DISTRICT PRAIRIES: It can provide information on some 100 prairies. The district is broken up into conservation departments as follows: 708/771-1330 – main office. Northeast Cook County: call the River Trail Nature Center at 847/824-8360 or 847/381-6592.
Southeast Cook County: call the Sandridge Nature Center at 708/868-0606.
Southwest Cook County: call the Little Red Schoolhouse at 708/839-6897.

CRABTREE NATURE CENTER: 500-acres of restored and recreated wet and high ground tallgrass prairie is located in the 1,100-acres of preserve land. The site lies on rolling, glacier-formed land that was forest, prairie and marsh until after 1830 when the landscape was plowed under, the trees cut and the wet prairies and marshes drained for farming or dredged to make lakes. The Cook County Forest Preserve District restored the site to approximate its natural state. There are several miles of self-guiding trails and an exhibition building plus a prairie restoration unit. Turkey-foot Prairie and Phantom Prairie have trails. The Center is located on the North side of Palatine Rd, 1-mile west of Barrington Rd in the extreme northwest corner of Cook County, in Barrington Hills, IL. Call Crabtree Nature Center at 847/381-6592.

THE DES PLAINES DIVISION TRAIL: The trail begins at Touhy Ave (connecting with the Indian Boundary Division Trail, see below) where it continues north along the Des Plaines River for a total of 10-miles. Along the way lie the remains of an Indian Village, an Indian Trail Tree, the site of a pioneer cabin among the cottonwoods, Indian portage to the North Branch of the Chicago River, Indian Charcoal pits, and the River Trail Nature Center (see below) with parking, exhibits and bathrooms. Here, Native Americans paddled their canoes along the Des

Plaines River and hunted bear, deer and elk along its banks. Next came white trappers and fur traders searching for beaver. Call the Cook County Forest Preserve at 312/261-8400.

DOLTON PRAIRIE: A privately owed site on the south side of Dolton Ave and east side of US 94 in Dolton, IL. The prairie has a high floristic quality and diversity. There is no contact information.

DROPSEED PRAIRIE: (See Indian Boundary Prairies below).

EAST RIVER ROAD PRAIRIE: 2-acres of managed prairie located on the north side of Ballard Rd east of US 294 in DesPlaines, IL in northeast Cook County. There is no contact information.

EDENS EXPRESSWAY: Prairie plantings along Eden's Expressway (Route 94) at Niles Center Road planted by the IDOT. Call the IDOT, Bureau of Operations in Schaumberg, IL at 847/705-4000.

EDGEBROOK FLATWOODS: 10-acre prairie bounded by Caldwell and Devon Aves and the Chicago River in northwest Cook County (see Bunker Hill Prairie above). Call the North Branch Restoration Project at 847/679-4289 or the Cook County Forest Preserve at 312/261-8400.

GREENBAY ROAD PRAIRIE: Prairie plantings along the east side of Greenbay Rd from the Wilmette/Evanston line to McCormick Blvd in Evanston, IL. Call Evanston, Streets and Sanitation Division, at 847/866-2940.

GENSBURG-MARKHAM PRAIRIE NATURE PRESERVE: 105.6-acres plus 6.2-acre buffer provides an unusual example of sandy loam prairie that combines the characteristics of black silt loam prairies with true sand prairies. Classified as lacustring prairie, it lies on one of the few untouched remnants of the bed of ancient Lake Chicago. Dr. Robert Betz, a noted prairie authority, accidentally discovered it and then worked to save this virgin prairie. Northeastern Illinois University biologist Ron Panzer has successfully reintroduced the Franklin's ground squirrel, an original inhabitant of these prairies whose local populations had become extinct. The Preserve is in Markham, IL east of Kedzie Ave, west of Interstate 294 and between 155th and 157th Sts. The prairie is open to the public, but visitors are encouraged to stay on the trails. Call Northeastern Illinois University at 312/583-4050 or TNC, IL in Chicago, IL at 312/346-8166. (This is one of the 4 prairies that makeup the Indian Boundary Prairies, see below).

GLENBROOK NORTH HIGH SCHOOL PRAIRIE NATURE PRESERVE: 1.6-acre remnant of original mesic black soil prairie plus 0.7 acres of buffer in the Village of Northbrook, IL at the Glenbrook North High School. The school is ½-mile north of Willow Rd on Shermer Rd. Call Glenbrook North High School at 847/272-6400, ext 274.

(The) GROVE NATIONAL HISTORIC LANDMARK: 125-acres includes restored prairie originally owned by the Kennicott family, early Illinois naturalists. The site is located at 1321 Milwaukee Ave in Glenview, IL. It has self-guided trails. Call the Grove at 847/299-6096.

(DEWEY) HELMICK NATURE PRESERVE: 12.83-acre natural area featuring more than 100 species of natural and restored prairie. The Preserve is west of Cicero Ave in Matteson, IL on the Old Plank Road Trail. Call the Old Plank Road Trail Matteson, IL at 708/748-1559 or Thorn Creek Audubon at 708/798-3115.

INDIAN BOUNDARY PRAIRIES: 300-acres of tallgrass prairie in the City of Markham, IL. The prairies are called: Dropseed, Paintbrush, Sundrop and Gensburg-Markham. A National Natural Landmark, it sits on the plain formed by the gradually receding ancient Chicago Lake waters at the end of the Wisconsin Glaciation. An ancient beach ridge runs throughout. Named for the 1800s boundary-line between whites and Indians, it escaped development because of the 1930's depression, becoming a critical habitat for endangered grassland plants and birds such as the bobolink and eastern meadowlark. Call TNC, IL at 312/346-8166 or Northeastern Illinois University at 312/583-4050.

INDIAN BOUNDARY DIVISION TRAIL: The trail begins at Madison Street, River Forest, IL and follows the Des Plaines River northward, past Trailside Museum, through Thatcher Woods to North Ave. It then goes along an old Indian Trail to Grand Ave, through the historic La Framboise and Robinson reservations, and on to Touhy Ave (a total length of about 10¾-miles), where it connects with the Des Plaines Division trail. The trail passes many habitats including prairie. Call the Cook County Forest Preserve at 312/261-8400.

INDIGO PRAIRIE: 5-acres located between Oakton and Dempster Sts on the east side of Waukegan Rd in Morton Grove, IL in northwest Cook County. Call River Trail Nature Center at 847/824-8360 or the Forest Preserve District of Cook County-Conservation Department, Land Management Section at 630/257-2045.

JEDLICKA PRAIRIE: 2-acres of restored prairie in southwest Cook County. Call the Forest Preserve District of Cook County-Conservation Department, Land Management Section at 630/257-2045.

KLOEMPKEN PRAIRIE: 175-acre site in the Cook County Forest Preserve being restored as a prairie, with approximately 20-acres restored so far. The prairie is located at 1600 E. Golf Road, Des Plaines, IL and accessible from the Oakton Community College parking lot C. Call the Cook County Forest Preserve at 708/771-1330.

LITTLE RED SCHOOLHOUSE NATURE CENTER PRAIRIE: 35-

acres of restored prairie located in southwest Cook County on 104th Ave, ½-mile south of 95th St. Before the written history of man, Indian hunters followed the receding glacier that covered northern Illinois and found the swampy southern end of Lake Michigan teeming with game. Flint chips and occasional arrow points are often found here. In 1804, the area supported two Indian villages, one at the intersection of Archer Ave and 107th St and one about where the town of Palos Park, IL now stands. Archer Ave was a very important Indian and early settler trail. (See Chuck's Meadow and Longjohn Slough, now a wildlife refuge, a wet prairie that farmers used to cut wild hay). Call the Forest Preserve District of Cook County-Conservation Department, Land Management Section at 630/257-2045 or the Nature Center at 708/839-6897.

MANNHEIM PRAIRIE: 10-acres of black soil prairie located south of 87th St between Kean and Mannheim Rds in Hickory Hills, IL in southwest Cook County. Call the Forest Preserve District of Cook County, Conservation Department, Land Management Section at 630/257-2045.

MIAMI WOODS PRAIRIE: 3-acre prairie located on the east side of Caldwell Ave 2 blocks north of Oakton St in Morton Grove, IL. Call the River Trail Nature Center at 847/824-8360 or the Forest Preserve District of Cook County, Conservation Department, Land Management Section at 630/257-2045.

MORTON GROVE PRAIRIE PRESERVE: 1.9-acre remnant of mesic and wet mesic tallgrass prairie in Morton Grove, IL at the northeast end of the 16-acre Prairieview Park, just east of Caldwell Rd on Dempster and Newcastle Sts. Call the Morton Grove Park District at 847/965-1200.

NILES WEST HIGH SCHOOL CONSERVATION & NATURE RESEARCH PRAIRIE RESTORATION PROJECT: The project is located south of Oakton St on Gross Point Rd in Skokie, IL. Call the school at 847/568-3900.

NORTH BRANCH RESTORATIOH PROJECT: Wet-mesic prairie restoration by volunteers along the bicycle path in the Cook County Forest Preserve on the north branch of the Chicago River in Chicago and Morton Grove IL. Call North Branch Restoration Project at 847/679-4289 or the Cook County Forest Preserve at 312/261-8400.

NORTH PARK VILLAGE NATURE CENTER: 9-to 10-acres of re-created prairies lie next to woodlands and wetlands in this 46-acre urban wilderness in the City of Chicago, IL. The Center is located at 5801 North Pulaski Ave. 1½-miles of trails wind through the Center. Parking and toilets are available. Call the Center at 312/ 744-5472.

OAKTON COLLEGE PRAIRIE: 20-plus acres of prairie restoration owned and managed by Oakton College at the south side of Central St in Des Plaines, IL in the northwest portion of the county. Call Oakton College at 847/635-1600.

OLYMPIA FIELDS COUNTRY CLUB: A golf course that is certified by the Audubon Society Cooperative Sanctuary Program of Selkirk, NY located at 2800 Country Club Dr Olympia Fields, IL. It has a 1.75-acre demonstration prairie. Call the Club at 708/748-0495.

PAINTBRUSH PRAIRIE: (See Indian Boundary Prairies above).

PALATINE PRAIRIE: 7.5-acre prairie characteristic of the "swell and swale" topography that once encompassed much of the Morainal Section of the Morainal Division of northeastern Illinois. Call the Palatine Park District at 847/991-0333.

PALOS FEN NATURE PRESERVE: 48-acres of graminoid fen, marsh and oak savanna located north of 107th St and west of 88th Ave in Palos Hills, IL. There are many prairie plants here in the only graminoid fen to survive on the Chicago Lake Plain. Call the Cook County Forest Preserve at 708/771-1330.

PAXTON AVENUE PRAIRIE: A small prairie located in the Sand Ridge Nature Center (see below). The Pines Trail passes by a prairie located at 15890 Paxton Ave in Calumet City, IL and east of Torrence Ave. Call the Sand Ridge Nature Center at 708/868-0606.

PHANTOM PRAIRIE TRAIL: 1.66-mile trail in the Crab Tree Nature Center (see above) that moves through a reconstruction of the tallgrass prairie that once covered 90% of Cook County and more than ½ of Illinois, which then supported bison, wolf, curlew and prairie grouse. The true prairie is gone but Phantom Prairie represents a man-made ghost or phantom of what once was. Deer, fox, bobolinks, Henslow's sparrows, short-billed marsh wrens, ants, bees, butterflies and grasshoppers can be spotted. The entrance to the Center is on Palatine Rd 1-mile west of Barrington Rd in Barrington, IL. Call Crabtree Nature Center at 847/381-6592.

POPLAR CREEK PRAIRIE/SAVANNA: 800-acre prairie restoration project, one of the Midwest's largest, is located in the City of Hoffman Estates, IL. The restoration is located in Popular Creek Forest Preserve, which is located on the west side of Hwy 59 between Golf and Shoe Factory Rds. Call the TNC, IL in Chicago, IL at 312/346-8166 or Cook County Forest Preserve District Conservation Department, Land Management Section at 630/257-2045.

POWDERHORN LAKE AND PRAIRIE: 7-acres of wet and sand ridge prairie located at Powderhorn Lake on Brainard Ave ½-mile east of

Burnham Ave in southeast Cook County. This site is part of the proposed Calumet National Heritage Area. Call the Forest Preserve District of Cook County Conservation Department, Land Management Section at 630/257-2045 or the Calumet Ecological Park Association at 773/374-8543.

ROGAN-WITTUR PRAIRIE: 7-acres of prairie restored by the Northbrook Garden Club on land owned by two corporations located on Commercial Ave close to Sanders Rd in Northbrook, IL. Call Julie Hansen at the Northbrook Park District at 847/291-2995.

RIVER TRAIL NATURE CENTER PRAIRIE: 10-acres of managed prairie located ½-mile south of Lake (Euclid) Ave on the east side of River Rd in northwest Cook County. The Nature Center and parking lot are located at 3120 Milwaukee Ave, Wheeling, IL. A self-guided trail that runs along the Des Plaines River runs through this site. (See the Indian Boundary Division Trail and The Des Plaines Division Trail above). Call the River Trail Center at 847/824-8360.

SAND RIDGE PRAIRIE NATURE PRESERVE: 15-20-acres of prairie in the 70-acre Sand Ridge Nature Preserve near Calumet City, IL. The Preserve is between 154th and 159th Sts and west of Torrence Ave. This prairie provides a fine example of dry-mesic and wet sand prairie growing on the very sandy soil deposited 5 to 6,000 years ago by the gradually receding glacial Lake Chicago. Its low sandy ridges supports sand prairies, scattered black oak savannas, and tall and short grasses. The Nature Center provides slide shows, a pioneer cabin reproduction, and trails and bathrooms. Call the Cook County Forest Preserve's Sand Ridge Nature Center at 708/868-0606.

SANTA FE PRAIRIE: 10-acres of prairie along the Des Plaines River line of the railroad in Hodgkins, IL in southwest Cook County's. Call the DNR, IL at 217/785-8774 or the Cook County Forest Preserve at 312/261-8400.

SAUGANASH PRAIRIE: 6-acres of wet prairie located at Bryn Mawr and Kostner Sts on Chicago's northwest side. Call the Forest Preserve District of Cook County-Conservation Department, Land Management Section at 630/257-2045.

SCHILLER WOODS PRAIRIE: 1-acre wet prairie located off Irving Park Rd west of Cumberland Ave in Schiller Park, IL in northwest Cook County. Call the Forest Preserve District of Cook County Conservation Department, Land Management Section at 630/257-2045.

SHOE FACTORY ROAD PRAIRIE NATURE PRESERVE: 10-acres of dry to dry mesic gravel prairie on a hill top in northwest Cook County east of Elgin, IL. Over 100 prairie species have been identified at this site on the crest and slopes of a kame. The prairie is on the south side of Shoe Factory road just west of Sutton Rd. Access is by permission only. This is the cornerstone of an adjacent 600-acre prairie and oak savanna restoration project by the Forest Preserve District and TNC, IL. Call the Forest Preserve District of Cook County Conservation Department, Land Management Section at 630/257-2045.

SOMME PRAIRIE NATURE PRESERVE: 70-acres of tallgrass prairie in Northbrook, IL, ¼-mile north of Dundee Rd on Waukegan Rd in the Somme Woods Forest Preserve. The Preserve includes wet and mesic prairie restored by the cooperative efforts of the Cook County Forest Preserve, TNC, IL and the North Branch Restoration Project. There is parking but no trails. Call TNC, IL in Chicago, IL at 312/346-8166 or Cook County Forest Preserve at 708/771-1330 or at 630/257-2045.

SPRING LAKE PRAIRIE: 20-acres of wet-black soil prairie located in the 560-acres Spring Lake Nature Preserve's mosaic of plant communities. There are also two glacial lakes. The prairie is west of Sutton Rd on County Line Rd about 3½-miles west of Barrington, IL in the northwest portion of county. Access is by permission only. Call the Cook County Forest Preserve District Conservation Department, Land Management Section at 630/257-2045 or Crab Tree Nature Center at 847/381-6592.

SPRING VALLEY POPLAR CREEK PRAIRIE: (See Poplar Creek Prairie above).

ST. MIHIEL AREAS: Part of the Cook County Forest Preserve's Tinley Creek Division, it holds small fragments of native prairie. The preserve is situated on a ridge of glacial drift known to geologists as Tinley Moraine. The Wisconsin Glacier, the last retreating glacier deposited it. To the northeast lies the flat Chicago Plain, a lower area that was the bed of the ancient Lake Chicago. To the southwest previously wet prairies were known as the "Deep Prairie." Call the Cook County Forest Preserve, Tinley Creek Division at 708/385-7650 or 7654.

SUPERIOR STREET PRAIRIE LAND AND WATER RESERVE: 33.5-acre tract owned by the Calumet Memorial Park District on Calumet City's Superior St. The property encompasses 10 city blocks and is one of the last remnants of the Chicago Lake Plain of dry-mesic sand savanna, mesic sand prairie and sedge meadow. Contact Brian Reilly at 815/423-6370.

SUNDROP PRAIRIE: (See Indian Boundary Prairie above).

THATCHER WOODS: 77 plus-acres of oak savanna located at Thatcher Ave and Washington Blvd in River Forest, IL. This is a restoration project. Call the Forest Preserve District of Cook County,

Conservation Department at 800/870-3666.

THORNTON FRACTIONAL NORTH HIGH SCHOOL PRAIRIE: A privately owned prairie located south of 154th St and east of Penn-Central RR tracks in Calumet City, IL. It is an Illinois Natural Inventory site and considered by botanists to be superior in quality to the nearby Sand Ridge Nature Preserve. Call at 708/585-1000

TURKEY-FOOT PRAIRIE: One of the prairies of the Crabtree Nature Center. (See Crabtree Nature Center above). Call the center at 847/381-6592.

UNDERWRITER'S LABORATORY: 9-acres being turned into prairie around the company's building located at 333 Pfingston Rd, Northbrook, IL. Call the Openlands Project (Julia Plumb) in Chicago, IL at 312/427-4256 or Volker Kotscha at 847/664-2100.

VAN VLISSINGEN PRAIRIE: 117-acre prairie that is earmarked as the northernmost parcel in the proposed 4,000-acre Calument Open Space Reserve. The site is located east of Van Vlissingen Rd between 97th and 103rd Sts. Call Corlands/Openlands Project at 312/427-4256.

WALKER SCHOOL DEMONSTRATION PRAIRIE: A small school prairie project at the corner of Central Park and Church in Skokie, IL. Call Walker Elementary School at 847/492-7970.

WATERSMEET PRAIRIE: A prairie on Winnetka Rd in Northfield, IL. Call North Branch Restortation Project at 847/679-4289.

WAYSIDE WOOD PRAIRIE: 3-acres of wet and black soil prairie located on the north side of Dempster St east of Waukegan Rd in Prairie View Park, Morton Grove, IL. Call the River Trail Nature Center at 847/824-8360.

WENTWORTH PRAIRIE: A privately owned site located north of 154th St and east of Penn-Central RR tracks in Calumet City, IL. This is a part of the proposed Natural Heritage Area. Call the Calumet Ecological Park Association at 773/374-8543.

WILLIGAN ROAD PRAIRIE: 10-acres of wet and upland prairie located south of Thornton-Lansing Rd across from entrance to Wampum Lake Forest Preserve in Thornton, IL in southeast Cook County's Thorn Creek Division. Thornton-Lansing Rd and Glenwood-Dyer Rd were Indian trails that followed the crests of sand dunes marking beaches at the southern limits of Lake Chicago when, during the last glacial epoch, it stood at levels much higher than the present Lake Michigan. Call Thorn Creek Division at 708/474-1221 or call the Forest Preserve District of Cook County Conservation Department, Land Management Section at 630/257-2045.

WOLF ROAD PRAIRIE NATURE PRESERVE: 44-acres plus 16-acres Hickory Lane Buffer Site in Westchester, IL located at the Northwest corner of 31st Street and Wolf Road. It represents the largest original tallgrass prairie in the Chicago area. This glorious remnant is located in the Salt Creek Division of the Cook County Forest Preserve District in Bemis Woods Forest Preserve. There is also a savanna community dominated by bur oak with wild hyacinth, groundnut and meadow rue beneath the trees. This is a restoration project by the Save the Prairie Society. A buffer to the prairie is being added. Visit its Franzosenbusch Prairie House Museum/Nature Center. Call Save the Prairie Society at 708/865-8736, read its publication "Prairie Roots" and visit its website at www.SaveThePrairie Society.org. Call DNR, IL at Silver Springs State Park in Yorkville, IL at 708/553-1372.

(JAMES) WOODWORTH PRAIRIE PRESERVE: 5.3-acres of virgin tallgrass prairie in Glenview, IL off Greenwood Rd on the east side of Milwaukee Ave north of Golf Rd. Speeding cars and a fast food restaurant surround this remnant of the former Peacock Prairie. Too wet to plow and loved for its flowery beauty, the original acreage escaped being farmed, but most fell to suburban development. Call the Preserve's Interpretative Center at 847/965-3488 in summer. Year round, call the University of Illinois in Chicago, Biological Sciences at 312/996-2643 or 8673 or email at csnp@uic.edu.

YANKEE WOODS: A part of the Cook County Forest Preserve's Tinley Creek Division, it holds small fragments of native prairie. Yankee Woods is located at Central Ave and 167th St in Chicago, IL. Call the Cook County Forest Preserve Tinley Creek Division at 708/385-7650 or 7654.

DeKalb County:
For information on prairie in pre-settlement DeKalb, the Forest Preserve District recommends booklets such as *Natural Prairie in the DeKalb Area, 1840 to present* by Don Murray available from the Gurler Heritage Association, 205 Pine St., DeKalb, IL 60115. For natural education, programs in DeKalb call the Natural Resource Center, which is located in Russell Wood Forest Preserve at the University of Illinois Extension, at 815/758-8194.

AFTON FOREST PRESERVE: 240-acres supporting a variety of wildlife habitats and recreation areas. Prairie grasses are planted along the Afton Forest Preserve Nature Trail along which numbered benches correspond to a guide pamphlet about the general area. A mowed path runs through the 4-acre re-created prairie. The site once supported Indians, bison and prairie chickens. The prairie was planted in 1984 by the forest preserve staff and is located on Crego Rd, between Perry and McGirr Rds south of DeKalb, IL. Call the DeKalb County Forest

Preserve District at 815/756-6633 or 815/895-7191.

AFTON TOWNSHIP CENTRE CEMETERY: 3-acres located on Perry Road 5-miles south of the city of Dekalb, IL, between Waterman Rd and South First St. Call the Afton Township supervisor at 815/758-8387.

MERRITT PRAIRIE: 56-acres of rolling terrain with native prairie and wetland restorations located on Keslinger Rd east of Somonauk Rd. Call the DeKalb County Forest Preserve District at 815/895-7191.

THE GREAT WESTERN TRAIL: 17-mile trail dotted with prairie plants begins just east of Sycamore, IL and extends eastward through Kane County to the Fox River Trail to St. Charles, IL, following the old railroad line. The DeKalb/Sycamore Trail (connects to the Illinois Prairie Path) links the DeKalb Park District Trail from Lions Park on DeKalb's south side to the City of Sycamore for 2-miles and then to the Great Western Trail that extends into Kane County. Shopping, restaurants and museums are interspersed with natural areas including prairies. Call the DeKalb Forest Preserve District at 815/895-7191.

WILKINSON-RENWICK MARSH NATURE PRESERVE: 47-acres of prairie potholes left from the glaciers located about 5-miles north of the City of DeKalb, IL. The marsh that formed in the pothole was too large to tile. This inability to drain the wetland saved it from farming. The Preserve also contains a prairie restoration area. Call the DeKalb County Forest Preserve at 815/895-7191.

DuPage County:
BELMONT PRAIRIE NATURE PRESERVE: 10.4-acre preserve is designated an Illinois Nature Preserve, and one of the last original prairies in Illinois. The site is part of the Valparaiso Moraine, formed by the Wisconsin Glacier 10,000-years ago. This is a high quality remnant of the dry to wet prairies typical of the Northeastern Morainal Natural Division. The dry mesic prairie has a high forb diversity. Dominant grass species are porcupine grass and Canada blue-joint grass. The small wet prairie contains such moisture-loving species as cordgrass, sedges, and blue-joint grass. Fauna sightings include coyote, woodchuck, meadow vole, ground squirrel and white-tailed deer. The prairie is located in Downers Grove, IL west of Belmont Rd and south of Ogden Ave near the intersection of Haddow and Cross Sts. To volunteer, obtain materials about this prairie, or make reservations for organized groups call Downers Grove Park District at 630/963-1304.

CHURCHILL PRAIRIE NATURE PRESERVE: 65-acres of gently rolling topography supports mesic and dry-mesic prairie, upland forest, savanna and sedge meadow and features a maintained 1-mile trail through the native grassland. The prairie is off the Western Trail at St Charles Rd and US 355. Call the DuPage County Forest Preserve

District in Wheaton, IL at 630/933-7200.

DANADA FOREST PRESERVE: 753-acre preserve is home to the esteemed Danada Equestrian Center. It also has trails and a restored prairie patch. The entrance is on Naperville Rd, ½-mile north of US 88, in Wheaton, IL. Call the Preserve at 630/668-6012.

FERMILAB PRAIRIE RECONSTRUCTION PROJECT: 1,200-acres of recreated pre-Columbian tallgrass prairie in various stages of restoration support bison (a herd of bison is maintained on the site), mink, beaver, muskrat, falcon, foxes, coyotes and grassland birds. Prairie ponds harbor the increasingly rare Blanding's turtle. This remarkable effort in the City of Batavia, IL to reconstruct a large acreage of native American grassland was undertaken by Fermi National Accelerator Laboratory (Fermilab) in 1974 under the guidance of Robert Betz, a noted biologist. Over 3,000 years ago, Native Americans hunted on the savanna where Fermilab is now located. Displays include implements unearthed by archeologists at the site. The entrance to Fermilab Prairie is at the east side of Batavia, IL at Kirk Rd and Pine St in Kane County. Part of the prairie is in Kane County. The lab was closed to all visitors after the September 11, 2001 terrorist attack. Call Fermilab at 630/840-3351 for its present status.

FULLERSBURG WOODS FOREST PRESERVE: 222-acres with an interpretive trail that lead visitors through lowland woods and the restored prairie. The Preserve is located on Spring Rd about ¼-mile north of Ogden Ave in Oak Brook, IL. Call the Preserve at 630/850-8110.

GREAT WESTERN PRAIRIE: 6-acres adjacent to the Illinois Prairie Path (see below), located in Elmhurst, IL and is 8-blocks long from Spring Rd to Salt Creek. Call Elmhurst Park District at 630/993-8913.

GREENE VALLEY FOREST PRESERVE: 1,425-acres of natural environments and open fields that provide a home for many of the county's native plants and animals. From golden prairies to misty marshes, the Preserve offers visitors a beautiful setting in which to enjoy the great outdoors and has multi-use trails, parking and picnic areas. The Preserve is located off Greene Rd, between Hobson Rd and 75th St, in Woodridge, IL. Call the DuPage County Forest Preserve District in Wheaton, IL at 630/933-7200.

ILLINOIS PRAIRIE PATH (IPP): 55-mile long hiking, biking, and equestrian nature trail (mainly made for bicycling) that extends into Kane County. The path starts 20-miles west of Chicago following the right-of-way of the former Chicago, Aurora and Elgin Railway and connects many nature areas, including prairies. The path was extended into Cook County by acquiring an additional 4.5 miles of right-of-way.

The path now begins at First Avenue in Maywood, IL. There are plans to extend it into DesPlaines County. Parking is available at several locations. Call the IPP Corporation at 630/752-0120 or visit the web site at www.ipp.org/

LYMAN WOODS: 135-acres of original landscape including 17-acres of oak savanna and a glacial kame support a remnant native prairie. Sightings from its 2-mile trail include deer, fox, coyote, great horned owls and waterfowl. The Woods is located in Downers Grove, IL, east of Highland Ave, north of the Good Samaritan Hospital and south of 31st St, with parking on 33rd St off Highland Ave. Call the Downers Grove Park District at 630/963-1304.

MAPLE GROVE FOREST PRESERVE: 82-acres that contains among other things a remnant black maple savanna and upland maple forest communities that have existed for hundreds of years. Maple Grove is a very special place. From Illiniwek hunters in the 1500s to modern-day hikers, people have enjoyed this forest for centuries. Native Americans lived around Maple Grove for hundreds of years. The entrance to the Preserve is on Maple Ave 1-mile west of Main St and 1-mile east of Belmont Rd in Downers Grove, IL. Call the DuPage Forest Preserves District in Wheaton, IL at 630/933-7200.

MORTON ARBORETUM: 100-acres of re-created tallgrass prairie in a 1,700-acre preserve, which features 12-miles of walking trails and 11-miles of scenic roads. The Arboretum is located within metropolitan Chicago in the City of Lisle, IL, ½-mile north of Hwy 5 on Hwy 53. Repairing a leaky water pipe raised the water level and rid the preserve of the unwanted and invasive imported reed canary grass. The Arboretum has a Visitor Center, Gift and Coffee Shops, Sterling Morton Library and Thornhill Education Center. A Fall Color Festival welcomes you to "the most beautiful time of the year" with colorful trees and "golden prairie grasses." Call the Arboretum at 630/968-0074 or 630/719-2465.

ST. STEPHEN CEMETERY PRAIRIE: 2-acre prairie in a cemetery located in Carol Stream, IL between Gary Ave and Schmale Rd. The cemetery is locked, but a key can be obtained from the Milton township offices, 1492 N. Main St., Wheaton, IL. Call the office at 630/668-1616. Information is also available from Bill Gunderson at 630/665-5183.

SPRINGBROOK PRAIRIE FOREST PRESERVE: 1,787-acres including open fields, wetlands and restored prairie. The Preserve is located in Naperville, IL near Hwy 59 and 75th St with parking off Plainfield-Naperville Road ¼-mile south of 75th St. Call the DuPage Forest Preserves in Wheaton, IL at 630/933-7200.

WATERFALL GLEN FOREST PRESERVE: 2,474-acres of some of the

most diverse plant and animal populations in the area, along with some of the most rugged landscape, including prairie and savanna. In addition, there are trails and many recreational opportunities here. Wildlife watching is also possible. The Preserve surrounds the Argonne National Laboratory. The entrance to the Preserve is at Cass Ave and Northgate Rd off US 55 in Darien, IL. Call the DuPage Forest Preserve in Wheaton, IL at 630/933-7200.

WHEATON WARRENVILLE SOUTH HIGH SCHOOL: 2.5-acres of student restored prairie located at 1920 S Wiesbrook Rd, Wheaton, IL. Call the school at 630/682-2120.

WEST CHICAGO PRAIRIE FOREST PRESERVE: 313-acres in West Chicago, IL with parking near the intersection of Industrial Dr and Western Dr. The site contains 500 native plant species and numerous wildlife species in its assortment of prairies, wetlands and savannas. This site captures the feeling of the land's original prairie wilderness. Call the DuPage Forest Preserve in Wheaton, IL at 630/933-7200.

Effingham County:
BALLARD NATURE CENTER: 210-acres, including 100-acres of woodland, 15-acres of restored prairie, 10-acres of shallow water wetlands, 85-acres of agricultural land and an interpretive center. The center is located 2¼-miles east of Altamont, IL on US 40. Call the center at 618/483-6856.

TWELVE-MILE PRAIRIE: Mesic black soil prairie located from Watson, IL to Kinmundy, IL between the Illinois Central RR tracks and Hwy 37. The prairie extends into Fayette and Marion Counties. Call IDOT at 217/782-7231.

INTERSTATE 57: Prairie plantings in highway median of Interstate 57 just south of Little Wabash River Bridge. Call IDOT at 217/782-7231.

Fayette County:
TWELVE-MILE PRAIRIE: (See Effingham County, above).

Ford County:
PAXTON ROAD PRAIRIE: A strip of native prairie along Hwy 45 between the highway and the railroad for a distance of about 600 feet. The prairie is located south of Paxton, IL and north of the Ford/Champaign County Line. Call the Illinois Nature Preservation Commission at 217/688-2622.

PROSPECT CEMETERY PRAIRIE NATURE PRESERVE: 5-acres of mesic black soil prairie supporting some prairie is located at the southeast edge of Paxton, IL on Green St. Call the Paxton Township Cemetery Association at 217/379-2676.

Grundy County:
GOOSE LAKE PRAIRIE STATE PARK (known as Illinois' "Prairie State Park"): 1,537-acres, plus 90.8 acres of buffer, include dry-mesic, wet-mesic and wet prairie and prairie potholes. This prairie is the only remnant of the once vast and famous untimbered Grand Prairie. This is the largest prairie remnant in Illinois with both prairie and marsh communities. The Park's Interpretive Center features dioramas depicting the prairie and early pioneer life on the prairie. A trail system takes the visitor through several prairie communities, and across a prairie pothole and marsh via a boardwalk. The prairie is large enough to provide a mile long prairie vista and to support prairie wildlife such as coyotes, marsh hawks and short-eared owls. Bird watchers can see now-rare grassland birds such as Henslow sparrow, bobolink and grasshopper and savanna sparrows. Waterfowl abound in spring and fall. Wildflowers and grasses are at their peak in August and September. The park is southeast of Morris, IL. Call the Park at 815/942-2800 or the DNR, IL at 217/782-7454.

SHORT PIONEER CEMETERY PRAIRIE: 1.3-acres of dry-mesic sand prairie southeast of Goose Lake Prairie State Park off of Erickson Rd on a dirt road. Call the DNR, IL at 217/782-7454.

Hamilton County:
KARCHER'S POST OAK WOODS NATURE PRESERVE: 40-acre tract contains old-growth post and white oak trees, some of which date back to the American Revolution. The savanna-like, open woodland supports many interesting forbs. This is one of the last remaining examples of old-growth post oak woods in Illinois. Generally closed to the public. Call the Illinois Audubon Society in Danville, IL at 217/446-5085.

Hancock County:
MISSISSIPPI RIVER SAND HILLS NATURE PRESERVE: 45-acres that includes a small dry prairie at the top of a hill. Access is by permission only. The Preserve is south-southwest of junction of highways 96 & 136 south of a blacktop road. Call the DNR, IL at 217/785-8774.

Henderson County:
BIG RIVER STATE FOREST: 200-acre state forest, located 8-miles north of Oquawka, IL on the Oquawka-Keithsburg blacktop. Prairie wildflowers are scattered in openings that appear throughout the forest, but are best seen in the prairie natural area along Landfill Rd. Call the DNR, IL at 217/785-8774 or Big River Forest at 309/374-2496.

Henry County:
GREENLEE CEMETERY PRAIRIE NATURE PRESERVE: 1.2-acres of relatively undisturbed dry-mesic black soil prairie lying near the top of a ridge and draining into a tributary of Spring Creek. The cemetery

is northeast of Cambridge, IL on a county road. Call Supervisor of Munson Township at 309/944-3707 or Henry County Natural Area Guardians % Henry County Soil and Water Conservation District at 309/937-3376 or the DNR, IL at 217/785-8774.

MUNSON TOWNSHIP CEMETERY PRAIRIE NATURE PRESERVE: 5-acres of black soil prairie. According to historical accounts, the site once was mowed for hay. The Preserve is southwest from the south edge of Geneseo, IL. There is a trail through the cemetery. Call Supervisor of Munson Township at 309/944-3707 or the DNR, IL at 217/785-8774.

Iroquois County:
BONNIE'S PRAIRIE NATURE PRESERVE: 10.6-acres that includes a high quality sand pond and wet sand prairie. Found here are two very uncommon native bee species that gather pollen exclusively from pickerel weed. The Preserve is northeast of Watseka, IL on Co Rd 2200N. Contact the Grand Prairie Friends of Illinois at gpf@prairienet.org, or call the DNR, IL at 217/785-8774.

HOOPER BRANCH SAVANNA NATURE PRESERVE: 483-acres supporting five biotic communities including rare shrub prairie and sand prairie. This savanna is a part of the 2,480-acre Iroquois County Wildlife Area and is considered the largest single tract of rare native savanna in Illinois (see below). The Wildlife Area and Savanna is northeast of Beaverville, IL in the northeast corner of the county. Call the Site Superintendent Iroquois County Wildlife Area at 815/435-2218 or the DNR, IL at 217/785-8774.

IROQUOIS COUNTY WILDLIFE AREA: 2,480-acres that includes a 2,000-acre wildlife area, open for hunting, and a 480-acre savanna (see above). This WA features dry, mesic, and wet prairie areas. The 2,000-acre hunting area is available for hiking and nature study during periods when hunting is not permitted. See above for location. Call the Site Superintendent Iroquois County Wildlife Area at 815/435-2218 or the DNR, IL at 217/785-8774.

LODA CEMETERY PRAIRIE NATURE PRESERVE: 3.4-acres that are an outstanding example of original mesic black soil prairie. The Preserve is northeast of Loda, IL. The cemetery was mowed but never cultivated or pastured. The site escaped being converted into additional burial space through the efforts of the Natural Land Institute. Call TNC, IL in Chicago, IL at 312/346-8166.

Jackson County:
DESOTO PRAIRIE: A dry-mesic prairie remnant preserved as a right-of-way strip adjacent to Hwy 51 north of DeSoto, south of Elkville, IL. Characteristic species include little bluestem, Indian grass, and wood-

Prairie Directory

land sunflower. The prairie is owned by the Illinois Central Gulf RR, but has been used by classes from SIU plant biology department for many years. The prairie is managed by the DNR, IL. Call the DNR, IL at 217/785-8774 or the SIU, College of Science, at 618/536-2331.

GREEN EARTH II: 3-hectare nature preserve near Carbondale's Oakland Cemetery dedicated to the restoration of a natural prairie environment. Green Earth acquired the site from the city of Carbondale, IL. Half of the site was seeded with prairie plants donated by the U.S. Soil Conservation Service. The SIU Botany Department provided seedlings of prairie dock. Call the Southern Illinois University, College of Science, at 618/536-2331 or write to Green Earth, PO Box 441, Carbondale, IL 62903.

GREEN EARTH WETLAND: Another small nature preserve in Carbondale, IL. This wetland prairie was established in the early 1990s with a tallgrass prairie seed mix. Call the Southern Illinois University, College of Science, at 618/536-2331 or write to Green Earth, PO Box 441, Carbondale, IL 62903.

Jasper County:
JASPER COUNTY PRAIRIE CHICKEN SANCTUARY: 200-acre sanctuary adjacent to the Newton Lake Fish and Wildlife Area. The sanctuary was established in order to enhance the management and conservation of the greater prairie chicken. Newton Lake served as one of two release points for the DNR's efforts to reintroduce the river otter back into Illinois. The Wildlife Area and Sanctuary is located south of Wheeler, IL. Call the DNR, IL at 618/783-2685.

PRAIRIE RIDGE STATE NATURAL AREA PRAIRIE CHICKEN SANCTUARIES: 2,000-acres of restored prairie and other grasses supporting greater prairie chicken and other grassland birds. Another 1,000-acres lies in Marion County. The area is southwest of the junction of Hwys 33 & 130 in the southwest portion of the county. Access is by permission only so as not to disturb the prairie chickens. For permission to visit, call DNR, IL at 618/783-2685.

Jefferson County:
INTERSTATE 57: Prairie grasses planted in the interchange at the junction of Interstate 57 and 64 south of Mt. Vernon, IL. Call IDOT at 217/782-7231.

Jersey County:
PERE MARQUETTE NATURE PRESERVE: 297-acre preserve is in the north part of the 8,000-acre Pere Marquette State Park. The Preserve holds 5 virgin hill, loess or bluff prairies. They are named Goat Cliff, McAdams Peak, Twin Mounds, Twin Shelters and First Lookout. Though glaciers never covered the park, melt waters from the

66

last glacier deposited soil or loess up to 150-feet deep upon which these prairies grow. Especially in August and September, when the Indian grass, lead plant, and little bluestem are blooming, the hill prairies provide another aspect of the prairie, one different from the tallgrass landscape that dominated the state. Moreover, hill prairies were prominent features of the landscape along most of the major Illinois River systems. Although often large and conspicuous, they were not mentioned in the early scientific literature or mapped by the Government Land Office Surveyors during the 1820s and 1830s, and were first described in 1868 by Worthen, a geologist with the Illinois Geological Survey. In 1937, the five prairies covered 25.01 acres. In 1974, overgrowth had reduced them to 9.78 acres. To survive, the sites require burning.

The Park is named in memory of Father Jacques Marquette. This French Jesuit missionary was, in 1673, along with explorer Louis Jolliet, the first known European to enter what is now Illinois. Occupied by the Illini Confederacy, the region had been home to Native Americans for at least 10,000 years and their prehistoric habitation sites have been excavated. Overlooking the Illinois River on the Great River Rd, the park is 5-miles from Grafton, IL and about 25-miles northwest of Alton. The park maintains trails, a visitor center and interpretative programs, lodge, cottages, restaurant and riding stables. Call the park at 618/786-3323 regarding the prairie or 618/786-2331 for reservations.

Jo Davies County:
APPLE RIVER CANYON STATE PARK: 1,485-acres near the towns of Stockton and Galena, IL supports a native prairie community dotting the edges of the bluffs overlooking the Apple River. The park is located northwest of Rockford, IL on Canyon Rd at 8763 E. Canyon Rd, Apple River, IL. Call the park at 815/745-3302.

HANOVER BLUFF NATURE PRESERVE: 361.7-acres first described by the geologist W. H. Keating in 1832 includes dry dolomite and sand hill prairies lying in a geographical-biological "Driftless Area" that escaped direct impact by the Pleistocene Glaciation. The Preserve is southeast of Hanover, IL on Whitton Rd. Call the DNR, IL at 217/785-8774.

SAVANNA ARMY DEPOT: (Lost Mounds NWR see Carroll Co above)

Johnson County:
CAVE CREEK GLAD NATURE PRESERVE: 2-acres of limestone glade prairie within a 25-acre natural area that is mostly dry upland forest. The Preserve is located 3½-miles south of Vienna, IL on the eastside of Hwy 45. Call the DNR, IL at 217/785-8774.

HERON POND-LITTLE BLACK SLOUGH NATURE PRESERVE:

1,861-acres plus 78-acres of buffer support several natural communities including a 5.9-acre limestone glade prairie on Wildcat Bluff (see below). Heavy rains sometimes flood the trails within the natural area. The Preserve is 4-miles southwest of Vienna, IL. Call DNR, IL at 217/785-8774.

SIMPSON BARREN: 69-acre tract in the National Forest containing high quality dry upland forest and limestone glade communities. Set amidst a dry upland forest of black oak and post oak, 3 distinct glade communities total approximately 10-acres. Common plants include: little bluestem, Indian grass, tick trefoil, woodland sunflower, elm-leaved goldenrod, tall boneset, rattlesnake master, drooping coneflower, rosinweed, and prairie dock. Call the Southern Illinois University, College of Science, at 618/536-2331.

WILDCAT BLUFF GLADE PRAIRIE: 2-hectare natural forest opening that is southwest of Vienna, IL. The glade is part of the Heron Pond-Little Black Slough Nature Preserve (see above). Call the Southern Illinois University, College of Science, at 618/536-2331.

Kane County:
ALMON UNDERWOOD PRAIRIE NATURE PRESERVE: 2-acres of high-quality dry gravel prairie and 12-acres of buffer to be restored to prairie. The site is also the northwestern terminus for the Kaneville Esker, a significant geological feature identified on the Illinois Natural Areas Inventory. Call the Forest Preserve District of Kane County at 630/232-5980.

BINNIE WOODS FOREST PRESERVE: 127-acre forest preserve with wetland prairie pockets being its outstanding feature. The Preserve is on Binnie Rd, about 1-mile west of Randall Rd in Dundee, IL. Call the Preserve at 847/683-2836.

BIG ROCK FOREST PRESERVE: 456-acre preserve with a 60-acre field of restored prairie in progress with a small wooded brook at the north end that joins the fine 80-acre Oak Hickory savanna woodland which overlooks Welsh Creek Fen and the southerly stem of Big Rock Creek. The Preserve is located on Jericho Rd south of Aurora, IL. Call the Forest Preserve District of Kane County at 630/232-5980.

BLACKHAWK FOREST PRESERVE: 284-acres of wetland and forest with little wisps here and there of original prairie remnants and exposed rock ledges and outcroppings. The Preserve is located on Hwy 31 in South Elgin, IL 1-mile north of McLean Blvd. Call the Forest Preserve District of Kane County at 630/232-5980.

BLISS WOODS FOREST PRESERVE: 330-acres in three areas. The Preserve is mostly wetland and forest, but west of Bliss Rd broad expanses of sedge meadows meet little drumlin-like hills, holding five different species of oak and many fine prairie edge plants such as pussy toes, spring beauties, and shining bed straw. The Preserve is located just east of the junction of Bliss Rd and Hwy 47. Call the Forest Preserve District of Kane County at 630/232-5980.

BRUNDIGE ROAD PRAIRIE: 3-acre prairie at Brundige Rd and the Union Pacific Railroad tracks southwest of Geneva, IL. This is a fine dry prairie that was being degraded and is now being restored. Call the Kane County Environmental Dept at 630/208-5118.

BURLINGTON PRAIRIE NATURE PRESERVE: 35-acre prairie and wetland (in a 429-acre preserve) is one of those very rare parcels of land that through a series of fortunate land use events, remains as totally undisturbed prairie. It is an isolated bit of raised, sandy alluvial soil separated from the west, north and east by a wetland moat, and from the rest of the parent farm on the south by a 20-foot high railroad embankment. The 60+ acres of farmland with its extensive, poorly drained soils and wetlands, south of the railroad is presently undergoing a restoration process. Call the Forest Preserve District of Kane County at 630/232-5980.

FERMILAB PRAIRIE RECONSTRUCTION PROJECT: (See DuPage County above).

HEALY ROAD PRAIRIE: A 10,000 year old prairie moved to Bluff Spring Fen in Elgin, IL to save it from being destroyed by mining. For more information call TNC, IL in Chicago at 312/346-8166.

ELBURN FOREST PRESERVE: 87-acre morainal gravel hill at the county watershed divide, which separates the Fox and Kishwaukee River Basins. It is a high quality savanna woodland dominated by white, black and bur oak andshagbark hickory. The Preserve is on Hwy 38 about ½-mile west of Hwy 47. Call the Forest Preserve District of Kane County at 630/232-5980.

ELGIN, GENEVA AND BATAVIA BRANCHES OF THE PRAIRIE PATH: An 8½-mile path that travels easterly into DuPage County. The path travels past prairie remnants. Call the Forest Preserve District of Kane County at 630/232-5980.

ELGIN SHORES FOREST PRESERVE: 50+ acres where there are extensive sand deposits, which permitted the survival of such prairie plants as Naked Sunflower and Purple Coneflower. The Fox River Trail (see below) joins the Illinois Prairie Path at this preserve. The Preserve is on Hwy 20 east of Hwy 31. Call the Forest Preserve District of Kane County at 630/232-5980.

FOX RIVER TRAIL: A hiking, biking, cross-country skiing, and jogging

Trail that stretches from Algonquin to Aurora, IL along the Fox River. The Trail winds through many preserves including prairies. Call the Forest Preserve District of Kane County at 630/232-5980.

GARFIELD FARM AND INN MUSEUM: (See Mill Creek Prairie below).

(VIRGIL L.) GILMAN TRAIL: An 11-mile trail that runs from Ohio St, south of Montgomery St in Aurora, IL to the Waubonsee Community College. The trail crosses the Fox River on a covered bridge and crosses Waubonsee Creek and passes wetlands and small patches of native prairie. On the way can be seen birds and wildflowers. Call the Forest Preserve District of Kane County at 630/232-5980.

(THE) GREAT WESTERN TRAIL: (See DeKalb County above).

JOHNSON MOUND FOREST PRESERVE: 185-acre heavily wooded classic example of a stratified gravel hill known as a "kame", which was deposited some 10,000 years ago. The Preserve was expanded in the 80's by adding some open fields on the north, where woodland and prairie restorations are underway. The Preserve is southeast of Elburn, IL on Hughes Rd. Call the Forest Preserve District of Kane County at 630/232-5980.

LEROY OAKES FOREST PRESERVE: 264-acre preserve located at 37W370 Dean Street, St Charles, IL. 20-acres locally referred to as "Horlock Hill" once held a cornfield. This dry prairie preserve is part of an end moraine composed chiefly of well drained sand and gravel. This site is considered one of the finest dry prairies in the Chicago area. Adjacent to the Preserve is a mesic and wet-mesic prairie created by Preservation Partners of Kane County and the Pioneer Sholes School Society. Call the Forest Preserve District of Kane County at 630/232-5980 or the Preserve at 630/584-5988.

LONG GROVE FOREST PRESERVE: 117-acres where the pre-settlement prairie forbs and grasses have intermixed with the traditional herbaceous woodland carpet plants. Here is an enclave of great biodiversity, an island of ever changing form and color throughout the seasons. The Preserve is 2½-miles northwest of Hwy 47 in Kaneville, IL. Call the Forest Preserve District of Kane County at 630/232-5980.

MILL CREEK PRAIRIE: 31-acre restored prairie includes 20 unplowed acres next to the 281-acre Garfield Farm and Inn Museum. Additional woodland, prairie and wetlands are being restored at the farm. The Garfield Farm is on Garfield Rd just north of Hwy 38 between Geneva and Elburn, IL. The farm conducts monthly-guided prairie walks. Call the farm at 630/584-8485.

MURRAY PRAIRIE: 2.5-acres along The Great Western Trail within

70

the LeRoy Oakes Forest Preserve (see above). This outstanding example of a dry prairie has been used as a gage on which to evaluate other dry prairies. Call the Forest Preserve District of Kane County at 630/232-5980.

PINGREE GROVE FOREST PRESERVE: 396-acres of basically wetlands, contains rich fen edges, prairie and wooded shorelines, bur oak-covered islands and peninsulas, and isolated wetland pockets each with a different high quality plant community. The Preserve is located on Hwy 20 near Pingree Grove, IL. Call the Forest Preserve District of Kane County at 630/232-5980.

PRAIRIE KAME FOREST PRESERVE: 82-acres of prairie lie upon a gravel pile around 30' high, situated on the leading edge of the great glaciers that moved through and retreated from this area some 12,000 years ago. Area high school, college and university science classes visit it today, for it is regarded as one of the best examples remaining of this glacial form. The prairie is located west of Harter Rd off of Hwy 47. Call the Forest Preserve District of Kane County at 630/232-5980.

RACEWAY WOODS FOREST PRESERVE: 95-acre open area with the central core of the tract having a fine savannah and mesic woodland with steep banks where pocket seeps trickle down into a clear rippling brook that wanders through several pristine natural areas. The Dundee Park District owns a portion of the Preserve, but the Kane County Forest Preserve manages the natural areas. The Preserve is located on Hwy 31 near Carpentersville, IL. Call the Forest Preserve District of Kane County at 630/232-5980.

UNDERWOOD PRAIRIE FOREST PRESERVE: 18-acre wetland and prairie. The Preserve is a beautiful assemblage of prairie covered, sandy knolls that have never been plowed, grazed or otherwise disturbed. It is a dedicated State Nature Preserve with a wide spectrum of dry prairie plants, and the 20-acre surrounding farmland is being restored to prairie. The Preserve is located on South Lorand Rd about ¾-mile south of Main St and ½-mile north of Seavy Rd near Kaneville, IL. Call the Forest Preserve District of Kane County at 630/232-5980.

Kankakee County:
AROMA FOREST PRESERVE LAND AND WATER RESERVE: 46.5-acre site on Hieland Rd near Hwy 17. The property includes one of the few known examples of high quality dry sand prairie remaining in the region. Contact Brian Reilly at 815/423-6370 or the Kankakee River Valley Forest Preserve District at 815/935-5630.

GRAND KANKAKEE MARSH NATIONAL WILDLIFE REFUGE: A planned 30,000-acre refuge with wetlands, prairies, and oak savanna stretching from Momence, IL in Kankakee County through Porter and

Prairie Directory

La Porte County IN to Sand Bend, IN. There is a proposal to change the name. Call Tim Bodeen, Project Leader, in Plymouth, IN at 219/935-3411.

KANKAKEE SANDS: 640-acres of woodlands, black oak barrens and agricultural fields. The old fields will be restored to savanna. The area is near St Anne, IL. Call TNC, IL at 312/346-8166.

Kendall County:
KLERONOMOS PRAIRIE: 15-acre privately owned prairie adjacent to Yorkville Prairie (see below). Call the DNR, IL at 217/782-6752.

MILLHURST FEN: 7-acre site located approximately 3-miles southwest of Plano, IL. Call the DNR, IL at 217/785-8774.

YORKVILLE PRAIRIE: 26-acre wet-mesic prairie remnant located in the floodplain of the Fox River. Call the DNR, IL at 217/782-6752.

Knox County:
KNOX COLLEGE GREEN OAKS FIELD STATION: 760-acres of forest, grassland and aquatic habitat includes the second-oldest restored tallgrass prairie in North America (see Curtis Prairie, Dane County, WI). The station is 20-miles east of Knox College's campus in Galesburg, IL on Co Rd 15, 4½-miles south of Victoria, IL. Non-academic uses are limited to Knox students, faculty and alumni, and rules for use of the station is strictly enforced. The station can probably be observed from the road. Call Stuart Allison at 309/341-7185 or Knox College at 309/341-7000.

I-57 SPOON RIVER REST AREA: Prairie restoration by the IDOT. Call IDOT, Bureau of Operations in Springfield, IL at 217/782-7231.

Lake County:
BERKELEY PRAIRIE: 18-acres of mesic prairie in Highland Park, IL on the south side of Berkeley Ave, west of Ridge Rd. Call Lake County Forest Preserve District at 847/367-6640.

BUFFALO CREEK FOREST PRESERVE: 396-acres of prairie and wetlands located near Buffalo Grove and Long Grove, IL on Arlington Heights Rd. Originally a tallgrass prairie dotted with wetlands, restoration of the prairie began in the 1980's because it had been degraded by farming. Today much of the Preserve is managed for flood control, but Bobolinks, Meadowlarks, and other grassland birds can be observed. Call the Lake County Forest Preserve at 847/689-1600.

BUFFALO GROVE PRAIRIE: A virgin prairie located on Hastings Rd under the ComEd power lines about 1-mile west of Milwaukee Rd. Call the North Branch Restoration Project at 847/679-4289.

CUBA MARSH FOREST PRESERVE: 779-acres of marsh, prairie,

woodland and savanna located in southwestern Lake County on Cuba Rd, just west of Ela Rd. The dry-hill prairie on the southeast side of the Preserve is accessible during guided nature tours and contains plants found nowhere else in the area such as prairie smoke and seneca snakeroot. Call the Lake County Forest Preserve at 847/689-1600.

DES PLAINES RIVER TRAIL: The trail parallels the Des Plaines River and will eventually span all of Lake County. Access can be obtained at Half Day Forest Preserve (see below). The trail meanders through open areas such as savannas and prairies. Call the Lake County Forest Preserve at 847/689-1600.

FARM TRAILS NORTH NATURE PRESERVE: 20-acres including wet to wet-mesic prairie. The Preserve is located at the intersection of Roberts and River Rd. Call Citizens for Conservation at 847/382-7283.

FLINT CREEK SAVANNA: The savanna is located on Hwy 21 just west of Harbor Rd. Call Citizens for Conservation at 847/382-7283.

GAVIN BOG AND PRAIRIE NATURE PRESERVE: 104.7-acres plus 31.8-acres of buffer contains a variety of wet habitats plus forest and prairie. The bog is 0.7-miles east of the junction of Wislon and Rollins Rd in Ingleside, IL on Rollins Rd and located in Grant Woods (see below). Call the Lake County Forest Preserve District at 708/367-6640.

GRANT WOODS FOREST PRESERVE: 974-acres in two sections located in northeastern Lake County near Lake Villa and Fox Lake, IL one entrance on Monaville Rd, just east of Hwy 59. The Preserve has a gently rolling landscape of woods, prairie and marsh; one area was never farmed. Call the Lake County Forest Preserve at 847/689-1600.

GRIGSBY PRAIRIE: 38-acre site located at the intersections of Oak Knoll and Buckley Rd near BarringtonHills, IL. Call Citizens for Conservation at 847/382-7283.

HALF-DAY WOODS: 201-acres of oak woods and savanna located in southeastern Lake County near Vernon Hills, IL on Hwy 21. Call the Lake County Forest Preserve at 847/689-1600.

HELLER NATURE CENTER: 5-acres of re-created tallgrass prairie lie in this 100-acre park in Highland Park, IL. Parking is north of Half Day Rd off Ridge Rd. Call the center at 847/433-6901.

HIGHMOOR PARK NATURE PRESERVE: 10-acres of various habitats including mesic to wet prairie are contiguous to the 27-acre privately owned Hibernia Nature Preserve (see below). Access is by a wood chip path. The Preserve is south of intersection of Half Day and Ridge Rd off Ridge Rd. Call the Park District of Highland Park at 847/831-0818.

HIBERNIA NATURE PRESERVE: 27-acres of complex wetlands, prairies and mesic savanna, located adjacent to Highmoor Nature Preserve (see above) and west of Highwood, IL on Half-day Rd. Call Red Seal Development Corp at 847/272-6280.

ILLINOIS STATE BEACH PARK AND NORTH DUNES NATURE PRESERVE: 4,000-acres located in Zion, IL, with the southern area supporting about 829-acres of wet to dry sand prairie (called North Dunes Nature Preserve), on Lake Michigan. Visit the interpretive center and, from trails, observe warblers and hawks during fall and spring migrations. Access to North Dunes Nature Preserve south of Dead River is by permission only. Designated as a National Natural landmark, the Preserve was the first Illinois Nature Preserve. Call the site superintendent at 847/662-4811 or DNR, IL at 217/785-8774.

LAKE BLUFF OPEN LANDS ASSOCIATION PRESERVES: The association manages many preserves and some have prairie. One 4-acre prairie is off of Greenbay Rd in Lake Bluff, IL. Call the association at 847/735-8137.

LAKE FOREST OPEN LANDS: 700-acres in 12 preserves and conservation easments that include woodland, savanna, and prairie. Call at 847/234-3880.

LIBERTY PRAIRIE NATURE PRESERVE: 47.1-acre NA that includes a small virgin prairie has no developed access. The native insects present here include six remnant butterflies and moths. The smooth green snake inhabits the prairie and several wetland birds nest in the Preserve, which is a part of a 2,500-acre macrosite being planned by public and private landowners. Call Libertyville Township Open Space District at 847/816-6800.

LYONS PRAIRIE AND MARSH NATURE PRESERVE: 259.2-acres plus 54.2–acres of buffer includes a wet prairie situated on a glacial outwash in a low area along the Fox River. The Preserve is on County Line Rd north of Three Oaks Rd. Call the McHenry County Conservation District at 815/338-6223 or DNR, IL at 217/785-8774.

LYONS WOODS FOREST PRESERVE: 264-acres of prairie, savanna, forest, and fen, located near Waukegan and Beach Park, IL on Blanchard Rd just west of Sheridan Rd. The prairie supports dropseed, big bluestem and goldenrod. This preserve is very good for bird watching. Yellowthroat, ovenbird and the blue-winged warbler nest here. Call the Lake County Forest Preserve at 847/689-1600.

MIDDLE FORK SAVANNA: 1,235-hectare Lake County Forest Preserve District and Lake Forest Open Lands Association preserve located at the western edge of Lake Forest, IL with a 500-acre remnant black-soil savanna considered to be one of the finest in the United States. A restoration program is underway at the site. Call the Lake Forest Open Lands Association at 847/234-3880.

NORTH DUNES NATURE PRESERVE: (See Illinois Beach State Park, above).

PRAIRIE CROSSING: 667-acre residental development holding nearly 175-acres of restored native prairie and wetland at Hwy 45 and Casey Rd in Grayslake, IL. Call at 847/548-5400.

SKOKIE RIVER NATURE PRESERVE: 100-acres plus 10-acres of buffer are remnants of a once large community of wetlands, mesic and wet-mesic prairie and woodlands situated along both sides of the Skokie River. A former owner, Mr. Shaw, found his 15-acre site of high quality prairie so beautiful he set it aside for preservation. Here, one can glimpse what the prairie looked like when it covered much of the Illinois landscape. The Preserve supports compass plant, lead plant, prairie phlox, hoary puccoon and Indian plantain. Parking is located at the end of Laurel Ave, west of Greenbay Rd in Lake Forest, IL. Call the Lake Forest Open Lands Association at 847/234-3880.

SPRING BLUFF NATURE PRESERVE: 274-acres that includes sand prairie formed 3,000 to 4,000 years ago when Lake Michigan was 20 feet higher than it is today. The Preserve is located in Winthrop Harbor, IL on 7th St east of Main St. Call the Lake County Forest Preserve District at 847/367-6640 which saved this area from being destroyed.

VAN PATTON WOODS: 972-acres of prairie, native oak and sedge meadows being restored by volunteers. The Woods are near Wadsworth, IL in northeast Lake County on Hwy 173. Call 847/948-7750 or the Lake County Forest Preserve District at 847/689-1600.

WADSWORTH PRAIRIE NATURE PRESERVE: 176-acre marsh and prairie that lies in a glacial valley formed during the Wisconsin stage of the Pleistocene Glaciation. The Preserve is located east of US 41, and west of the Milwaukee Road Railroad, and ¼-mile north of Wadsworth Rd. Call the Lake County Forest Preserve District at 847/367-6640 before entering the site.

LaSalle County:
PECUMSAUGAN CREEK-BLACKBALL MINES NATURE PRE-SERVE: 205-acres plus 6.1-acres of buffer support a dolomite prairie. The Preserve is north of the Illinois & Michigan Canal near Utica, IL. Entrance is by permission only. Call DNR, IL at 217/785-8774.

Lawrence County:
CHAUNCEY MARSH NATURE PRESERVE: 155-acres of outstanding

marsh, prairie and bottomland forest located east of Chauncey, IL. The Preserve is threatened by drainage in the area, which may cause the marsh to disappear. Call DNR, IL at 618/783-2685.

US ROUTE 50: Little bluestem prairie grass planted along roadside at US 50 along the north side near Bridgeport, IL. Call IDOT at 217/782-7231.

Lee County:
GREEN RIVER STATE WILDLIFE AREA: 2,565-acre wildlife restoration area. The area varies from flat to gently rolling. Swampy slough areas dominate nearly a third of the acreage, but the remaining portions are prairie restorations, open fields, cultivated areas or timberlands. Many of these areas have been specially planted and managed to provide more food and cover for a variety of wildlife species. Native prairie plants are found in many portions of the Green River Area. The WA is located about 6-miles northwest of Ohio, IL, off Hwy 26. One entrance is on Maytown Blacktop. Call the WA in Harmon, IL at 815/379-2324.

FOLEY SAND PRAIRIE NATURE PRESERVE: 15.2-acres of dry mesic and dry sand prairie, recovering from grazing, located east of County Line Rd, and north of Foley Rd. Call DNR, IL at 217/785-8774.

NACHUSA GRASSLANDS: 1,000-acres of tallgrass prairie formed from high grade prairie and restored areas, near Dixon, IL on Lowden Rd north of Hwy 88. Home to-endangered birds, snakes and other creatures. Call TNC, IL at 312/346-8166.

TEMPERANCE HILL CEMETERY PRAIRIE NATURE PRESERVE: 0.8-acre mesic prairie, representing the landscape that once prevailed, is preserved in a cemetery, located on US 52 northwest of intersection of US 30 and US 52. Call Lee County Natural Area Guardians c/o Lee County Soil and Water Conservation at 815/857-3223.

Livingston County:
SUNBURY PRAIRIE: 209-acres of mesic prairie within the abandoned right-of-way of the Illinois Central Gulf RR located 8.5-miles west of Dwight, IL. Call TNC, IL at 312/346-8166.

SUNBURY RAILROAD PRAIRIE NATURE PRESERVE: 12-acre prairie on a gently rolling topography formed during the Wisconsin Glacier. The Preserve is 9-miles west of US 55 off Hwy 17. Call DNR, IL at 217/782-6302 and Prairie Lands Foundation (Richard Miller) at 815/832-5573.

Macon County:
ROCK SPRINGS CENTER FOR ENVIRONMENTAL DISCOVERY:

1,350-acres of prairie, forest and aquatic habitat. Homestead Prairie Farm is within the complex and adjacent to a 20-acre replicated prairie and has been developed to present a living visual impression of middle class rural farm life of Illinois in the year 1860. The Center is off Rock Springs Rd in southwest Decatur, IL. Call Macon County Conservation District at 217/423-7708.

SAND CREEK RECREATION AREA: 755-acres of forest, open grasslands, floodplain forests and restored tallgrass prairie south of the city of Decatur, IL. Call Macon County Conservation District at 217/423-7708.

Macoupin County:
DENBY PRAIRIE NATURE PRESERVE: 2.5-acres containing critical habitat for prairie plants, birds and small mammals. This part of Illinois was 80% forest and 20% prairie before European settlement. The site is characteristic of the prairie portion with big bluestem, Indian grass, flowering spurge, tall gayfeather, shooting star, and false white indigo, as the principle species. The prairie is located south of Carlinville, IL between Shipman Blacktop and the railroad right of way. Call the DNR, IL at 217/785-8774.

GILLESPIE PRAIRIE LAND AND WATER RESERVE: 78-acre reserve that is 7.28-miles long and 100 feet wide and was a former railroad corridor that is adjacent to Hwy 16. The reserve extends into Montgomery County. Call the DNR, IL at 217/785-8774.

Madison County:
CAHOKIA MOUNDS STATE HISTORIC SITE: 2,200-acre site named after the Cahokia, a sub-tribe of the Illini Confederation, preserves the central section of the largest prehistoric Indian city north of Mexico. The site's 65 man-made earthen burial and ceremonial mounds, wooden sun calendar, and Interpretive Center present the sophisticated culture whose city was centered here on an expansive flood plain near the confluence of the Mississippi and Missouri Rivers. When French explorers visited Illinois, this "City of the Sun" had been long abandoned by its Mississippian culture builders. The Monks Mound, the great platform mound, was named for French Trappist monks who lived nearby in the early 1800s, and covers 14-acres. Along with the Pyramids in Egypt, the City of Rome in Italy, the Taj Mahal in India and the Great Wall of China, Cahokia is designated a United Nation World Heritage site. Prairie, the original landscape, has been reintroduced along interpretative hiking trails, and near the Interpretive Center parking lot. Special education programs are available. Also in St Clair County. Call the Site Manager in Collinsville, IL at 618/346-5160.

HEARTLAND PRAIRIE: (See Gordon F. Moore Park below).

MISSISSIPPI SANCTUARY NATURE PRESERVE: 15-acres plus 26.2-acres of buffer including a small loess hill prairie. This site is privately owned and requires prior permission to enter. Call Illinois Nature Preserves Commission in Springfield at 217/785-8686.

(GORDON F.) MOORE PARK: 33-acre prairie restoration in Moore Park off the north side of Hwy 111 on the east side of Alton, IL and west of the soccer fields. Called the Heartland Prairie (see above) and owed by the City of Alton. Call Alton Park District at 618/463-3580 or the Nature Institute at 618/466-9930.

(JOHN M.) OLIN NATURE PRESERVE: 213-acres plus 79.6-acres of buffer including a small hill prairie. The site is located in the City of Godfrey, IL on South Levis Ln. Call the Nature Institute at 618/466-9930.

Marion County:
(KARL) BARTEL WILDLIFE SANCTUARY: 80-acre sanctuary of former cropland that is being converted to native grasses which will benefit greater prairie chickens and other grassland-dependent birds. The sanctuary is located south of Kinmundy, IL and near the Prairie Ridge State Natural Area. Call the Illinois Audubon Society at 217/446-5085.

PRAIRIE RIDGE STATE NATURAL AREA PRAIRIE CHICKEN SANCTUARIES: 1,000-acres of restored prairie and other grasses supporting greater prairie chicken and 6 other Illinois endangered breeding grassland birds: greater prairie chicken, northern harrier, short-eared owl, barn owl, upland sandpiper and Henslow's sparrow. Another 2,000-acres lies in Jasper County. For permission to visit call DNR, IL at 618/783-2658.

(ROBERT) RIDGWAY GRASSLAND SANCTUARY: 40-acres of restored prairie being managed as an integral part of the Prairie Ridge State Natural Area. The Illinois Audubon continues purchasing nearby land to enlarge the preserve. This area of the preserve will be open to the public without prior permission and enable visitors to walk an interpretive trail through the restored prairie and around the wetland. An observation deck was scheduled to be completed in the summer of 2001. Call the Illinois Audubon Society at 217/446-5085.

TWELVE-MILE PRAIRIE: (See Effingham County above).

Marshall County:
HOPEWELL HILL PRAIRIES NATURAL AREA: 78-acres that includes high quality glacial drift hill prairie. The NA is located about 18-miles northeast of Peoria, IL. For more information, contact Tom Lerczak 309/535-2185 or the DNR, IL at 217/782-8774.

WIER HILL PRAIRIE NATURE PRESERVE: 2.5-acres containing a

steep glacial drift hill prairie. The Preserve is privately owned and permission is required to visit. Call Illinois Nature Preserves Commission in Springfield at 217/785-8774.

Mason County:
BARTON-SOMMER WOODLAND: 52.5-acre tract is located approximately 15-miles west of Lincoln, IL along Salt Creek in Mason and Menard Counties. Management intends to restore the savanna community. Call the DNR, IL at 217/782-8774.

(HENRY ALLAN) GLEASON NATURE PRESERVE: 110-acres within the Sand Ridge State Forest contains dunes, blowouts and sand prairie. (See the Sand Ridge State Forest below). Call Site Superintendent at Sand Ridge State Forest in Forest City, IL at 309/579-2260.

LONG BRANCH SAND PRAIRIE: 93-acres of rolling dunes prairie located northeast of Kilbourne, IL and west of Hwy 97. In 1989, 10-acres of pine was removed and the restoration of this area is underway. Call the DNR, IL at 217/782-8774.

MANTANZAS PRAIRIE: 27.6-acres of high quality wet prairie located northeast of Bath, IL. Call DNR, IL at 217/782-8774.

REAVIS HILL PRAIRIE NATURE PRESERVE: 454-acres of loess hill prairie and other types of prairie. This preserve is one of the largest and finest hill prairies in Illinois. Animal inhabitants include two that are unique to the tallgrass prairie belt, namely the western hognose snake and the pocket gopher whose mounds clearly stand out across the prairie landscape after the site is burned. The Preserve is located 5½-miles south of Easton, IL and 8-miles east of Kilbourne, IL and south of Co Hwy 5. Call the DNR, IL at 217/785-8774.

SAND PRAIRIE-SCRUB OAK NATURE PRESERVE: 1,460-acres located in the SAND RIDGE STATE FOREST which consists of 7,500-acres of forest (3,916 acres of native oak-hickory forest and 3,492 acres of pine) and the dry sand prairie typical of western states. The Preserve is located west of Forest City, IL and north of Hwy 136, and has parking, and trails. Contact the site superintendent at Sand Ridge State Forest at 309/597-2212.

SAND RIDGE STATE FOREST: (see above).

McHenry County:
BYSTRICKY PRAIRIE NATURE PRESERVE: 18-acre dedicated Illinois nature preserve containing the only high quality black soil prairie remaining in this county. It is privately owned and requires permission for entry. The prairie is located east of Hwy 47 and north of Woodstock, IL. Call Illinois Nature Preserves Commission in

Springfield at 217/785-8686.

CARY COUNTRY CLUB: A public golf course with prairie plants scattered at various locations. The Club is located at 2400 Grove Ln, Cary, IL. Call the Club at 847/639-3161.

CARY JUNIOR HIGH SCHOOL NATURE PRESERVE: 4.6-acres of dry to dry-mesic gravel prairie, one of the few gravel prairies protected in Illinois. The Preserve is on the hillside south of the school. Call the Principal, Cary Junior High School in Cary, IL at 847/639-2148 or Cary Prairie Management Committee in Cary at 847/639-4099.

COTTON CREEK MARSH NATURE PRESERVE: 247.4-acres that includes a wet prairie among other natural communities. The Preserve is southwest of Hwy 176. Access is by permission only. Call McHenry County Conservation District in Woodstock, IL at 815/338-6223.

GLACIAL PARK CONSERVATION AREA: 330-acres located at 6512 Harts Road in Ringwood, IL. The area features a bog, an oak savanna, a marsh, restored prairies and a nursery for prairie plants. The area has restrooms, parking, trails, canoeing, and picnic facilities.
Note! Glacial Park Nature Preserve is located within the larger Glacial Park. Call the McHenry County Conservation District at 815/338-6223 or 815/678-4431.

HICKORY GROVE: 440-prairie acres named Lyons Prairie and Marsh resides in this grove in Cary, IL at 700 Hickory Nut Grove Rd. Call the McHenry County Conservation District at 815/338-6223 or 815/653-2297.

HILLSIDE PRAIRIE PARK: 7.7-acre park in Cary, IL. Call the Cary Park District at 847/639-6100.

HOLLOWS: Call the McHenry County Defenders at 815/338-0393 or the McHenry County Conservation District at 815/338-6223.

HUNTLEY-UNION-MARENGO RAILROAD PRAIRIES: Prairie remnants discovered in a railroad right-of-way. The remnants are located at the positions listed below. Call the McHenry County Conservation District at 815/338-6223.
The remnants were found at the following:
a. Coyne Station Rd
b. Milepost 58.
c. Milepost 59.
d. Milepost 61.
e. West of Marengo, IL.

LAKE-IN-THE-HILLS FEN NATURE PRESERVE: 207.1-acres contain 9 distinct native plant communities including dry gravel and mesic gravel prairies. The middle of the Preserve presents a sense of stepping back into pre-settlement time. The Preserve is located at the north side of lake in the Hills, IL. A trail begins at Barbara Key Park, which has parking and public facilities. Call the McHenry County Conservation District in Woodstock, IL at 815/338-6223 and Cary Park District at 847/639-6100 or Al & Barbara Wilson at 847/658-0024.

LARSEN PRAIRIE AND FEN: Call the McHenry County Defenders at 815/338-0393 or the McHenry County Conservation District at 815/338-6223.

LYONS PRAIRIE AND MARSH: (See Hickory Grove, above).

OLD WATERTOWER PRAIRIE: 5.7-acre park in Cary, IL near Cary Country Club on High Rd. Call the Cary Park District at 847/639-6100.

PLEASANT VALLEY PRAIRIE: Call the McHenry County Defenders at 815/338-0393 or the McHenry County Conservation District at 815/338-6223.

PRAIRIE TRAIL: Call the McHenry County Conservation District for a map at 815/338-6223.

QUEEN ANNE PRAIRIE-ECKERT CEMETERY CONSERVATION AREA: 1-acre pioneer cemetery mesic prairie with interpretive trail on Queen Anne Rd north of Charles Rd, and northeast of Woodstock, IL. Call the McHenry Conservation District in Woodstock, IL at 815/338-6223

(CARL AND MARIE) SANDS/MAIN STREET PRAIRIE NATURE PRESERVE: 114.9-acres including high quality gravel hill prairie supporting plants characteristic to this ecosystem and also restored mesic prairie whose open grassland provides habitat for grassland birds. The NA is located in Cary, IL on Main St east of Decker Dr. Call the Cary Park District at 847/639-6100.

STERNE'S FEN NATURE PRESERVE: 46.5-acre nature preserve and 134.0-acres of uplands as nature preserve buffer. A prairie trail is proposed through the upland preserve buffer. The NA is in Crystal Lake, IL off Hillside, Rd. Call the Crystal Lake Park District at 815/459-0680.

VETERANS ACRES PARK: 140-acres with hiking trails through natural areas including Sterne's Woods and Wingate Prairie (see below). McHenry County Conservation District's Prairie Trail South also winds through this Park. The Park is in Crystal Lake, IL with the entrances off Hwy 176 and Walkup Rd. Call the Crystal Lake Park District at 815/459-0680.

VOLO BOG: 850-acres of land, which includes marshes, prairie restoration areas, woodlands, and two other bogs. The bog is the State's only floating bog. The area has parking. One of the trails passes the prairie. The bog is located on Brandenburg Rd off Hwy 12 north of Volo, IL. Call the DNR, IL at 217/785-8774.

WHEELER FEN LAND AND WATER RESERVE: 26.4-acre area that is characterized by its early successional grasslands. The City of McHenry and the County of McHenry own the reserve. Call the DNR, IL at 217/785-8774 or Contact Steven Byers at 815/385-9074.

WINGATE PRAIRIE: 39-acres of precious gravel hill prairie in Veterans Acres Park (see above). An additional 38.8 acres of land was designated around the prairie as Nature Preserve buffer. This unique prairie land, with its rolling terrain, oak savanna and conifer groupings, is home to many prairie plants and is also home to the Silvery Blue Butterfly, and the Franklin Ground Squirrel. Call the Crystal Lake Park District at 815/459-0680.

McLean County:
COLMARA COUNTY PARK: 30-acre park, with a 3-acre and a 10-acre recreated prairie, located north of Normal-Bloomington, IL off Hwy 39. Call the McLean County Dept of Parks and Recreation at 309/785-8774.

FUNK'S GROVE: a moist prairie grove 2-miles north of McLean, IL off Hwy 55. Call the DNR, IL at 217/785-8774.

WESTON CEMETERY PRAIRIE NATURE PRESERVE: 5-acre mesic prairie remnant of the vast blacksoil tallgrass prairie that covered more than 13-million Illinois acres. The Preserve is located ½-mile east of Weston, IL and north of Hwy 24. Call the Illinois State University's Department of Biological Science in Normal, IL at 309/438-5567 or contact ParkLands Foundation in Bloomington, IL at 309/454-3169.

Menard County:
WITTER'S BOBTOWN HILL PRAIRIE: 5.5-acres typical of the extensive prairies in pre-settlement times that lay on steep, exposed, south to west-facing hills and bluffs along major river valleys. This prairie is 2-miles west of Hwy 97 south of Oakford, IL on Whites Crossing Rd. The preserve is privately owned and permission is required to visit. Call Illinois Nature Preserves Commission in Springfield at 217/785-8686.

Mercer County:
BROWNLEE CEMETERY PRAIRIE NATURE PRESERVE: 1.4-acre preserve with 1.6-acre buffer contains a remnant of mesic prairie. The Preserve is northwest of Alexis, IL. Call the Mercer County Soil and Water Conservation District in Aledo, IL at 309/582-5154.

Monroe County:
FULTS HILL PRAIRIE NATURE PRESERVE: 532-acre preserve, with trails, that has been designated a National Natural Landmark by the

US Department of the Interior, features a variety of natural communities including the largest complex of the highest quality undisturbed loess hill prairie along the Mississippi River in Illinois. The Preserve is located southeast of Fults, IL near Bluff Rd. Call DNR, IL at 217/785-8774 or IL Dept of Natural Resources, Natural Heritage Biologist at 618/462-1181.

Montgomery County:
(H & B) BREMER SANCTUARY: 203-acres of oak-hickory upland, with ponds, a creek, and a small prairie area and marked hiking trails. The sanctuary is located just north of Hillsboro, IL. Call the Illinois Audubon Society at 217/446-5085.

ROBERTS CEMETERY SAVANNA NATURE PRESERVE: 1.7-acre savanna. Difficult to find, it is east of US 55 off the 108 exit. Call the Illinois Nature Preserves Commission at 217/785-8686.

Morgan County:
MEREDOSIA HILL PRAIRIE NATURE PRESERVE: 30-acres of dry hill prairie containing a rich assemblage of plant species. The Preserve is northeast of Meredosia, IL. Call DNR, IL at 217/785-8774.

Moultrie County:
CONEFLOWER HILL PRAIRIE: 4-acres of hill prairie located south of the laboratory building on Lake Shelbyville Fish and Wildlife Management Area (see below). In 1990, a rare butterfly, the Ottoe Skipper, was found here, one of only ten sites in the state. Coneflower Hill Prairie is included in the Illinois Natural Areas Inventory, a list of high quality natural areas of statewide significance. Call DNR, IL at 217/785-8774 or Nick Owens at 217/348-0629.

LAKE SHELBYVILLE FISH AND WILDLIFE AREA: The WA is composed of two separate units. The Kaskaskia (eastern) Unit covers 3,700-acres and the West Okaw (western) Unit contains about 2,500 acres. The two areas contain over 6,000-acres of mixed habitats including forests, prairies, restored grasslands, old fields, brush, wetlands, rivers, streams, and cropland. All are situated in the upper reaches of the 34,000-acre Lake Shelbyville project area. The WA is located along the Kaskaskia and West Okaw Rivers near Sullivan, IL. Call the WA in Bethany, IL at 217/665-3112.

Ogle County:
BEACH CEMETERY PRAIRIE NATURE PRESERVE: 2.5-acre dry-mesic prairie located south of Davis Junction, IL on the north side of Big Mound Rd. The plant community includes little bluestem, prairie dropseed, porcupine grass, pasqueflower, puccoons, lead plant, and coneflowers. Call the Natural Land Institute in Rockford, IL at 815/964-6666.

CASTLE ROCK STATE PARK: (See George B. Fell Nature Preserve, below.) Call the Site Superintendent in Caledonia, IL at 815/885-3612 or DNR, IL at 217/782-6302.

(JOHN) DEERE HISTORIC SITE NATURAL PRAIRIE: 2-acres of re-created prairie in Grand Detour, IL near an archaeological site where, in 1837, John Deer developed the steel plow that could cut through the unyielding prairie sod, dooming it forever. There is also a visitor center, blacksmith shop and Deere's home located in Grand Detour, Illinois. Call the Historic Site at 815/652-4551.

(GEORGE B.) FELL NATURE PRESERVE: 685.6 acres plus 23.4 acres of buffer resides within Castle Rock State Park (see above) and contains a tremendous diversity of natural communities including prairie. The Preserve is protected and is restricted to scientific study and limited interpretation activities. Castle Rock State Park is located 2 miles south of Oregon IL on Hwy 2. Call Site Superintendent in Caledonia, IL at 815/885-3612 or DNR, IL Biologist in Oregon, IL at 815/732-6185 or the park at 815/732-7329.

HEEREN PRAIRIE: 1.9 acres of high quality prairie. For more information, contact the DNR, IL at 217/785-8774.

JARRETT PRAIRIE NATURE PRESERVE: 115.8-acres plus 25.2-acre buffer feature a large complex of dry dolomite and dry mesic dolomite prairie remnants. Parking, trails, and trail maps are available at the Jarrett Prairie Center at the top of the hill. This preserve is part of the bigger Byron Forest Preserve District "Prairie Preserve" and is located south of Byron, IL off Hwy 72. Call Byron Forest Preserve District in Byron, IL at 815/234-8535.

PINE ROCK NATURE PRESERVE: 59-acres of mesic and wet-mesic prairie dominated by big bluestem grass and various sedges. The Preserve is located 4-miles east of Oregon, IL on Hwy 64. Call Northern Illinois University, Lorado Taft Field Campus, Oregon, IL at 815/732-2111.

(DOUGLAS E.) WADE NATURE PRESERVE (Formally called Bicentennial Prairie Nature Preserve): 11.2-acres named in honor of a leader of the prairie preservation movement contains original dry-mesic gravel and dolomite prairie. The Preserve is located ½-mile south of the intersection of Crestview and Kishwaukee Rds in the northeastern part of the county. Call Prairie Preservation Society of Ogle County c/o Oregon Township Public Library in Oregon at 815/732-2724.

Peoria County:
DETWEILLER PARK: (See Detweiller Woods Nature Preserve below).

DETWEILLER WOODS NATURE PRESERVE: 246-acres containing 2

small glacial drift hill prairies in Detweiller Park. The park is located on North Galena Rd (Hwy 29). Call the Forest Park Nature Center, Peoria Park District in Peoria, IL at 309/686-3360.

FOREST PARK NATURE CENTER: 500-acre nature preserve with a restored prairie (see below) and a visitor center, trails and a naturalist. The Nature Center is northwest of Peoria, IL on Forest Park Dr. Call Forest Park Nature Center in Peoria at 309/686-3360.

FOREST PARK SOUTH NATURE PRESERVE: 134.6-acres including a remnant glacial drift hill prairie found on a steep upper slope. This preserve is south of Forest Park Nature Center on Forest Park Drive. Call Peoria Park District in Peoria at 309/682-1200 or DNR, IL at 217/782-6302.

ROBINSON PARK HILL PRAIRIES NATURE PRESERVE: 151.5-acres include a series of small high quality glacial drift hill prairies. Public access is not available from any public road so one must call the Forest Park Nature Center for access directions at 309/686-3360.

ROCK ISLAND TRAIL PRAIRIE NATURE PRESERVE: 5.1-acres of mesic prairie on an abandoned railroad right of way located north on Hwy 91 from intersection of Hwys 90 & 91 then east on County Line Rd for ½-mile. Call the DNR, IL Natural Heritage Biologist at 309/347-5119.

(W H) SOMMER PARK: 320-acre park with oak barrens where native grasses are being restored. The Park is located at 6329 Koerner Rd, Peoria, IL. Call the Park at 309/691-8423 or the Forest Park Nature Center, Peoria Park District in Peoria, IL at 309/682-1200.

SPRINGDALE CEMETERY SAVANNA: 20-acre oak savanna in the heart of Springdale Cemetery, one of central Illinois' largest and most historic cemeteries. This increasingly rare ecological community once dominated the bluffs overlooking the Illinois River in the Peoria area. Volunteers are restoring the savanna. The cemetery is located at 3014 N Prospect Rd, Peoria, IL. Call the DNR, IL at 217/785-8774.

WILDLIFE PRAIRIE PARK: 2,000-acres with a zoological park containing prairie animals such as bison and elk and bobcats with a restored prairie is open to the public for a fee. The Park is 10-miles west of Peoria, IL off US 74 at exit 82. There is parking and a gift shop. Call the Park at 309/676-0998.

Pike County:
GRUBB HOLLOW PRAIRIE: 50-acres of loess hill prairie perched on limestone bluffs that overlook the Mississippi River floodplain and supports some plants that are more typical of the western prairies. The prairie is located north of New Canton, IL on a county road. Call the

DNR, IL Natural Heritage Biologist at 217/285-2221 or DNR, IL at 217/785-8774.

Putnam County:
MT. PALATINE CEMETERY PRAIRIE NATURE PRESERVE: 1.5-acre remnant of the tallgrass prairie. The Preserve is northeast of McNabb, IL on an access lane. Call Putnam County Conservation District in Hennepin, IL at 815/882-2319.

MILLER-ANDERSON WOODS NATURE PRESERVE: (See Bureau County above).

St Clair County:
CAHOKIA MOUNDS: (See Madison County above).

DESPAIN WETLANDS LAND AND WATER RESERVE: 164.5-acre tract including 50-acres of reconstructed wetlands, surrounded by reconstructed prairie, reforested flatwoods, bottomland and upland woods and remnant forest that is privately owned by the DesPain family. The property is adjacent to the 2,000-acre Peabody River King State Fish and Wildlife Area located east of New Athens, IL. Contact Debbie S. Newman at 618/758-3808.

Sangamon County:
ADAMS WILDLIFE SANCTUARY: A small prairie restoration with easy walking trails. The sanctuary is located on the east side of Springfield, IL on Clear Lake Ave. The sanctuary is open to small groups by appointment. Contact the Illinois Audubon Society in Danville, IL at 217/446-5085.

INTERSTATE 55: Big Bluestem prairie grass planted within the interchange loops at intersection of Interstate 55 and Toronto Rd south of Springfield, IL. Call the IDOT at 217/782-7301 or 217/782-7231.

UIS PRAIRIE RESTORATION PROJECT: 1-acre prairie restoration project on the campus of the University of Illinois at Springfield. The campus consists of 746-acres with nearly 400 currently leased out to local farmers. The entire campus was previously agricultural fields, and before that, prairie. The campus is on the south edge of Springfield, IL. Call the school at 800/252-8533.

Stephenson County:
FREEPORT PRAIRIE NATURE PRESERVE: 4.5-acres of dry dolomite prairie with parking and trails located at the south edge of Freeport, IL on Walnut Rd. This is one of the last remnants of the original upland Prairie known as Shannon Prairie. Call Highland Community College at 815/235-6121 or Jane Addamsland Park Foundation of Freeport, IL at 815/235-5253.

WIRTH PRAIRIE NATURE PRESERVE: 2.1-acres of dry dolomite prairie formed during the advance and stagnation of the Wisconsin Glacier whose "domed' presence results from a glacial feature called an "ice-shove." The site is privately owned and requires permission for entry. Call the Illinois Nature Preserves Commission in Springfield at 217/785-8686.

Tazewell County:
FORT CREVE COEUR PARK: (See Creve Coeur Nature Preserve below).

CREVE COEUR NATURE PRESERVE: 23-acres of glacial till hill prairie at the south end of Fort Creve Coeur Park in the village of Creve Coeur, IL. Call the Village of Creve Coeur at 309/699-6714 or the Park at 309/694-3193.

INTERSTATE 474: Prairie grass plantings throughout the interchange and the right of way at the junction of US 474 and 74 and for several miles west along US 474. Call the IDOT at 217/782-7231.

MANITO PRAIRIE NATURE PRESERVE: 19.6-acres of gravel hill and sand prairie formed during the post-glacial period of the Wisconsin Glacier. The Preserve is on a terrace above the Illinois floodplain and is located 7½-miles north of Manito, IL. Call the Site Superintendent in Spring Lake State Park at 309/968-7135 or DNR, IL, Natural Heritage Biologist at 309/347-5119.

Union County:
BERRYVILLE SHALE GLADE: A small glade with prairie grasses. The glade is south of Brown Barrens (For location and contact information see below).

BROWN BARRENS NATURE PRESERVE: A small nature preserve that has xeric grassland species, such as poverty grass, little bluestem, and muhly. The Preserve is west of Jonesboro, IL on Hwy 146. Call Andy West (Trail of Tears Forest) at 618/833-4910.

LARUE-PINE HILLS ECOLOGICAL AREA: A Part of the Shawnee National Forest that covers 268,400 acres in southern Illinois. Prairie and wild flowers bloom in this US Forest Service Area. Call the USFS at 800/699-6637 or DNR, IL 217/785-8774.

MCCLURE SCHOOL SHALE GLADE: A small glade with prairie grasses. The glade is south of Brown Barrens (For location and contact information see above).

Vermilion County:
FAIRCHILD CEMETERY SAVANNA: 0.5-acre savanna remnant supporting over 35 species of prairie plants. The savanna is located outside

87

of the Kennekuk County Park on Indian Springs Rd. Call Vermilion County Conservation District in Danville, IL at 217/662-2142 or the Vermilion County Audubon Society in Danville, IL at 217/427-5563.

FOREST GLEN PRESERVE: 1,800-acre preserve 7-miles east of Westville, IL on Co Hwy 5. There are 4 registered Illinois Nature Preserves within the Preserve including the 40-acre (Doris) Westfall Prairie. (See below). In addition, there is a 22-acre savanna restoration area. Forest Glen Preserve serves as the Illinois State Headquarters for the Illinois Native Plant Society and the Illinois Walnut Council. For information about these organizations or the park call 217/662-2142.

KENNEKUK COUNTY PARK: 3,000-acre park in east central Illinois located 5-miles west of Danville, IL and is the headquarters for the Vermilion County Conservation District. The site houses an oak and hickory forest, with native tallgrass prairie areas. It contains three Illinois Nature Preserves within its boundaries (Windfall Prairie, Horseshoe Bottoms and Fairchild Cemetery). Also in the Park is the sparkling Middle Fork River, marshes, wetlands, prairie patches, a Woodland Prairie Trail, a prairie restoration area, archaeological site, visitors center with a Native American display and the Bunker Hill Historic Area. Windfall Prairie is located on the western boundary of the Park (see below). Call the Park at 217/442-1691 or the Vermillion County Conservation District at 217/442-1691.

(DORIS) WESTFALL PRAIRIE PRESERVE: 40-acre recreated prairie including salvaged native plants from prairie remnants about to be bulldozed. Once the Grand Prairie "appeared boundless as the ocean," wrote Chester A. Loomis in 1825, now only these remnants and restorations remain. Call Vermilion County Conservation District at 217/662-2142 and the Vermilion County Audubon Society at 217/446-5085. One can also ask about *The Prairie in Vermilion County* by Doris Westfall and Marilyn Campbell.

WINDFALL PRAIRIE NATURE PRESERVE: 32-acre glacial drift prairie plus 29-acre buffer. Access is by permission only. Call Vermilion County Conservation District at 217/662-2142.

Warren County:
MASSASAUGA PRAIRIE NATURE PRESERVE: 6.2-acres of wet and mesic prairie that escaped the plow because of its sleep slopes. The prairie is northeast of Roseville, IL. Call the DNR, IL Natural Heritage Biologist at 309/347-5119.

SPRING GROVE CEMETERY PRAIRIE NATURE PRESERVE: 1.1-acre mesic black soil prairie deeded for church use in 1859. The prairie is located from the intersection of US 67 & 34 north on US 67 for about 6-miles then west on a gravel road for 1/8 of a mile. Call Spring Grove

Cemetery Trustees, c/o the Department of Biology, Monmouth College, Monmouth, IL at 309/457-2349.

Whiteside County:
LYNDON PRAIRIE NATURE PRESERVE: 21.8-acre preserve and 8.7-acres as a nature preserve buffer along a 3-mile corridor of abandoned railroad right-of-way northeast of Lyndon, IL in the central part of Whiteside County. Scattered remnants of dry-mesic, mesic and wet-mesic prairie occur there. Contact The Natural Land Institute at 815/964-6666.

THOMSON-FULTON SAND PRAIRIE NATURE PRESERVE: 37-acre sand prairie that is recovering from past grazing. The Preserve is located northwest of Fulton, IL. Call DNR, IL at 217/785-8774 or Site Superintendent, Morrison-Rockwood State Park in Morrison, IL at 815/772-4708.

Will County:
BRAIDWOOD DUNES AND SAND RIDGE SAVANNA: 259-acres that includes 145-acres of sand prairie and savanna located 1-mile southeast of Braidwood, IL and south of Hwy 113. This is a remnant of dry-mesic, sand savanna, mesic and wet mesic sand prairie, sedge meadow and marsh. Call Will County Forest Preserve District in Joliet, IL at 815/727-8700.

GRANT CREEK PRAIRIE NATURE PRESERVE: 78-acre mesic and wet prairie near Bloomington, IL located east of US 55, and ½-mile south of Blodgett Road. Call Site Superintendent at Des Plaines Fish and Wildlife Area in Wilmington, IL at 815/423-5326 or DNR, IL at 217/785-8774.

HITS SIDING PRAIRIE NATURE PRESERVE: 261.3-acre site contains high quality examples of mesic/wet mesic prairie, wet prairie, mesic sand prairie, marsh, mesic sand savanna and sedge meadow. 57-acres of this site are of such high quality that they are considered to have statewide significance. The NA is southwest of Wilmington, IL on Hwy 53. Call the DNR, IL at 217/785-8774.

INTERSTATE 57: prairie grass plantings behind US 57 rest area south of Monee, IL. Call IDOT at 217/782-7231.

LOCKPORT PRAIRIE NATURE PRESERVE: 254-acres of prairie sit on the floodplain along the DesPlaines River. The Preserve is southeast of Lockport, IL. This unusual location, which required plants to adapt to a high water table during much of their growing season, explains its unique prairie plant community. Call the Forest Preserve District of Will County in Joliet, IL at 815/727-8700.

MESSENGER WOODS NATURE PRESERVE: 180-acre nature preserve and 227-acres nature preserve buffer. The Preserve has high quality, dry-mesic and mesic upland forests. Other plant communities present within the Preserve include shrub, swamp, and wet prairie. The Preserve is located on Bruce Rd, north of Hwy 6 and east of Cedar Rd, in rural Lockport, IL. Call the Forest Preserve District of Will County in Joliet, IL at 815/727-8700.

MIDEWIN NATIONAL TALLGRASS PRAIRIE: 40,000-acres carved out of the former Joliet Arsenal is named for the Potawatomi word for healing and is the first national tallgrass prairie. Bird watchers can view upland sandpipers, loggerhead shrikes, bobolinks and mocking-birds. The prairie is located on Hwy 53 near Wilmington IL. Contact the Open Lands Project at 312/427-4256 or Midewin National Tallgrass Prairie at 815/423-6370.

O'HARA WOODS NATURE PRESERVE: 70-acres plus 10-acres of buffer contain a natural prairie grove of undisturbed mesic forest and savanna once typical of the region. It appeared, in pre-settlement days, as an island of trees in the midst of a vast sea of prairie and marsh. The Preserve is located by taking Romeoville Rd west from Romeoville, IL for a mile then north for 0.3 mile. Call Romeoville Department of Recreation in Romeoville, IL at 815/838-8223.

RACCOON GROVE NATURE PRESERVE: This preserve is a prime example of a prairie to forest transition. The Preserve is near Frankfort, IL. Call the Forest Preserve of Will County at 815/727-8700.

ROMEOVILLE PRAIRIE NATURE PRESERVE: 108.4-acres plus 15.1-acres of buffer located where once lay an outlet for Glacial Lake Chicago at the end of the last glacial period. The Preserve contains wet to mesic dolomite prairie and other natural communities. The Preserve is located 3-miles east of the junction of Hwy 53 and Romeoville Rd on Romeoville Rd. Call Forest Preserve District of Will County in Joliet at 815/727-8700 or the DNR, IL at 217/785-8774.

(ERIS L) RUDMAN PRAIRIE: 4-acre community created project at the Public Library at 21119 Pfeiffer Rd in Franfort, IL. Call 815/469-2423.

THORN CREEK WOODS NATURE PRESERVE: 471-acres plus 90.6-acres of buffer include several natural communities including a small wet and mesic recreated prairies. There is a Nature Center, double loop trail and interactive brochure. Call Thorn Creek Nature Center in Park Forest, IL at 708/747-6320 or the DNR, IL at 217/785-8774.

WILMINGTON SHRUB PRAIRIE NATURE PRESERVE: 146-acres containing one of the few remaining examples of Illinois shrub prairie. The Preserve is northeast of Braidwood, IL. Call the DNR, IL at

217/785-8774.

Winnebago County:
BELL BOWL PRAIRIE: 15-acres of dry gravel prairie located at the southwest edge of the Greater Rockford Airport, north of Belt Line Rd. Access is by permission only. Call Natural Land Institute at 815/964-6666.

BLACKHAWK SPRINGS FOREST PRESERVE: 950-acres that is heavily forested. A new 2-mile paved recreation trail winds through woods and prairie. The Preserve is just southeast of Rockford, IL. Call the Winnebago County Forest Preserve District at 815/887-6100.

COLORED SANDS FOREST PRESERVE: 114-acre preserve that contains a dedicated Illinois Nature Preserve, the Sand Bluff Bird Observatory and a restored sand prairie. The Preserve is northeast of Durand, IL on the north county line. Call the Winnebago County Forest Preserve District at 815/887-6100.

DEER RUN FOREST PRESERVE: 593-acre preserve includes forest, prairie, and a large lawn area south of Rockford, IL off of Hwy 11. Call the Winnebago County Forest Preserve District at 815/887-6100.

HARLEM HILLS NATURE PRESERVE – LOVES PARK: 53-acre dry-mesic gravel hill prairie. This is the state's largest and finest remaining example of a gravel hill prairie. It is located east of Hwy 173, south of Nimtz Rd, and 1-mile southwest of Rock Cut State Park. Call site superintendent at Castle Rock State Park in Caledonia, IL at 815/885-3612 or the DNR, IL 217/785-8774.

KIESELBURG FOREST PRESERVE: 211-acres including the largest prairie restoration in the district and is east of Machesney Park on Swanson Rd. Call the Winnebago County Forest Preserve District at 815/887-6100.

KISHWAUKEE GORGE NORTH FOREST PRESERVE: 128-acres of diverse woodlands and prairie openings located south of Rockford, IL near Kishwaukee Rd and Hwy 60. Call the Winnebago County Forest Preserve District at 815/887-6100.

(CARL AND MYRNA) NYGEN WETLAND: 705-acre complex that is the latest project of the Natural Land Institute that intends to restore this area to wetlands, savanna and prairie. The complex is located at the confluence of the Pecatonica and Rock Rivers just west of Rockton, IL. Call the Natural Land Institute at 815/964-6666 for information or to volunteer for one of their projects.

OAK RIDGE FOREST PRESERVE: 650-acres of former farmland on the Kishwaukee River. A beautiful oak grove overlooks flood plain prairie. The Preserve is southeast of Rockford, IL off Blomberg Rd. Call the Winnebago County Forest Preserve District at 815/887-6100.

(EMILY J.) SEARLS PARK PRAIRIE NATURE PRESERVE: 66-acres of wet to mesic prairie with parking and trails located at northwest edge of City of Rockford on Central Ave. Call the Rockford Park District at 815/987-8800.

SUGAR RIVER FOREST PRESERVE: 426-acre preserve that has woodlands, sand prairie, wetlands, river, extensive trails, picnic areas, campgrounds and shelterhouses. The Preserve is located west of Hwy 15 on Hwy 9. Call the Winnebago County Forest Preserve District at 815/887-6100.

WILSON PRAIRIE NATURE PRESERVE: 20-acre dry prairie whose location serves as a wildlife movement corridor. The Preserve is 15-miles west of Rockford, IL and just north of Hwy 20. Entrance to the Preserve is by permission only. Call Illinois Nature Preserves Commission in Springfield at 217/785-8686.

Woodford County:
RIDGETOP HILL PRAIRIE NATURE PRESERVE: 16-acres plus 1.4-acre buffer contain glacial drift hill prairie and forest, once abundant in the region. Prairie grasses adapted to dry sites including little bluestem and sideoats grama dominate the hill prairie. The Preserve is located on the Mackinaw River about 5-miles southeast of Eureka, IL. Contact the ParkLands Foundation in Bloomington, IL at 309/454-3169.

INDIANA

Blacksoil prairie and sand prairie once covered 15% of the state.

Because prairie resists drought, benefits wildlife, and controls erosion, the Indiana DNR supports planting prairie plants. The Division of Nature Preserves (DNP) refers gardeners to the *Prairie Propagation Handbook*, Wehr Nature Center, Franklin, WI telephone number 414/425-8550.

Below are some prairie remnants that remain in Indiana:

Allen County:
METEA PARK: (See Meno-Aki Nature Preserve below).

MENO-AKI NATURE PRESERVE: 120-acre preserve containing several natural communities among them a hill prairie, dry-mesic, mesic upland forest, and floodplain forest. Prairie vegetation is scattered along the south-facing bluffs overlooking Cedar Creek. These hill prairies are rare this far east in Indiana. The Preserve is part of Metea Park west of Cedarville, IN. Call the Allen County Parks and Recreation Dept at 219/627-3289 or the IDNR, Division of Nature Preserves (DNP) at 317/232-4052.

Crawford County:
HARRISON-CRAWFORD FOREST: (See the Leavenworth Barrens below).

LEAVENWORTH BARRENS NATURE PRESERVE: This preserve is a small part of the larger (25,600-acre) Harrison-Crawford Forest. The Barrens is a form of savanna. The main entrance to the forest is to the west of Wyandotte Woods State Recreation Area on Hwy 62 south of US 64. The forest is also in Harrison County. Call the IDNR at 317/232-4020.

Harrison County:
HARRISON-CRAWFORD FOREST: (See above and Post Oak-Cedar NA below).

POST OAK-CEDAR NATURE PRESERVE: 266-acres of forest with some glades or barrens supporting prairie. The Preserve is near the Harrison-Crawford Forest. The Preserve is on Hwy 462 and just before entering the forest one turns south onto Cold Friday Rd (there is a small sign) and drives about a mile to a marked parking lot. A self-guiding nature trail winds through the Preserve. Call the IDNR at 317/232-4020.

Henry County:
PIONEER CEMETERY PROJECT: 2-acres of tallgrass prairie in three small pioneer cemeteries managed in agreement with Stoney Creek Township by Central Indiana Land Trust Inc (CILTI). For more information, call CILTI at 317/921-5528, in Indianalopis, IN.

Jackson County:
KNOBSTONE GLADE NATURE PRESERVE: 60-acres in three separate tracts of land each with a glade. The driest glade is a savanna supporting prairie plants. The Preserve is south of Brownstown, IN from the intersection of Hwy 135 and US 50 on Hwy 135 for 3½-miles than to the Starve Hollow Recreation Area. There is no easy access to all the glades. One can be reached by following the hiking trail from the north end of the campground. Call the IDNR, DNP at 317/232-4052.

Jasper County:
JASPER-PULASKI STATE FISH AND WILDLIFE AREA: (See Tefft Savanna below).

NIPSCO SAVANNA: 840-acres of high quality black oak sand savanna and savanna flats with a rich diversity of plants, including prairie plants. The Savanna is located 3-miles north on Hwy 49 from the junction of Hwys 10 & 49 and then east ½-mile on Co Rd 1500. Call TNC, IN in Indianapolis, IN at 317/923-7547.

STOUTSBURG SAVANNA: A black oak savanna with a prairie remnant. The savanna is located from US 65 on Hwy 10 east about 7-miles to Co Rd 350W, and then south and then for 1-mile to Co Rd 1100N east then for about ¾-mile, where the prairie begins. Call the IDNR, DNP at 317/232-4052.

TEFFT SAVANNA NATURE PRESERVE: 480-acres in 2 parcels of sand dunes and black oak savanna with some prairie openings. The Preserve is located in the northwest portion of the Jasper-Pulaski State Fish and Wildlife Area and northwest of Medaryville, IN. Call the IDNR, DNP at 317/232-4052.

LaGrange County:
MONGOQUINONG NATURE PRESERVE: A part of the Pigeon River Fish and Wildlife Area (see below). Call the WA at 219/367-2164 or the IDNR, DNP at 317/232-4052.

PIGEON RIVER FISH AND WILDLIFE AREA: 11,500-acres of restored prairies, tamarack swamps, fens, creeks and the Pigeon River. The office is in Mongo, IN on Co Rd 300N. Call the WA at 219/367-2164 or IDNR, DNP at 317/232-4052.

Lake County:
BIESECKER PRAIRIE: 34-acres of mesic grass prairie. The prairie is at the extreme northeast portion of the State where US 41 and US 231 intersect. Call the IDNR, DNP at 317/232-4052.

CRESSMOOR PRAIRIE NATURE PRESERVE: 38-acres of blacksoil

prairie, which, plus sand prairie, once covered 15% of the state. This is the largest protected example of a silt-loam or "black soil" prairie in Indiana. Black soil prairies were once the most common prairies in Indiana, but because they made the best farmland most were plowed under. This is just a part of a larger preserve. From exit #258 of Business US 6 go east on Ridge Rd about 2½-miles to Lake Park Ave and then turn south about ½-mile. Call Shirley Heinze of the Environmental Fund at 219/879-4725 or the IDNR, DNP at 317/232-4052.

GERMAN METHODIST CEMETERY PRAIRIE: 1-acre remnant of excellent black soil prairie supporting over 70 species of native prairie plants. This acre was never used as a cemetery. The dominant grass is Prairie Dropseed, an indicator of virgin prairie. The Cemetery is 1-mile south of Cedar Lake, IN. Call TNC, IN in Indianapolis at 317/923-7547.

GIBSON WOODS NATURE PRESERVE: 120-acres containing several communities of plants: dry-mesic sand savanna with an overstory of black oak, mesic sand prairie dominated by big bluestem and tall coreopsis, and wet-mesic forest. The Preserve is north of the intersection of US 80/94 and Kennedy Ave. Call the Preserve at 219/844-3188 or the IDNR, DNP at 317/232-4052.

HOOSIER PRAIRIE NATURE PRESERVE: 548-acres make up a significant natural area that supports great ecological diversity and is a National Natural Landmark. Wet prairie and sand prairie flourish minutes from steel mills and oil refineries in the Calumet region. This is Indiana's largest high-quality prairie remnant reminding one of days long ago. A 1-mile self-directed trail runs into the part open to the public. The Preserve is located east of US 41 on Main St and is considered a part of the Indiana Dunes National Lakeshore. Call TNC, IN in Indianapolis at 317/923-7547 or the IDNR, DNP at 317/232-4052.

INDIANA DUNES NATIONAL LAKESHORE: Within the park's boundaries are sand dunes, forest, wetlands and prairies. (See Hoosier Prairie above).

IVANHOE DUNE AND SWALE: 114-acres of globally rare inland dune and swale, features savanna, dry and mesic sand prairies, cattail marshes and buttonbush-filled swales. The dune is located on 4th Ave in Gary, IN. Call TNC, IN in Indianapolis at 317/923-7547.

La Porte County:
GRAND KANKAKEE MARSH NATIONAL WILDLIFE REFUGE: A proposed 30,000-acre refuge with wetlands, prairie and oak savanna that extends into Kankakee County IL (see Illinois above) and Porter County IN. Call Tim Bodeen, Project Leader, in Plymouth, IN at 219/935-3411.

Newton County:
(BILL) BARNES NATURE PRESERVE: (See the Willow Slough below).

BEAVER LAKE PRAIRIE PRESERVE: 640-acres of mostly prairie that is probably a remnant of the Grand Kankakee Marsh and Prairie. The Preserve is northeast of Enos, IN on Co Rd 200W. Permission is required to visit this Preserve. Call the LaSalle Fish and Wildlife Area at 219/922-3019.

CONRAD SAVANNA: 800-acres of dunes sculpted by the wind following the last glaciations now supporting high-quality black oak savanna, scattered trees, grasses and sedges. The Savanna is south of Lake Village, IN on Co Rd 700N. Call TNC, IN in Indianapolis, IN at 317/923-7547.

HOLLEY SAVANNA: 79-acres of oak woodland and former savanna mix with flowers from both communities. The Savanna is located northwest of the junction of US 65 and Hwy 114 on Co Rd 150 (Northstar Road). Call TNC, IN in Indianapolis, IN at 317/923-7547.

KANKAKEE SANDS: 7,209-acres near the Illinois state line are being restored to prairie and wetland and will recapture a small portion of the million-acre Grand Kankakee Marsh landscape as it was in the early 1800's. The TNC is connecting eleven square miles of publicly owned conservation area to form this area; the preserves being connected are the 800+ acre Conrad Savanna, the 640-acre Beaver Lake Prairie, and the 12,000+ acre Willow Slough State Fish and Wildlife Area. TNC, IL also has a restoration project not far from the Indiana's project to someday connect the two. (See Kankakee Sands, Kankakee County, IL above) Call TNC, IN in Indianapolis, IN at 317/923-7547 regarding visiting this area.

WILLOW SLOUGH STATE FISH AND WILDLIFE AREA: 1,200+ acres of sand dunes, wetlands, a shallow lake and the Bill Barnes Nature Preserve containing some remnant prairie. The WA is north west of Morocco, IN on State Line Rd. Call the Indiana Division of Fish and Wildlife at Morocco, In at 219/285-2704.

Porter County:
GRAND KANKAKEE MARSH NATIONAL WILDLIFE REFUGE: (See La Porte County above).

Pulaski County:
SANDHILL NATURE PRESERVE: 120-acres of mainly forest with a few open areas, caused by prior disturbance, that now support prairie. An effort is being made to maintain these prairies by burning. The Preserve is located at the north end of the 180-acre Tippecanoe River

State Park. The park is 4-miles north of the town of Winamac, IN on Hwy 35. Call the park at 219/846-3213 or the IDNR, DNP at 317/232-4052.

TEFFT SAVANNA: 480-acres of black oak savannas with prairie openings that are remarkable for their rare plants that are commonly found along the Atlantic Ocean. The savanna is located on the northwest side of the Jasper Pulaski Fish and Wildlife Area (see above) north of Medaryville, IN. Call the IDNR, DNP at 317/232-4052.

TIPPECANOE RIVER STATE PARK: (See Sandhill Nature Preserve above)

St. Joseph County:
KANKAKEE FEN: 13-acres of fen or "wet prairie." Call TNC, IN in Indianapolis, IN at 317/923-7547 for permission to visit.

Starke County:
KOONTZ LAKE NATURE PRESERVE: 148-acres of open water, marsh, bogs, remnant stands of tamaracks, and uplands of prairie and savanna. The Preserve is north of Koontz Lake, IN on Co Rd 1150E and is adjacent to and north of Koontz Lake Wetland Conservation Area. Call the IDNR, DNP in Indianapolis, IN at 317/232-4052.

OBER SAVANNA: 90-acres of high quality black oak sand savanna. The savanna is southwest of Ober, IN on Co Rd 200S. Call TNC, IN in Indianapolis, IN at 317/923-7547.

Tippecanoe County:
LOOKOUT POINT GRAVEL HILL PRAIRIE: 15-acres of gravelhill prairie with a panoramic view of the Wabash River Valley. At the time of this printing, there was no visitation. Call TNC, IN at 317/923-7547 for present status.

White County:
SPINN PRAIRIE NATURE PRESERVE: 29-acres of Indiana-endangered bluestem-Indian grass tallgrass prairie remnant between the road and the railway right-of-way. By Indiana standards, this is a relatively large remnant. The Preserve contains both mesic prairie and oak savanna. The prairie is located northeast of Reynolds, IN off Co Rd 200N. This is a good place to bird watch. Call TNC, IN in Indianapolis, IN at 317/923-7547 or IDNR, DNP at 317/232-4052.

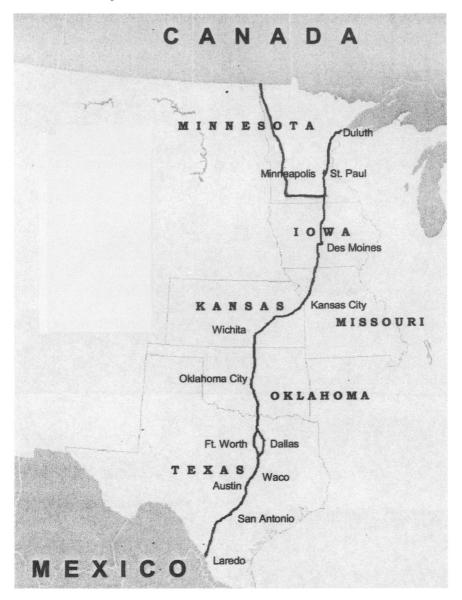

Fig 9 "Prairie Passage" I-35 (US 35)

The Prairie Passage is a planting of prairie along I-35 from Canada to Mexico by State Depts of Transportation. For more information see each participating state.

Map by Bernard L Schwartz

IOWA

"We had heard so much of the beautiful prairies of Iowa," wrote a Pennsylvania girl in the 1840s. "We could see for miles and all my longings for the vast open spaces were satisfied." (*Western Women,* by Sandra L Myres, 1982).

Today, little remains of what that girl saw. However, many organizations are working to protect and restore prairie and other natural areas in Iowa. These include the Audubon Society of Iowa, the Loess Hills Preservation Society, the Iowa Department of Natural Resources (Iowa DNR), The Nature Conservancy (TNC), AmeriCorps, the Iowa Prairie Network, the Volunteer Conservation Corps, and the Iowa Natural Heritage Foundation (INHF). The INHF alone has preserved about 65,000-acres of land in Iowa since 1979, including the Cedar River Greenbelt, Faulkes Heritage Woods, the Cedar Valley, and the Hoover Nature Trails in Linn County.

In 1983 Iowa's Department of Transportation (Iowa DOT) joined "The Prairie Passage," a national project to plant prairie plants along a designated roadside from the Canadian to the Mexican Border in Minnesota, Iowa, Missouri, Kansas, Oklahoma, and Texas. Around 1993, the federal highway administration provided funds for a survey and plan. US 35, was chosen as the route since it is the major federal highway common to all participating states. Because US 35 does not run through former prairie in Minnesota, the Minnesota Department of Transportation (MN DOT) is planting other roadsides with prairie plants to the Canadian Border (see Minnesota below).

The Iowa DOT is planting US 35 with prairie plants and plans to plant all state highways with roadside prairie plants. Further, 77 of the 90 counties in Iowa plan to plant their roadsides with prairie plants. It is anticipated that all counties will eventually join in these plans. Iowa DOT has a substantial budget allocated for prairie plantings although only 25% of their plans have been completed. The Iowa DOT also has a very sensible mowing policy. Only one pass of the mower is used on the shoulder of the road with no mowing beyond that until grassland birds have completed their nesting. All in all, Iowa's roadside prairie plan is the most extensive in the USA. Contact the Iowa DOT at 515/239-1424 for additional information.

Still, Iowa's long neglected prairies have been invaded by noxious weeds and woody plants and many need help in order to restore them to a more healthy state. The Iowa Natural Heritage Foundation (INHF) has led the way but needs volunteers to help. Other organizations have joined INHF in this effort to restore prairies, and are working on "prairie rescue sites," many of which are designated below. For more information and contact information to volunteer see INHF's web site: http://www.inhf.org/rescuesites2.htm.

Below are some of Iowa's remaining prairies:

Allamakee County:
EFFIGY MOUNDS NATIONAL MONUMENT: 2,526-acres with 195 Indian mounds including 31 effigies, and conical, linear, and compound mounds. Eastern Woodland Indians built mounds from about 500 BC until the early European contact period. Natural features in the Monument include forests, tallgrass prairies, wetlands and rivers. The park extends into Clayton County and is located at 151 Hwy 76, Harpers Ferry, IA. Call the Monument at 563/873-3491.

IVERSON BOTTOMS WILDLIFE MANAGEMENT AREA: 3-acre site is a "hill prairie" or "goat prairie," which favor dry species. Woods surround the prairie. This is a prairie rescue site. The site is very difficult to find. Contact the Iowa Native Plant Society at 515/294-9499. If you have questions or would like a map of how to get to the hill prairie from Hwy 76, contact Mark Leoschke at 515/281-5951. One can also contact the Iowa DNR at 515/281-8681.

Black Hawk County:
CEDAR HILLS SAND PRAIRIE: 90-acres of sand prairie located about 10-miles northwest of Cedar Falls, IA. A large sedge meadow and a small fen occupy a swale that traverses the property, and small marshes occupy depressions in the southwest portion of the property. These diverse habitats support over 360 species of native plants, 107 species of birds, over 50 species of butterflies and over 90 species of leafhoppers. It was originally bought by TNC, but is now a State Preserve. Call TNC, IA at 515/244-5044 or the Iowa DNR at 515/281-8681.

HARTMAN RESERVE NATURE CENTER: (See Shirey Sand Savanna below).

SHIREY SAND SAVANNA: 5-acre site located on a low terrace in the floodplain of the Cedar River in the North Unit of Hartman Reserve Nature Center in Waterloo, IA. This is a prairie rescue site. Call the Hartman Reserve Nature Center at 319/277-2187.

Bremer County:
BRAYTON-HORSLEY PRAIRIE: 36-acre mesic-wet prairie. The prairie is located about 2-miles south of Sumner, IA. The property is privately owned and permission must be obtained before visiting. Call TNC, IA in Des Moines, IA at 515/244-5044.

Buchanan County:
BEARBOWER SAND PRAIRIE: 40-acre prairie located 5-miles east of Brandon, IA on the southern border of the county. Call the Buchanan County Conservation Board at 319/636-2617.

Butler County:
CLAY PRAIRIE: 3-acres of an unused cemetery still in prairie vegeta-

tion and one of many pioneer cemeteries. From the intersection of US 20 & Hwy 14, one goes 8½-miles north on Hwy 14 and then 1-mile east on Co Rd C45 to reach the prairie. Call the University of Iowa, Biology Dept at 319/273-2456.

LEEPAR PRAIRIE RESERVE: 41-acre wildlife prairie 5-miles southwest of Clarksville, IA. Call Butler County Parks at 319/278-4237.

SKILLEN'S CORNER HABITAT DEMONSTRATION AREA: This area located at the intersection of Co Rds C13 & T24 is designed as a teaching area. The Butler County Conservation Board Staff has planted trees, shrubs, and prairie grasses to demonstrate how good planning and proper maintenance can help enhance wildlife habitat. Call Butler County Parks 319/278-4237.

WOLTERS PRAIRIE PRESERVE: 44-acre wildlife refuge and native prairie area 3-miles southwest of Clarksville, IA. Call Butler County Parks at 319/278-4237.

Calhoun County:
JOHNSON PRAIRIE MARSH: 120-acre area consisting of an old farmstead and a pasture/prairie that is being restored to native grasses and flowers. Part of the area has never been plowed and contains many native species. A small pond was constructed in the prairie, which attracts many kinds of wildlife and waterfowl. The area is located on Traer Ave 2-miles south of Hwy 20, southeast of Rockwell City, IA. Call the Calhoun County Conservation Board at 712/297-7131.

MUNSON PRAIRIE: 11-acres of virgin prairie abounding with the native wildflowers and grasses that once covered all of Iowa's prairies. The site is 3½-miles northwest of Munson, IA and is north of the railroad tracks and access is gained only by walking in from Quartz Ave from the east. The site is only a few miles from the state-owned Kalsow Prairie in Pocahontas County (see below). Call the Calhoun County Conservation Board at 712/297-7131.

SHILLING SANCTUARY: 15-acres of disturbed prairie and wildlife plantings. When gravel mining ceases, the area will have a small pond. The Sanctuary is 3½-miles south of Knierim, IA. Call the Calhoun County Conservation Board at 712/297-7131.

SHERMAN SCHOOL AND PRAIRIE: This old school is 3-miles west of Manson, IA on Hwy 7. The small cemetery is from the 1800's and early 1900's. The north end of the area is an undisturbed native prairie that features many species of wildflowers and grasses found in only a few places in Calhoun County. Call the Calhoun County Conservation Board at 712/297-7131.

Cerro Gordo County:

BLAZINGSTAR PRAIRIE: 10.5-acre remnant of native prairie. The Prairie is located 2-miles north of Rockwell, IA on Hwy 65 and ½-mile east of 180th Street. Call Cerro Gordo County Parks at 641/423-5309.

HAUGEN WILDLIFE AREA: 75-acre mix of wetland, oak timber and native prairies. The WA is 1-mile west of intersection of Co Rds B20 and S14 near Fertile, IA. This WA is used for hunting and wildlife viewing. Call Cerro Gordo County Parks at 641/423-5309.

HOFFMAN PRAIRIE: 36-acre wetland/prairie community. Vegetation ranges from cattail and sedge wetlands to big bluestem uplands. Several rare butterflies are found here. The prairie is located 2½-miles west of the water tower in Clear Lake, IA on US 18. The Prairie is north of the highway. Call TNC, IA at 515/244-5044.

INGEBRETSON PARK: Located on the south edge of Thornton, IA along Beaver Dam Creek, the site includes a prairie display, shelter houses, playground equipment, picnicking, and restrooms. Call the Park at 515/423-5309.

LIME CREEK CONSERVATION AREA AND NATURE CENTER: 400-acres of woods, prairies and wetlands. The area is located just north of Mason City, IA off Hwy 65. There are trails and parking. Call the Center at 641/423-5309.

WHITE WILDLIFE AREA: 34-acre tract along the Shellrock River. A boardwalk trail loops through open marsh, wooded swamp, restored Prairie and streamside timber. The area, open to public hunting and trapping in season, is located just north of Rock Falls, IA on Co Rd S62. Call Cerro Gordo County Parks at 641/423-5309.

Cherokee County:

NESTOR STILES PRAIRIE: 10-acres of mesic tallgrass prairie dominated by big bluestem, porcupine grass and prairie dropseed. The Prairie is located west of Aurelia, IA south on CR 43. Call the Cherokee County Conservation Board 712/225-6709.

STEELE PRAIRIE: 160-acre site and separate 40-acre tract of mesic to wet tallgrass prairie. The tract has a diverse array of prairie plants and provides habitat for many species of birds, mammals and butterflies. The prairie is located 10½-miles north of Cherokee, IA. The Prairie was purchased by TNC and is managed by the Cherokee County Conservation Board. Call the Board at 712/225-6709.

Clay County:

KIRCHNER PRAIRIE: This site is located south of Landon, IA at the intersection of 310th St and 280th Ave. Call the Iowa DNR at 515/281-8681.

MORI PRAIRIE: 40-acre blacksoil prairie and sedge meadow. The prairie is west of Fosteria, IA. Call TNC, IA at 515/244-5044.

Clayton County:
EFFIGY MOUNDS NATIONAL MONUMENT: (See Allamakee County above).

Clinton County:
DUKE PRAIRIE: 20-acre mesic tallgrass prairie. The Prairie is located 4-miles southwest of Grand Mound, IA. Call the Clinton County Conservation Board at 319/847-7202.

GOOSE LAKE WILDLIFE MANAGEMENT AREA: 886-acres of wetland with 520-acres of wetland and 366-acres of upland with a small portion in native grasses. The WMA is located 1-mile west of Goose Lake, IA along Hwy 136. Call the Clinton County Conservation Board at 319/847-7202.

LOST NATION PUBLIC HUNTING AREA: 260-acre wildlife area that is favored by local pheasant hunters. The Area is being replanted in native grasses because "these native grasses provide much better winter and nesting cover for pheasants and other wildlife." So far, 20% of the area has been replanted. The Area is 1-mile west and 3-miles north of Lost Nation, IA. Call the Clinton County Conservation Board at 319/847-7202.

(MARIE) KETELSEN LEARNING CENTER: 40-acre park and wildlife area is operated by a private trust in honor of Marie Ketelsen, a school teacher who lived on the land. The park features a 26-acre restored prairie, 2-miles of trails, a picnic shelter, a pond and a small oak woodland. The Center is east of Lost Nation, IA with access on 150th St. Call the Clinton County Conservation Board at 319/847-7202.

MALONE PARK: 30-acre park that features a swimming beach, fishing, playground, picnicking, large shelter, small wetland, and a restored prairie in the southwest corner of the park. There is also a 1-mile trail and a parking lot. The Park is located 5-miles east of DeWitt, IA. Call the Clinton County Conservation Board at 319/847-7202.

MANIKOWSKI PRAIRIE: 46-acre virgin limestone prairie is a dedicated state preserve. It is the largest limestone prairie left in Iowa. The Prairie is located 1-mile north and ¼-mile east of Goose Lake, IA. Access is across private land. Call the Clinton County Conservation Board at 319/847-7202.

WAPSI RIVER ENVIRONMENTAL EDUCATION CENTER: 225-acre nature area devoted to provide environmental education. The area contains a small prairie. The Center is located 2-miles northwest of Dixon, IA. Call the Clinton County Conservation Board at 319/847-7202.

Crawford County:

Crawford County's Roadside Vegetation Management Program was established to evaluate, develop, improve, and maintain vegetation cover in 1,200 miles of road-right-of-ways. The goal is to enhance the vegetative stability of the roadsides with the establishment of native prairie, control of noxious weeds, and the improvement of the roadside's natural beauty.

(JOSEPH) AHART/JOHN RUDD NATURAL RESOURCE AREA: 20-acres of re-established prairie, trees and 7-acre pond 2-miles southwest of Dow City, IA. Call the Crawford County Conservation Board at 712/263-2748.

BUCK GROVE CEMETERY PRAIRIE: 2-acre native prairie cemetery located 1½-miles southeast of Buck Grove, IA. Call the Crawford County Conservation Board at 712/263-2748.

KING CEMETERY PRAIRIE: 2-acre native prairie cemetery located 5-miles northwest of Vail, IA. Call the Crawford County Conservation Board at 712/263-2748.

NECOM CEMETERY PRAIRIE: The Prairie is located southeast of Boyer, IA on 320th St. Call the Crawford County Conservation Board at 712/263-2748.

NEWCOM DALE RIGGLEMAN NATURAL RESOURCE AREA: 100-acres of hilly ground which has never been cultivated and is being restored to native prairie through activities such as burning to stimulate growth of original prairie vegetation. The remaining acres consist of a pond and about 39-acres of woodland. Call the Crawford County Conservation Board at 712/263-2748.

OLD CATHOLIC CEMETERY PRAIRIE: 2-acre native prairie cemetery located 1-mile east of Dension, IA. Call the Crawford County Conservation Board at 712/263-2748.

VAIL CEMETERY PRAIRIE: 5-acre native prairie cemetery located ½-mile west of Vail, IA. Call the Crawford County Conservation Board at 712/263-2748.

WILOW CEMETERY PRAIRIE: 3-acre native prairie cemetery located 6-miles southwest of Charter Oak, IA. Call the Crawford County Conservation Board at 712/263-2748.

Dallas County:

RACCOON RIVER VALLEY RECREATIONAL TRAIL: 34-mile hard-surface, multi-purpose trail starts in Waukee, IA and crosses the county to Yale, IA. The Trail is noted for its vistas of agricultural land, river crossing, woodlands, savannas, prairies and unique geologic formations. Call the Dallas County Conservation Board at 515/465-3577.

VOAS NATURE AREA: 260-acre restored wetland/prairie/woodland area. Ideal environment for nature walks, birding, and photography in an area noted for its diverse migrating and endemic wildlife. The Area is located southwest of Minburn, IA off of Co Rd F31 at 1930 Lexington Rd. Call the Dallas County Conservation Board at 515/465-3577.

WAGNER PRAIRIE: This site is located west of the Dallas Center along Hwy 44 and west of US 169. Call the Dallas County Conservation Board at 515/465-3577.

Des Moines County:
BIG HOLLOW RECREATIONAL AREA: 768-acres making it Des Moines County's largest park. An extensive trail system passes through woods, prairies, and around ponds. The park is located 7-miles southwest of Mediapolis, IA. Call the Des Moines Conservation Board at 319/753-8260.

LUCKENBILL WOODS: 76-acre natural area located 4¾-miles northeast of Mediapolis, IA. The trail system winds its way through young and mature woodlands, ponds and wetlands, and restored prairie. This area is being restored to its pre-settlement vegetation patterns of woodlands and prairie. Call the Des Moines Conservation Board at 319/753-8260.

STARR'S CAVE PARK AND PRESERVE: 200-acre area ¼-mile north of Burlington, Iowa. Features include an extensive trail system through mature woodlands, prairie remnants and the limestone bluffs along Flint Creek. Three caves are also located within the preserve. Call the Des Moines Conservation Board at 319/753-8260.

Dickinson County:
FLOWERING HILL PRAIRIE: The Prairie is located near Lake Park, IA. This site is privately owned and there is no contact information.

CAYLER PRAIRIE: 160-acres of wet and dry prairie supporting 40 species of butterfly. Some of the site is marsh dominated by slough grass, sedges and cattail. The prairie is a National Natural Landmark and is located southwest of Sprint Lake, IA on Co Rd M38 (a gravel road). Call the Iowa DNR at 515/281-8681 or John Pearson at the Iowa DNR at 515/281-3891.

CAYLER PRAIRIE ADDITION: This addition is located 4-miles west of Okoboji Lake and adjoins Cayler Prairie State Preserve on the Little Sioux River. Call the Iowa DNR at 515/281-8681.

(FREDA) HAFFNER KETTLEHOLE PRESERVE: 110-acre wet and dry prairie growing on Ice Age kettleholes that were formed by gravel deposited around an isolated block of glacial ice that broke off 14,000 years ago. Over 50-acres of prairie have been restored on portions of the Preserve that were previously farmed. A diverse mix of prairie seed was collected and used from the preserve and Cayler Prairie 4-miles to the north. The prairie supports a very diverse number of plants and animals. The site is a State Preserve and is located west of Hwy 71 near Spencer, IA. Call TNC, IA at 515/244-5044 or Iowa DNR at 515/237-1386.

Dubuque County:
HORSESHOE BLUFF: 15-acre site of hilltop and savanna prairie that is threatened with tree growth. The Bluff is southeast of Dubuque, IA. This is a prairie rescue site. Call the Iowa DNR at 515/281-3891.

KAUFMANN AVENUE PRAIRIE: 9.3-acre "goat" or hill prairie, which typically occurs as forest openings on the crests and south-to-west facing slopes of steep bluffs. This high quality prairie features spectacular displays of forbs and is located on Kaufmann Ave in the city of Dubuque, IA. For access, call TNC, IA at 515/244-5044.

INTERSTATE POWER FOREST PRESERVE: 78-acres was donated to the Dubuque County Conservation Board by the Interstate Power Company, which maintains a substation on the site. The area contains approximately 8-acres of restored prairie, 15-acres of gently rolling grassland, and the rest is made up of heavily forested woodland dissected by deep ravines containing spring-fed streams. A 1½-mile trail directs hikers through the area and is the only development planned for this natural area. The Preserve is located approximately 3½-miles southeast of Dubuque, IA on Olde Davenport Rd near the intersection with Schueller Heights Rd. Call the Dubuque County Conservation Board at 319/556-6745.

LITTLE MAQUOKETA RIVER MOUNDS PRESERVE: 41-acre preserve features 32 ancient Indian burial mounds that are protected by fencing. Situated high atop a limestone ridge, overlooking the Little Maquoketa River just north of Dubuque, IA on Hwys 52 & 3, this preserve also harbors a mature forest containing numerous wildflowers and a small remnant of native blufftop prairie. This site is a classic example of a place to observe "stream piracy" and the route that took the Little Maquoketa from its original bed. A trail up the 200-foot steep bluff continues at the top to circle the Indian Mounds that range from 13 to 42 feet across and 6.5 to 50 feet high. Over 15 Native American tribes were consulted in the development of the site. Informational kiosks at the parking lot and blufftop explain about the significant archaeological, geological, and natural resources found at the site. Call the Dubuque County Conservation Board at 319/556-6745.

POHLMAN PRAIRIE PRESERVE: 23-acre site consisting of native bottomland forest and native prairie remnants on the high bluffs overlooking the Little Maquoketa River valley and the Heritage Trail. This "goat prairie" is in bloom for much of the spring, summer, and fall starting with Pasque flowers in early April and ending in a blush of color from Cylindrical Blazing Stars and various asters in the autumn. The Preserve is located adjacent to Hwy 3 & 52 just south of Durango, IA. A small parking area exists adjacent to the highway, with a steep ½-mile switchback trail leading to the top of the limestone bluffs where the prairie remnants are located. Call the Dubuque County Conservation Board at 319/556-6745.

Emmet County:
ANDERSON PRAIRIE: 200-acres that contains a wide variety of habitats from dry prairie to wetlands, from oak savanna to floodplain woodland. The prairie is located west of Estherville, IA, 9 miles on Hwy 9 and then 1½-mile north at the rest stop. Call the Iowa DNR at 515/281-3891.

IOWA LAKE WILDLIFE AREA: 16-acre camping area sits on an 802-acres Iowa Lake of which 308-acres lie in Iowa and 494-acres lie in Minnesota. This is a small and quiet area with some restored wetlands and native prairie areas. This site is 6-miles north of Armstrong, IA on Hwy 15 and west on 110th Street. Call the Emmet County Conservation Board at 712/362-2510.

RINGHAM HABITAT AREA: 76-acres of which a third is timbered, and two-thirds are native prairie vegetation. Untouched Native American burial mounds are here. The Area is located north of Estherville, Iowa on Co Rd 360th Ave. Call the Emmet County Conservation Board at 712/362-2510.

Floyd County:
ROCKFORD FOSSIL AND PRAIRIE PARK: 187-acres for fossil hunting and study, and a walking trail with native wildflowers. The Park is located ¾-miles southwest of Rockford off Co Rd B47. Call the Floyd County Conservation Board at 515/257-6214.

Fremont County:
WAUBONSIE STATE PARK: The park's prairie remnants have been provided public land protection since 1926, but have received minimal ecosystem management through fire or clearing of invading species. This is a prairie rescue site. The Park is 6-miles south of Sidney, IA. Call Mark Edwards, Iowa DNR at 515/281-8959.

Grundy County:
BEAVER TOWNSHIP CEMETERY & PRAIRIE: The stones on this 3-acre cemetery have been lost and destroyed, but the prairie vegetation that was present when early pioneers were laid to rest still remain. A stone and bronze marker stands in one corner naming the people

believed buried here. The remainder of the area is managed for native grasses and flowers. Call the Grundy County Conservation Board at 319/345-2688.

MELROSE TOWNSHIP CEMETERY: Once the site of a Methodist Church, the building is long gone but native grasses and flowers remain. The Cemetery and stones are well cared for, and interesting stories can be gleaned from a study of the dates and names they hold. The undisturbed east third of the area contains the finest representative remnant of native prairie found to date in Grundy County! The Conservation Board staff offers public interpretive walks each summer. Call the Grundy County Conservation Board at 319/345-2688.

Guthrie County:
Our history tells us that prairie grasses and forbs evolved and became the dominant vegetation for this area. Roadsides in Guthrie County are being seeded with prairie grasses and forbs, which out compete noxious weeds, reduce the amount of chemical applications and create beautiful roadsides and wildlife habitat.

BUNDT PRAIRIE: 3-acre native prairie located 3½-miles northwest of Guthrie Center, IA just off Hwy 25 holds a wide variety of prairie grasses and forbs. Call the Guthrie County Conservation Board at 515/755-3061.

GREENWOOD CEMETERY PRAIRIE: 3-acre cemetery prairie remnant, supporting a variety of prairie grasses and forbs, is located 1-mile east and ½-mile south of Panora, IA. Call the Guthrie County Conservation Board at 515/755-3061.

RACCOON RIVER VALLEY TRAIL: (See Dallas County above).

SHEEDER PRAIRIE: 25-acre mesic prairie with several draws dominated by shrubs and trees. Fire is being used as a management tool to restore prairie vegetation to these areas. The Prairie is northwest of Guthrie Center, IA. Call the Iowa DNR at 515/281-3891.

Hancock County:
CRYSTAL LAKE PARK: 263-acre park with a natural lake, features wildlife habitat and grasslands. The Park is located at Crystal Lake, IA, ¼-mile north of the former Iowa Hwy 111 (now called Co Rd R35). Call the Hancock County Parks at 641/923-2720.

LAU WILDLIFE AREA: 60-acre grassland located 2-miles south of Klemme, IA. Call the Hancock County Parks at 641/923-2720.

RUSS WILDLIFE AREA: 98-acre tract with wetlands, timber, and grassland located 2-miles north and a ½-mile east of Crystal Lake Park (see above). Call the Hancock County Parks at 641/923-2720.

Harrison County:
DESOTO NATIONAL WILDLIFE REFUGE: 7,823-acres (3,499-acres in Iowa and 4,324-acres in Nebraska) along the Missouri River bottom and north of Council Bluffs, Iowa. Partial restoration from cornfields to tallgrass prairie has been accomplished. Red tail hawk and eastern meadowlark can be viewed here. Call the NWR at 712/642-4121.

Howard County:
CROSSMAN PRAIRIE: 10-acres of mesic to wet prairie dominated by big bluestem, prairie dropseed, and Indian grass in the drier areas. The Prairie is about 5-miles northeast of Riceville, IA. Call TNC, IA at 515/244-5044.

HAYDEN PRAIRIE: 240-acres constitute Iowa's largest black soil prairie, which originally covered vast expanses of Iowa, but only a few small fragments remain. This prairie is a National Natural Landmark and a state preserve. The Prairie is located 4-miles west on Hwy 9 from the junction of Hwy 9 and US 63, then north on Co Rd V26 for 4½-miles to the preserve. Call the Iowa DNR at 515/281-3891.

Humboldt County:
HUMBOLDT RAILROAD PRAIRIE: The Prairie is located 1-mile north and 2-miles east of Livermore, IA. Call the Humboldt County Conservation Board at 515/332-4087.

PIONEER PRAIRIE POTHOLE: This site is located approximately 3-miles south and 7-miles west of Humboldt, IA. Call the Humboldt County Conservation Board at 515/332-4087.

Iowa County:
BERSTLER WOODS: 69-acre oak-hickory timber and grassland area rich in Native American history as well as an excellent wildlife area. The woods are 2-miles south of Millersburg, IA. Call the Iowa County Conservation Board at 319/655-8465.

ENGLISH RIVER WILDLIFE AREA, FULLER ADDITION: 60-acres of wetlands, upland and lowland timber and grasslands, which are excellent wildlife habitat. This area adjoins the 330-acres owned by Washington County and is located 6-miles east of North English, IA on S Ave and the Keokuk/Iowa Rd. The WA is also in Keokuk and Washington Counties (see below). Call the Iowa County Conservation Board at 319/655-8465.

I-80 WILDLIFE AREA: 13-acres of open grassland. The area is located just off US 80, exit 216, 3-miles northwest of Williamsburg, IA. Call the Iowa County Conservation Board at 319/655-8465.

PILOT GROVE STATE PRESERVE: 7-acre remnant includes an oak-hickory savanna and evidence of pioneer wagon trails through the timber. The Preserve is southwest of Williamsburg, IA. Call the Iowa County Conservation Board at 319/655-8465.

Jasper County:
KISH-KE-KOSH PRAIRIE: 16.65-acre prairie on sand, which mantles an unusual upland projection into the South Skunk River valley. The sand blew out of the river valley about 4,000 years ago. Big and little bluestem, Indian grass, and prairie dropdseed dominate the prairie. The Prairie is southeast of Reasnor, IA. Call the Jasper County Conservation Board at 641/792-9780.

NEIL SMITH (WALNUT CREEK) NATIONAL WILDLIFE REFUGE: 8,654-acre restoration in Prairie City, IA 20-miles east of Des Moines, IA. This is one of the most ambitious projects to restore farmland to prairie and oak savanna. The project intends to transform uniform rows of corn and soybeans into a tallgrass prairie supporting elk and buffalo. Call the NWR at 515/994-3400.

ROCK CREEK STATE PARK & STEPHENS STATE FOREST, REICHELT UNIT: 602-acre Rock Creek Lake is the center of the park. This is a prairie rescue site. Contact Roger Thompson, Iowa DNR, at 641/236-3722.

Johnson County:
FINKBINE PRAIRIE: A chain of five small but moderately diverse native tallgrass prairie remnants on the west side of the University of Iowa campus between Iowa City and Coralville, Iowa mostly located on the hillside along the bicycle trail between Hawkins Dr and Mormon Trek. As you drive by on US 6, these prairies are clearly visible as open meadows on the hillside to the south. Parking is available in the lot serving the softball field, accessible from Mormon Trek about a block south of US 6, just north of the railroad underpass. There is also a new parking lot off US 6, serving the University's soccer fields; a wood-chip jogging trail connects this to the bike trail. Call the Johnson County Conservation Board at 319/645-2315.

KENT PARK, VALLEY VIEW WEST PRAIRIE: 12-acre site is one of several relict prairies in Kent Park threatened by invading woody plants and desperately in need of some TLC. This is a prairie rescue site. The prairies are located 6-miles west of Carolville, IA on Hwy 6. Call the Iowa Natural Heritage Foundation at 515/288-1846.

SOLON PRAIRIE: 3-acre prairie on the west edge of Solon, IA. Call the Johnson County Conservation Board at 319/645-2315.

WILLIAMS PRAIRIE: 20-acre wet sedge prairie located within a shallow, poorly drained bowl, which frequently remains wet through the spring and summer. The prairie is northwest of Oxford, IA. Call TNC, IA at 515/244-5044.

Jones County:
BREEN PRAIRIE FARM: The prairie is located 3-miles north of Monticello, IA, on Hwy 38. This is a prairie rescue site. Call the Iowa Natural Heritage Foundation at 515/288-1846.

ROCHESTER CEMETERY PRAIRIE: Rochester Township set aside a beautiful tract of virgin prairie savanna for a Township Cemetery not long after Iowa became a state. It remains one of Iowa's best-preserved tracts of native vegetation and is a remnant of Iowa's tallgrass prairie savanna. The Cemetery is south of Rochester, IA on Cemetery Rd. Call the Cedar Counter Conservation Board in Tiption IA at 319/886-6930.

Keokuk County:
ENGLISH RIVER WILDLIFE AREA: (See Iowa County above). Call the Keokuk County Conservation Board at 641/622-3757.

Kossuth County:
STINSON PRAIRIE: 32-acres ranging from prairie potholes to dry prairie hold a very diverse community of prairie plants. The preserve is on the conspicuous south-facing edge of the Algona end moraine. The preserve is northwest of Algona, IA. Call the Kossuth County Conservation Board at 515/295-2138.

UNION SLOUGH NATIONAL WILDLIFE REFUGE: 3,309-acres devoted to resting, nesting and feeding for waterfowl and other migratory birds that include restored prairie. The NWR is Located just south of the Minnesota border, about 50-miles west of Mason City, IA. Call the USFWS at 515/928-2230.

Louisa County:
FLAMING PRAIRIE PARK: 72-acre site is managed for camping, picnicking and wildlife habitat, which includes a shallow pond, wetland, forest and prairie. The Park is east of Grandview, IA and along the Mississippi River and is submerged when the Mississippi River level is high. Call the Louisa County Conservation Board at 319/523-8381.

INDIAN SLOUGH WILDLIFE AREA: 1,049-acre area is managed for wildlife habitat, which contains wetlands, forest, prairie, crop ground and food plots. There is a parking lot and trails. The area is 2-miles north of Wapello, IA and adjacent to the Iowa River and may be flooded when the river level is high. Call the Louisa County Conservation Board at 319/523-8381.

Madison County:
JENSEN MARSH: 190-acres of wet, mesic and dry prairie. The prairie is southwest of Bevington, IA on 228th Lane. Contact Iowa Prairie

Network at www.iowaprairienetwork.org.

Lucas County:
STEPHENS STATE FOREST, WHITE BREAST UNIT: This unit of the State Forest is southwest of Lucas, IA. This is a prairie rescue site. Contact Jeff Goerndt, Iowa DNR, at 515/774-4559.

Lyons County:
GITCHIE MANITOU: 91-acres of prairie, woodland and old-field and contains wind-polished outcrops of Sioux quartzite, the oldest exposed rock bed in Iowa. The area has been a favorite of Iowa botanists since the late 1800's. The preserve can be reached from the south edge of Larchwood, IA by taking Co Rd A18 west 6½-miles and then turning north on Co Rd K10 for another 4½-miles. Call the Iowa DNR at 515/281-3891.

Mahaska County:
EDDYVILLE DUNES: 1,200-acres of sand deposits, up to 69 feet thick having depressions forming numerous open water wetlands and wet meadows. This is a prairie rescue site. This is an area protected by the Sierra Club. Call the Sierra Club, Iowa at 515/277-8868 or the Mahaska County Conservation Board at 641/673-9327.

Marion County:
ELK ROCK STATE PARK: The park is 7-miles north of Knoxville, IA. This is a prairie rescue site. Call Mark Edwards, Iowa DNR at 515/281-8959.

Marshall County:
MARIETTA SAND PRAIRIE PRESERVE: 17-acre prairie and woodland located on an upland deposit of windblown sand. The vegetation ranges from dry upland prairie to wet prairie and wet woodland. The Preserve is located 2-miles west and 1-mile south of Albion, IA. Call the Iowa DNR at 515/281-8681 or the Marshall County Conservation Board at 641/754-6303.

Mills County:
FOLSOM POINT PRAIRIE: 281-acres near Lewis and Clark's Council Bluffs where the United States held its first council with Native Prairie Indians, protects the core of the loess hills tallgrass prairie area. The Prairie's unique dry ridges are associated with the Missouri River and the site extends into Pottawattamie County. This is a prairie rescue site. The Prairie is southeast of Council Bluffs, IA. Call TNC, IA at 515/244-5044 or contact Susanne Hickey, TNC, IA at 402/558-8099.

VINCENT BLUFF PRESERVE: 31-acre site located on top of a loess hill near the intersection of Woodbury Ave and Harry Langdon Blvd, on the southern edge of Council Bluffs, IA. It is one of the few undeveloped blufftops remaining within the city limits. The bluff contains high-quality prairie remnants and provides wildlife habitat. This is a prairie rescue site. Contact Glenn Pollock, Loess Hills Preservation Society, at 402/571-6230 or the INHF at 800/475-1846.

Mitchell County:
MARKHAM'S POND: 33-acre area containing Mitchell County's last prairie pond. The Pond is located 1½-miles northwest of Otranto, IA on Co Rd S70. Call the Mitchell County Conservation Board at 641/732-5204.

NEW HAVEN POTHOLES: 168-acre area provides a variety of habitat such as marsh, prairie, woodland, river and several small potholes with 4 self-guided trails. The Potholes are southeast of Osage, IA. Call the Mitchell County Conservation Board at 641/732-5204.

Monona County:
BEAVER RUN: 65-acre wildlife management area is located along Co Rd L37. Beaver dams have created a picturesque wetland, bordered on the west by native prairie grasses. Call the Monona County Conservation Board at 712/423-2400.

THE DAVIS WETLAND: 54-acre property was planted with native grasses and woody plants to attract wildlife. This marsh lies in the Little Sioux River floodplain just below the loess hills 1-mile north of Turin, IA on the Larpenteur Rd. Call the Monona County Conservation Board at 712/423-2400.

LOESS HILLS WILDLIFE MANAGEMENT AREA: 3,896-acres contains significant amounts of prairie including Turin Preserve and Sylvan Runkel Preserve (see below). Call the Iowa DNR at 712/458-2428.

THE MONONA ARBORETUM: 11-acre area is located at the east edge of Onawa, IA and is the location for many environmental education programs offered by the Board. In the north field, seven windbreak designs show the diversity possible with windbreaks, and also offers shelter for the native prairie grass plot, the nut tree display, a demonstration wildlife habitat area and a stand of short-grass prairie. Call the Monona County Conservation Board at 712/423-2400.

PRAIRIE TRAIL: This linear park is an abandoned railroad right-of-way that has been smoothed and planted to native short grasses and wildflowers. The 2-mile trail begins on the west side of the Maple River and follows Hwy 183. Call the Monona County Conservation Board at 712/423-2400.

PREPARATION CANYON RIDGE TOP PRAIRIES: 346-acre park contains remnant and restored prairies and is located 5-miles southwest of Moorhead, IA. Call the Iowa DNR at 712/458-2428.

SYLVAN RUNKEL PRESERVE: 330-acre preserve within the 3,900-acre Loess Hills Wildlife Management Area (see above), which includes prairie on a prominent ridge of deep loess typical of the Loess Hills. The preserve is named after a well-known Iowa naturalist and conservationist. This site is located east of Onawa, IA. Call the Iowa DNR at 515/281-3891. See Folsom Point Prairie above (Mills County) for similar loess hill prairies.

TURIN LOESS HILLS PRESERVE: 220-acres of dry prairie with encroaching woodland. The prairie is 1½-miles north of Turin, IA on a gravel road. Call the Iowa DNR at 515/281-3891. See Folsom Point Prairie above (Mills County) for similar loess hill prairies.

Muscatine County:
GREINER FAMILY NATURE PRESERVE: 97-acre site containing Oak savanna, sand prairie, and open sandy areas required by nesting turtles, which are being restored through intensive management efforts. The Preserve is located about 6-miles northwest of Muscatine, IA. Call TNC, IA at 515/244-5044.

SWAMP WHITE OAK PRESERVE: This site sits on a low sand terrace along the Cedar River. The understory has diverse wetlands, sedge dominated woodlands and dry sand prairie ridges, which support an array of plants, birds, amphibians and reptiles. This is a prairie rescue site. The preserve is located west of Muscatine, IA. Call TNC, IA at 515/244-5044.

Plymouth County:
BROKEN KETTLE GRASSLANDS: 4,000-acre preserve protects the largest known native tallgrass prairie in Iowa. The extensive prairie ridgetops feature a variety of plants and animals typically found further west in the Great Plains, and also provide critical habitat for many species of prairie butterflies. By releasing flea beetles, the preserve is attempting "biocontrol" of the invasive non-native, leafy spurge. The preserve is located north of Sioux City, IA on Butcher Rd, about 1-mile east of Hwy 12. Call TNC, IA at 515/244-5044.

DURHAM PRAIRIE PRESERVE: 30-acre prairie near Akron, IA. Call the Plymouth County Conservation Board at 712/947-4270.

FIVE RIDGE PRAIRIE: 790-acres of dry prairie and woodland on a steep wind-blown loess deposits, of which 300-acres of prairie lie along the ridgetops and on south and west facing slopes in this area. The site is located northwest of Sioux City, IA on Co Rd C43. Call the Plymouth County Conservation Board at 712/947-4270.

HILLSIDE RECREATION AREA: 230-acres of open grassland, reconstructed prairie, and woodlands. The area is 1-mile west of Hinton IA on Co Rd C60. Call the Plymouth County Conservation Board at 712/947-4270.

KNAPP PRAIRIE: 25-acres of dry-mesic loess hills prairie growing on the lower portions of a moderate slopes and is dominated by tallgrass prairie species adapted to deeper soils and higher moisture. The Prairie is northeast of Sioux City, IA. Call TNC, IA at 515/244-5044.

MOUNT TALBOT: 90-acres exemplifying the loess hills landform which can be seen in western Iowa from the Missouri border to Five Ridge Prairie State Preserve north of Sioux City, IA. The prairie extends into Woodbury County and is on the north side of the 1,069-acre STONE STATE PARK, (see below) which is the northwest corner of Sioux City, IA along Hwy 12. Call the Iowa DNR at 515/281-3891.

O'BRIEN PRAIRIE: 40-acre black soil native tallgrass prairie remnant that is indicative of what Plymouth County was like at the time of the settlers. The prairie is located at Noble Ave & 260th Street. Call the Plymouth County Conservation Board at 712/947-4270.

STONE STATE PARK: 1,069-acres of ridgetop and hillside prairies and bottomland forest. The park contains fine examples of prairies and woodlands, including rare species from each. Late April and early May are the best times to view woodland wildflowers. Rare butterflies, such as the Pawnee skipper, Ottoe skipper, and Olympia white, can be found in the prairies. The Park is on Talbot Rd in Sioux City, IA. This is a prairie rescue site. Contact Chuck Johnson, Loess Hills Audubon Society, at 712/258-3501 or call the Park at 712/255-4698.

Pocahontas County:
KALSOW PRAIRIE: 160-acres including prairie pothole wetlands lie near the center of the buried Mason Crater that was formed by a meteor impact in pre-glacial times. This tallgrass prairie ranges from mesic to wet with potholes. The site is northwest of Manson, IA. Call the Iowa DNR at 712/458-2428.

WIEGERT PRAIRIE FARM: The Farm is located 4-miles southeast of Palmer, IA and is intended to depict farm life as it used to be. Two miles south of the farm is Kalsow Prairie (see above). Call the Pocahontas County Conservation Board at 712/335-4395.

Polk County:
ENGELDINGER MARSH: 81-acre wildlife area has been described as a "geological and ecological museum" because of its rare prairie pothole and sedge meadow. It is located 5-miles northeast of Bondurant, IA on Hwy 65. A yearlong survey at the marsh counted 314 species of plants, 19 species of mammals, 15 species of reptiles and amphibians, and 82

species of birds. A small parking area off NE 120th Street offers access for wildlife viewing and hunting in the area. Call the Polk County Conservation Board at 515/999-2557.

SNYDER FARM: 151-acre farm being restored to prairie, oak savanna and wetlands by the Iowa Natural Heritage Foundation (INHF). The property lies 2-miles east and 1-mile south of Elkhart, IA. Call INHF at 515/288-1846.

Pottawattamie County:
FOLSOM POINT PRAIRIE. (See Mills County above).

HITCHCOCK NATURE AREA: 660-acre site located 5-miles north of Cresent, IA on Ski Hill Loop, and just 15 minutes from downtown Omaha, NE. Located in the heart of the geologically unique Loess Hills, this area was "rescued" from developers planning a landfill and now sits as a crown jewel in the Loess Hills. This area is one of the best wildlife viewing areas in Iowa; it is not uncommon to see turkeys, deer, coyotes, and birds of all kinds. Call the Pottawattamie County Conservation Board at 712/328-5638.

Ringgold County:
KELLERTON/RINGGOLD WILDLIFE AREA: This is a prairie rescue site located southwest of Kellerton, IA near the Kellerton Bird Conservation Area. Call the INHF at 515/288-1846.

Shelby County:
DERALD DINESEN PRAIRIE: 20-acres representing the tallgrass prairie of western Iowa. Hilltops in this rolling landscape are capped by loess, which was blown from the Missouri River valley over 12,000 years ago. This rolling terrain is typical of the Southern Iowa Drift Plain. The Prairie is 3-miles north and 1¼-miles east of Harlan, IA. Call the Shelby County Conservation Board at 712/755-2628.

Story County:
AMES HIGH SCHOOL PRAIRIE: A 22-acre rare example of urban native tallgrass prairie. This is an example of the more xeric type of tallgrass found on drier, well drained hillsides. Heavily used for teaching in central Iowa, Ames High School Prairie is located in Ames, IA off 20th St west of Hwy 69 and is entered from a small parking lot at the back of the high school. Call the TNC, IA at 515/244-5044.

DOOLITTLE PRAIRIE PRESERVE: 25-acre mesic to wet prairie that includes several potholes formed by slow melting of the Des Moines Lobe ice sheet about 13,000 years ago. This is so recent that drainage is not well developed, and wet areas like these potholes remain. The Prairie is located southwest of Story City, IA. Call the Story County Conservation Board at 515/232-2516.

DOOLITTLE PRAIRIE PRESERVE ADDITION: The addition is located 8-miles north of Ames, IA and 3-miles south of Story City, IA. Call Story County Conservation Board at 515/232-2516.

Warren County:
MEDORA PRAIRIE: 60-acres of rolling topography features native tallgrass prairie dissected by wooded ravines, located about 10-miles southwest of Indianola, IA. It supports a diverse array of prairie plants typical of prairie communities in the Southern Iowa Drift Plain, numerous bird species, and rare prairie butterflies such as the regal fritillary and the state threatened byssus skipper. Rolling Thunder Prairie State Preserve, (see below) a 123-acre tallgrass prairie preserve owned and managed by the Warren County Conservation Board, is within 1½-miles of Medora Prairie. These two preserves make a significant contribution to the conservation of tallgrass prairie in southern Iowa. Call the TNC, IA at 515/244-5044.

MCRAE PARK: This city park is a remnant oak savanna, an ecosystem whose plant composition is related to both prairie and oak forest communities. Oak savanna may be the most endangered of our native plant communities. This is a prairie rescue site. The park is 1-mile south of Des Moines, IA. Call the Iowa Natural Heritage Foundation at 515/288-1846.

ROLLING THUNDER PRAIRIE: 123-acres of tallgrass prairie growing on steeply rolling landscape last glaciated over 500,000 years ago. The vegetation ranges from dry to mesic. The site is located southwest of Indianola, IA. Call the Warren County Conservation Board at 515/961-6169.

Washington County:
ENGLISH RIVER WILDLIFE AREA: 330-acres (see Iowa County above). Call the Washington County Conservation Board at 319/657-3457.

Webster County:
BRUSHY CREEK STATE PARK: 6,000-acre park. This is a prairie rescue site. The park is northeast of Lehigh, IA. Contact Greg Van Fosson, Iowa DNR at 515/543-8298.

LISKA-STANEK PRAIRIE: 20-acre mesic prairie containing two potholes with wet prairie vegetation. The site is southwest of Fort Dodge, IA. Call the Webster County Conservation Board at 515/576-4258.

Winnebago County:
(C A) BLOCK WILDLIFE AREA: 99-acres of Winnebago River bottom, native prairie, uplands and timber, and is a popular waterfowl hunting area located north of Leland, IA. Call Winnebago County Parks at 641/565-3390.

HOGSBACK WILDLIFE AREA: 154-acres of bluffs, marshlands, oak forest, woodland wildflowers and native grasses located 3-miles north of Lake Mills, IA on Co Rd A16. Call Winnebago County Parks at 641/565-3390.

LARSON-TWEED WILDLIFE AREA: 74-acre public hunting area includes a prairie and is located 1-mile north of Lake Mills, IA on Co Rd R74. Call Winnebago County Parks at 641/565-3390.

LUKE ROSSITER WILDLIFE AREA: 51-acre area features a public hunting area with wetlands and a native restored prairie and is located southwest of Thompson, IA on Co Rd R34. Call Winnebago County Parks at 641/565-3390.

RUSS WILDLIFE AREA: 100-acres lying adjacent to THORPE PARK, a 40-acre marsh, oak timber, natural and restored prairie grasses, and a trail with observation deck. The WA is located northwest of Forest City, IA on Co Rd B14. Call Winnebago County Parks at 641/565-3390.

THOMPSON ROADSIDE PRAIRIE: A former rest area is now a restored prairie located ½-mile north of Thompson, IA on Hwy 9. Call Winnebago County Parks at 641/565-3390.

THORPE RECREATION AREA: 82-acres adjacent to THORPE PARK. A prairie, which is popular with bow hunters, is located here. (See Russ Wildlife Area for location) Call Winnebago County Parks at 641/565-3390.

WINNEBAGO RIVER TRAIL: The trail starts at the intersection of Hwys 9 & 69 in Forest City, IA and runs to Co Rd A44. The trail lies mostly along an abandoned railroad right-of-way. The 2½-mile trail winds through oak timber, wetlands and prairie areas. Call Winnebago County Parks at 641/565-3390.

Winneshiek County:
CHIPERA PRAIRIE: 77-acre site located 3½-miles southwest of Fort Atkinson, IA. Call the Winneshiek County Conservation Board at 319/534-7145.

Woodbury County:
MOUNT TALBOT: (See Plymouth County above).

SIOUX CITY PRAIRIE: 157-acre dry-mesic Loess Hills prairie located in the northern portion of the Loess Hills and within the metropolitan area of Sioux City, IA and just west of Briar Cliff College. The Prairie provides an excellent outdoor classroom for students from area schools. This is a prairie rescue site. Contact Chuck Johnson, Loess Hills Audubon Society, at 712/258-3501 or call TNC, IA at 515/244-5044 or the Woodbury County Conservation Board at 712/258-0838.

KANSAS

"If you should get the chance to visit the Flint Hills, it is truly an inspiration knowing there is still a place where the tallgrass prairie has a chance to function," writes Greg Wingfield of TNC, Kansas. The Flint Hills region encompasses much of eastern Kansas from near the Kansas-Nebraska border south into northeast Oklahoma.

"The Prairie Passage, i.e., US 35" runs through Kansas, which involves the Kansas Department of Transportation (KDOT) in the project. However, budget restraints and other problems have led Kansas to take a different approach than some other states. Instead of large scale planting, Kansas is protecting and enhancing those prairies along the roadsides that already exist. Further, small demonstration prairies have been planted at some of the rest stops along US 35. And prairie plants are planted along those roadsides where there is new construction. KDOT's policy is to restore present prairies and where budgets allow plant more. Its mowing policy is to mow 15 to 30 feet from the shoulder. Call the KDOT, Environmental Services at 785/296-0853.

The Kansas State flower is the wild native sunflower, the state bird is the western meadowlark, and the state animal is the American Buffalo (Bison).

Note!
The Kansas Department of Wildlife and Parks (KDWP) provides prairie chicken blinds for people who want to see prairie chickens during their courtship ritual. For more information and to reserve a blind call the Pratt Office at 316/672-5911 or the Valley Center Office at 316/755-2711 or the Emporia Office at 316/342-0658.

"The name - Kansas - is derived from the name of the dominant tribe of Indians found in the Territory when first visited by white men. They were variously spoken of by early explorers as Kanzas, Canceas, Cansez, Kansez, Canzas, Canzes, Okanis, Kansies, Canses, Canzon, Kanzon, Konza, Konzas, Kasas, Kanzan, Kanzans and by other varied spellings, all having a similar phonetic expression," stated William G. Cutler's *History of the State of Kansas,* first published in 1883 by A. T. Andreas, Chicago, IL.

"The Missouri territory (including Kansas) is a vast wilderness, resembling a desert, extending from the state of Missouri and the river Mississippi, to the Rocky Mountains. It is a region of open elevated plains, generally destitute of forest trees, and interspersed with barren hills," stated *A System of Modern Geography for Schools, Academies and Families,* by Nathaniel G. Huntington, A. M., Hartford, 1836.

Today this vast "desert" is no more, and only remnants remain. As in other prairie states, organizations are involved in protecting and restoring existing prairies, and in some cases creating prairies where they used to exist.

Below is a list of some remnant prairies that can be seen today in

Kansas:

Allen County:
THE PRAIRIE SPIRIT TRAIL: This new trail runs through Anderson and Franklin Counties (see below) with a proposed extension into Allen County into the Town of Iola, KS. The Trail starts in Ottawa, KS going through Princeton, Richmond, Garnett, and presently ending in Welda, KS. The section from Welda to Iola, KS is still waiting for construction funds. When completed, it will total 50 miles. At the present, it is 33 miles. The Trail is 10 feet wide and winds through prairies and woodlands following US 59 and US 169. For more information, call the Trail Manager's Office at 785/448-6767.

Anderson County:
THE PRAIRIE SPIRIT TRAIL: (See Allen County above).

WELDA PRAIRIE: 128-acre tallgrass prairie located between the towns of Welda and Garnett, KS. This prairie has a population of Henslow's sparrow, a grassland bird whose numbers are declining. Call TNC, KS in Topeka, KS at 785/233-4400.

Bourbon County:
BOURBON STATE FISHING LAKE AND WILDLIFE AREA: 277-acres in a forest-prairie mosaic area. The WA is east of Elsmore, KS. Call the KDWP at 316/362-3671.

Butler County:
BUTLER STATE FISHING LAKE: 546-acres lying in the heart of the Flint Hills tallgrass prairie area. The Lake is northwest of Latham, KS. Call the KDWP at 316/321-7180.

EL DORADO STATE PARK: 4,600-acres supporting lots of prairie and wildlife, including prairie chickens and meadowlarks. The Park is located just northeast of the city of El Dorado, KS at the edge of the Flint Hills. Call the Kansas Department of Wildlife and Parks at 316/321-7180.

FLINT HILLS SCENIC BYWAY (K177): 47.2 mile drive across the Flint Hills of Kansas on Co Rd K177 between Council Grove and Cassoday, KS. The byway extends through Butler, Chase, and Morris Counties, and is a beautiful drive year-round showing off the panoramic vistas of the tallgrass prairie. Historic sites abound in Council Grove from the Kaw Mission and the Last Chance Store. Call the KDOT at 785/296-3585.

FLINT HILLS TALLGRASS PRAIRIE PRESERVE: 2,200-acres of typical upland prairie located on the Butler-Greenwood County line supports eagles, prairie chickens, bison, cattle, armadillos, bobcats and badgers. The Preserve extends into Chase County. For permission to visit, call TNC, KS in Topeka, KS at 785/233-4400.

Chase County:
CHASE STATE FISHING LAKE: 383-acres of tallgrass prairie surrounding a beautiful lake is a wonderful place to hike. The Lake is west of Cottonwood Falls, KS on Main St. Call the KDWP at 316/767-5900.

FLINT HILLS SCENIC BYWAY (K177): (See Butler County above).

FLINT HILLS TALLGRASS PRAIRIE PRESERVE: (See Butler County above).

TALLGRASS PRAIRIE NATIONAL PRESERVE: Also known as the Z BAR/SPRING HILL RANCH contains 11,000-acres within the Flint Hills region and is designated a National Historic Landmark. ThePreserve is dedicated to preserving the prairie environment. A nature trail is named in honor of the Kansa Indians known as the People of the South Wind. The Preserve is located 1-mile west of Strong City, KS on Hwy 177. Parts of the Preserve are open to the public along with bus tours of the Preserve. Call the Superintendent, Tallgrass Prairie National Preserve at 316/273-6034.

Z BAR/SPRING HILL RANCH: (See Tallgrass Prairie National Preserve, above).

Cherokee County:
MINED LAND WILDLIFE AREAS NOS 20 to 23: 2,000-acres of restored shrublands, woodlands, and restored native grasses. The Area is northwest of Columbus, KS. Call the KDWP at 316/827-6135.

Clark County:
BIG BASIN PRAIRIE PRESERVE: 1,818-acres of short to mid-grass prairie containing steep-sided sink holes and a permanent pond that never goes dry even during severe drought, known as St. Jacob's Well. Fossils are found here. This National Natural Landmark supports a bison herd, and has a short trail and parking. The Preserve is 15-miles south of Minneola, KS on US 283. US 283 bisects the Big Basin, which is 1-mile in diameter and 100 feet deep with two-thirds of the basin lying east of the road and within the confines of the Preserve. The remaining western third of the basin is privately owned. Call TNC, KS at 785/233-4400.

Coffey County:
FLINT HILLS NATIONAL WILDLIFE REFUGE: 18,463-acres at the northern end of the John Redmond Reservoir (see below) is known for its diverse habitat of wetlands, cropland, and tallgrass prairie. The NWR is northwest of Burlington, KS while the headquarters is in Hartford, KS. Call the USFWS at 316/392-5553.

(JOHN) REDMOND RESERVOIR: 10,870-acres with bluestem pasture surrounding the reservoir. The Reservoir is northwest of Burlington, KS. Call the KDWP at 913/828-4933.

Cowley County:
CHAPLIN NATURE CENTER: 200-acres with 5-miles of walking trails winding through bottomland timber, prairie, a spring-fed creek, and the Arkansas River. The Center is northwest of Arkansas, KS. Call the Wichita Audubon Society at 316/442-4133.

COWLEY STATE FISHING LAKE: 197-acres of tallgrass prairie surrounding the lake, which is east of Arkansas, KS on US 166. Call the KDWP at 316/321-7180.

SAND PRAIRIE NATURAL HISTORY RESERVATION: (See Harvey County below).

WINFIELD CITY LAKE: 2,000-acres of tallgrass prairie surrounding the lake with the north shore having wooded draws, hedgerows, and bushy areas. The lake is northeast of Winfield, KS on Co Rd 8. Call the City of Winfield at 316/221-4249.

Dickinson County:
HERINGTON CITY LAKES: 1,600-acres with prairie and cropland surrounding these city lakes, which are just east of Herington, KS. Call the City of Herington at 913/258-2271 or 3051.

Douglas County:
BAKER WETLANDS: 573-acre preserve just south of Lawrence, KS on 31st St. The north half of the preserve is wetland, while the south half has two prairie areas with a total of 45-acres. Call either the University of Kansas at 913/864-4180 or Baker University at 913/594-3172.

(IVAN) BOYD PRAIRIE PRESERVE: 18-acre remnant prairie located 3-miles east of Baldwin, KS on Hwy 56. ThePreserve is adjacent to the site of the Civil War battle of Black Jack. Some wagon ruts remain here from the days of the Santa Fe Trail. Call Dr. Boyd at Butler University 800/873-4248.

CLINTON RESERVOIR: 18,856-acres of high limestone bluffs, clear water, wooded shoreline, tallgrass prairie, croplands, and miles of hiking trails. The Reservoir is west of Lawrence, KS on Co Rd 13. Call the KDWP at 913/842-8562.

PRAIRIE PARK NATURE CENTER: 72-acres of prairie, woodland, and wetland on the east side of Lawrence, KS with walking trails that are excellent for bird watching and wildlife viewing. Call the Lawrence Dept of Parks and Recreation at 785/832-7985.

Ellsworth County:
KANOPOLIS RESERVOIR: 18,000-acres that includes the reservoir, Kanopolis State Park, and parks operated by the Corp of Engineers. The Buffalo Track Canyon Nature Trail takes one past 423 species of plants of which many are prairie plants. The Reservoir is west of Venango, KS with the State Park at the north and south end of the lake. Call the USCE at 913/546-2294 or the KDWP at 913/546-2565.

Franklin County:
THE PRAIRIE SPIRIT TRAIL: (See Allen County above).

Finney County:
FINNEY GAME RESERVE: 3,670-acres of sandsage prairie, one of the last remnants of this habitat that once covered much of western Kansas, which supports about 100 bison. Access to the Reserve is by arranged tour only. The Reserve is just south of Garden City, KS. Call the reserve at 316/276-9400 or 800/879-9803.

Geary County:
KONZA PRAIRIE: 8,616-acres of tallgrass prairie located in the Flint Hills region and approximately 6-miles south of Manhattan, KS and Kansas State University. This is perhaps North America's largest area of virgin unplowed tallgrass prairie. It supports a bison herd, 208 species of birds and a wide variety of wildflowers, reptiles, mammals and amphibians. The Prairie has hiking trails, and extends into Greenwood and Riley Counties. Call TNC, KS at 785/233-4400 or call the Director, Konza Prairie Biological Station, Kansas State University at 785/587-0441.

MILFORD RESERVOIR: 37,000-acres including the reservoir, Milford State Park, and a large wildlife area (18,000-acres) operated by the Corp of Engineers. In back of the Nature Center is the tallgrass nature trail. The Reservoir is northwest of Junction City, KS and extends into Clay County. Call the US Corp of Engineers (USCE) at 913/238-5714 or the Nature Center at 913/238-3014.

Greenwood County:
KONZA PRAIRIE: (See Geary County, above).

FALL RIVER RESERVOIR: 10,270-acres situated in the rolling tallgrass prairie and wooded valleys of Flint and Chautauqua Hills includes Fall River State Park, the Fall River Wildlife Area and other land owned by the Corp of Engineers. The Reservoir is northwest of Fall River, KS. Call the USCE at 316/658-4445 or the KDWP at 316/637-2213.

FALL RIVER STATE PARK: (See above).

Harvey County:
HARVEY COUNTY WEST PARK: 310-acres on the Arkansas River with woodlands, a small lake and pond, and a sand prairie. The Park is northeast of Burrton, KS on Co Rd 566. Call Harvey County at 316/835-3189.

SAND PRAIRIE NATURAL HISTORY RESERVATION: 80-acre reserve between the Arkansas River and the Little Arkansas River. The sand dunes, marshes, and sand prairie of the area have never been cultivated and are rich in plant and animal life. The prairie is 14-miles from the Bethel College Campus in North Newton, KS. An additional tract of prairie in Cowley County has been deeded to the college. Call Bethel College in North Newton, KS at 800/522-1887.

Jefferson County:
PERRY RESERVOIR: 22,134-acres includes Perry State Park and Perry Wildlife Area and rolling bluestem prairie in the area of the reservoir. The park office is on Hwy 237 west of Perry, KS. Call the KDWP 913/246-3449.

Jewel County:
LOVEWELL RESERVOIR: 6,275-acres of reservoir and Lovewell State Park. The Reservoir is situated in the Chalk Hills region with chalk bluffs, oak-covered hillsides, and upland prairies, northeast of Mankato, KS off Hwy 14. Call the KDWP at 913/753-4971.

Johnson County:
(ERNIE) MILLER NATURE CENTER: 113-acres on the west edge of Olathe, KS off Hwy 7 and near the Prairie Center (see below). Nature and walking trails wander through woodlands and native prairie. Call Johnson County Parks and Recreation at 913/831-2255.

PRAIRIE CENTER: 300-acres of tallgrass prairie. 45-acres of virgin prairie, 75-acres of restored prairie, rare bison wallows, and a great variety of species of birds and wildflowers, make this property an ideal place for Kansas citizens to experience the beauty of the prairies. The Center is near downtown Olathe, KS; at 26235 W 135th St. Call the Kansas Department of Wildlife and Parks at 316/321-7180.

SHAWNEE MISSION PARK: 1,250-acre park at 7900 Renner Blvd in Shawnee, KS. The 8-mile asphalt Mill Creek Streamway Trail passes along the stream and through oak-hickory forest and upland native prairie. Call Johnson County Parks and Recreation at 913/831-2255.

Kingman County:
CHENEY RESERVOIR: 16,700-acres with Cheney State Park and Wildlife Area. Native grasses and forbs have been planted in the wildlife area. The Reservoir and land area is also in Reno and Sedgwick

Counties. Call Cheney Wildlife Area at 316/459-6922.

(BYRON) WALKER WILDLIFE AREA: 4,530-acres of woodland, native prairie, food plots, shrub plantings, several ponds, a lake, and a wetland. The WA is 7-miles west of Kingman, KS on US 54. Call the KDWP at 316/532-3242.

Labette County:
BIG HILL WILDLIFE AREA: 13.75-acre area of tallgrass prairie and hedges around the Big Hill Reservoir east of Cherryvale, KS. Call the KDWP at 316/331-2741.

Leavenworth County:
LEAVENWORTH STATE FISHING LAKE: 940-acres with the lake surrounded by tallgrass prairie and woodland with the uplands being tallgrass prairie is northwest of Tonganoxie, KS. Call the KDWP at 913/842-8562.

Linn County:
DINGUS NATURAL AREA: 167-acres largely undisturbed, neither grazed nor plowed. Though some tallgrass prairie remnants still exist on the property, most of the area has become forested due to the absence of naturally-occurring prairie fires. The Area is open to the public for hiking. Call TNC, KS at 785/233-4400 or contact the Kansas Ornithological Society at http://ksbirds.org/.

Logan County:
SMOKY VALLEY RANCH: 16,800-acres dominated by short-grass prairie supports prairie dogs, swift fox, pronghorn, burrowing owls, ferruginous hawks and golden eagles. Here, TNC may reintroduce the endangered black-footed ferret to Kansas. As part of a long-range plan, a local rancher released a herd of 150 bison on a portion of the ranch, which is located south of Oakley, KS. Call TNC, KS at 785/233-4400.

Lyons County:
LYON STATE FISHING LAKE: 582-acres in the tallgrass prairie area. However, much of the lake is bordered with woods. The Lake is northeast of Emporia, KS. Call the KDWP at 913/828-4933.

Miami County:
MIAMI STATE FISHING LAKE AND WILDLIFE AREA: 267-acres of wooded farm country with remnant tallgrass prairie as one approaches the area. The WA is about 6-miles north of La Cygne, KS. Call the KDWP at 913/783-4507.

Montgomery County:
ELK CITY RESERVOIR: 13,000-acres around the reservoir that includes Elk City State Park and Wildlife Area, and land owned by the Corp of Engineers. The Reservoir is located in an area where oak-hick-

ory woodland meets meadows of big bluestem and Indian grass. The reservoir is northwest of Independence, KS. Call the KDWP at 316/331-6295.

Morris County:
FLINT HILLS SCENIC BYWAY (K177): (See Butler County above).

Morton County:
CIMMARON NATIONAL GRASSLANDS: 108,000-acres of short to mid-grass prairie supporting elk, antelope, white tail and mule deer. The route of the Santa Fe Historic Trail runs through this site. 920-acres are in Stevens County. This National Grasslands is located in the extreme southwest corner of Morton County near the town of Elkhart, KS at the intersection of Hwys 56 & 27. Call the Cimmaron National Grasslands at 316/697-4621.

Norton County:
PRAIRIE DOG STATE PARK: 7,850-acres includes the state park and the Norton Wildlife Area that is around the Keith Sebelius Reservoir. The area is rolling mixed-grass prairie and holds a sizable black-tailed prairie dog town. The Park is southwest of Norton, KS. Call the KDWP at 913/877-2953.

Osage County:
OSAGE STATE FISHING LAKE: 506-acres of riparian woodland and upland native bluestem prairie surrounding the lake. The area is east of Carbondale, KS. Call the KDWP at 913/828-4933.

MELVERN RESERVOIR: 24,800-acres includes Eisenhower State Park, the Melvern Wildlife Area, and other land owned by the Corp of Engineers around the reservoir, which cuts through gently rolling hills of tallgrass prairie and has marshes along its shores. The Reservoir is south of Osage City, KS off US 75. Call the USCE at 913/549-3318 or the KDWP at 913/828-4933.

POMONA RESERVOIR: 10,500-acres includes the Pomona State Park and other land owned by the US Corp of Engineers around Pomona Reservoir. Here tallgrass prairie adjoins valleys of woodlands. The Park is at the southern end of the Reservoir and the Corp of Engineers Information Center is 2-miles east of the park office. Call the USCE at 913/453-2202 or the KDWP at 913/828-4933.

Ottawa County:
OTTAWA STATE FISHING LAKE: 711-acres with tallgrass prairie surrounding the woodland that borders the lake, which is east of Minneapolis, KS on Hwy 93. Call the KDWP at 913/658-2465.

Phillips County:
KIRWIN NATIONAL WILDLIFE REFUGE: 10,778-acres that includes

a lake, woodlands, 4,000-acres of mixed-grass prairie, and 2,000-acres of cultivated land. The NWR is southeast of Glade, KS off Hwy 9 on a county road. Call the USFWS at 913/543-6673.

Pottawatomie County:
POTTAWATOMIE STATE FISHING LAKE PARK NO 1: 190-acre lake with surrounding bluestem prairie and bordered by woods. The Lake is 5-miles north of Westmoreland, KS on Hwy 99. Call the KDWP at 913/539-7941.

POTTAWATOMIE STATE FISHING LAKE PARK NO 2: A 249-acre lake in a heavily wooded valley surrounded by tallgrass prairie. The Lake is north of Manhattan, KS. Call the KDWP at 913/539-7941.

TUTTLE CREEK RESERVOIR: 26,800-acres including the reservoir, Tuttle State Park, and Fancy Creek State Park, areas owned by the Kansas State University, and areas owned by the Corp of Engineers. Wooded valleys surround the reservoir with the uplands being tallgrass prairie. The Reservoir is northwest of Manhattan, KS and it is on the border of Pottawatomie and Riley Counties. Call the USCE at 913/539-8511 or the KDWP at 913/539-7941.

Reno County:
CHENEY RESERVOIR: (See Kingman County above).

SAND HILLS STATE PARK: 1,123-acre park that is rolling sand hill prairies. The Park is northeast of Hutchinson, KS with one parking lot off 56th St and another on 69th St. Call the KDWP at 316/663-5272.

Riley County:
FORT RILEY: 67,000-acres of grassland include tallgrass prairie managed by the US Army. The free ranging elk herd reintroduced for prairie diversity is the largest in the state. The site supports greater prairie chicken, a large breeding population of Henslow sparrow, logger shrike and upland sandpipers, and other typical prairie birds. There are nature trails here. Fort Riley is located north of US 70 near Junction City, KS. To visit, call the conservation division at 785/239-6211.

KONZA PRAIRIE: (See Geary County above).

TUTTLE CREEK RESERVOIR: (See Pottawatomie County above).

Rooks County:
WEBSTER RESERVOIR: 10,380-acres including the reservoir and Webster State Park, holding mixed-grass prairie, shrubs, river, lake and marsh. The Reservoir is west of Stockton, KS off US 24. Call the KDWP at 913/839-4326.

Russell County:
WILSON RESERVOIR: 10,086-acres including the state park (see below) and Lucas Park with the Rocktown Natural Area. The Rocktown Natural Area is on the east end of the lake and has a trail that loops through it where one can see the mixed-grass prairie. Call the USCE at 913/658-2551 or the KDWP at 913/658-2551.

WILSON STATE PARK: The park is located on the south shore of Wilson Reservoir. One of the better ways to see the prairie and Wilson Lake is by taking the self-guided Dakota trail. The Kansas Dept of Wildlife and Parks (KDWP) is trying to re-introduced golden eagles. The Park is southwest of Sylvan Grove, KS. Call the KDWP at 913/658-2551.

Saline County:
LAKEWOOD PARK NATURAL AREA: 99-acre park in the northeast section of Salina, KS with a hiking trail that weaves through areas of prairie, woodland, and water, all in an urban setting. The Park is east of Ohio St between North and Iron St. Call the City of Salina at 913/-823-1245.

Sedgwick County:
CHENEY RESERVOIR: (See Kingman County above).

CHISHOLM CREEK PARK: 280-acre park located at 3238 North Oliver in Wichita, KS. The Park contains a 2-mile paved trail that winds through woodlands, native tallgrass prairie, and a small wetland. Call the City of Wichita at 316/264-8323.

PAWNEE PRAIRIE PARK: 400-acre park in west Wichita, KS with the Nature Center entrance at 2625 South Tyler Rd. The Park has woodland and prairie, which provides habitat for wildlife. Call the City of Wichita at 316/264-8323.

Shawnee County:
GREEN MEMORIAL WILDLIFE AREA: 83-acres of restored prairie, oak-hickory hillside, and a stream. The WA is southeast of Willard, KS on Gilkerson St. Call the KDWP at 913/246-3499.

SHAWNEE STATE FISHING LAKE AND WILDLIFE AREA: 640-acres of prairie with prairie animals surrounding the lake. The Area is northwest of Topeka, KS on 86th St. Call the KDWP at 913/246-3449.

Stevens County:
CIMMARON NATIONAL GRASSLANDS: (See Morton County above).

Summer County:
SLATE CREEK WILDLIFE AREA: 667-acres of wetland, woodland, cropland, and prairie, but only for the hearty as some hiking is

required. The WA is southwest of Oxford, KS. Call the KDWP at 316/321-7180.

Woodson County:

TORONTO RESERVOIR: 5,840-acres that includes the state park, (see below) the Toronto Wildlife Area, and other land owned by the Corp of Engineers. The land around the reservoir includes prairie and other habitats. The Reservoir is southwest of Yates Center, Ks. Call the USCE at 316/658-4445 or the KDWP at 316/637-2213.

TORONTO STATE PARK: 1,075-acres of forest flood plain surrounded by terraces of prairie and hills of oak savanna. The park is about 12-miles southwest of Yates Center, KS. Call the KDWP at 316/637-2213.

WOODSON STATE FISHING LAKE AND WILDLIFE AREA: 2,850-acres with post oak, blackjack oak and some prairie grasses surrounding the lake while, upland bluestem prairie dominates the wildlife area. The WA is southwest of Yates Center, KS. One travels 7-miles southwest on US 54 and than 3-miles south on a gravel road and then 1.25-miles east. Call the KDWP at 316/637-2213.

YATES CENTER RESERVOIR: 500-acres of upland native grasses surrounding the reservoir. Here one can get the open tallgrass prairie feeling. The Reservoir is southwest of Yates Center, KS. Call the City of Yates Center at 316/625-2118.

Fig 10

Compass Plant. See Fig 2 for root structure.

Illustration by Charlotte Adelman

KENTUCKY

"The buffaloes were more frequent than I have seen cattle in the settlements, browsing on the leaves of the cane, or cropping the herbage of those extensive plains, fearless, because ignorant of the violence of man. Sometimes we saw hundreds in a drove, and the numbers about the salt springs were amazing," said Daniel Boone in 1769. [*The Discovery, Settlement and Present State of Kentucke*" (1784) by John Filson].

Although Kentucky is not a state that one associates with the Great Plains and the prairie, it held and still holds areas where prairie plants grow. Listed below are some of those places:

Boyle County:
JACKSON PRAIRIE RESTORATION: 23.2-acre project on private land re-introduced native grasses and forbs (big and little bluestems, Indiangrass, switchgrass, prairie cordgrass, lobelia, several sunflower species, and smartweed). Also used in the restoration are mast producing upland trees. Approximately 18.9-acres were restored to prairie/wet meadow, 9-acres to tallgrass prairie, 5.2-acres of wet meadow, 3.1-acres of short-grass prairie, 1.6-acres of savannah, and 4.3-acres of upland hardwood. It is estimated it takes from 5 to 10 years for the prairie to become established. Contact the USFWS at the Jackson Ecological Field Office at 601/629-4900.

Bullitt County:
PINE CREEK BARRENS PRESERVE: 150-acres of open woodland with remnant prairie supporting little bluestem, pale purple coneflower, blazing star and obedient plant. The Preserve is located 10-miles north of Bardstown, KY. Due to the sensitivity of the site, the Preserve is open to the public only through Conservancy guided hikes. For permission to visit, call TNC, KY in Lexington, KY at 859/259-9655.

Christian County:
FORT CAMPBELL: 25,000-acres of tallgrass prairie support endangered Henslow and grasshopper sparrows. The Fort extends into Trigg County, Kentucky, and extends also into Montgomery and Stewart Counties, Tennessee. Call the Fort at 270/798-9855.

Fleming County:
BUFFALO TRACE PRESERVE: 15.5-acres located near Blue Licks Battlefield State Park, an important buffalo area before European settlement. The Preserve extends into Nicholas and Robertson Counties. For permission to visit, call TNC, KY at 859/259-9655.

Grayson County:
BAUMBERGER BARRENS PRESERVE: 80-acres with some grassland. Several grassland species are found in the openings of primarily oaks with a very open understory. These grasslands, which once cov-

ered most of mid-western Kentucky, have all been virtually replaced by farmland, making this preservation especially important. Due to the sensitivity of the site, the preserve is open to the public only through Conservancy guided hikes. For permission to visit, call TNC, KY in Lexington, KY at 859/259-9655.

Hardin County:
EASTVIEW BARRENS STATE NATURE PRESERVE: 120-acre remnant of the "Big Barrens" pre-settlement prairie that covered much of Kentucky. Due to the sensitivity of the site, the Preserve is open to the public only through Conservancy guided hikes. For permission to visit call TNC, KY in Lexington, KY at 859/259-9655.

(JIM) SCUDDER STATE NATURE PRESERVE: 58-acre glade and prairie complex. Visitation is by written permission only. Contact the Kentucky State Nature Preserves Commission at 801 Schenkel Lane, Frankfort, KY 40601, or call at 502/573-2886.

Jackson County:
HORSE LICK CREEK BIORESERVE: 62-square mile watershed partly on Daniel Boone National Forest supports remnant prairie plants. Remnant salt licks, Indian petroglyphs and broad open meadows indicate buffalo once traveled Horse Lick Creek Road. Call the National Forest at 606/745-3100 or TNC, KY at 859/259-9655.

Larue County:
THOMPSON CREEK GLADES STATE NATURE PRESERVE: 64-acre preserve is a very high quality, dry limestone hill glade developed on thin-bedded Salem limestone. The natural community is a remnant of the rich and diverse prairie/glade flora that graced over 2 million-acres of Kentucky before European settlement. Visitation is by written permission only. Contact the Kentucky State Nature Preserves Commission at 801 Schenkel Lane, Frankfort, KY 40601, or call at 502/573-2886.

Livingston County:
MANTLE ROCK PRESERVE: 240-acre sandstone glade-type prairie with a trail. The Preserve is located northwest of Joy, KY on Hwy 133. Call TNC, KY in Lexington, KY at 859/259-9655.

(AIMEE) ROSENFIELD MEMORIAL PRESERVE: 69-acre prairie. The Preserve is open to the public only through Conservancy guided hikes. To visit, call TNC, KY in Lexington, KY at 859/259-9655.

Logan County:
(RAYMOND) ATHEY BARRENS STATE NATURE PRESERVE: 156-acre preserve supports several plant communities with a high diversity of associated species. The open-grown post and black jack oaks that

dominate the woodland canopy typify the barrens. Glades occur as small openings within the woods and the soils are characteristically thin with bedrock at or near the surface. Visitation is by written permission only. Contact the Kentucky State Nature Preserves Commission at 801 Schenkel Lane, Frankfort, KY 40601, or call at 502/573-2886.

LOGAN COUNTY GLADE STATE NATURE PRESERVE: 41-acres of limestone glades in Russellville, KY. The glade openings occupy the southwest facing mid-slope of an 810-foot high knob located within the city limits. Prairie grasses such as little bluestem and side-oats grama, dominate the steep rocky slope. Call the Kentucky State Nature Preserves Commission at 502/573-2886.

Lyon County:
LAND BETWEEN THE LAKES: 170,000-acre national recreation area in Western Kentucky and Tennessee includes prairie restoration that demonstrates the area's look before settlement. 700-acres of prairie lie in its Elk and Bison Prairie located north of the Golden Pond Visitors Center. The area is located in the City of Golden Pond, KY near US 24 about 90-miles north of Nashville, TN and just south of Paducah, KY. The area extends into Trigg County Kentucky and into Tennessee. It has lodging, a Visitors Center, Nature Station, and Civil War sites. Call the USFS at 270/924-2000 or visit their website at www.lbl.org.

McCracken County:
WEST KENTUCKY WILDLIFE MANAGEMENT AREA: 7,000 acres, half in tallgrass prairie. This WMA is northwest of Future City, KY and is just 1 of 38 WMAs in Western Kentucky. Call Kentucky Fish and Wildlife at 800/858-1549.

Simpson County:
FLAT ROCK GLADE STATE NATURE PRESERVE: 99-acre glade supports prairie plants. Visitation is by written permission only. Contact the Kentucky State Nature Preserves Commission at 801 Schenkel Lane, Frankfort, KY 40601, or call at 502/573-2886.

Trigg County:
FORT CAMPBELL: (See Christian County above).

LAND BETWEEN THE LAKES: (See Lyon County above).

Warren County:
WOODBURN GLADE STATE NATURE PRESERVE: 20-acre tract consists of several rocky glade openings. Visitation is by written permission only. Contact the Kentucky State Nature Preserves Commission at 801 Schenkel Lane, Frankfort, KY 40601, or call at 502/573-2886.

Fig 11
Pale Purple Coneflower (with goldfinch). See Fig 2 for root structure.

Illustration by Charlotte Adelman

LOUISIANA

Less than 100 virgin prairie acres, mostly along railroads, remain of pre-settlement Louisiana's 2.5 million acres of tallgrass, coastal prairie that lined the western gulf coast of the United States into southeast Texas, just inland from the coastal marsh. Settled by early 19th century exiled Acadian settlers, it is often called the "Cajun Prairie."

Below are some prairie areas in Louisiana:

Caldwell Parish:
COPENHAGEN PRAIRIE: 440-acres managed with an agreement with the former International Paper Company. Call TNC, LA in Baton Rouge, LA at 225/338-1040 for location and other information.

Cameron Parish:
CAMERON PRAIRIE NATIONAL WILDLIFE REFUGE: 1,200-acres of prairie located in a designated National Wildlife Refuge managed by U. S. Fish and Wildlife. This refuge, the first formed under the North American Waterfowl Management Plan, a treaty among Canada, Mexico and United States, supports over l, 200 bird species. The Visitor Center is located 11-miles south of Holmwood, LA on Hwy 27. Call the NWR at 318/598-2216.

Evangaline Parish:
DURALDE PRAIRIE: 350-acres of restored tallgrass prairie lies northwest of Eunice, LA. Call the Cajun Prairie Habitat Preservation Society at 318/342-1814.

EUNICE PRAIRIE: 10-acres representing a 1988 pioneering effort to restore coastal prairie. Call the Cajun Prairie Habitat Preservation Society at 318/342-1814.

Winn Parish:
KEIFFER PRAIRIE POCKET OF KISATCHIE NATIONAL FOREST, WINN DISTRICT: 350-scattered acres of prairie constitute one of the most significant prairie areas in the state. Similar to tallgrass prairies of the Midwest, it has been tentatively classified as a type of "bluestem prairie." The Winn District also contains a group of prairies called Packton Prairies. Call the USFS at 318/628-4664.

PACKTON PRAIRIES: (See Keiffer Prairie Pocket above).

MASSACHUSETTS

The Prairie Peninsula Theory holds that prairie species in Massachusetts are remnants of the prairie that once stretched to the Atlantic Ocean due to a climatic period of heat and aridity that extended between 3,000 and 8,000 years ago. Some of the areas that remain are listed below:

Dukes County:
KATAMA PLAINS: 200-acres, in Martha's Vineyard, of sand plain grassland with prairie forbs and grasses such as little bluestem. Prescribed burns and mechanical clearing maintain the area. The Nature Conservancy manages this property for the town Edgartown, MA. Open to visitors by prior arrangement only. Call TNC, MA in Boston, MA at 617/227-7017.

HAZY ACRES: 830-acres of the largest remaining coastal sandplain habitat left on Martha's Vineyard. TNC is attempting to restore this property to its original grassland and woodland habitat. The area is near Edgartown, MA. Call TNC, MA at 617/227-7017.

HOMER-WATCHA: 142-acre ecologically significant sandplain grassland surrounded by oak woodlands near West Tisbury, MA. Call TNC, MA in Boston, MA at 617/227-7017.

Nantucket County:
HEAD OF THE PLAINS AND RAM PASTURE: Several hundred acres include sand plain grassland. Call Nantucket Conservation Foundation at 508/228-2884 for location and other information.

MICHIGAN

Although the Mississippi river is considered the eastern boundary of the Great Plains, prairie lands existed east of that boundary. Prairies in the Great Plains states are considered short-grass prairies and those found in states east of the Mississippi River are considered tallgrass prairies, by some. However, tallgrass prairie grew west of the Mississippi. Prairies found between these two areas are called mixed-grass prairies. Before settlement, prairie lands were found as far east as Wisconsin, Illinois, Indiana, and even Michigan. Each of these states had their own prairie regions.

There was an area in Michigan that was called the desert, but was really tallgrass prairie. Efforts by local farmers and the federal government caused it to disappear. Without fire to keep the trees in check, the original prairie habitat is fragmented and unhealthy. On prairie land altered by human activities, prairie grasses struggle to occupy their former range. Today some of the healthiest prairie remnants are usually found on private property that has never been farmed or has not been planted with trees. Few prairie remnants contain the full complement of prairie plant species that would once have been common. In Michigan many prairie plants, insect, and animal species are rare or endangered.

Below are some of the prairies that still exist in Michigan:

Allegan County:
ALLEGAN STATE GAME AREA: 50,000-acres that includes prairie species. The area is west of Allegan, MI. Call the DNR, MI at 616/673-2430.

Berrien County:
FERNWOOD NATURE CENTER: 105-acre Nature Center with facilities. The center offers a unique opportunity for environmental study and enjoyment. Within the center there is a 55-acre Nature Preserve, a 5-acre reconstructed prairie, 8-acres of gardens, a 40-acre naturalistic Arboretum, and 3-miles of hiking trails. No pesticides are used and wildlife is commonplace. The Nature Center is located on Range line Rd, Niles, MI. Contact Wendy Jones, Naturalist at the Center, at 616/695-6491.

Chippewa County:
MAXTON PLAINS PRESERVE: 828-acre preserve on Drummond Island. The preserve is the site of one of the world's foremost examples of alvar grassland, a unique mixture of Arctic tundra and Great Plains prairie plant species, living in the shallow soil atop a massive 140-million-year old slab of limestone. The mix of grassland, forest and shoreline attracts a multitude of butterflies and birds, including osprey, upland sandpiper, and northern harrier. The Preserve is open to the public. Call TNC, MI in East Lansing, MI at 517/332-1741.

Clinton County:
SLEEPY HOLLOW STATE PARK: 2,600-acres situated on Price Rd off US 27 near St. Johns, Ovid and Laingsburg, MI. Lake Ovid is a 410-acre lake in the middle of the park, which developed from the Little Maple River. There are 16-miles of trails that take you through prairie grasses, hardwood forest and stands of pine trees. Call the Park at 517/651-6217.

Kalamazoo County:
CONSUMERS POWER PRAIRIE PRESERVE: 13-acre preserve located on the north side of B Ave, east of the US 131 overpass in Kalamazoo, MI. Call the Southwest Michigan Land Conservancy at 616/324-1600.

MARC'S MARSH: 11-acre marsh is in Comstock Township on Lyon's Lake, just east of the intersection of East Main and 26th St. Some plants that live here are blazing star, fringed gentian, pitcher plant, grass-of-Parnassus, and swamp milkweed. Milkweed is vital for monarch butterflies and many butterflies use the plants and flowers on the preserve. Call the Southwest Michigan Land Conservancy at 616/324-1600.

Lenawee County:
GOOSE CREEK GRASSLANDS PRAIRIE NATURE SANCTUARY: 70.4-acre prairie remnant along Goose Creek. Surrounded by fenland that carpets the valley floor lies a marly wet meadow rich in attractive forbs and grasses, which is embellished with a scattering of trees and shrubs. The Sanctuary is located south of Cement City, MI. Call Michigan Nature Association (MNA) at 810/324-2626.

IVES ROAD FEN PRESERVE: 406-acre preserve is one of the largest and least disturbed fen wetlands in Michigan. Calcium-rich groundwater maintains the prairie fen, while spring floods on the river maintain the floodplain forest. The Preserve is home to the prairie rose, showy coneflower, prairie Indian-plantain, yellow-breasted chat and blue-winged warbler. Visitation is by Conservancy field trip only. Call TNC, MI at 517/332-1741.

WILLOW LAKE PRAIRIE SLOUGH PLANT PRESERVE: 70.4-acre wet prairie supports 221 native plant species and 38 nesting bird species. Call the MNA at 810/324-2626. To avoid summer race weekends, call 800/354-1010 for schedule.

WILLOW LAKE PRAIRIE SLOUGH PLANT PRESERVE: 0.7-acre remnant of original prairie surrounds a "water hole." This preserve is south of Cement City, MI off US 233 east of Harold Rd. Call the MNA at 810/324-2626.

Luce County:
MCMAHON LAKE PRESERVE: 2,919-acres includes patterned fen, dry coniferous forest, northern hardwoods, and rich and dry coniferous swamp. The northern end of the site is open to the public, though visitors should avoid the fragile wetlands. Call TNC, MI at 517/332-1741.

Jackson County:
LEFGLEN NATURE SANCTUARY: 210.5-acres of wooded upland, cattail marsh, swale, lakes, tamarack bog, oak groves, and prairie. The Sanctuary is south of Grass Lake, MI on Rexford Rd. Call the MNA at 810/324-2626.

Mackinac County:
PURPLE CONEFLOWER PLANT PRESERVE: 21-acres support prairie species including the purple coneflower that is uncommon to Michigan. The Preserve is northwest of Moran, MI on M123. Call the MNA at 810/324-2626.

Monroe County:
MINONG PRAIRIE: 9-acres of prairie that once covered 57,000-acres in Monroe County. One school in Monroe County is working with The Nature Conservancy and the Michigan Department of Natural Resources to preserve this small, fragile remnant, which is actually an oak opening. Patrick Schoen's science classes at Summerfield Middle School are both studying the unique features of these prairie remnants and are working to preserve them. Mr. Schoen stated, " I started theses studies to get the students excited about the world around them." This study involves the students discovering the importance of these areas to both Native Americans and the pioneers. The Prairie is not far from Petersburg, MI. Call the DNR, MI at 616/673-2430.

Montcalm County:
(GERORE & JESSIE) KRUM MEMORIAL PLANT PRESERVE: 17-acre preserve with a small prairie garden next to the parking lot. The Preserve is 4-miles east of Stanton, MI on Co Rd 522. Call the MNA at 810/324-2626.

Newaygo County:
NEWAYGO PRAIRIE NATURE SANCTUARY: 110-acres established by MNA to preserve prairie vegetation including prickly pear cactus, needle grass and a grass with no common name. The Sanctuary is west of Croton, MI. Call the MNA at 810/324-2626.

Oakland County:
BURR MEMORIAL PRAIRIE: Managed to maintain its 15-inch wide, Indian style footpath, but still highly prized for its prairie plants. Call the MNA at 810/324-2626.

Oscerola County:
PRAIRIE CHICKEN NATURE SANCTUARY: 47-acres set aside to preserve the prairie chicken, but failed to save the bird from extinction in Michigan. Call the MNA at 810/324-2626.

St. Joseph County:
SAUK INDIAN TRAIL PRAIRIE PLANT PRESERVE: ¼-acre of unplowed prairie located between the railroad track and highway US 12 about 4-miles west of Co Rd M66. This remnant was an Indian trail that settlers used in the 1800s. Call the MNA at 810/324-2626.

Van Buren County:
JEPTHA LAKE FEN: 49-acre fen. Fens are typically rich in plant species including some species also found in bogs (acidic wetlands), such as the pitcher plant and sundew, along with many species also found in wet prairies. Call the Southwest Michigan Land Conservancy at 616/324-1600.

Washtenaw County:
ANN ARBOR CITY PRAIRIES:
1. Barton Park Prairie: 15-acres consisting of wet and dry prairie.
2. Furstenberg Park Prairie: 5-acre prairie. The Park is across Fuller Rd from Huron High School, along the banks of the Huron River and is one of the richest natural areas in the city. It includes a variety of ecosystems and has been the target of intensive restoration work, mainly directed at removing invasive species (primarily Buckthorn and Honeysuckle in the woodlands and the Spotted Knapweed in the prairie), by both cutting and burning.
3. Gallup Park Wet Prairie: 10-acre prairie.
Call Ann Arbor Parks and Recreation at 734/994-4834 or 734/996-3266 for prairie locations within the city.

BARTON PARK PRAIRIE: (See Ann Arbor City Prairies above).

DOW PRAIRIE at the UNIVERSITY OF MICHIGAN'S NICHOLS ARBORETUM: 27-acres of never-plowed native tallgrass prairie in the City of Ann Arbor, MI. Call the Arboretum at 734/998-9540.

FIRSTENBERG PARK PRAIRIE: (See Ann Arbor City Prairies above).

GALLUP PARK WET PRAIRIE: (See Ann Arbor City Prairies above).

MINNESOTA

"To partake in the magic of prairie life, all you have to do is gaze at a blazing sunrise or sunset, listen to the wind and birds in the tall bluestem grass, watch the seemingly eternal approach of a prairie thunderstorm and smell its freshness after the rejuvenating rain," states the DNR, MN. "To those that come to know it, the prairie can be a spiritual tapestry that connects us to the land." Because "the prairie is a living sense of history for those who take the time to explore it," the state celebrates an annual "Minnesota Prairie Day" and sells "A Guide to Minnesota's Scientific and Natural Areas hereinafter referred to as SNA." At some of the SNA's one can see unusual species of prairie animals, such as prairie voles and greater prairie chicken. Call DNR, MN at 888/646-6367 or 651/296-6157 for a list of interesting animals and where they can be seen.

Note!

Minnesota has hundreds of Wildlife Management Areas (WMA), but has not completed a habitat survey. A map of these WMAs can be obtained from the DNR, MN. In addition, many western and southern WMAs may have prairies, but these have not yet been designated.

The Minnesota Department of Transportation (MN DOT) is taking part in the "Prairie Passage" a national prairie wildflower route that travels from the Canadian to the Mexican Border (See Iowa above). Minnesota's "The Prairie Passage" should be (US 35) which is basically in the eastern part of the State, and not in the location of the original prairie. Therefore, the MN DOT is planting prairie plants along the roadsides in the western or prairie part of the State, from the Canadian border to US 90 and then east to US 35, which uses a variety of roads. The "Prairie Passage" starts at the Canadian Border with US 75 then Co Hwy 102, Hwy 132, Hwy 9, US 59, US 212, US 23 and finally US 75 to US 90 over to US 35. Although Minnesota has only completed about 1% of this project, the state intends to eventually complete it, and, in addition, plant many other roadsides with prairie plants. Call Kathy Bolin, 'Prairie Passage Coordinator, MN DOT at 651/284-3767.

Minnesota's tallgrass prairie once covered 18-20 million acres, less than 1% (180,000-acres) remains. Below are some of those remnants:

Anoka County:

(HELEN) ALLISON SAVANNA: 86-acre savanna named for Helen Allison Irvine, "Minnesota's grass lady." Habitats include oak sand savanna, dry prairie with bur oak and pin oak, thickets of willow and aspen, and sedge marshes in scattered depressions, and trees and shrubs characteristic of a savanna. Pasque flowers bloom in the spring and prairie grasses are at their finest in late summer. This savanna is located east of Bethel, MN on Co Rd 15. Call the DNR, MN at 888/646-6367 or 651/296-6157.

Big Stone County:
BIG STONE LAKE STATE PARK: (See Bonanza Prairie below).

BIG STONE NATIONAL WILDLIFE AREA AND WETLAND MAN-AGEMENT AREA: 11,521-acres of wetlands and grasslands of which over 6,000-acres are grassland, including large tracts of native prairie. The refuge is committed to restoring the area to its original prairie and wetlands state. The refuge is located 3-miles southeast of Ortonville, MN on Hwy 7. Call the WMD in Odessa, MN at 320/273-2191.

BONANZA PRAIRIE: 85-acre prairie located in the Big Stone Lake State Park. The site contains an example of undisturbed, glacial till hill prairie, dry prairie, and bur oak savanna. Visitors can see into South Dakota from this site and enjoy that state's prairie. In summer, prairie plants bloom and butterfly species are abundant. The Prairie is about 14-miles northwest of Ortonville, MN. Call the DNR, MN at 888/646-6367 or 651/296-6157.

CLINTON PRAIRIE: 160-acres contains a previously disturbed glacial till hill blacksoil prairie. The rare powesheik skipper can be found here and on other Minnesota prairies but details of its life history remain unknown. The Prairie is west of Clinton, MN on Co Hwy 6. Call the DNR, MN at 888/646-6367 or 651/296-6157.

Brown County:
COTTONWOOD RIVER PRAIRIE (PRAIRIE SKY UNIT): 181-acre Prairie Sky Unit of the Cottonwood River Prairie is on ridges between the present Cottonwood River and an older, abandoned channel on Mound Creek. The area is adjoined by a large wetland and wet prairie and several old fields nearby have been planted to native species. The site provides a wonderful view and has a diversity of flora and fauna. Its forbs include purple coneflowers, lead plant, puccoon, and blazing stars. The site is located southwest of Springfield, MN. Call the DNR, MN at 888/646-6367 or 651/296-6157.

(JOSEPH A) TAUER PRAIRIE: 80-acre prairie preserved because Tauer (the owner) used only horses to farm until the 1980s, and also refused to drain the low portions of his land. He restricted his farming to the high, dry uplands, which are being restored to prairie. The undisturbed prairie supports many prairie plants. The Prairie is located southwest of New Ulm, MN on Co Rd 22. Call the DNR, MN at 888/646-6367 or 651/296-6157.

Carver County:
UNIVERSITY OF MINNESOTA, MINNESOTA LANDSCAPE ARBORETUM: 1,000-acre arboretum where one can enjoy miles of hiking trails in summer and cross-country ski trails in winter through northern woodlands, native prairie and natural marshes. The

142

Arboretum is located at 3675 Arboretum Dr, Chanhassen, MN. Call the Arboretum at 952/443-1400.

Chippewa County:
CHIPPEWA PRAIRIE: 1,143-acres of tallgrass prairie was home to the Dakota Indians who harvested wild plants and followed the vast herds of buffalo. Part of the prairie is in Swift County. The prairie is south of Appleton, MN and near Lac qui Parle Lake. Call TNC, MN in Minneapolis, MN at 612/331-0700 or the DNR, MN at 888/646-6367.

GNEISS OUTCROPS: 241-acre Gneiss outcrops, which were formed approximately 3.6 billion years ago, are among the oldest known rock on the earth's surface. This unusual combination of geological rock and prairie plants is located southeast of Granite Falls, MN on Co Rd. 40. Call the DNR, MN at 888/646-6367.

Clay County:
BLUESTEM PRAIRIE: 4,658-acres making it one of the largest remnants of northern tallgrass prairie in the Midwest. It is located on the eastern edge of the Red River Valley on several beachlines of Glacial Lake Agassiz. The prairie has about 313 plant species and rare fauna species. Blinds for viewing the greater prairie chickens' courtship behavior in April are available by reservation through TNC, Bluestem Prairie office at 218/498-2679. This prairies location next to other prairies allows one to experience the vastness of the native prairie that once covered a great portion of western Minnesota and the Dakotas. The prairie is southwest of Moorehead, MN on 17th Ave. Call TNC, MN at 612/331-0700 or 0750.

BUFFALO RIVER STATE PARK: 1,367-acres located near Bluestem Prairie (see above). Undisturbed virgin prairie supports prairie flora and fauna. Buffalo once wintered at this site. Call the DNR's Natural Heritage Program at 651/296-6157 about this park, and many other prairies.

FELTON PRAIRIE: 761-acre gravel prairie complex consisting of four units that all lie within a large beach-ridge complex of Glacial Lake Agassiz. The complex includes mesic and wet blacksoil prairie along with gravel prairie and scattered glacial erratics. Needle grass, side oats grama, pasque flowers, blazing stars, and prairie chickens can be seen here. The complex is located southeast of Felton, MN. Call the DNR, MN at 888/646-6367 or 651/296-6157.

MARGHERITA PRESERVE-AUDUBON PRAIRIE: 479.63-acres located in the lakebed of what once was Glacial Lake Agassiz. Mesic and wet mesic prairie dominates this site, along with meadow and aspen woodland. The Prairie is located southeast of Moorhead, MN. Call TNC, MN in Minneapolis, MN at 612/331-0700 or 0750.

143

Cottonwood County:
RED ROCK PRAIRIE: 611-acre prairie underlain by Sioux Quartzite with moisture conditions ranging from dry, mesic to wet. The Prairie is northeast of Windom, MN. Call TNC, MN at 612/331-0700 or 0750.

Dodge County:
HYTHECKER PRAIRIE: 40-acre mesic tallgrass prairie protected from the plow by its namesake. Former old fields have been planted with seeds of native prairie species collected from the site. Prairie plants include rattlesnake master, valerian, and blazing star. The Prairie is located southeast of Claremont, MN on Co Hwy 1. Call the DNR, MN at 888/646-6367 or 651/296-6157.

IRON HORSE PRAIRIE: 35-acre site between two railroad tracks and thus protected by the "iron horses." This large mesic prairie has very high species diversity. This site is located south of Hayfield, MN on Co Rd M where parking is available. Call the DNR, MN at 888/646-6367 or 651/296-6157.

RICE LAKE STATE PARK: 1,040-acres representing a historic transition zone between the woods and prairie. The Park is also in Steele County and is located 7-miles east of Owatonna, MN on Rose St. Call the DNR, MN at 888/646-6367 or 651/296-6157.

Douglas County:
STAFFANSON PRAIRIE: 95-acres of dry and high quality mesic black-soil prairie with unaltered "prairie pothole" surrounded with marsh plants near its center. The Prairie is northwest of Kensington, MN. Call TNC, MN at 612/331-0750.

Dakota County:
BLACK DOG NATURE PRESERVE: 126-acre preserve is named after the great Dakota Sioux chief and contains mesic prairie and a degraded calcareous fen. The preserve lies within the Minnesota Valley Wildlife Refuge and has many spring and summer blooming mesic prairie flowers and fen species. Visitation to posted portion of this SNA is by permission only. Apply to Minnesota SNA Program at (651) 296-2835. This preserve is north of Burnsville, MN on Co Rd 32. Call the DNR, MN at 888/646-6367 or 651/296-6157.

MINNESOTA VALLEY WILDLIFE REFUGE: (See Black Dog Preserve above).

Faribault County:
OSMUNDSON PRAIRIE: 6-acre prairie survived through the efforts of the Albert Lea Audubon Society and the subsequent donation of land to the State of Minnesota by Mildred Osmundson Wickman. Prairie forbs include pasque flowers, prairie smoke, blazing stars, rattlesnake

master, and sunflowers. The SNA is near the Iowa/Minnesota State line and is east of Kiester, MN. Call the DNR, MN at 888/646-6367 or 651/296-6157.

Fillmore County:
(RICHARD J.) DORER MEMORIAL HARDWOOD STATE FOREST: (See the Rushford Sand Barrens below and Mound Prairie in Houston County, below).

RUSHFORD SAND BARRENS: 230-acre SNA was spared by the last period of glaciation. The site features a complex of rare natural communities nestled in the Root River Valley within the Richard J Dorer Memorial Hardwood State Forest including dry oak savanna and jack pine savanna. The six-lined racerunner, a small lizard, runs across the sand barrens and through the bluff prairies. This site is west of Rushford, MN on Hwy 16. One must walk to the site through a field. Call the DNR, MN at 888/646-6367 or 651/296-6157.

Goodhue County:
RIVER TERRACE PRAIRIE: 84-acre gravel prairie with many native prairie forbs and grasses. The long-range management plan includes restoration of old fields to native prairie. The Prairie is located southeast of Cannon Falls, MN on Sunset Trail. Call the DNR, MN at 888/646-6367 or 651/296-6157.

SPRING CREEK PRAIRIE: 145-acre prairie including a bedrock bluff prairie and sandstone and limestone outcrops and streams that flow to the Mississippi River. Small burrowing mammals, skinks, and several snakes (garter, milk, blue racer) thrive among the outcrops. The SNA is located west of Red Wing, MN. Call the DNR, MN at 888/646-6367 or 651/296-6157.

Houston County:
MOUND PRAIRIE: 257-acre site located within the Richard J Dorer Memorial Hardwood State Forest, (see Fillmore County above) just south of the Root River. The site contains three southwest facing "goat prairies" on the north side of Hwy 16 and three 'goat prairies' on the south side, all supporting a highly diverse plant community with many late summer blooms. Wonderful views from the "goat prairies" make the climb worthwhile. Look for the prairie vole. The Forest is located 4-miles west of Hokah, MN on Hwy 16. Call the DNR, MN at 888/646-6367 or 651/296-6157.

Jackson County:
DES MOINES RIVER PRAIRIE: 210-acre hill prairie has numerous Prairie plant species. Some old fields are being restored to prairie. The prairie is located southwest of Windom, MN on Co Rd. 30. Public access is east of the river and the road. Call the DNR, MN at 888/646-6367 or

651/296-6157.

HOLTHE PRAIRIE: 148-acre site with a hill prairie and calcareous seepage fen with many prairie flowers. Plant species include porcupine grass, grama, plains muhly, and prairie dropseed. The combination of native fen plants and upland grass and wildflowers create an unusual site. The SNA is located southwest of Windom, MN off of Co Rd. 19 on a low maintenance road. Call the DNR, MN at 888/646-6367 or 651/296-6157.

KILEN WOODS STATE PARK: (See Prairie Bush Clover SNA below).

LINDGREN-TRAEGER BIRD SANCTUARY: 91-acres of marsh and prairie. At normal water levels, marsh and low-grass habitat covers nearly half the preserve creating a classic prairie lake. Spring and fall migration provide good bird watching. The Sanctuary is southeast of Lake Heron, MN on a gravel road. Call TNC, MN at 612/331-0750.

PRAIRIE BUSH CLOVER SNA: 25-acre prairie is located entirely within Kilen Woods State Park (see above), along Des Moines River with a small calcareous fen on one of the prairie hillsides. Many prairie forbs can be seen here. This prairie is not far from Holthe Prairie and is located southeast of Windom, MN on Co Hwy 24, in the Kilen Woods State Park. Call the DNR, MN at 888/646-6367 or 651/296-6157.

Kandiyohi County:
REGAL MEADOW: 385-acre prairie located 8-miles west of Paynesville, MN on a gravel road off Hwy 23. Call TNC, MN at 612/331-0750.

(HENRY HASTINGS) SIBLEY PARK: 2,300-acres where the western grasslands meet the eastern Big Woods. Some of the fields are being restored to native prairie grasslands and oak savanna. The Park is northwest of New London, MN on Hwy 9. Call the DNR, MN at 888/646-6367 or 651/296-6157.

Kittson County:
WALLACE C. DAYTON CONSERVATION & WILDLIFE AREA: 9,758-acre preserve is a mosaic of aspen and balsam poplar groves, prairies, fens, dotted with willow and bog birch. Created by Glacial Lake Agassiz, this broad, unfragmented woodland-prairie is largely intact, and represents the northernmost example of the transition between tallgrass prairie and forest ecosystems. TNC has targeted 140,000-acres in this region, which extends into Manitoba Canada, to try to protect by easements, purchase and cooperation with private landowners. The WA is 18-miles northeast of Lancaster, MN. Call TNC, MN at 612/331-0750.

LAKE BRONSON PARKLAND: The 196-acre site is an example of the aspen parkland landscape and contains a mixture of prairie and aspen woodland with wet brush prairie. The site contains both woodland and prairie species. The SNA is located 4-miles east of the intersection of US Hwy 56 & Co Hwy 10. Call the DNR, MN at 888/646-6367 or 651/296-6157.

NORWAY DUNES: 320-acres of sand dunes, oak savanna/lowland forest, and mesic prairie located in extreme northwest Minnesota near Halma, MN. Call TNC, MN at 612/331-0750.

Lac Qui Parle County:
LAC QUI PARLE STATE PARK: 1,057-acre park contains river floodplain and prairie hillsides with Lac qui Parle Lake providing a diverse wildlife habitat and dramatic spring and fall bird migration. The park is approximately 5-miles northwest of Watson, MN off U.S. 59 and Hwy 7. Call the Park at 320/752-4736. Also, see Lac Qui Parle Wildlife Management Area at the end of this section.

PLOVER PRAIRIE: 655-acre prairie in two units along the Minnesota River Valley, providing a continuum from upland prairie to wet prairie, and supporting the plains pocket mouse, prairie vole and northern grasshopper mouse and western harvest mouse. The Prairie is located north of Bellingham, MN near Hwy 75. Call TNC, MN at 612/331-0750.

YELLOW BANK HILLS: 80-acre dry, sand-gravel prairie on the gravelly, coarse-textured soil kames with plant communities typical of the Great Plains. This site has the prairie vole, an animal that agriculture has generally replaced with the meadow vole. During spring migration, waterfowl can be seen at the nearby Pegg Lake. This prairie is located 1-mile east of Nassau, MN on Co Hwy 24. Call the DNR, MN at 888/646-6367 or 651/296-6157.

Le Sueur County:
KASOTA PRAIRIE: 42-acres of prairie, wet meadow, oak woodland, and lowland hardwood plant communities thrive in the thin soils. Kasota is an Indian word meaning "cleared-off place." The site is southwest of Kasota, MN on a gravel road. Call the DNR, MN at 888/646-6367 or 651/296-6157.

OTTAWA BLUFFS: 63-acre prairie and woodland located 5-miles north of St Peter, MN. Call TNC, MN at 612/331-0750.

Lincoln County:
ALTONA STATE WILDLIFE MANAGEMENT AREA: (See Hole-in-the-Mountain Prairie below). Call the DNR, MN at 888/646-6367 or 651/296-6157.

HOLE-IN-THE-MOUNTAIN PRAIRIE: 590-acre large prairie remnant situated on a steep valley along the outer edge of the glacial

147

escarpment known as the Prairie Coteau. This site is a part of a 4,300-acre prairie area that begins at the south end of the City of Lake Benton and runs south toward the Altona State Wildlife Management Area (see above). 3,400-acres of this prairie area ecosystem are privately owned and managed. The preserve is located 1½-miles south of the Lake Benton, MN. Call TNC, MN at 612/331-0750.

Lyon County:
GLYNN PRAIRIE: 80-acre site with a 35-acre level mesic blacksoil prairie with much of it sloping toward a stream channel creating a wetter prairie. Butterflies are plentiful here in summer. The Prairie is located northwest of Tracy, MN on Co Hwy 9. Call DNR, MN at 888/646-6367 or 651/296-6157.

Mahnomen County:
SANTEE PRAIRIE: This is a 442-acre diverse prairie that adjoins the Wambach Wildlife Management Area and together forms part of an extensive prairie and wetland complex. This is a good birding spot for, among others, the greater prairie chicken. Blazing stars, purple coneflower, and sunflowers can be seen here. The site is one of the best prairies in the area and is located northeast of Mahnomen, MN and east of US 59. Call the DNR, MN at 888/646-6367 or 651/296-6157.

WAMBACH WILDLIFE MANAGEMENT AREA: (See Santee Prairie above).

Marshall County:
AGASSIZ NATIONAL WILDLIFE REFUGE: 61,500-acres located in eastern Marshall County are situated in the aspen parkland region of northwest Minnesota. Originally named Mud Lake Migratory Waterfowl Refuge, this refuge was established in 1937 primarily for waterfowl production and maintenance. This area is the transition zone between the coniferous forests, tallgrass prairie, and the prairie pothole region of the Red River Valley. The refuge lies in the bed of Glacial Lake Agassiz resulting in a very flat terrain. Before man changed the landscape, this was a paradise for waterfowl and other wildlife. Today, Agassiz contains 40,000-acres of wetlands, 10,000-acres of shrublands, 7,000-acres of forestland, 4250-acres of grassland, and 150-acres of cropland. In 1976, 4,000-acres were established as Wilderness; otherwise the refuge habitat is actively managed.

A diversity of wildlife species inhabits the NWR, including 280 bird species, 49 mammals, 12 amphibians and 9 reptiles. A Franklin's gull colony numbers 20,000 breeding pairs. Agassiz has the distinction of being one of only two refuges in the lower 48 states with resident packs of eastern gray wolves. The resident moose herd of approximately 110 animals has long attracted refuge visitors from many states and countries. Contact the NWR at Route 1, Box 74, Middle River, MN, 56737, Phone: 218/449-4115, or email at margaret_anderson@fws.gov.

Mcleod County:
SHAEFER PRAIRIE: 160-acre preserve of dry, mesic, and wet prairie and wetland. The prairie is 7-miles southwest of Glencoe, MN. Call TNC, MN at 612/331-0750.

Mower County:
RACINE PRAIRIE: 6-acre remnant of mesic prairie along the abandoned Chicago & Northwestern Railroad right-of-way. The Prairie is 1-mile north of Racine, MN on US 63. Call the DNR, MN at 888/646-6367 or 651/296-6157.

SHOOTING STAR PRAIRIE: 8-acre tallgrass prairie remnant is named for the prairie wildflower that once grew here and is being reintroduced. The Prairie is located on an abandoned Milwaukee Railroad right-of-way northwest of Leroy, MN on Hwy 56. Call the DNR, MN at 888/646-6367 or 651/296-6157.

WILD INDIGO PRAIRIE: 150-acres of mesic tallgrass prairie on an abandoned Chicago-Milwaukee right-of-way between Ramsey and Dexter MN contains many fine examples of blacksoil prairie, including over 340 native plant species. Call the DNR, MN at 888/646-6367 or 651/296-6157.

Murray County:
LUNDBLAD PRAIRIE: 80-acres of mesic prairie is one of the largest and best mesic prairie remnants in southwestern Minnesota. The site includes about 40-acres of upland prairie, 30-acres of wet prairie, meadow, and cattail marshes and a field that is being restored to prairie. Prairie plants include prairie-clover, goldenrod, aster, sunflower, milkweed, lead plant, and prairie rose. The site is located southeast of Slayton, MN on a gravel road. Call the DNR, MN at 888/646-6367 or 651/296-6157.

Nicollet County:
GUSTAVUS ADOLPUUS COLLEGE, LINNAEUS ARBORETUM: The three major natural ecosystems found in Minnesota are represented in the Arboretum: the conifer forest in the north, the prairie in the south and west, and the deciduous forest in between. The Arboretum's Uhler Prairie contains grasses and flowers native to the drier areas of Minnesota. At the time of European settlement, the Gustavus campus was prairie. The College is located at 800 West College Ave, Saint Peter, MN. Call the College at 507/933-8000.

Nobles County:
COMPASS PRAIRIE: 20-acre prairie with many compass plants lies on

the two slopes facing a creek coursing its way to the Rock River. The very rare powesheik skipper is also found here. The site is west of Worthington, MN on a gravel road. Call the DNR, MN at 888/646-6367 or 651/296-6157.

Norman County:
AGASSIZ DUNES: 435-acre site is located within the largest dune field in Minnesota associated with Glacial Lake Agassiz. The dunes sands were deposits 9,000 to 12,000 years ago on the deltas of the Sand River near Glacial Lake Agassiz's eastern shore. This site features a variety of plant community types; among them are dry sand savanna, dry sand prairie, and the unique sand blowouts with bur oak. This is one of TNC's most beautiful sites with old, gnarly bur oaks growing out of sand dunes that are carpeted with grama and bluestem grasses. The SNA is also in Polk County and is 2-miles southwest of Fertile, MN. Call TNC, MN at 218/498-2679 or the DNR, MN at 888/646-6367 or 651/296-6157.

FRENCHMAN'S BLUFF: 50-acre prairie on a prominent hill that was deposited by glaciation some 9,000 to 12,000 years ago and now supports an unusual mix of tallgrass prairie. 26 butterfly and 48 bird species have been recorded here. The hill is located southeast of Syre, MN on Co Rd 36. Call the DNR, MN at 888/646-6367 or 651/296-6157.

PRAIRIE SMOKE DUNES: 1,107-acres of dry sand savanna, sedge meadow, wet prairie, and wet-mesic prairie communities. The state flower, the showy lady slipper, is found here. The site is located northwest of Twin Valley, MN on Co Hwy 7. Call the DNR, MN at 888/646-6367 or 651/296-6157.

SANDPIPER PRAIRIE: 320-acres of dry, wet, and dry mesic prairie communities. Prairie plants provide a season-long variety of butterflies, birds, and animals as well as an endless variation of color. The Prairie is located southwest of Twin Valley, MN. Call the DNR, MN at 888/646-6367 or 651/296-6157.

TWIN VALLEY PRAIRIE: 499-acres of plant communities ranging from wet to dry prairie with sedge meadow and marsh communities occupy the poorly drained swales alongside the beach ridge. Also, 150-acres of choice mesic blacksoil prairie is dominated by big bluestem and prairie cordgrass. This site is one of several in the area that are important to the long-term survival of the prairie chicken. This SNA is located southwest of Twin Valley, MN. Call the DNR, MN at 888/646-6367 or 651/296-6157.

Olmsted County:
ORONOCO PRAIRIE: 80-acre kame and its gravelly outwash contain oak savanna, dry gravel prairie and bedrock bluff prairie. Rattlesnake

master, at its northernmost range here, is scattered throughout the site, assisting the survival of the endangered rattlesnake master butterfly. Some old fields are being restored to prairie. The site is located southeast of Oronoco, MN on Co Rd 112. Call the DNR, MN at 888/646-6367 or 651/296-6157.

Otter Tail County:
OTTERTAIL PRAIRIE: 320-acre site is a wet to wet-mesic prairie interlaced with shallow, seasonally inundated pools and supporting greater prairie chickens, upland sandpipers, and bobolink. This prairie can be visited throughout the year. The site is southwest of Fergus Falls, MN. Call the DNR, MN at 888/646-6367 or 651/296-6157.

SEVEN SISTERS PRAIRIE: 136-acres of gravel prairie with plants characteristic of western short-grass prairie with bur oak savanna. The Prairie is near the town of Ashby, MN. Call the DNR, MN at 651/296-6157 or 888/MINNDNR.

Pipestone County:
PRAIRIE COTEAU: 329-acre prairie occupies an area of steep slopes and valleys, which cuts through the Bemis glacial moraine. The 1800s American artist George Catlin called this area the Couteaus des Prairies, or highland of the prairies. Dry prairie vegetation grows on the higher elevations wet prairie species flourish in the lowlands. The site is rich in grasses, sedges, rushes and wildflowers species. This prairie is located 10-miles northeast of Pipestone, MN on Hwy 23. Call DNR, MN at 888/646-6367 or 651/296-6157.

Polk County:
AGASSIZ DUNES: (See Norman County above).

GULLY FEN: 1,610-acres of wetland seepage communities, where east meets west on the Glacial Lake Agassiz lakebed, including seepage fens, tamarack and shrub seepage swamps, conifer and hardwood swamps. This site is northeast of Gully, MN. Call the DNR, MN at 888/646-6367 or 651/296-6157.

MALMBERG PRAIRIE: 80-acre site has both mesic and wet prairie within the southern basin of the ancient Glacial Lake Agassiz. Bison once roamed on this very sod, among the big and little bluestem, the mat muhly, and the cordgrass. The Prairie is located southwest of Crookston, MN on Co Rd 56. Call the DNR, MN at 888/646-6367 or 651/296-6157.

PANKRATZ MEMORIAL PRAIRIE PRESERVE: 920-acre preserve in two units. The north unit is 468-acres while the south unit has 452-acres. ThePreserve is largely mesic prairie with low swales that contain wet prairie species. It is about 7-miles southeast of Crookston, MN. Call

TNC, MN in Minneapolis, MN at 612/331-0750 or 0700.

PEMBINA TRAIL PRESERVE SCIENTIFIC AND NATURAL AREAS: 2,360-acres in northwest Minnesota, an area associated with a trail over which fur and buffalo-hide traders transported their goods by ox cart to St. Paul, MN, until the Winnipeg-to-St. Paul railroad was built in the 1870s. The Preserve includes wet and mesic tallgrass prairie, gravel prairie, willow thickets, mixed prairie, sedge meadow, aspen woods, marsh, and old fields and scatter granite boulders, which served as buffalo rubbing rocks. Many bird, butterfly, and mammal species can be seen here. The SNA is west of Mentor, MN on Co Hwy 45. Call TNC, MN at 612/331-0750 or the DNR, MN at 888/646-6367 or 651/296-6157.

RYDELL NATIONAL WILDLIFE REFUGE: 2,120-acre refuge is situated between the flat Red River Valley floodplain to the west and a rolling hardwood forest and lake region to the east creating a mosaic of ecosystems with 657-acres of wetlands, about 500-acres of trees and shrubs, 590-acres of grassland, and 293-acres of cropland. The NWR is west of Erskine, MN on Co Rd 210. Call the NWR at 218/847-4431.

Pope County:
GLACIAL LAKES STATE PARK: 1,880-acre park with some prairie. Here one can experience the vast, open prairie that once dominated western Minnesota and its abundant wildflowers and prairie grasses. The Park is located south of Starbuck, MN on Co Rd 41. Call the DNR, MN at 888/646-6367 or 651/296-6157.

(KATHERINE) ORDWAY PRAIRIE: 581-acres in a region of rolling hills and lakes in west central Minnesota, is an undulating terrain of tallgrass and dry gravel hill prairies, calcareous fens, wetlands, and maple, basswood, and oak forests. This site is owned and managed by TNC, MN, which recognized the ecological significance of this landscape nearly 30 years ago. However, habitat fragmentation, destruction, water quality degradation, and other significant threats to this relatively intact region have pushed it to the front of their conservation agenda. The Conservancy wants to acquire lands to expand its existing ownership within this 130,000-acre area. Local landowners are included in the TNC's plans. The Prairie is southwest of Brooten, MN on Hwy 104. Call TNC, MN 612/331-0750.

STRANDNESS PRAIRIE: 40-acre mesic, blacksoil prairie containing small wetlands and named for Elizabeth Strandness. The preserve is south of Lowry, MN. Call TNC, MN 612/331-0750 or 0700.

Ramsey County:
TRI-DISTRICT SCHOOL RESTORATION PROJECT: 28-acre cattail marsh/wetland, oak areas, aspen and willow areas, and open hillside,

which is being converted to prairie. The school is located at 30 East County Rd B, Maplewood, MN, a suburb of St. Paul, MN. Contact the School at 651/487-5450.

Redwood County:
WAHPETON PRAIRIE: 80-acre preserves a now rather rare ecological features the transition between upland, mesic prairie and bottomland, wet prairie. Crossing from the west side of the preserve to the east, the plant communities gradually change, reflecting the increased water content of the soils. The Prairie is north of Walnut Grove, MN. Call TNC, MN 612/331-0750.

Rice County:
CARLETON COLLEGE, COWLING ARBORETUM: 800-acres of wetland, forest, oak savanna, and prairie. Hillside Prairie and Postage Stamp Prairie have been restored along with the oak savanna. Carleton College is located at One North College Street, Northfield, MN. Call the College at 507/646-4000.

HILLSIDE PRAIRIE: (See Cowling Arboretum above).

POSTAGE STAMP PRAIRIE: (See Cowling Arboretum above).

Rock County:
BLUE MOUNDS STATE PARK: 1,500-acres of prairie and grassland support a small herd of bison, and a 1,250-foot long line of east-west aligned rocks built by persons and reasons unknown. This is one of the few places in Minnesota where cactus grows. The Park is located northeast of Luverne, MN on Co Rd 20. Call DNR, MN at 888/646-6367, 651/296-6157, or the Park at 507/283-1307.

Roseau County:
TWO RIVERS ASPEN PRAIRIE PARKLAND: 1,333-acres of prairie parkland, which has a diversity of prairie forbs, in northwestern Minnesota, whose swells and swales support extensive areas of wet and wet-mesic brush prairie, shrubby wet meadow, and aspen woodland. This SNA is located is northeast of Pelan, MN on Hwy 11. Call the DNR, MN at 888/646-6367 or 651/296-6157.

Scott County:
SAVAGE FEN: 45-acre fen community that is very sensitive to disturbance. The Fen is located southeast of Savage, MN. Call the DNR, MN at 888/646-6367 or 651/296-6157.

Sherburne County:
(HARRY W.) CATER HOMESTEAD PRAIRIE: 133-acres of upland oak savanna, mesic and wet-mesic prairie openings in aspen groves, and floodplain forest along the Elk River, wet meadow and marsh. Parking is on Co Rd 3 southeast of St Cloud, MN from which the Prairie is

153

accessible by boat down stream on the Elk River. Call the DNR, MN at 888/646-6367 or 651/296-6157.

RICE LAKE SAVANNA: 80-acre open, grassy landscape dotted with bur and pin oak, a classic savanna. The nearly level site includes scattered wetlands and 60-acres of dry, bur oak savanna carpeted with native grasses and wildflowers. The SNA is located 10-miles north of Becker, MN on Hwy 25. Call the DNR, MN at 888/646-6367 or 651/296-6157.

SHERBURNE NATIONAL WILDLIFE REFUGE: 30,665-acres of federal land dedicated to the conservation, management, and where appropriate, restoration of fish, wildlife, and plant resources and their habitats for the benefit of present and future generations of Americans. Sherburne, one of ten NWRs in Minnesota, is located in the east central region of the state, approximately 50-miles northwest of the Minneapolis/St Paul metropolitan area and 30-miles southeast of St Cloud, MN. The primary mission of the Refuge is to represent a diverse biological community characteristic of the transition zone between tallgrass prairie and forest. Today's focus is on the restoration of oak savanna, wetland and big woods habitats. Call the NWR in Zimmerman, MN at 763/389-3323.

UNCAS DUNES: 745-acres of dunes located within the Anoka Sandplain, and contains a relic dune field associated with Glacial Lake Grantsburg. The SNA contains oak savanna, oak forest, and wetland with the savanna supporting asters and goldenrods. This site is located southwest of Zimmerman, MN and near the Sand Dunes State Forest Campgrounds. Call the DNR, MN at 888/646-6367 or 651/296-6157.

Stearns County:
COLD SPRING HERON COLONY: 62-acres of open floodplain meadow, floodplain forest, and a small prairie hill. Until 1989, the site was home to a large heron colony that was studied longer than any other in the state. Visitation is by permit only. Apply through Minnesota SNA Program at 651/296-2835 or through the Nongame Wildlife Specialist at New Ulm, MN at 507/359-6000. The site is located northeast of Cold Spring, MN on Hwy 23. Call the DNR, MN at 888/646-6367 or 651/296-6157.

QUARRY PARK: 133-acre site has granite bedrock along with high quality wet meadow, wet prairie, oak woodland, and oak forest. The site, on the southwestern edge of St Cloud, MN, is in the south part of the Stearns County Quarry Park and Nature Preserve (see below), a 250-acre park depicting the granite industry, historically significant to the area. Prairie plants can be found here. Call the DNR, MN at 888/646-6367 or 651/296-6157.

ROSCOE PRAIRIE: 57-acre prairie that has nearly 25-acres of undisturbed blacksoil prairie and has good bird watching opportunities. The SNA is located southwest of Roscoe, MN off Co Hwy 16. Call the DNR, MN at 888/646-6367 or 651/296-6157.

SAINT JOHN'S ABBEY AND UNIVERSITY: 160-acre restoration project of wetlands, prairie, and oak savanna. The success of the project is evident by 115 species of birds, 28 species of butterflies, and over 100 species of native plants. The Abbey is in Collegeville, MN. Contact the guest master at 320/363-2573.

STEARNS COUNTY QUARRY PARK AND NATURE PRESERVE: 553-acres park includes scenic woodlands, open prairie, wetlands, and unquarried bedrock areas. The Park is at the southwestern portion of Waite Park, MN. Call the Park at 320/255-6172.

Steele County:
RICE LAKE STATE PARK: (See Dodge County above).

Stevens County:
VERLYN MARTH MEMORIAL PRAIRIE: 34-acre prairie named after Verlyn Marth, a citizen known locally for his botanical skills and his advocacy of prairie protection. Despite his years of trying to restore this site Mr Marth concluded that it was more efficient to preserve existing prairie than to try to restore prairie. The SNA is located at the intersection of MN Hwys 9 & Co Rd 76 approximately 3-miles north of Donnelly, MN. Call the DNR, MN at 888/646-6367 or 651/296-6157.

Swift County:
CHIPPEWA PRAIRIE: (See Chippewa County above).

Wabasha County:
KELLOGG-WEAVER DUNES: 1,004-acres of dunes that encompasses a diversity of successional stages ranging from blowouts with bare sand, to mature dunes with dry, mesic, or wet prairie species. An oak savanna, with pin oak, bur oak, and jack pine, occurs along the edges. The rare Blanding's turtle nest at this site. This SNA is located southeast of Kellog, MN on Co Rd 84. Call the DNR, MN at 888/646-6367 or 651/296-6157.

ZUMBRO FALLS WOODS: 300-acre site is mainly forest but it has small areas of gravel prairie. This SNA is located southeast of Zumbro Falls, MN. Call the DNR, MN at 888/646-6367 or 651/296-6157.

Washington County:
GREY CLOUD DUNES: 220-acre site encompasses two sandy terraces along the Mississippi River with distinctive species adapted to a dry, sandy environment. Blue racers, an uncommon Minnesota snake, and prairie skinks live here. The Dunes is located at the intersection of Hadley and 103rd streets in Cottage Grove, MN. Call the DNR, MN at 888/646-6367 or 651/296-6157.

LOST VALLEY PRAIRIE: 200-acre bluff prairie located in the southern oak barrens landscape region containing a series of limestone ridges and dry swales and prairie wildflowers. This site is located close to the Twin Cities off Co Rd 78 (110 St) and at the end of Nyberg Ave. Call DNR, MN at 888/646-6367 or 651/296-6157.

ST. CROIX SAVANNA: 112-acre savanna at the top and side of a south-facing bluff with scattered bur oak and pin oak on the open gravel prairie become increasingly dense toward the northeast and northwest, forming first an oak woodland and then an oak forest. The Savanna has a significant diversity of grasses in the savanna and is about a ½-mile south of Bayport, MN on Hwy 95. Call the DNR, MN at 888/646-6367 or 651/296-6157.

Wilkin County:
FOXHOME PRAIRIE: 240-acre preserve that is predominantly a wet and mesic prairie and marsh. This preserve is located 10-miles northwest of Fergus Falls, MN. Call TNC, MN at 612/331-0750.

(RICHARD M. & MATHILDA) RICE ELLIOT SNA: 497-acre prairie is located within the basin of Glacial Lake Agassiz contains undisturbed tallgrass and wet communities, with small-scattered sedge meadows and willow thickets. Occasional boulders, called erratics, rest in earthen pits where they were deposited by a passing glacier long ago. The prairie vole and greater prairie chicken are found here. This site is located northwest of Rothsay, MN on Co Rd 188. Call the DNR, MN at 888/646-6367 or 651/296-6157.

(ANNA) GRONSETH PRAIRIE: 1,300-acre marshy prairie supports some plants rare or distinctive to Minnesota. In early spring, the greater prairie chicken booms or courts. Here one can experience the vast, unbroken acres of tallgrass prairie seen by Dakota Indians and early settlers. Call TNC, MN at 612/331-0750.

TOWN HALL PRAIRIE: 240-acre mesic and wet prairie located 3½-miles southwest of Rothsay, MN. Call TNC, MN at 612/331-0750.

WESTERN PRAIRIE SOUTH: 320-acre SNA is located within the basin of Glacial Lake Agassiz between two former shorelines and contains moist sedge meadows, tallgrass prairie, and prairie wetlands. Greater prairie chickens court in early spring and one can listen for meadowlarks among the blooming prairie grasses and wildflowers in late summer. The site is located northwest of Rothsay, MN with parking on Co Rd 165. Call the DNR, MN at 888/646-6367 or 651/296-6157.

Winona County:
KING'S AND QUEEN'S BLUFF: 178-acres of mixed oak forest, second

growth forest, goat prairie, and moist shaded cliff. King's Bluff, open all year round, is a "goat prairie" on the southwest slopes and is northwest Queen's Bluff. Queen's Bluff is designated as an educational unit and requires a permit. The SNA is 12-miles southeast of Winona, MN on US 61. Call the DNR, MN at 888/646-6367 or 651/296-6157.

Yellow Medicine County:
BLUE DEVIL VALLEY: 30-acre preserve contains a granite outcrop community within the Minnesota River Valley with xeric prairie species common among the outcrops and scattered bur oak. Spring through fall is a good time to view the wildflowers. The SNA is located ½-mile southwest of Granite Falls, MN off Hwy 23. Call the DNR, MN at 888/646-6367 or 651/296-6157.

SWEDES FOREST, HOMME-KOLLIN UNIT: 202-acre SNA is located within the Minnesota River Valley in Swedes Forest township and contains the granite outcrop community type that supports the rare five-lined skink. The Minnesota populations of these small, blue tailed lizards (sometimes called "blue devils") are isolated from the main range of this species, which is in the eastern United States. Several undisturbed wetlands are also found on the site. The SNA is located southwest of Sacred Heart, MN. Call the DNR, MN at 888/646-6367 or 651/296-6157.

Wildlife Refuge Areas: All the wildlife areas listed below share the goals of providing areas for wildlife to flourish, and restoring the areas to their natural states, including prairie.

Note! The following areas are not listed by county.

DETROIT LAKES WETLAND MANAGEMENT AREA: 39,558-acres in 154 units of Waterfowl Production Areas (WPA) totaling Wetland Easements: 324 totaling 12,100-acres in Becker, Clay, Mahnomen, Norman and Polk Counties. The WMA is committed to restoring the areas by providing habitat for native plants and animals, especially prairie songbirds, and assisting private landowners with restoration of wetlands and grasslands, among other things. The District office is located 2-miles north of Detroit Lakes, MN. Contact the District Manager: Mark Chase e-mail: mark_chase@fws.gov or 26624 North Tower Rd, Detroit Lakes, MN 56501-7959, Phone: 218-847-4431.

HAMDEN SLOUGH NATIONAL WILDLIFE REFUGE: 3,150-acres currently and authorized to 5,944-acres consists of rolling hills, grassland and small wetlands located in a transitional zone between flat tall-grass prairies and rolling hardwoods. Restoration efforts have brought back many native plants, waterfowl and other prairie wildlife. The goal is to restore the prairie wetland ecosystem of native grass and wetlands. Contact the Refuge Manager: Michael Murphy email:

mike_t_murphy@fws.gov or Call Audubon, MN at 218/439-6319.

LAC QUI PARLE MANAGEMENT WILDLIFE AREA: 31,000-acres or over 48-sq miles of land and water that lies in Big Stone, Chippewa, Lac qui Parle and Swift Counties. It is about 25 miles long, 1 to 3 miles wide that is made up of wetlands, brushlands, woodlands, native prairie, and other grasslands and cropland. Lac qui Parle Lake (6,400-acres) and Marsh Lake (5,100-acres) are the most prominent features. The WMA is located about 140 miles west of the Twin Cities in the Minnesota River Valley, northwest of Montevideo. Its headquarters is on the northeast side of Lac qui Parle Lake between the towns of Watson and Milan, MN. For more information contact the WMA at Route 1, Box 23 Watson, MN 56295, Telephone: 612/734-4451.

LITCHFIELD WETLAND MANAGEMENT DISTRICT: 146 units totaling 32,828-acres and 417 easements totaling 33,283-acres in Kandiyohi, McLeod, Meeker, Nicollet, Renville, Stearns, Todd and Wright Counties. Contact the District Manager, Barry Christenson at his e-mail address: barry_christenson@fws.gov or at 971 East Frontage Road, Litchfield, MN 55355, Telephone: 320/693-2849. The District office is located in Litchfield, MN on Hwy 12.

WINDOM WETLAND MANAGEMENT DISTRICT: 59 units totaling 11,445-acres and 51 wetland easements totaling 2,556-acres that cover Brown, Cottonwood, Faribault, Freeborn, Jackson, Martin, Murray, Nobles, Pipestone, Redwood, Rock, and Watonwan Counties. The landscape is dotted with thousands of small wetlands or "prairie potholes," created by glaciers. The objectives include:
1) Providing habitat for native plants and animals, especially prairie songbirds.
2) Assisting private landowners with restoration of wetlands and grasslands.
3) Providing wildlife-dependent recreation and education.
Non-game species of grassland birds are also monitored for abundance and diversity. The District office is located 1½-miles south of Windom, MN, on Hwy 71. Call the District at 507/831-2220.

MISSISSIPPI

Tallgrass prairie once extended into Alabama and Mississippi. Fire suppression enabled the forest to invade and agriculture devoured what prairie remained. For information about Mississippi prairies, call Ron Wieland at the Mississippi Museum of Natural Sciences at 601/354-7303.

Following are some of the prairies that still exist in Mississippi:

Jasper County:
JACKSON PRAIRIE OPENINGS IN JACKSON PRAIRIE REGION: 100 scattered acres of prairie and the 150-acre HARRELL HILL PRAIRIE located in the 178,000-acre BIENVILLE FOREST that lies halfway between Jackson and Meridian, MS and is bisected by US 20. To enter, call Bienville National Forest at 601/469-3811.

Mississippi State University characterized the soils of four prairie remnants in the Jackson Prairie Belt of gently rolling upland approximately 9 to 31 miles wide. The selected sites are:
DURAND OAK PRAIRIE: (10-acres)
HARRELL PRAIRIE HILL: (47-acres) in Scott County.
FIVE-ACRE PRAIRIE: (10-acres) in Smith County.
EUREKA CHURCH PRAIRIE: (1-acre) in Newton County. The study sites were selected on the basis of their size, degree of disturbance, and proximity to other prairie sites. Call the University at 662/325-5119.

Lowndes County:
BLACKLAND PRAIRIE WILDLIFE MANAGEMENT AREA: 5,000-acres of degraded blackland prairie being restored that supports quail, turkey, rabbit, bobcat (trapped seasonally) and deer. Call area managers at Mississippi State University at 662/325-5119.

Newton County:
JACKSON PRAIRIE OPENINGS IN JACKSON PRAIRIE REGION: (See Jasper County above).

Oktibbeha County:
SEC 16 PRAIRIE OR OSBORN PRAIRIE: 30-acres of original, but degraded, due to lack of burning, black belt prairie that once extended into Tennessee, Alabama, and Georgia. Call Richard Brown at the Mississippi Entomology Museum at 662/325-2085.

Scott County:
JACKSON PRAIRIE OPENINGS IN JACKSON PRAIRIE REGION: (See Jasper County above).

Smith County:
HARRELL PRAIRIE HILL BOTANICAL AREA: 150-acres of prairie surrounded by forest. Contact the US Forest Service at 601/469-3811 or

the Mississippi Department of Wildlife, Fisheries and Parks at 601/432-2400.

Note! The Mississippi Natural History Program has identified many prairies in the Jackson Prairie Region. For information contact:
Mississippi Natural Heritage Program
Mississippi Museum of Natural Science
Department of Wildlife, Fisheries and Parks
2148 Riverside Drive
Jackson, MS 39202
601/354-7303

MISSOURI
"Nature is an open book for those who care to read it. Each grass-covered hillside is a page on which is written the history of the past, conditions of the present and predictions of the future. Some see without understanding, but let us look closely", wrote John Weaver in "North American Prairie" (1954). He also wrote, "The disappearance of a major natural unit of vegetation from the face of the earth is an event worthy of causing pause and consideration by any nation. Yet so gradually have the breaking plow, the tractor, and the overcrowded herds of man conquered the prairie, and so intent has he been upon securing from the soil its last measure of innate fertility, that scant attention has been given to the significance of this endless grassland or the course of its destruction. Civilized man is destroying a masterpiece of nature without recording for posterity that which he has destroyed."

The Missouri Department of Conservation (MDC) publishes "Public Prairies of Missouri." Call 573/751-4115 for the publication, which gives detailed information on those prairies managed by the MDC, and other organizations. Their latest printing indicates that since the last edition, more native and restored prairies have become available for public viewing. This indicates that Missouri has organizations working to save and restore its prairies.

Missouri is one of the States involved in the "Prairie Passage"(See Iowa above). The Missouri DOT (MO DOT) is actively planting prairie plants along US 35 and other highways within the state whenever there is new construction or the roadside is re-seeded. Further at least one rest area will have a prairie demonstration area. The state's mowing the roadside policy is quite different from other states. Where the prairie is planted along the roadside, MO DOT mows the first 30 feet, which it does not plant in natives. Each county has its own policy. The state as of yet has not surveyed its remnant roadside prairies. For more information on such prairie plantings call the MO DOT at 888/275-6636.

There are many areas in Missouri where one can see prairie chickens and hear and maybe see prairie mole crickets; for those locations contact the MDC.

The state once supported 15-million acres of prairie; today only remnants remain. Below are some of Missouri's remaining prairie remnants:

Atchison County:
BRICKYARD HILL CONSERVATION AREA: 2,262-acres with associated prairies (see Brickyard Hill NA below).

BRICKYARD HILL LOESS MOUND NATURAL AREA: 41-acre prairie in a 125-acre NA within Brickyard Hill Conservation Area is an upland dry prairie with many prairie plants. The site is 8-miles south of the Missouri/Iowa state line on Co Rd RA near Watson, MO. Call the MDC, Northwest Regional Office at 816/271-3100.

STAR SCHOOL HILL PRAIRIE CONSERVATION AREA: 289-acre area with loess mound prairies (see Star School Hill Prairie NA below).

STAR SCHOOL HILL PRAIRIE NATURAL AREA: 70-acres within Star School Hill Prairie Conservation Area has dry prairies located on loess mounds adjacent to the Missouri River floodplain. The site is about 1½-miles south of the Iowa state line and 12-miles north of Rockport, MO. Call the Missouri Department of Conservation (MDC), Northwest Regional Office at 816/271-3100.

TARKIO PRAIRIE CONSERVATION AREA: 560-acres with some prairie present and hiking trails (see Tarkio Prairie NA below).

TARKIO PRAIRIE NATURAL AREA: 57-acre natural area with prairies of varying quality and diversity. A creek flows through the area, bisecting the prairie. The Area is 5-miles east of Westboro, MO off Hwy C. Call the MDC, Northwest Regional Office at 816/271-3100.

Barton County:
BETHEL PRAIRIE: 260-acre upland prairie with a small seasonal branch of the North Fork Spring River crossing it and adding to the diversity of the site. Grassland wildlife can be seen in the area. The Prairie is located northwest of Jasper, MO on Hwy126. Call the MDC, Southwest Regional Office at 417/895-6880, ext. 1078.

BUFFALO WALLOW PRAIRIE CONSERVATION AREA: 1,113-acres, in 2 portions, named for its remnant buffalo wallow, supports greater prairie chickens. Some of the area was previously farmed and is being restored to prairie. The native prairie units have a rich flora and fauna. The larger of the 2 parts of the prairie is north of Irwin, MO on US 71. The smaller unit is southwest of the larger. Call the MDC, Southwest Regional Office at 417/895-6880, ext. 1078.

BUSHWHACKER LAKE CONSERVATION AREA: 4,217-acres of tall-grass prairie, timber draws and streams that straddle Barton and Vernon Counties. The Area is southwest of Nevada, MO. Call the MDC in Springfield, MO at 417/895-6880.

BUSHWHACKER PRAIRIE: 665-acres in the Bushwhacker Lake Conservation Area (see above).

CATLIN PRAIRIE: 160-acres with 148-acres of upland prairie and 12-acres of cropland. The area contains a rich prairie flora, which is divided by a drainage break with mature hardwood timber. Prairie chickens, coyotes and deer use the area. The Prairie is south of Sheldon, MO on a gravel road. Call the MDC, Southwest Regional Office at 417/895-6880, ext. 1078.

CLEAR CREEK CONSERVATION AREA: 762-acres of prairie and forest that extends into Vernon County. This prairie supports a diverse prairie flora and wildlife. The Area is southeast of Sheldon, MO. Call the MDC, Southwest Regional Office at 417/895-6880, ext. 1078.

COMSTOCK PRAIRIE CONSERVATION AREA: 320-acres of upland prairie with a stream running through the site. There are diverse habitats, which support wildlife, including greater prairie chickens. The Area is north of Liberal, MO. Call the MDC, Southwest Regional Office at 417/895-6880, ext. 1078.

(SHELTON L.) COOK MEMORIAL MEADOW: 185-acres of prairie in an area of 280-acres. Most of the prairie is dry-mesic and some is mesic. The prairie has very diverse prairie flora with its nearly 400 species of native flowering plants. The prairie is located northwest of Golden City, MO. Call the MDC, Southwest Regional Office at 417/895-6880, ext. 1078.

(EDGAR AND RUTH) DENISON PRAIRIE: 160-acre upland prairie. Greater prairie chickens and wild turkeys can be seen here. The site is southwest of Sheldon, MO and adjacent to the Lattner Prairie (see Vernon County below). Call the Missouri Prairie Foundation at 888/843-6739.

DORRIS CREEK PRAIRIE CONSERVATION AREA: 160-acre flat to rolling upland prairie and lakes that help attract wildlife. Greater prairie chickens can be seen. The Area is west of Golden City, MO off Hwy 126. Call the MDC, Southwest Regional Office at 417/895-6880, ext 1078.

GOLDEN PRAIRIE: 320-acres of prairie including restored prairie. Greater prairie chickens can be found here along with numerous plant species. The Prairie is southwest of Golden City, MO. Call the Missouri Prairie Foundation at 888/843-6739.

MO-NO-I PRAIRIE CONSERVATION AREA: 302-acre upland prairie plus the adjacent 320-acres of private prairie make it one of Missouri's larger prairies. Greater prairie chickens can be seen here. The Area is northwest of Lamar, MO on Hwy DD. Call the MDC, Southwest Regional Office at 417/895-6880, ext. 1078.

MON-SHON PRAIRIE CONSERVATION AREA: 80-acres that is primarily upland prairie. The Area is located north of Asbury, MO, on a gravel road. Call the MDC, Southwest Regional Office at 417-895-6880, ext. 1078.

PA SOLE PRAIRIE CONSERVATION AREA: 240-acre upland prairie and cropland supporting grassland wildlife. The Prairie is located northwest of Golden City, MO off Hwy T. Call the MDC, Southwest Regional Office at 417/895-6880, ext. 1078.

PAWHUSKA PRAIRIE NATURAL AREA: 77-acres of upland prairie with a small creek in southwestern corner of the NA. Buffalo once frequented this area. The prairie is northeast of Lamar, MO. Call TNC, MO in St Louis, MO at 314/968-1105.

PRAIRIE STATE PARK: 3,702-acres containing a variety of native prairie grasses, flowers and distinctive prairie animals, including prairie chickens, bison, southern plain's skink, and free-roaming elk. The Park has several natural areas (see below):
1. REGAL PRAIRIE NATURAL AREA (240-acres),
2. TZI-SHO PRAIRIE NATURAL AREA (240-acres),
3. EAST DRYWOOD CREEK NATURAL AREA (50-acres), and
4. HUNKAH PRAIRIE NATURAL AREA (160-acres). Regal Prairie, Hunkah and Tzi-Sho (Sky People) Prairie NAs feature undisturbed tallgrass prairie. The park is south of Liberal, MO on a gravel road. Call DNR, MO at 417/843-6711 or at 800/334-6946.

REDWING PRAIRIE: 160-acres, with 111-acres native prairie and 49-acres of restored prairie at the entrance. This upland prairie has a fine spring display of forbs. The site is east of Liberal, Mo along a gravel road. Call the MDC, Southwest Regional Office at 417/895-6880, ext. 1078.

(EDWARD B. & MARIE O.) RISCH CONSERVATION AREA: 163-acres of rolling to hilly upland prairie with some cropland for wildlife. The Area is east of Sheldon, MO off Hwy B. Call the MDC, Southwest Regional Office at 417/895-6880, ext. 1078.

TREATY LINE PRAIRIE CONSERVATION AREA: 168-acres of upland prairie supporting much prairie flora and fauna. The Prairie is located southeast of Lamar, MO. Call the MDC, Southwest Regional Office at 417-895-6880, ext. 1078.

Bates County:
RIPGUT PRAIRIE NATURAL AREA: 280-acres of ripgut wet prairie, forest and cropland with some cropland being restored to prairie. The area has a diversity of wildlife. The NA is northeast of Rich Hill, MO. Call the MDC, West Central Regional Office at 660/885-6981, ext. 230.

Benton County:
HI LONESOME PRAIRIE CONSERVATION AREA: 627-acre prairie that is the largest prairie in this area of Missouri. Greater prairie chicken can be seen here. This area is located northwest of Cole Camp, MO. Call the MDC, West Central Regional Office at 660/885-6981, ext. 230.

ROCK HILL PRAIRIE: 68-acres with about 40-acres of native prairie and about 28-acres of restored prairie supporting a good variety of prairie plants. The Prairie is north of Warsaw, MO on US 65. Call TNC,

MO in St Louis, MO at 314/968-1105.

(HARRY S) TRUMAN STATE PARK: 1,440-acre park located on a peninsula and almost surrounded by the Harry S Truman Reservoir (see below). This park has open oak woodlands, natural grasslands, towering limestone bluffs and oak savannas. The Park is northwest of Warsaw, MO. Call the DNR, MO at 800/334-6946.

(HARRY S) TRUMAN RESERVOIR: 55,000-acre lake in an area where the forest meets the prairie. The area includes the state park (see above). Call the USCE in Warsaw, MO at 816/885-6981.

Boone County:
KATY TRAIL STATE PARK: (See Callaway County below).

MARK TWAIN NATIONAL FOREST CEDAR CREEK TRAILS: 16,000-acres of prairies and white oak forests border limestone caves and bluffs located southeast of Columbia, MO. Call the National Forest, District Ranger in Fulton, MO at 573/592-1422.

Callaway County:
DANVILLE CONSERVATION AREA: 2,654-acres with rocky meadows and glades that support Indian paintbrush, pale purple coneflower and prairie grasses. The area is southeast of Kingdom City, MO on Co Rd RB. Call the MDC in Williamsburg, MO at 573/254-3330.

KATY TRAIL STATE PARK: A 47-mile hiking or biking trail built on the abandoned MKT railway the runs from Jefferson City, MO to Franklin, MO in Callaway, Boone, and Howard Counties. The trail passes crop fields, wetlands, forests, cliffs, springs, caves, prairies and glades. Call the DNR, MO at 800/334-6946.

TUCKER PRAIRIE NATURAL AREA: 146-acre upland prairie used by the University of Missouri for research purposes. Many plant species have been found here. This NA is west of the junction of US 70 and Hwy 54 on US 70. Call the University of Missouri, Dept of Biological Sciences at 573/882-7541 or 573/882-6659.

Camden County:
HA HA TONKA SAVANNA NATURAL AREA: 953-acre portion of Ha Ha Tonka State Park located south of Camdenton, MO is an excellent example of pre-settlement landscape. Scattered oaks, prairie grasses and wildflowers, open rocky glades and valley woodlands form a savanna mosaic. The NA contains one of the largest publicly owned savanna landscapes left in Missouri and has a self-guided interpretive trail. Call the Park Superintendent, Ha Ha Tonka State Park at 573/346-2986.

HA HA TONKA STATE PARK: (See Ha Ha Tonka Savanna NA above).

LAKE OF THE OZARKS STATE PARK: 17,203-acres of lake with the ridges and hills coated with dense forests of oak-hickory and sprinkled with sunny glades. Several areas are covered by savanna, which has scattered trees and ground cover of colorful flowers and prairie grasses. The Park extends into Miller County and is south of Osage Beach, MO. Call the DNR, MO at 800/334-6946.

Cass County:
DORSETT HILL PRAIRIE CONSERVATION AREA: 79-acres of prairie, woods and fields. The site is located northeast of Everett, MO. Call the MDC, Kansas City Regional Office at 816-655-6250, ext. 246.

Cedar County:
SKY PRAIRIE CONSERVATION AREA: 200-acre area is an upland prairie and woodland supporting both prairie and forest plants and animals. The Area is southwest of El Dorado Springs, MO. Call the MDC, West Central Regional Office at 660/885-6981, ext. 230.

MONEGAW PRAIRIE: 240-acres of rolling upland with gentle, south facing slopes is officially classed as a dry to mesic sandstone and shale prairie. Local areas of mesic to wet soils contribute to a high diversity of native plants here. Over 220 plant species have been recorded at the site, which is home to upland sandpipers and scissor-tailed flycatchers, both of which breed here, as well as smaller beings like the rare prairie mole cricket. The Prairie was named for the Osage Chief Monegaw and is east of El Dorado Springs, MO on US 54. Call the TNC, MO in St Louis, MO at 314/968-1105 or the MDC, Southwest Regional Office at 417-895-6880, ext. 1078.

WAH'KON-TAH (GREAT SPIRIT IN OSAGE) PRAIRIE: 2,858-acres that is also in St Clair County, which is the second largest prairie in the state. This upland tallgrass prairie contains a diverse flora and fauna, including greater prairie chicken and upland sandpipers and other grassland birds and animals that live in tallgrass prairies. The Prairie is north of El Dorado Springs, MO on Hwy 82. Call TNC, MO in St Louis, MO at 314/968-1105 or the MDC, West Central Regional Office at 660/885-6981, ext. 230.

Charitan County:
NEHAI TONKAYEA PRAIRIE NATURAL AREA: 90-acre prairie on private land about 12-miles southeast of Marceline, MO. This is a dry-mesic prairie of the Grand River Section of the Glaciated Plains Natural Division. It is one of only a few prairies remaining on the Kansan glacial till plain. Contact the Nehai Property Owners Association, Inc, at 816/222-3453.

Clark County:
FROST ISLAND CONSERVATION AREA: 1,178-acre conservation

area (see Steyermark Sand Prairie below).

ILLINIWEK VILLAGE STATE HISTORIC SITE: This site is believed to be the Illiniwek village in a prairie visited by explorers Marquette and Jolliet in 1673. To see the kind of extremely rare sand prairie that surrounded that village, visit the nearby 6-acre Steyermark Sand Prairie in Frost Island Conservation Area (see below). The Historical Site is Southeast of St Francisville, MO. Call the DNR, MO State Parks Division at 660/877-3871.

STEYERMARK SAND PRAIRIE: 6-acre (within the Frost Island Conservation Area) sand prairie. This is one of the few sand prairies left in Missouri. The Prairie is immediately east of St Francisville, MO. Call the MDC, Northeast Regional Office at 660/785-2420.

Crawford County:
ONONDAGA CAVE STATE PARK: 1,317-acre park with trails that pass springs, rocky bluffs, glades and an oxbow lake. The Park is southwest of Sullivan, MO on Co Rd H. Call the DNR, MO at 800/334-6946.

Dade County:
BURNS TRACT: 320-acres of upland areas and wet-mesic prairie. The Tract is northwest of Lockwood, MO on Hwy D and adjacent to the Stony Point Conservation Area. Call the Missouri Prairie Foundation at 888/843-6739.

GREENFIELD GLADE: 47-acres of open glade and wooded areas. The glade is south of Greenfield, Mo. Call TNC, MO at 314/968-1105.

HORSE CREEK PRAIRIE CONSERVATION AREA: 80-acres of upland prairie with many prairie plants and animals. This site is northwest of Lockwood, MO. Call the MDC, Southwest Regional Office at 417/895-6880, ext. 1078.

INDIGO PRAIRIE CONSERVATION AREA: 40-acres of upland prairie that contains some shrubs. The Prairie is southeast of Lockwood, MO. Call the MDC, Southwest Regional Office at 417/895-6880, ext. 1078.

NIAWATHE PRAIRIE CONSERVATION AREA: 320-acre dry mesic upland prairie with some mesic prairie that contains a wide range of prairie flora and fauna. The site is north of Lockwood, MO on Hwy E. Call the TNC, MO at 314/968-1105 or the MDC, Southwest Regional Office at 417/895-6880, ext. 1078.

PENN-SYLVANIA PRAIRIE: 160-acre upland prairie that supports greater prairie chickens as well as a large variety of plants and animals. The Prairie is north of Lockwood, MO. Call the Missouri Prairie Foundation at 888/843-6739.

STONY POINT PRAIRIE CONSERVATION AREA: 640-acres of prairie and forest that supports the prairie mole cricket. The site is north of Lockwood, MO on Hwy D. Call the MDC, Southwest Regional Office at 417/895-6880, ext. 1078.

Greene County:
SPRINGFIELD CONSERVATION NATURE CENTER: 80-acres within the city limits of Springfield. The nature center trail crosses forests, a restored prairie, a glade, creeks, small marshes and Lake Springfield. The Center is on Frontage Rd in Springfield, MO near the Glenstone exit of US 60. Call the MDC in Springfield, MO at 417/888-4237.

Harrison County:
DUNN RANCH: 2,991-acres of tallgrass prairie on rolling hills on which prairie chickens still perform their colorful spring "booming"; the upland sandpiper's ghostly call carries in the wind; and regal fritillary butterflies alight on coneflowers. TNC sees this largely unplowed site as an anchor site in its plans to protect the native diversity in a 33,000-acre grassland project of the Central Tallgrass Prairie Region. This northern Missouri site is among the best large tallgrass prairie between Nebraska and Indiana and plans include introducing bison to compliment its wealth of wildlife. The ranch is located north of Bethany, MO. Call TNC, MO at 314/968-1105.

(WAYNE) HELTON MEMORIAL WILDLIFE AREA: 2,560-acres that contains some prairie (See Helton Prairie Natural Area below).

HELTON PRAIRIE NATURAL AREA: 30-acres of native and restored prairie within Wayne Helton Memorial Wildlife Area, which supports a good variety of plant species. The WA and NA are east of Bolton, MO. Call the MDC, Northwest Regional Office at 816/271-3100.

PAWNEE PRAIRIE: 910-acre jointly owned prairie included in the Pawnee Prairie Conservation Area (see below). Its diversity of grassland birds makes it a good birding location. The Prairie is south of Hatfield, MO. Call TNC, MO at 314/968-1105 or the MDC, Northwest Regional Office at 816/271-3100.

PAWNEE PRAIRIE CONSERVATION AREA: (See Pawnee Prairie above).

Henry County:
CHAPEL VIEW PRAIRIE CONSERVATION AREA: 384-acres of prairie and forest with ponds and also a large diversity of prairie flora and fauna. The site is southwest of Deepwater, MO. Call the MDC, West Central Regional Office at 660/885-6981, ext. 230.

Holt County:
MCCORMACK CONSERVATION AREA: 242-acres of prairie and

woodland (See the McCormack Loess Mound NA below).

MCCORMICK LOESS MOUND NATURAL AREA: 158-acre upland prairie within the McCormack Conservation Area in the Loess Mound Natural Area supports some typical Great Plains prairie plants. The NA is located south of Mound City, MO. Call TNC, MO at 314/968-1105 or Call the MDC, Northwest Regional Office at 816/271-3100.

SQUAW CREEK NATIONAL WILDLIFE REFUGE: 7,350-acre refuge that includes areas of loess bluff hills, an unusual geological formation caused by wind deposited soil. These bluffs have some of the remnants of the once vast native prairie. During migration, great numbers of waterfowl stop at this NWR. The NWR is south of Mound City, MO. Call the NWR at 816/442-3187.

Howard County:
KATY TRAIL STATE PARK: (See Callaway County above).

Howell County:
TINGLER LAKE CONSERVATION AREA: 240-acres, of which a large portion is being restored to prairie (See Tingler Lake Wet-Mesic Prairie below).

TINGLER LAKE WET-MESIC PRAIRIE: 10-acre native prairie within the Tingler Lake Conservation Area supporting very diverse flora. One can view the area from trails. The Prairie is located south of West Plains, MO. Call the MDC, Ozark Regional Office at 417/256/7161, ext. 234.

Iron County:
TAUM SAUK MOUNTAIN STATE PARK: 6,888-acres with wooded igneous rock knobs dotted with glades covered in thick mantels of prairie grass. The Park extends into Reynolds County and is southwest of Ironton, MO on Hwy CC. Call the DNR, MO at 800/334-6946.

Jasper County:
WAH-SHA-SHE PRAIRIE NATURAL AREA: 160-acre flat prairie contains a 10-acre marsh lake that attracts spring and fall flights of waterfowl. This NA has diverse vegetation and also has a flock of prairie chickens. The NA is located north of Asbury, MO on Hwy M. Call TNC, MO in St Louis, MO at 314/968-1105.

Jackson County:
BURR OAK WOODS CONSERVATION AREA AND NATURE CENTER: 1,071-acres of hardwood forests, tallgrass prairie planting and glade. The Nature Center is northwest of Blue Springs, MO on NW Park Rd. Call the Center at 816/228-3766.

JAMES A. REED MEMORIAL WILDLIFE AREA: 2,456-acres with trails through prairies, forests, and other habitats. The WA is southeast of Kansas City, MO on Ranson Rd. Call the MDC in Lee's Summit, MO at 816/524-1656.

Jefferson County:
VALLEY VIEW GLADES NATURAL AREA: 227-acres with a trail leading to rocky slopes with prairie grasses. The NA is northwest of Hillsboro, MO on Co Rd B. Call the MDC in Glencoe, MO at 314/458-2236.

Johnson County:
JOHNSON COUNTY PARKS: Several prairie remnant sites. Call MDC at 816/655-6250, ext 246.

KNOB NOSTER STATE PARK: 3,600-acre park with prairie, savanna, and forest. The park is south of Knob Noster, MO on Hwy 132. Call the DNR, MO at 800/334-6946.

Laclede County:
BENNETT SPRINGS SAVANNA: 920-acres of scattered oaks and hickories raise full, gnarled canopies with tall bottlebrush grass, Indian grass and blazing stars below. This high quality savanna preserve is being restored to pre-settlement times. Explore ravines and creeks for the chance of meeting a shy turtle, delicate ferns or elusive birds. Look for downy blue gentian, pink milkwort, royal catchfly, stiff aster, red milk snake, dogface and Baltimore-checker-spot butterflies. The Savanna is west of Lebanon, MO. Call TNC, MO at 314/968-1105.

Lawerence County:
KICKAPOO PRAIRIE CONSERVATION AREA: 160-acre upland prairie with diverse flora and fauna. The site is west of Miller, MO off Hwy 97. Call the MDC, Southwest Regional Office at 417-895-6880, ext. 1078.

MOUNT VERNON PRAIRIE NATURAL AREA: 40-acre upland dry prairie has diverse flora and fauna. The NA is northeast of Mount Vernon, MO. Call TNC, MO at 314/968-1105.

PROVIDENCE PRAIRIE CONSERVATION AREA: 197-acres that is mostly prairie with many forbs and prairie grasses. The site is east of Red Oak, MO. Call the MDC, Southwest Regional Office at 417-895-6880, ext. 1078.

WOODS PRAIRIE: 40-acre upland prairie with mima mounds. An area of the site is being restored to prairie. The Prairie is located east of Mt. Vernon, MO. Call the Ozark Regional Land Trust in Carthage, MO at 417/358-0852.

Lincoln County:
CUIVRE RIVER STATE PARK: 6,393-acres that includes about 123-acres of contiguous native prairies named Sherwood, Sac, Northwoods and Dry Branch Prairies (see below) and savanna, glades, and bottomland forests. The Park is located 3-miles east of Troy, MO off Hwy 47. Call the DNR, MO, Division of State Parks at 800/334-6946.

SHERWOOD, SAC, NORTHWOODS AND DRY BRANCH PRAIRIES 70-acres within Cuivre River State Park.
Sherwood Prairie: 8-acres
Sac Prairie: 20-acres
Northwoods Prairie: 25-acres and
Dry Branch Prairie. These native prairie restoration areas feature remnant and restored upland dry-mesic prairie bordered by savanna and woodland and preserve many plants indicative of Lincoln Hill's original diversity. The park is located 3-miles east of Troy, MO off Hwy 47. Call the DNR, MO, Division of State Parks at 800/334-6946.

Linn County:
CORDGRASS BOTTOMS NATURAL AREA AND LOCUST CREEK PRAIRIE: 800-acres of wet prairie within Pershing State Park (see below), which is home to the endangered Massasauga rattlesnake. The NA is west of Brookfield, MO. Call the DNR, MO at 660/963-2299.

PERSHING STATE PARK: 3,257-acre park with a meandering stream with oxbow sloughs and cutoffs, a gently sloping upland forest, a mature bottomland forest and an expansive river bottom prairie, marshland and swamps (see Cordgrass Bottoms Natural Area above).

Macon County:
BEE TRACE & LITTLE CHARITON GRASSLANDS: 200-acres of prairie remnants scattered within the Long Branch State Park (see below) of which the largest is 100-acres. The easily located grasslands remind one of the once vast prairies. The park is west of the junction of Macon, MO. Call the DNR, MO Parks Division at 660/773-5229.

LONG BRANCH STATE PARK: 1,834-acre park with wooded areas, restored rolling prairie, and savannas. (See Bee Trace &Little Chariton Grasslands above).

HIDDEN HOLLOW CONSERVATION AREA: 1,228-acre area has a 41-acre prairie, which contains typical prairie grasses and forbs. The site is north of Elmer, MO. Call the MDC, Southwest Regional Office at 417/895-6880, ext. 1078.

Madison County:
AMIDON MEMORIAL CONSERVATION AREA: 1,630-acres of forest and glades with the 1-mile Cedar Glade Trail descending to glades

171

where prairie grasses and wildflowers grow on the granite landscape. The site is southeast of Fredricktown, MO on Co Rd 253. Call the MDC in Perryville, MO at 573/547-4537.

Mercer County:
CHLOE LOWRY MARSH CONSERVATION AREA: (See Chloe Lowry Marsh Natural Area below).

CHLOE LOWRY MARSH NATURAL AREA: 115-acres of prairie, marsh, savanna, woods, restored prairie, and a ½-mile hiking trail within Chloe Lowry Marsh Conservation Area. The NA is northwest of Princeton, Mo. Call the MDC, Northwest Regional Office at 816/271-3100.

Miller County:
LAKE OF THE OZARKS STATE PARK: (See Camden County above).

Mississippi County:
TOWOSAHGY STATE HISTORIC SITE: 64-acre site preserves the remains of a Mississippian culture fortified Indian village on a prairie. The town of East Prairie is all that is left of the area known historically as Little Prairie. Call the Historic Site at 573/649-3149.

Morgan County:
HITE PRAIRIE CONSERVATION AREA: 102-acres of native and restored prairie with many prairie species. The Prairie is located near the southwest edge of Versailles, MO. Call the MDC, West Central Regional Office at 660/885-6981, ext. 230.

Newton County:
(GEORGE WASHINGTON) CARVER NATIONAL MONUMENT: 210-acres with woodlands, prairie, and a trail. The Monument is southwest of Diamond, MO on Carver Rd. Call the National Park Service in Diamond, MO at 417/325-4151.

DIAMOND GROVE PRAIRIE NATURAL AREA: 611-acre upland tallgrass prairie that is home to a variety of wildlife including greater prairie chickens and is one of the few large prairies in the region. This site is northwest of Diamond, MO. Call the MDC, Southwest Regional Office at 417/895-6880 ext. 1078.

Ozark County:
CANEY MOUNTAIN CONSERVATION AREA: 6,694-acres of glades, savannas, forests and small spring-fed creeks. The site is northeast of Gainesville, MO on Hwy 181. Call the MDC in Gainesville, MO at 417/679-4218.

MARK TWAIN NATIONAL FOREST GLADE TOP TRAIL: A self-guided driving tour of the National Forest Scenic Byways System. The trail has pull-offs at Hayden Bald Natural Area, Three Sisters Glades and Caney Lookout Tower. Each offer beautiful views of the landscape, including glades and savannas. The Trail follows forest roads 147 and 149 that are south of Smallett, MO. Call the USFS in Ava, MO at 417/683-4428.

Pettis County:
DROVERS' PRAIRIE: 80-acre prairie in two parcels is home to greater prairie chicken and has many flora species. This site is located north of Ionia, MO on Hwy 52. Call the MDC at Sedalia, MO at 816/530-5500.

FRIENDLY PRAIRIE: 40-acre upland prairie with a large number of bird and plant species located north of Ionic, MO off US 65. Call the MDC at Sedalia, MO at 816/530-5500.

GOODNIGHT-HENRY PRAIRIE: 40-acre upland prairie with diverse forb species. The Prairie is located north of Cole Camp, MO on Hwy U. Call TNC, MO at 314/968-1105.

GRANDFATHER PRAIRIE CONSERVATION AREA: 78-acre upland prairie and wooded area with many spring flowering plants located north of Cole Camp, MO. Call the MDC in Sedalia, MO at 816/530-5500.

PAINT BRUSH PRAIRIE CONSERVATION AREA: 314-acres that is basically prairie and supports prairie flora and fauna and is northeast of Ionia, MO off US 65. Call the MDC in Sedalia, MO at 816/530-5500.

Polk County:
LA PETITE GEMME NATURAL AREA: 37-acres of upland prairie with a great diversity of prairie wildflowers located south of Bolivar, MO. Call MDC, Southwest Regional Office at 417/895-6880 ext. 1078.

Reynolds County:
TAUM SAUK MOUNTAIN STATE PARK: (See Iron County above).

Ray County:
FOXGLOVE CONSERVATION AREA: 55-acres of native and restored prairie located southeast of Lawson, MO. Call the MDC, at the Northwest Regional Office at 816/271-3100.

Ripley County:
BALD HILL GLADE NATURAL AREA: 332-acre area within the Mark Twain National Forest. This site is the largest dolomite glade complex known from the Lower Ozarks Section of the Ozark Natural Division. The glade's flora is exceptionally diverse with more than 160 species observed. It is north of Gatewood, MO with access by Forest Service Roads 3213 and 3194. Contact the District Ranger, Doniphan/Eleven Point Ranger District at 573/996- 2153.

Prairie Directory

Saline County:
VAN METER STATE PARK: 983-acres once home to Missouri Indians after whom Missouri is named. The prairie that supported their burial mounds has not been restored. The Park is 12-miles northwest of Marshall, MO on Hwy 122. Call the Park at 660/886-7537.

St Charles County:
RIVERLANDS ENVIRONMENTAL DEMONSTRATION AREA: 1,200-acres of bottomland between the Missouri and Mississippi Rivers with small lakes, wet prairies and marshes. The Area is just south of West Alton, MO. Call the Riverlands Area Office at 314/355-6585.

St Clair County:
LICHEN GLADE: 30-acres of open glade with prairie plants being managed by TNC located west of Osceola, MO. Call TNC, MO in St Louis, MO at 314/968-1105.

TABERVILLE PRAIRIE CONSERVATION AREA: 1,680-acres of prairie and open fields (see Taberville Prairie Natural Area below).

TABERVILLE PRAIRIE NATURAL AREA: 1,360-acre native prairie is the largest prairie within the Taberville Prairie Conservation Area (see above). The NA supports a diverse plant species and is north of El Dorado Springs, MO on Hwy H. Call the MDC, West Central Regional Office at 660/885-6981, ext. 230.

SAC-OSAGE ROADSIDE PARK: The Park's prairie grasses, such as little bluestem and sideoats grama, grow on a rocky glade home to thirteen-lined ground squirrel and fence lizard. The Park is 3-miles west of Osceola, MO on Hwy 82. Call the MO, DOT in Osceola, MO at 417/876-4232.

SCHELL-OSAGE CONSERVATION AREA: 8,663-acres of rich bottomlands of oak, hickory and pecan trees and natural oxbow sloughs along the Osage River as well as prairie areas (See Schell-Osage Prairies below).

SCHELL-OSAGE PRAIRIES: 171-acres of prairie in scattered sites within Schell-Osage Conservation Area, partly in Vernon County. The Prairies are northwest of El Dorado Springs, MO. Call the MDC, West Central Regional Office at 660/885-6981, ext. 230.

SCHWARTZ PRAIRIE: 240-acres of native prairie, restored prairie and woodland northeast of El Dorado Springs, MO. Call the Missouri Prairie Foundation at 888/843-6739.

WAH-KON-TAH PRAIRIE: (See Cedar County above).

St Francois County:
ST FRANCOIS STATE PARK: 2,734-acres of forest, glades, fens and

clear running streams. The park is south of Bonne Terre, MO on US 67. Call DNR, MO at 800/334-6946.

Stone County:
(RUTH & PAUL) HENNING CONSERVATION AREA: 1,534-acres where little bluestem and Indian grass make tufts of green on the thin glade soils. The Area is northwest of Branson, MO on Hwy 76. Call the MDC in Springfield, MO at 417/895-6880.

Sullivan County:
MORRIS PRAIRIE: 47-acre high quality prairie that is privately owned. Call MDC in Kirskville, MO at 660/785-2420

Taney County:
DRURY-MINCY CONSERVATION AREA: 5,699-acres of rocky glades and post oak savannas cover south and west hillsides which are habitat for tarantula, bluebird, spotted skunk and prairie plants, such as little bluestem, pale purple coneflower, blazing star and larkspur. The site is east of Mincy, MO. Call the MDC in Kirbyville, MO at 417/334-4830.

MARK TWAIN NATIONAL FOREST HERCULES GLADE WILDERNESS AREA: 12,315-acres of open prairie grasslands, forested knobs, steep glades and narrow valleys. The WA is north of Fairview, MO on Hwy 125. Call the National Forest in Ava, MO at 417/683-4428.

Vernon County:
BUSHWHACKER PRAIRIE: 665-acres of upland prairie in two tracts within the Bushwhacker Lake Conservation Area (see Barton County above). The prairies are southeast of Bronaugh, MO. Call the MDC, West Central Regional Office at 660/885-6981, ext. 230.

BUSHWHACKER LAKE CONSERVATION AREA: (See Barton County above).

CLEAR CREEK CONSERVATION AREA: (See Barton County above).

DOUGLAS BRANCH CONSERVATION AREA: 360-acres of native prairie, woods and open fields. The site is north of Nevada, MO off US 71. Call the MDC, West Central Regional Office at 660/885-6981, ext. 230.

FLIGHT LAKE CONSERVATION AREA: 159-acres including 54-acres of ripgut prairie, a 41-acre lake, 29-acres of old field, and 34-acres of woods. The site's primary feature is the ripgut (cord grass) wet prairie. The lake attracts shorebirds and a variety of waterfowl. The Area is northwest of Nevada, MO. Call the MDC, West Central Regional Office at 660/885-6981, ext. 230.

FOUR RIVERS CONSERVATION AREA: 6,696-acre forest, wetlands, savanna, and prairie (see Horton Bottoms Natural Area below).

GAMA GRASS PRAIRIE CONSERVATION AREA: 80-acres of flat hardpan prairie over silt loam to silty clay soils. The area contains the largest stand of eastern gama grass in the state. Shrubby and forested draws add to the wildlife diversity. This site is 4-miles south of Rich Hill, MO on Hwy 71, then 1-mile west on a gravel road to the parking lot. Call the MDC, West Central Regional Office at 660/885-6981, ext. 230.

GAY FEATHER PRAIRIE: 116-acre prairie is an upland Ozark border prairie over silt loam soils derived from shale and sandstone. A total of 305 plant species have been recorded on this site. The Prairie is southeast of Milo, MO on a gravel road. Call the MDC, West Central Regional Office at 660/885-6981, ext. 230.

HORTON BOTTOMS NATURAL AREA: 227-acres of prairie, savanna, marsh, and forest within Four Rivers Conservation Area. The NA is northeast of Nevada, MO off US 71. Call the MDC, West Central Regional Office at 660/885-6981, ext. 230.

LATTNER PRAIRIE: 80-acre upland prairie that is adjacent to Denison Prairies (see Barton County). The Prairie is west of Sheldon, MO. Call the Missouri Prairie Foundation at 888/843-6739.

LITTLE OSAGE PRAIRIE NATURAL AREA: 80-acre prairie upland prairie with many native plant species. The NA is south of Nevada, MO off Hwy 71. Call TNC, MO at 314/968-1105.

MARMATON RIVER BOTTOMS WET PRAIRIE: 609-acres of ripgut wet prairie, savanna, forest, old fields and restored prairie located northwest of Nevada, MO. Call TNC, MO at 314/968-1105.

OSAGE PRAIRIE CONSERVATION AREA: 1,506-acres of upland prairie and fields. This site is south of Nevada, MO off Hwy 71. Call the MDC, West Central Regional Office at 660/885-6981, ext. 230.

STILWELL PRAIRIE: 376-acres of rolling upland prairie not far from the Kansas border with a high diversity of prairie plants. The Prairie is northeast of Richards, MO. For information about this and its other prairies, call the Missouri Prairie Foundation at 888/843-6739 or visit its website at http://www.moprairie.org

Washington County:
HUGHES MOUNTAIN NATURAL AREA: 330-acres with igneous glades that are rough, rocky meadows supporting common glade plants. The NA is south of Potosi, MO on Co Rd 521. Call the MDC in Sullivan, MO at 573/468-3335.

MONTANA
Especially east of the Continental Divide, prairie comprised 65% of the state. It is widely accepted that plowing, overgrazing, fire suppression, tree encroachment, invasive exotics (non-native) plants, altered predator populations, and the slaughter of black-tailed prairie dogs (considered a keystone species) have all combined to make native grasslands the most extensively altered biome on the planet. Montana landowners and the Fish and Wildlife Service both acknowledge the role ranching has played in maintaining productive grassland-wetland landscapes and stable wildlife populations.

Below are some prairies that can be seen in Montana:

Beaverhead County:
RED ROCK LAKES NATIONAL WILDLIFE REFUGE: 44,157-acres of a vast shallow lake/marsh complex, along with subirrigated meadows, sagebrush grasslands, and coniferous forests. The Refuge is east of Monida, MT. Call the NWR in Lima, MT at 406/276-3536.

Bighorn County:
BIGHORN CANYON NATIONAL RECREATION AREA: 63,000-acres including canyon, and tall and short-grass prairie supporting wild horses, black bears, falcons, red-tail and rough legged hawks, badgers, and white tail and mule deer. The park Headquarters is near Ft. Smith, MT. The Park extends for 70-miles straddling the Montana-Wyoming border. Call 406/666-2412 or call Rick Lasko at 307-548-2251, ext. 305.

LITTLE BIGHORN BATTLEFIELD NATIONAL MONUMENT: 640-acres of short-grass prairie and sagebrush where Native Americans defeated Lt Col George Armstrong Custer. The Monument is 1½-miles northwest of Crow Agency, Montana. Call the park at 406/638-2621.

TONGUE RIVER RESERVOIR STATE PARK: 640-acre park with short-grass prairies. The Park is 7-miles from Decker, MT, nearly on the border with Wyoming. Call 604/232-0900.

Blaine County:
FORT BELKNAP AGENCY: 670,000-acre reservation of short-grass prairie, which is partly in Philips County, and is located between the Milk River and Little Rocky Mountains. The agency is home to Gros Ventre and Assiniboine (Nakoda) nations and supports a herd of 400-head of buffalo and deer, antelope, upland birds and migratory waterfowl. To visit the Reservation call 406/353-2205 and ask for tourism.

Carter County:
MEDICINE ROCKS STATE PARK: 320-acre park with sandstone rock formations and forest and prairie. The Park is southwest of Willard, MT. Call the Park at 406/232-0900.

Cascade County:
BENTON LAKE NATIONAL WILDLIFE REFUGE: 12,383-acres of rich, shallow prairie marsh surrounded by intense agriculture. The "lake" is actually a 5,800-acre shallow marsh in a closed basin. The gently rolling refuge uplands are dominated by 6,000-acres of native short-grass prairie. A 9-mile wildlife viewing auto tour route is open to the public. The Refuge is located on the western edge of the northern Great Plains near Great Falls, MT. Call the NWR at 406/727-7400.

CROWN BUTTE PRESERVE: This geologic formation rises 900 feet above the foothill prairies just east of Montana's Rocky Mountain Front. The southeast corner holds the remains of a Native American "eagle catch." Looking west transports the visitor to an era before the first wagon train moved west across the prairie. This site offers an exceptional opportunity to encounter an undisturbed grassland ecosystem. The four main grassland habitat types are grouped according to dominant plant species. They are:
1.Bluebunch wheatgrass/blue grama (on west-facing slopes and on the crest of small knolls).
2.Rough fescue/bluebunch wheatgrass (on slightly more moist sites).
3.Rough fescue/Idaho fescue (the most productive climax plant community on the butte).
4.Idaho fescue/bluebunch wheatgrass (found less frequently, usually on west-facing slopes, and includes needle-and-thread grass and thread-leaf sedge).
The preserve is 30-miles southwest of Great Falls, MT and can be approached from Simms, MT (on Hwy 200, just north of the butte) or from Cascade, MT (on US 15, southeast of the Butte, MT). Call TNC, MT in Helena, MT at 406/443-0303.

Chouteau County:
LONESOME LAKE: 15,600-acres of short-grass prairie and wetlands. The Lake is west of Rocky Crossing, MT. Call the BLM at 406/265-5891.

Fergus County:
(CHARLES M.) RUSSELL NATIONAL WILDLIFE REFUGE: 1.1 million acre refuge extending 125 airline miles up the Missouri River from Fort Peck Dam. The NWR includes the 245,000-acre Fort Peck Reservoir. Also included in the NWR are James Kipp State Park, UL Bend National Wildlife Refuge, Hell Creek State Park, Rock Creek State Park, and recreational areas (Crooked Creek, Devils Creek, The Pines, Fort Peck, Black Creek and Nelson Creek). These native prairies, forested coulees, river bottoms, and badlands were often portrayed in the paintings of Charlie Russell, the colorful western artist for whom the refuge is named. A 1,000-acre area called Manning Corral Prairie Dog Town is home to burrowing owls, rattlesnakes and the re-

introduced black-footed ferret that went extinct in the wild. The Refuge is extensively involved in the Prairie Pothole Joint Venture and Farm Bill programs in Montana. Call the NWR at 406/538-8706.

ULM PISHKUN STATE PARK: One of the largest Native American buffalo jumps in the US has a mile long-cliff over which the Indians herded buffalo. The Park, which has undisturbed prairie, is west of Great Falls, MT. Call the Park at 406/866-2217.

UPPER MISSOURI NATIONAL WILD AND SCENIC RIVER: 149-mile section of the river near Fort Benton supports bighorn sheep and prairie dogs. Adjacent to Charles M. Russell Refuge, the site extends into Petroleum County. Call the BLM at 406/538-7461.

Flathead County:
GLACIER NATIONAL PARK: 1,000,000-acres including prairies such as the 6-mile Cracker Lake Trail, the ½-mile Firebrand Pass Trail featuring prairie potholes, and the 2,600-acre Big Prairie. The Park is located in the northwestern part of the state on the Canadian border and extends into Glacier County. Call the Park at 406/888-7800.

Gallatin County:
MADISON BUFFALO JUMP STATE PARK: 640-acres with prairie remnants. Before the introduction of the horse, Native Americans of the Northern Great Plains stampeded herds of bison over the precipice. Today, buffalo occasionally wander out from Turner Ranch. The Park is northwest of Bozeman, MT. Call the Park at 406/994-4042.

Glacier County:
GLACIER NATIONAL PARK: (See Flathead County above).

Lake County:
WILD HORSE ISLAND ON FLATHEAD LAKE: 2,163-acre state park accessible by boat is noted for its prairie plants. The receding Wisconsin Glacier dredged out the lake. Call the Park at 406/751-4573.

NATIONAL BISON RANGE: 25-square miles with lots of palouse prairie providing habitat for bison, elk, big horn sheep, mountain goats, and black bears that can be viewed from Prairie Drive/West Loop and walking trails. The Range is near Moiese, MT and extends into Sanders County. Call the USFW at 406/644-2211.

Lame Deer County:
NORTHERN CHEYENNE INDIAN RESERVATION: Prairies and a buffalo jump not far from Little Bighorn Battlefield. The Reservation located in southeastern Montana, covers 445,000-acres and is bounded on the east by the Tongue River and on the west by the Crow Reservation. The tribal headquarters are in Lame Deer, MT. Call the Reservation at 406/477-6284.

Lewis and Clark County:
SUN RIVER WILDLIFE MANAGEMENT AREA: 19,200-acres of short-grass prairie supporting elk and deer, not far from the Sun River Canyon, where the northern Great Plain prairies abruptly meet the Rockies. The WMA is northwest of Augusta, MT. Call MFWP in Billings, MT at 406/247-2940.

Lincoln County:
DANCING PRAIRIE PRESERVE: 680-acre prairie "island" in the Tobacco Plains just north of Eureka, MT supports the last active dancing ground of Colombian sharp-tailed grouse. The Preserve is northeast of Eureka, MT. Call TNC, MT, at 406/443-0303.

Musselshell County:
LAKE MASON NATIONAL WILDLIFE REFUGE: The refuge is divided into three units: Lake Mason, Willow Creek and the North Unit. The Lake Mason Unit is 3,721-acres and includes a 1,300-acre marsh surrounded by rolling short-grass dry prairie hills. The Lake Mason Unit is 8-miles northwest of Roundup, MT. The Willow Creek Unit is 2,160-acres and features short-grass prairie and provides viewing of mountain plovers, burrowing owls, hawks and antelope and has a black-tailed prairie dog town on the north end. This unit is about 25-miles north of Roundup, MT. The North Unit is 5,323-acres and is about 26-miles north of Roundup, MT. Call the NWR at 406/538-8706.

Petroleum County:
UPPER MISSOURI NATIONAL WILD AND SCENIC RIVER: (See Fergus County above).

Phillips County:
BOWDOIN NATIONAL WILDLIFE REFUGE: 15,500-acres of short-grass prairie, wetlands and shrubs consisting of approximately half water and half uplands comprised mostly of native short and mid-grass prairie. The NWR is managed for migratory birds. The Mayfield duck has 50-60 percent nesting success. The American white pelican nests here and 150 bald eagles have been seen here. Further, the NWR is leading the effort to protect the Baird's sparrow, an important species in the grassland ecosystem. Call the NWR at 406/654-2863.

FORT BELKNAP AGENCY: (See Blaine County above).

MATADOR RANCH: 60,000-acres of mixed-grass prairie, sagebrush grasslands and streams. TNC and the Tranel family combined resources to meet a mutual goal of well-managed livestock grazing and the conservation of high quality and extensive native prairie and wildlife. The arrangement gives the Tranels over half of the deeded land and TNC the remainder of the ranch, which it leases to the Tranels for livestock grazing. TNC also hold a conservation easement on the Tranel's portion of the ranch. A wide variety of wildlife, including black-tailed prairie dog, and the black-footed ferret live on Matador Ranch, which is located 40-miles south of Malta, MT. Call TNC, MT 406/443-6735.

UL BEND NATIONAL WILDLIFE REFUGE: 46,245-acres which are adjoined on three sides by the Charles M. Russell National Wildlife Refuge and are a part thereof (see Fergus County above). The NWR is managed to promote wildlife especially wildfowl. However, the rolling prairie supports prairie dog towns attracting coyotes, badgers, burrowing owls, golden eagles, ferruginous hawks and merlins during fall migration as well as prairie rattlesnakes, sage grouse and elk. Call the NWR at 406/538-8706.

Ravalli County:
WILLOUGHBY ENVIRONMENTAL EDUCATION AREA: This area contains sagebrush grassland and forest. The site is northeast of Bell Crossing, MT. Call the USFS at 406/777-5461.

Roosevelt County:
FORT UNION TRADING POST HISTORIC SITE: 462-acre historic site (See North Dakota). Built in 1828 on the prairie near the confluence of the Yellowstone and Missouri Rivers by John Jacob Astor's powerful American Fur Company, it hosted John James Audubon, George Catlin, Karl Bodmer and Prince Maximilean. Prairie still is seen looking north from the fort. Fort Union is 15-miles southeast of Bainville, MT; 21-miles north of Sidney, MT; 25-miles southwest of Williston, ND. The Historic Site sits astride the Montana/North Dakota state line. Call the Historic Site at 701/572-9083.

Rosebud County:
ROSEBUD BATTLEFIELD STATE PARK: 3,052-acres of short-grass prairie where on June 17, 1876 the Sioux and Cheyenne Indians fought General Crook's infantry and cavalry about 40-miles from the Little Bighorn where "General" George Armstrong Custer died 8 days later fighting the same nations. The Park is adjacent to the Crowe Reservation. Watch for rattlesnakes here. The park is south of Busby, MT off Hwy 314. Call the Park at 406/232-0900.

Sanders County:
NATIONAL BISON RANGE: (See Lake County above).

Sheridan County:
MEDICINE LAKE NATIONAL WILDLIFE REFUGE: 31,457-acres consisting of two units in the prairie pothole region. The north unit contains the 8,700-acre Medicine Lake plus eight other small lakes. The Homestead Unit consisting of the 1,280-acre Homestead Lake and adjacent uplands is a prairie refuge, located in the transition zone between

the mixed and short-grass prairies. The NWR has the largest white pelican rookery (9000+) in Montana and produces over 2,300 young in an average year. The NWR supports an active breeding population of endangered piping plovers. The native mixed-grass prairie is still largely intact and home to many native grassland bird species such as Baird's and LeConte's sparrows, Sprague's pipit, ferruginous hawks and burrowing owls. Refuge headquarters is located 1-mile south of Medicine Lake, MT and 2-miles east of Hwy 16. Call the NWR at 406/789-2305.

COMERTOWN POTHOLE PRAIRIE PRESERVE: 1,130-acre prairie in a rolling landscape of native grasses and shallow "pothole" lakes that were formed over 10,000 years ago by the great continental glaciers. Sometimes referred to as the Missouri Coteau, a name for the low glacial moraine that formed at the southern edge of the glacial front, this land represents the largest unplowed stretch of pothole prairie ecosystem left in the state of Montana. While the native prairie extends into North Dakota and Canada, agricultural plowing continues to destory many acres each year. The Preserve is approximately 15-miles northeast of Plentywood, MT. Call TNC, MT, at 406/443-0303.

NOTE! TNC, MT intends to step up its work in eastern Montana to preserve an area that it describes this way: "One-half of Eastern Montana holds perhaps the largest and most significant native grassland communities remaining in the Northern Great Plains. South of Malta, MT in the glaciated plains is an area of native mixed-grass prairie that supports black-tailed prairie dogs, swift fox, mountain plover, bison, and the black-footed ferret -- the rarest mammal in the world. Most likely, it is the largest remaining assemblage of these prairie species in the Northern Great Plains."

Sweetgrass County:
GREYCLIFF PRAIRIE DOG TOWN STATE PARK: 98-acres that supports a black-tailed prairie dog community with short-grass prairie and sagebrush. The park is located in southeast Montana, 9-miles east of Big Timber, MT off US 90 at the Greycliff Exit. Call the Park at 406/247-2940.

Teton County:
BLACKLEAF WILDLIFE MANAGEMENT AREA: 19,340-acres of woods, rolling prairies, and marsh. The WMA is west of Bynum, MT. Call MFWP at 406/444-3750.

PINE BUTTE SWAMP PRESERVE: 24,000-acres of lush wetlands and rolling prairies adjacent to Blackleaf Wildlife Management Area (see above) in the Rocky Mountain Front. Grizzly bears foraging for cow parsnip venture onto the prairie, as great numbers did when Lewis and

Clark passed through. Pine Butte Swamp (or fen) is an extensive peatland fed by mineral-rich groundwater that differs from other such fens in its proximity to mountains, foothills, and grasslands. Wetlands and dry ground, flat prairie and steep mountain areas meet in a geologic sweep ranging from 4,500 to 8,500 feet in elevation. This site is at the western border of the High Plains grassland edging up against cliffs and talus slopes, alpine meadows and montane forests. The result is a remarkably diverse flora including 40 distinct plant communities. This wealth of vegetation provides habitat for an equally diverse fauna including 43 species of mammals and 150 species of birds. Sharp-tailed grouse use the wet meadows on the swamp's periphery for their "dancing grounds." In short, this site is a wildlife bonanza. The Preserve is adjacent to the Pine Butte Guest Ranch in Choteau that offers workshops on the Blackfeet Indian nation, grizzly bears, birds of the prairies and Rockies, dinosaur digs and mammal tracking. For the Ranch, call 406/466-2158. Call TNC, MT about this and other preserves at 406/443-0303.

THE THEODORE ROOSEVELT MEMORIAL RANCH: 6,040-acre working ranch purchased by the Boone and Crockett Club in prime wildlife habitat along Dupuyer Creek on the East Front of the Montana Rockies. Theodore Roosevelt founded the club to conserve the country's natural wildlife resources. In 1995 the ranch created a watchable wildlife trail, which passes through such varied habitats as wet meadows, cottonwood river bottoms, rolling hills of short-grass prairie, and pine ridges, which visitors are welcome to experience. The ranch is southwest of Dupuyer, MT. Call the Boone and Crockett Club at 406/472-3380.

Valley County:
BITTER CREEK WILDERNESS STUDY AREA: 59,660-acres in an Area of Critical Environmental Concern (ACEC). Short-grass prairie supports prairie dog, considered an indicator species, and pronghorn, and mule deer, and nesting prairie falcons, ferruginous hawks, sage grouse and sharp-tailed grouse. Call the ACEC at 406/228-3750 or 3761.

SOUTH RANCH CONSERVATION EASEMENT: 151,789-acres (19,189-acres owned by Montana, the rest in easements) of sagebrush/grassland habitat that is being enhanced for wildlife. South Ranch is about 35-miles southwest of Glasgow, MT. Call MFWP in Billings, MT at 406/247-2940.

TAMPICO CONSERVATION EASEMENTS: 3,770-acres of sagebrush/grassland habitat that is being enhanced for wildlife. This site is about 11-miles west of Glasgow, MT, along the Milk River. Permission to visit must be obtained from South Ranch. Call MFWP in Billings, MT at 406/247-2940.

Fig 12
Little bluestem (with damselflies). It is the state grass of Nebraska. See Fig 2
for root structure.

Illustration by Charlotte Adelman

NEBRASKA

Nebraska's state song opens with the line: "Beautiful Nebraska, peaceful prairieland." The state's grass is little bluestem, its flower the goldenrod, and its bird is the western meadowlark. All of these are associated with the prairie. [Nebraska Game and Parks Commission (NGPC) 2200 North 33rd Street Lincoln, NE 68503 phone 402/471-0641.]

"The early settlers of Nebraska looked out from the little fringe of woods along the streams upon a treeless prairie. Natural prairie groves like those of Iowa and Illinois were lacking. The far-sighted fathers of this state studied and thought much upon this question. All the early speeches and the early newspapers are filled with the thought that the prairie must be plowed and trees must be planted and made to grow before the people would have homes where they would like to live and bring up their children," states "History and Stories of Nebraska" by Addison Erwin Sheldon.

Today it can be seen that those early Nebraskans got their way, for very little of that prairie exists. However, organizations are working to protect, preserve and restore what is left of that treeless prairie.

Below are some places where prairie can be seen in Nebraska:

Adams County:
HARVARD WATERFOWL PRODUCTION AREA: 1,848-acres of land with some being restored to native grassland. The site is northeast of Hastings, NE. Call the USFWS at 308/236-5015.

Antelope County:
ASHFALL FOSSIL BEDS STATE HISTORICAL PARK: 360-acres situated in an area of rugged rangeland in the scenic Verdigre Creek Valley with some prairie. Some 10 million years ago, hundreds of rhinos, three-toed horses, camels and other animals died and were buried by volcanic ash around the edge of a watering hole in what is now northeast Nebraska. The amazingly well preserved skeletons of these prehistoric beasts lay undisturbed, until the 1970s, when scientific study of the fossilized remains began. Visitors can watch the ongoing excavation of this unique "time capsule." A "Rhino Barn" protects part of the deposit, where skeletons are uncovered and displayed exactly where they are found. Nature trails are being developed to interpret the geology as well as the flora and fauna of the area. The Park is 6-miles north of US 20 between Royal, and Orchard, NE. Call the Park at 402/893-2000.

GROVE LAKE WILDLIFE MANAGEMENT AREA: 2,000-acres of sandhills prairie, bur oak woodlands and cropland. The WMA is located 2-miles north of Royal, NE. Call Nebraska Games and Parks Commission (NGPC) at 402/471-0641.

Arthur County:
ARAPAHO PRAIRIE: 1,298-acres of short-grass prairie in the Nebraska sandhills. Recently, a Eurasian weevil widely released by the U S and Canada to control alien thistles has attacked the preserve's native Platte and other native thistles, as well as those on Niobrara River Valley Preserve (see Cherry County below). The Prairie is 30-miles from Cedar Point Biological Station (See Keith County below). The University of Nebraska, School of Biological Sciences, operates this site. Call the school at 402/472-2729 or call TNC, NE at 402/342-0282.

Blaine County:
SANDHILLS ADVENTURE INC: A private grassland and prairie in the heart of the sandhill country for hunting prairie chicken and grouse along the Loup River located near Brewster, NE. Call 308/547-2450.

Boone County:
OLSON NATURE PRESERVE: 112-acres of oak woodland, sandhills prairie, wetlands, and a stretch of Beaver Creek. This preserve is historically significant as the site where Logan Fontenelle, Chief of the Omaha, was slain in an 1855 encounter with the Sioux. Artifacts from early inhabitants of the Great Plains have been discovered in and near the preserve. The area is being developed as an outdoor classroom for area schools. The site is north of Albion, NE. Call PPRI 402/694-5535.

Brown County:
KELLER PARK STATE RECREATIONAL AREA: 196-acre recreational area, with small areas of native prairie. The site is located on scenic Bone Creek, just west of US 183, and northeast of Ainsworth, NE. Typical of terrain found along the Niobrara River, this park is nestled amid rugged bluffs covered with oak, pine and cedar. Call the Park at 402/684-2921.

NIOBRARA RIVER VALLEY PRESERVE: (See Cherry County below).

PINE GLEN WILDLIFE MANAGEMENT AREA: 960-acres with creeks, mixed-grass prairie, and woods. The WMA is north of Long Pine, NE. Call the NGPC at 402/471-0641.

Buffalo County:
PEARL HARBOR SURVIVORS PRESERVE: 320-acres of native virgin prairie, restored prairie, and cropland used as a laboratory for the University of Nebraska-Kearney. The Preserve is north of Riverdale, NE. Call PPRI at 402/694-5535.

(LILLIAN ANNETTE) ROWE SANCTUARY: 1,150-acres with cropland, wetland and river front land; the sanctuary has approximately 300 or so acres of undisturbed prairie with another 200 or so acres being restored to prairie. The Sanctuary encompasses some of the best remaining crane habitat along the Platte River and is a major staging area each spring for hundreds of thousands of Sandhill Cranes. Late March is the best time to see waterfowl. The Sanctuary is on the Platte River southwest of Gibbon, NE. Call Audubon Nebraska at 308/468-5282.

Chase County:
ENDERS LAKE STATE RECREATIONAL AREA: 5,300-acres including the 1,707-acre lake. The Enders Wildlife Refuge encompasses 2,146-acres at the southwestern portion of the lake with some sandsage prairie. The site is south of Enders, NE. Call the NGPC at 402/471-0641.

Cherry County:
(ARTHUR) BOWRING SANDHILLS RANCH STATE HISTORICAL PARK: 7,200-acre park in the Mystic Prairie Hills that is preserved as a working ranch. The Ranch is located northeast of Merriman, NE. Call the Park at 308/684-3428.

FORT NIOBRARA NATIONAL WILDLIFE REFUGE: 19,131-acres of sand hill and mixed-grass prairie supporting buffalo, elk, black-tailed prairie dogs and burrowing owls with blinds for grouse viewing in the spring. The Niobrara River flows through the refuge forming a wooded canyon in the prairie. The Refuge's location permits the growth of both tall and short-grass prairie. Most animals found here historically are still present. The NWR is located 4-miles east of Valentine, NE off Hwy 12. Call the NWR at 402/376-3789.

(SAMUAL R.) MCKELVIE NATIONAL FOREST: 115,960-acre National Forest, which despite its name is mostly a combination of mixed-grass prairie, shallow wetlands and meadows on Steer Creek plus pine plantings. The forest is located 26-miles southwest of Valentine, NE off of Hwy 97 and immediately north of Merritt Reservoir State Recreational Area, a 2906-acre reservoir with surrounding grassland. The Forest is not far from the Valentine National Wildlife Area. (See below). Contact the National Forest at 402/823-4154. The Merritt Reservoir can be reached at 402/376-3320 or call the NGPC at 402/471-0641.

MERRITT RESERVOIR STATE RECREATIONAL AREA: (See McKelvie National Forest above).

NIOBRARA RIVER VALLEY PRESERVE: 60,550-acres of mainly prairie in central Nebraska plus 1,400-acres of buffer along the river, located at the eastern edge of the Sandhills. The Preserve is also in Brown and Keya Paha counties. Trails wander through tallgrass and mixed-grass prairies that are grazed by bison and inhabited by rattlesnakes. One can view sharp-tailed grouse from blinds. The Preserve is recognized as one of the premiere biological reserves in the Great Plains. It encompasses majestic pine-clad canyons, extensive grasslands, and a 25-mile stretch of the Niobrara River. To date, 581 plant, 213 bird, 86 lichen, 70 butterfly, 44 mammal, 25 fish, 17 reptile and 8 amphibian species have been recorded. The Preserve is 11-miles north of Johnstown, NE. Call TNC, NE at 402/342-0282.

SMITH FALLS STATE PARK: 252-acre park that is a naturally occurring biological museum. As the last glacier retreated north some 12,000 years ago, Nebraska's climate turned warmer and drier. The spruce and birch forest covering the state could not survive in this new climate and was replaced by prairie, except in canyons. In these spring-branch canyons, remnants of the Ice Age fauna and flora still persist including a northern birch community. Additionally there are forest communities, and mixed-grass prairie on tablelands north of the river and on the north valley slope. South of the valley is sandhills prairie. In this relatively short stretch of the Niobrara River Valley, 160 species of plants and animals are at the very edge of their distribution. The Park is 15-miles east of Valentine, NE. An entry permit is required. Call the Park at 402/376-1306.

VALENTINE NATIONAL WILDLIFE REFUGE: 72,000-acres of sandhill prairie supports prairie grouse, deer, badgers and waterfowl. The NWR lies in the heart of the Sandhills Region in north central Nebraska where there is the largest remaining tract of mixed-grass prairie in the US. The Refuge has been designated a National Natural Landmark. Grasses blanket the meadows and shield the dunes from the force of the wind and provide a degree of stability to the shifting sands. Numerous lakes, marshes, and grass-covered hills and meadows provide habitat for many kinds of wildlife. More than 260 species of birds are present. This a good place for bird and wildlife watching and photography. The NWR is located 20-miles south of Valentine, NE, along Hwy 83. The main office is located 5-miles east of the city of Valentine. Call the NWR at 402/376-3789.

Custer County:
PRESSEY WILDLIFE MANAGEMENT AREA: 1,566-acres of riparian woodlands, wetlands and mixed-grass prairie along with the South Loup River. The WMA is about 4-miles north of Oconto, NE on Co Hwy N21. Call the WMA at 402/471-0641.

Dawes County:
CHADRON STATE PARK: 977-acre park surrounded by the Pine Ridge Division of the Nebraska National Forest is mostly forest, but has some prairie patches. The Park is not far from Fort Robinson State Park and the Oglala National Grasslands (see below) and is located 9-miles south of Chadron, NE. Call the Park at 308/432-6167.

FORT ROBINSON STATE PARK: 22,673-acre park, supporting bison on the half that is short-grass prairie. The Park extends into Sioux County (see below) and is located 3-miles west of Crawford, NE. Call the Park at 308/665-2900.

OGLALA NATIONAL GRASSLAND: 94,300-acres of prairie supporting prairie dogs and antelope. The Grassland extends into Sioux County (see below) and to the South Dakota Border and adjacent to the Buffalo Gap National Grasslands and is near the Badlands National Park (see South Dakota below) and is 15-miles north of Harrison, NE. Present here is short-grass prairie, badlands topography and the Toadstool Park Geological Site. Call the Grassland at 308/432-4475.

Dixon County:
PONCA STATE PARK: 892-acres of heavily forested rolling hills with prairie ridgetops. The Park is 2-miles north of the town of Ponca, NE, just off Hwy 12 on S26E. Call the Park at 402/755-2284.

Douglas County:
ALLWINE PRAIRIE PRESERVE: 160-acre tallgrass prairie located about 12-miles northwest of the University of Nebraska-Omaha. The University is taking the lead in the "Glacier Creek Prairie Project," an effort to expand the present prairie to a total of 760+ acres of diverse habitat. The site will be a single, integrated and continuous gradient from upland prairies to lowland springs, wetlands and aquatic habitats. This site and the environmental study center situated adjacent to it, will significantly improve the university's ability to provide high-quality, in-depth environmental education to students and particularly to those enrolled in their Environmental Studies Program. The focus on an urban-based environmental study center, within 30 minutes of most Omaha residents, is critical to this project as it is expected to be particularly beneficial to this urban population, which represents a significant proportion of the total Nebraska population. Call the University of Nebraska at Omaha, Biological Science Dept, at 402/554-3378.

BOYER CHUTE NATIONAL WILDLIFE REFUGE: 3,500-acre refuge which is an extension of the DeSoto National Wildlife Refuge from Iowa (See Harrison County, Iowa). Call the DeSoto NWR at 712/642-4121.

JESEN PRAIRIE: 13-acres, the south half is virgin prairie (never plowed) and the north half is old farm field, which is being replanted using seeds harvested form the virgin prairie and seed collected from other local prairies. The preserve is available as a research study site for all students and scientists. The Prairie has many species of forbs and grasses along with grassland birds, such as bobolink. To visit this site located at 6720 Bennington Street near 72nd and McKinley in Omaha, NE contact the Audubon Society Omaha office at 402/445-4138.

NEALE WOODS NATURE CENTER: 554-acres of forest, ridges, ravines, and restored prairie. A trail winds through forest and prairie. The center is north of Omaha, NE on Edith Marie Ave. Call the Fontenelle Forest Association at 402/453-5615.

Fillmore County:
MALLARD HAVEN WATERFOWL PRODUCTION AREA: 1,087-acres with 633-acres of wetland and 454-acres of upland with some restored prairie. This site is northwest of Stickney, NE. Call the USFWS at 308/236-5015.

Gage County:
HOMESTEAD NATIONAL MONUMENT NATIONAL PARK: 100-acres of tallgrass prairie in the 160-acre park make up the second oldest restored tallgrass prairie in the US. (For the first see Curtis Prairie, Dade County, WI) Complete with a restored one-room schoolhouse in the prairie, the park was created to commemorate the Homestead Act of 1862. The Monument is located west of Beatrice, NE. Call the National Park Service (NPS) at 402/223-3514.

WILDCAT CREEK PRAIRIE: 30 or so acres of prairie near Virginia, NE. Call the Wachiska Audubon Society at 402/486-4846.

Garden County:
ASH HOLLOW STATE HISTORICAL PARK: 1,000-acres of mixed-grass prairie and contains archaeological evidence that early man seasonally exploited this site at least 6,000 years ago for its rich resources of wood, water, shelter, berries, and game animals. The Plains Indians also valued the area for its life sustaining resources, as did the pioneers traveling along the Oregon Trail during their westward migration. The bones of extinct mammals such as the prehistoric rhinoceros, mammoth, and mastodon, which grazed on the rich prairie grasses of the Great Plains 10,000 years ago, have been found within the park. The Park also contains a distinctive geological feature known as the Ash Hollow Formation. Visitors can glimpse a bit of geology, paleontology, history of early man, and the story of the great pioneer trek west, as well as see prairie here. The Park is approximately 4-miles south of Lewellen, NE on US Hwy 26. Call the Park at 308/778-5651.

CRESCENT LAKE NATIONAL WILDLIFE REFUGE: 45,818-acres of rolling grass-covered sandhills. This largest continuous dune area in America was created from the wind blown sands of an ancient sea. 21 lakes and ponds are supported by an aquifer lying below the hills. The grasslands range from the densely vegetated meadows to the sparsely covered "choppies" and support a wide variety of wildlife. The NWR is located at the juncture of the eastern and western, the cool season and warm season ecotones, producing a unique mixture of plants and wildlife species, which are a blend of east and west, north and south. The lenghtly NWR bird list makes it a good bird watching location. This NWR is one of the best shorebird areas in the Great Plains. The Refuge is north of Oshkosh, NE on Hwy 27. Call the NWR in Ellsworth, NE at 308/762-4893.

Hall County:
CRANE MEADOWS NATURE CENTER: 250-acres of prime river habitat where the Platte River's north channel forms the property's northern border, providing river access along with close-up viewing of wetland wildlife. The southern border is marked by a slough. Between these two very different riverine habitats lies an abundance of native prairie interspersed with areas of riparian forest. The Meadows is southwest of Grand Island, NE. Call the Center at 308/382-1820.

STUHR MUSEUM OF THE PRAIRIE PIONEER: 200-acre complex with a 7-acre restored mixed-grass prairie sitting on recovering prairie. The Museum is located near the intersection of US 281 & Hwy 34 southwest of Grand Island, NE. Call the Museum at 308/385-5316.

Hamilton County:
LINCOLN CREEK PRAIRIE AND TRAIL: 16-acre wayside area along Lincoln Creek north of Aurora, NE. The long-range goal is to create a 3-mile long creek corridor greenway connecting Streeter Park, The Leadership Center, and Pioneer Trails Recreation Area with a system of trails, prairies, and woodlands. Call PPRI at 402/694-5535.

MARIE RATZLAFF PRAIRIE PRESERVE: 30-acres of virgin tallgrass prairie in the northeast part of the county, near Hordville, NE. Call PPRI at 402/694-5535.

Harlan County:
HARLAN COUNTY LAKE: 23,100-acre lake (the 2nd largest in Nebraska) with a 75-mile shore line surrounded by mixed-grass prairie. The Lake is south of Hwy 136 between the towns of Alma and Republican, NE. Call the USCE at 308-799-2105.

Jefferson County:
ROCK CREEK STATION STATE HISTORICAL PARK: 500+ acres of virgin tallgrass hilltop prairie and wooded ravines with visible Oregon Trail wagon wheel routes. The Park is located 6-miles east of Fairbury, NE. Call the NGPC at 402/729-5777 or 402/471-0641.

Kearney County:
SPEIDELL ISLAND PRESERVE: 596-acre prairie preserve on Dover Island in the Platte River, southeast of Kearney, NE. Call TNC, NE in Omaha, NE at 402/342-0282.

Keya Paha County:
NIOBRARA RIVER VALLEY PRESERVE: (See Cherry County above).

THOMAS CREEK WILDLIFE MANAGEMENT AREA: 1,154-acres of woods and mixed-grass prairie. The WMA is southeast of Springview, NE. Call the NGPC at 402/471-0641.

Knox County:
NIOBRARA STATE PARK: 1,260-acres of sand hill prairies providing sweeping vistas on the South Dakota border. The Park is located southwest of Niobrara, NE. Call thePark at 402/857-3373.

Keith County:
CEDAR POINT BIOLOGICAL FIELD STATION: This is a unique facility with a major emphasis on the study of natural systems. The site is located in a diverse and scenic habitat just below Lake McConaughy near Ogallala, NE. Furthermore, the station is at the juncture of four major grassland systems: short-grass prairie, sand/sage prairie, mixed-grass prairie, and sand hills and provides exceptional opportunities for study of the Great Plains systems. The Nebraska Sandhills is the largest sand dune area in the Western Hemisphere and, unlike many other large dune areas, is not a desert, but grassland. An incredible 340 bird species have been observed in the area, a number unmatched by any comparable area north of Texas. The Station is northeast of Ogallala, NE and near Lake McConaughy. Contact the University of Nebraska, School of Biological Sciences at 402/472-2729.

Lancaster County:
KELLER NATURAL HISTORY AREA: 80-acre tract 19-miles from University of Nebraska-Lincoln that provides an area for long-term research on tallgrass prairie. Contact the University of Nebraska, School of Biological Sciences at 402/472-2729.

MAXWELL ARBORETUM, UNIVERSITY OF NEBRASKA-LINCOLN: 5-acre site on the East Campus has a 1-acre prairie. Call the Arboretum at 402/472-2679.

NINE MILE PRAIRIE: 260-acres of never-plowed tallgrass prairie researched and made famous by prairie ecologist, J E Weaver, the "founding father of modern plant ecology," who began his study of the prairie in 1917. Beginning in the 1920's, Weaver and his students at the University of Nebraska-Lincoln used this prairie for their pioneering studies in plant ecology. Today, this prairie is the longest-studied natural area in Nebraska and has 350 plant species, which host a rich variety of insects. Biological science professionals and interested citizens manage the Prairie to inhibit weeds and foster the growth of native species. The Prairie is located northwest of Lincoln, NE. The Prairie was named in the 1930s for its location exactly nine miles from the

Lincoln City Square. Contact the University of Nebraska, School of Biological Sciences at 402/472-2729.

PIONEER PARK NATURE CENTER: 192-acres located west of Lincoln, NE containing tallgrass prairie. The Nature Center, in the southwest corner of the park, features 4-miles of walking trails through native Nebraska prairie grasses, woodlands and wetlands. The Park is on Coddington, and W Van Dorn Aves in Lincoln, NE. Call the City at 402/441-7895.

SPRING CREEK PRAIRIE (formerly the O'Brien ranch): 626-acre nature center and preserve consists of mostly never-plowed tallgrass prairie with 3-feet deep wagon wheel ruts from the Nebraska City Cutoff on the Oregon Trail. Miles of walking trails allows visitors to step back in time and experience the feel of more than 500-acres of unplowed tallgrass prairie. The Prairie is located 3-miles south of Denton, NE. Call the Nebraska Audubon at 402/797-2301.

WILDERNESS PARK: 1,445-acres containing wooded areas and some prairie. This is Lincoln, Nebraska's largest park and features 22-miles of bridle and hiking/biking trails that begin in southwest Lincoln, NE at South First and Van Dorn Sts. Call the City at 402/441-7895.

Merrick County:
BADER MEMORIAL PARK: 200-acre park with a specially designated 80-acre natural area that includes a stretch of the Platte River, riparian woodlands, sandpits, and tallgrass prairie. The Park is east of Chapman, NE. Call Prairie Plains Resource Institute (PPRI) at 402/694-5535.

Morrill County:
CHIMNEY ROCK NATIONAL HISTORIC SITE: 80-acres of mixed-grass prairie separated from its 8-acre headquarters by a 560-acre privately owned scenic-easement protected prairie. This site is the most recognized landmark along the Oregon and Mormon trail, which thousands followed as they traveled to the West beginning in the late 1840s. The prairie supports rattlesnake, hognose snake, eagles, deer, pronghorn antelope and bobcat and is 3½-miles southwest of Bayard, NE. Call 308/586-2581.

Nemaha County:
INDIAN CAVE STATE PARK: (See Richardson County below).

Otoe County:
(HENRY) DIEKEN PRAIRIE: 15-acre tallgrass prairie located near Unadilla, NE. Call the Wachiska Audubon Society at 402/486-4846.

Pawnee County:
BURCHARD LAKE WILDLIFE MANAGEMENT AREA: 400-acres of

tallgrass prairie with prairie chicken booming grounds and a 160-acre lake. The WMA is northeast of Burchard, NE. Call NGPC at 402/471-0641.

PAWNEE PRAIRIE WILDLIFE MANAGEMENT AREA: 1,130-acres of tallgrass prairie and riparian woodland supports a resident flock of greater prairie chickens. The WMA is located southeast of Burchard, NE. Call NGPC at 402/471-0641.

Phelps County:
FUNK WATERFOWL PRODUCTION AREA: 1,989-acres with 1,163-acres of wetland and 826-acres of upland and some areas planted in native grasses. The site is northeast of Holdredge, NE. Call the USFWS at 308/236-5015.

Richardson County:
INDIAN CAVE STATE PARK: 3,000-acres with Native American rock carvings and some re-created prairie. The Park is located 4-miles east of Barada, NE, and extends into Nemaha County. Call the Park at 402/883-2575.

RULO BLUFF: 445-acres that preserves a distinctive mingling of shady hardwood forest giving rise to oaks and hickories, and a sun-drenched prairie of big bluestem and blazing star. Rarely do two such divergent landscapes converge so abruptly and dramatically as they do at this preserve. In fact, this site has one of Nebraska's best surviving savanna communities containing chinkapin oak and little bluestem. The Bluff is near Rulo, NE. Call TNC, NE at 402/342-0282.

Saunders County:
MADIGAN PRAIRIE: 20-acre tract of tallgrass prairie was a 1979 gift from Dr. Marian Madigan to the University of Nebraska to be maintained in perpetuity as a natural area for environmental education and research. Contact the University of Nebraska, School of Biological Sciences at 402/472-2729.

Scotts Bluff County:
BUFFALO CREEK WILDLIFE MANAGEMENT AREA: 2,880-acre mixed-grass prairie and woodland. The WMA is southwest of Melbeta, NE. Call the NGPC at 402/471-0641.

NORTH PLATTE NATIONAL WILDLIFE REFUGE: 2,909-acre refuge that offers a migratory stopover for concentrations of up to 200,000 ducks. The refuge is superimposed over four Bureau of Land Reclamation projects: Lake Minatare Unit, Winters Creek Unit, Lake Alice Unit, and Stateline Island Unit. Approximately 1,000-acres are being restored as prairie. The NWR is situated 8-miles north of Minatare, NE and 10-miles northwest of the Scotts Bluff National

Monument (see below). Call the NWR at 308/635-7851.

SCOTTS BLUFF NATIONAL MONUMENT: 3,100-acre park contains what was a prominent natural landmark for emigrants on the Oregon Trail, Scotts Bluff, Mitchell Pass, and includes the adjacent prairie lands. This site preserves the memory of the historic Oregon, California and Mormon Trails. Short-grass prairie, ponderosa pine woodlands, badlands and an interpretive center are present at this site. The Monument overlooks the North Platte River and is just south of Scottsbluff, NE on US 26. Call the Monument at 308/436-4340.

Seward County:
TWIN LAKES WILDLIFE MANAGEMENT AREA: 1,270-acres of tall-grass prairie remnants re-seeded warm-season grass and the twin lakes. The WMA is northeast of Milford, NE. Call the NGPC at 402/471-0641.

Sheridan County:
METCALF WILDLIFE MANAGEMENT AREA: 3,068-acres of mixed-grass prairie and wooded canyons. The WMA is north of Hay Springs, NE. Call the NGPC at 402/471-0641.

Sioux County:
AGATE FOSSIL BEDS NATIONAL MONUMENT: 3,150-acre National Monument preserves Agate Fossil Beds and surrounding sandhills prairie. Once part of "Captain" James H. Cook's Agate Springs Ranch, the nearby beds are an important source for 19.2 million year-old Miocene epoch mammal fossils. The Monument is located south of Harrison, NE. Call the park at 308/668-2211.

FORT ROBINSON STATE PARK: (See Dawes County above).

OGLALA NATIONAL GRASSLANDS: (See Dawes County above).

SIOUX COUNTY RANCH: 5,000-acre working ranch that includes wetlands, needlegrass/threadleaf sedge prairie, rocky buttes, and Niobrara River headwaters. The Ranch is near Harrison, NE. Call PPRI at 402/694-5535.

SOLDIER CREEK WILDERNESS: 8,100-acre area was part of the Fort Robinson Military Reservation and used as a horse and mule pasture, a supply area for wood products and a recreation area for military personnel stationed at the fort. This area represents an environment characteristic of the Pine Ridge escarpment in northwest Nebraska. The ponderosa pine covered ridges give way to open upland parks containing native grasses such as western wheatgrass, prairie sandreed, big bluestem and little bluestem. Between July 8 and July 14 1989, the 48,000-acre Fort Robinson Fire burned the Wilderness and state and private lands west of Fort Robinson. The wildfires effect will be observed for years to come, because the Wilderness will be allowed to recover naturally. The Wilderness is west of Crawford, NE and must be entered through Fort Robinson State Park (see Dawes County above). Call the USFS at 308/432-4475.

Stanton County:
WOOD DUCK WILDLIFE MANAGEMENT AREA: 629-acres of wetlands, cottonwood flood plain, and grassy areas planted to native species and food plots. The WMA is southeast of Norfolk, NE. Call the NGPC at 402/370-3374.

Thomas County:
NEBRASKA NATIONAL FOREST-BESSEY DISTRICT: 90,444-acres of gently rolling sand hills prairie interspersed with 20,000-acres of man-planted tress and marked hiking trails. The Forest is located 2-miles west of Halsey, NE on Co Hwy N2. Call the Nebraska National Forest at 308/432-0300.

Thurston County:
OMAHA RESERVATION: 225-sq miles on former prairie now leased out for corn, beans and alfalfa. Along the Missouri River lies Blackbird Hill, the mound in which the infamous Omaha Chief Blackbird is buried, but it has passed out of Indian ownership. Call the Reservation at 402/837-5391.

Thayer County:
MERIDIAN WILDLIFE MANAGEMENT AREA: 400-acre area with some native grasses. The WMA is southwest of Alexandria, NE. Call the NGPC at 402/729-5777 or 402/471-0641.

Washington County:
FORT ATKINSON STATE HISTORICAL PARK: 157-acre park that was an important site for Lewis and Clark's encounters with the Indians, in the expansion of the fur trade, and in the early river traffic on the mighty Missouri River. Telling that story through reconstruction and interpretation is an awesome task that is being undertaken by the Nebraska Games and Parks Commission (NGPC). An interpretive trail runs through the prairie. The Park is located southeast of Blair, NE on US Hwy 75. Call the Park at 402/468-5611.

CUMING CITY CEMETERY PRAIRIE AND NATURE PRESERVE: 11-acre cemetery remnant of native prairie that reminds the viewer of a city that died after being bypassed by the railroad. This tract of land was set-aside in 1976 primarily as a preserve for native vegetation. The never plowed prairie looks much as it did to the Indians and to the first white men who settled Nebraska in the 1850's. The Cemetery is northwest of Blair, NE. Call Dana College at 402/426-9000 or 800/444-3262.

DESOTO NATIONAL WILDLIFE REFUGE: 8,000-acres located on a wide plain along the Missouri River bottoms. Ongoing restoration has converted 1,200-acres of cornfields to tallgrass prairie. The NWR lies midway between Blair, NE and Missouri Valley, IA on US 30. (See Boyer Chute National Wildlife Refuge in Douglas County above) Call the NWR at 712/642-2772.

Webster County:
(WILLA) CATHER MEMORIAL PRAIRIE: 610-acre prairie along the Nebraska-Kansas border preserves an example of the native grassland that once covered much of Nebraska. Typical prairie plants and animals flourish as they did before the first settlers arrived. This mixed-grass prairie, with sparsely wooded draws, described by some range ecologists as "Kansas Prairie," is located 5-miles south of Red Cloud, NE. Call TNC, NE at 402/342-0282 or the Nebraska Historical Society at 800/833-6747.

Fig 13
Stiff Goldenrod (with butterflies). See Fig 2 for typical prairie plant root structure.

Illustration by Charlotte Adelman

NEW MEXICO

New Mexico is the most westerly limit of the Great Plains so the eastern portion of the State is the most likely place to see prairie remnants. However, the most southern portion of the state also has native grasslands, which are officially designated as desert grasslands but have a lot in common with the prairie. Many of the same plants found in the prairie are found in the desert grasslands so this anthology has included some of those areas. The state grass is a short-grass prairie grass: Blue Grama Grass.

Below are some of the areas where prairie or other grasslands can be seen in New Mexico:

Chaves County:
BITTER LAKE NATIONAL WILDLIFE REFUGE: 24,500-acres of native grasses, sand dunes, brushy bottomlands, seven lakes, and a red-rimmed plateau containing habitat types ranging from a saline playa lake and wetland areas to short-grass prairie and desert uplands. The Refuge plays an important role in ecosystem management by protecting native grasslands and rare springs and streams along the corridor of the Pecos River and includes the 9,620-acre Salt Creek Wilderness Area. This is the only known nesting area in New Mexico for the interior least tern. The Refuge is located northeast of Roswell, NM on Pine Lodge Road. Call Ken Butts, Manager of the Refuge at 505/622-6755.

CAPROCK WILDLIFE HABITAT AREA: 645,800-acres much of which is short-grass prairie, 260,500-acres are public lands and the remainder is privately held, but managed by the Bureau of Land Management (BLM). To view the lesser prairie chickens at Mescalero Sands (see below) one must enter Caprock.

MESCALERO SANDS: This site has been divided into 4 units by the BLM. One is Caprock Wildlife Habitat Area (see above). Another is the 6,173-acre Mescalero Sands Outstanding Natural Area, that can only be viewed on foot and where one has the opportunity to see the lesser prairie chicken and its courtship ritual in a short-grass prairie setting. The other 2 units are the 241-acre Mathers Research Natural Area, and the 610-acre Mescalero Sands North Dune OHV (off-highway vehicle) Area. The Sands is 40-miles east of Roswell, NM. Call the BLM at 505/627-0270.

SALT CREEK WILDERNESS AREA: This area is the north tract of the three tracts that make up the Bitter Lake NWR (see above). Salt Creek itself runs through the center of the Wilderness, an area of native grassland, sand dunes, brushy bottomlands, and a northern boundary distinguished by its red-rimmed plateau, all just west of the Pecos River. See Bitter Lake NWR ab ove for location and contact information.

199

Colfax County:
KIOWA NATIONAL GRASSLANDS: 263,954-acres includes part of the Canadian River canyon west of Mills, New Mexico, a rugged 900-foot-deep canyon forming a wildlife habitat island in the prairie for mule deer, bear, Barbary sheep, Siberian Ibex, ducks and geese. The grasslands in New Mexico, Oklahoma and Texas are characteristically flat with some rolling low hills. The exception is the Kiowa National Grassland, which is bisected by the Canadian River Canyon. This grassland has no established or marked trails, and is part of the Cibola National Forest. The grassland extends into Harding and Mora Counties. Another section is located in Union County connected to the Rita Blanca National Grasslands (see below). This section is located near Mills, NM off Hwy 39. Call the Grassland at 505/374-9652.

MAXWELL NATIONAL WILDLIFE REFUGE: 3,000-acres of gently rolling prairie, playa lakes, and farmland managed for waterfowl. Several lakes on the refuge provide approximately 700-acres of roosting and feeding habitat for waterfowl. During wet years, the shoreline vegetation of the lakes is dense enough to aid waterfowl nesting. During dry years, the constantly changing shoreline is beneficial to shorebirds. The NWR is located southwest of Raton, NM. Call Dan Dinkler, Refuge Manager at 505/375-2331.

Dona Ana County:
DRIPPING SPRINGS NATURAL AREA: 2,850-acres where the Chihuahuan desert grasslands meet the Organ Mountains a dramatic locale of immense boulders, rocky peaks, narrow canyons, and open woodlands. The NA located east of Las Curces, NM. There is a $3/day fee. Call the BLM at 505/525-4300 or TNC, NM at 505/988-3867.

Harding County:
KIOWA NATIONAL GRASSLANDS: (See Colfax County above).

Hidalgo County:
THE GRAY RANCH: 321,000-acres spanning more than 50 natural communities, and containing more than 700 species of plants, 75 mammals, 50 reptiles and amphibians and more than 170 species of breeding birds. This site lies in a unique area of the county called the Sky Islands. Here, tall mountain ranges, northern extensions of Mexico's Sierra Madre Occidental, rise high above the grasslands of the Chihuahuan Desert. This landscape is home to the Mexican jaguar, Aplomado falcon, Baird's sparrow, white-sided jackrabbit, and pronghorn. The Ranch is 200-miles east of Tucson, AR and 200-miles west of El Paso, TX. Call TNC, NM in Santa Fe, NM at 505/988-3867.

Mora County:
KIOWA NATIONAL GRASSLANDS: (See Colfax County above).

Rio Arriba County:
EDWARD SARGENT FISH AND WILDLIFE AREA: 20,208-acres bordering the Chama River south of the New Mexico/Colorado state line. The WA holds a major portion of the Chamita River Valley and forms a broad basin of grassland and wildflowers, which provide excellent habitat for deer and elk. The WA is located just west of Chama, NM. Call the New Mexico Dept of Game & Fish at 505/827-7882.

Roosevelt County:
GRULLA NATIONAL WILDLIFE REFUGE: 3,236-acres with more than 2,000-acres in the saline lakebed of Salt Lake and the remainder grassland. Lesser prairie chickens can be seen here. The refuge is southeast of Portales, NM on the Texas border. Call Don Clapp, Manager Muleshoe NWR at 806/946-3341.

San Miguel County:
LAS VEGAS NATIONAL WILDLIFE REFUGE: 8,672-acres situated on the Great Plains where the prairie meets the Rocky Mountains. The NWR consists of native grassland, cropland, marshes, ponds, forested canyons, and streams. Las Vegas (Spanish for "the meadows") is as rich in history as New Mexico itself. Native Americans used the area for hunting, camping, and picking wild fruit. Coronado's journey into the southwest brought a Spanish influence and culture that is as prevalent today as it was 300 years ago. The golden eagle and the prairie falcon, among other birds use this refuge, as do mule deer, antelope, badger, coyote, and bobcat. The Refuge is located 6-miles southeast of Las Vegas, NM. Call Joe Rodriguez, Manager of the NWR at 505/425-3581.

Socorro County:
SEVILLETA NATIONAL WILDLIFE REFUGE: 229,700-acres managed as a Research Natural Area. The refuge has a wide range of ecosystem types, including Chihuahuan Desert, Great Plains Grassland, Great Basin Shrub-Steppe, Piñon-Juniper Woodland, Bosque Riparian Forests and Wetlands, Ponderosa Pine Forests, Mixed-Conifer Montane Forests, and Sub-alpine Forests and Meadows. Management is devoted to restoring the NWR to its turn of the century natural conditions. Native animals and a plethora of birds and reptiles are becoming more abundant and visible. A Mexican wolf captive management facility on the refuge enables this endangered species to acclimate, while in large pens to their historical habitat. Some of the wolves are candidates to be released into the wild in other parts of the southwest. A 22-mile driving loop enables wildlife viewing. The Refuge is located in the Chihuahuan desert 20-miles north of Socorro, NM. Call Terry Tadano, Manager of Sevilleta NWR at 505/864-4021.

Union County:
CAPULIN VOLCANO NATIONAL MONUMENT: 793-acre park with

the volcano, grasslands and forest surrounded by the high plains of northeast Montana. The park is north of Capulin, NM on Hwy 325. Call the Monument at 505/278-2201.

CLAYTON LAKE STATE PARK: Set among rolling grasslands, one can walk a ½-mile to the lake's spillway and see the internationally significant dinosaur trackway, containing more than 500 footprints dating back more than 100 million years. The Park is located southwest of Seneca, NM. Call the New Mexico State Parks at 1-888-NMPARKS.

KIOWA AND RITA BLANCA NATIONAL GRASSLAND: 229,327-acres of grassland is part of a 4-unit, restoration project. Originally plowed for farming, because of poor topsoil and other factors, it became part of the Great Plains dust bowl. It is also the Certified Site of the Santa Fe National Historic Trail. A two-mile section of the SFT Cimarron Route, identified by limestone posts, has been preserved here in this largely re-vegetated national grassland. Here can be found black tailed prairie dogs, prairie chickens, bobcat, black bear, pronghorn, mule deer and red and gray fox. The Rita Blanca National Grassland includes 77,463-acres in Texas and 15,860-acres in Oklahoma. This grassland is located northeast of Clayton, NM. Call the Grassland in Clayton, NM at 505/374-9652.

NEW YORK
Not a prairie state, although at one time tallgrass prairie extended east as far as the "Prairie Peninsula" into extensive areas of Illinois, parts of western Indiana, isolated areas of central Ohio, and western Pennsylvania, and, finally, across the New York lowlands to the Pine Bush near Albany, and south into the Hudson River valley to Long Island in the Hempstead Plains.

Below are some areas in New York that resemble prairie:

Jefferson County:
CHAUMONT BARRENS: 1,620-acres created by the retreating glaciers about 10,000 years ago support globally rare prairie plant communities. Spring floods and summer droughts prevent trees, so grassland birds thrive, safe from cats and lawn mowers. Call TNC, NY in Rochester, NY at 716/546-8030.

Monroe County:
RUSH OAK OPENINGS: 105-acres of rare oak opening, grassy, savanna-like landscape. Call TNC, NY at 716/546-8030.

Nassau County:
HEMPSTEAD PLAINS: 67-acres of prairie grassland that once covered 60,000 New York acres. Call TNC, Long Island Chapter, at 631/367-3225.

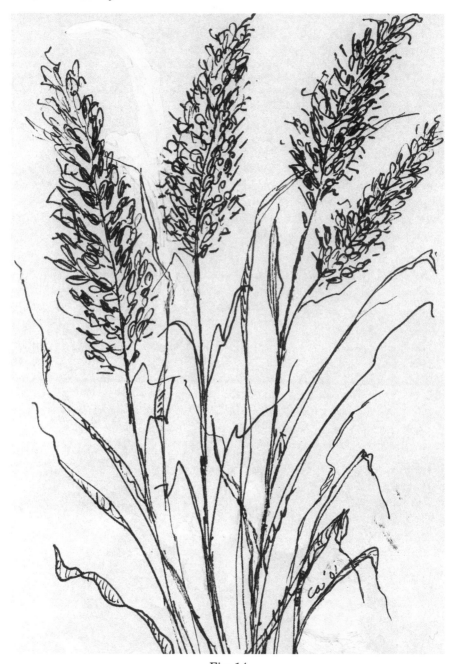

Fig 14

Indian Grass - the state grass of Oklahoma. See Fig 2 for root structure.

Illustration by Charlotte Adelman

NORTH DAKOTA

"Before Euro-American settlement of the Northern Plains began in the 19th Century, the land had been occupied for many centuries. Archeological investigations document the presence of big game hunting cultures after the retreat of the continental glaciers about 10,000 years ago and later settlements of both hunting and gathering and farming peoples dating ca. 2000 B.C. to 1860. When the first white explorers arrived, distinct Indian groups existed in what is now North Dakota. These included the Dakota or Lakota nation (called "Sioux" or "enemies"by those who feared them), Assiniboine, Cheyenne, Mandan, Hidatsa, and Arikara. Groups of Chippewa (or Ojibway) moved into the northern Red River valley around 1800, and Cree, Blackfeet, and Crow frequented the western buffalo ranges.

"These peoples represented two different adaptations to the plains environment. Nomadic groups depended primarily upon vast herds of American Bison for the necessities of life. When the horse was brought to the Northern Plains in the 18th Century, the lives of the Dakota, Assiniboine, and Cheyenne changed dramatically. These bands quickly adapted to the *horse,* and the new mobility enabled them to hunt with ease and consequently to live better than ever before. The horse became a hallmark of Plains cultures, and the images of these mounted Indians bequeathed a romantic image of power and strength that has survived in story, films, and songs. In contrast, the sedentary Mandan, Hidatsa, and Arikara lived in relatively permanent earthlodges near the Missouri River and supplemented produce from extensive gardens with hunting; their fortified villages became commercial centers that evolved into trading hubs during the fur trade of the 18th and 19th centuries.

"Indians and Euro-Americans came into contact during the 18th Century. The first recorded visitor was La Verendrye, a French explorer who reached the Missouri River from Canada in 1738 while searching for a water route to the Pacific Ocean. American settlement of the Northern Plains commenced in earnest after 1861, when the Dakota Territory was organized by Congress." The above excerpt is from "North Dakota History: Overview and Summary," by Larry Remele, Education & Interpretation Division, State Historical Society of North Dakota.

Before the settlers came, North Dakota was almost entirely grassland (prairie) and even today much of it remains prairie in varying states of degradation. Those areas being farmed, of course, have no native prairie, but those areas that have been grazed have more or less the same prairie plants that existed when only the Plains Indians were here.

"North Dakota prairie is starting to get the respect it deserves," comments Gerald Reichert of TNC, North Dakota. Many prairie areas exist in North Dakota and the State or the Federal Government owns many. Prairies exist in National Grasslands, National Wildlife Refuges,

Wildlife Management Areas and State Parks. This state preserves prairies for their beauty, environmental reasons, and for recreation, hunting and grazing. This mixed-use gets many people, who might not otherwise be, interested in protecting natural areas. However, this mixed-use causes conflict. It is not clear that these mixed-uses might not do more harm than good in protecting and restoring a prairie. TNC and others are involved in protecting and restoring prairie; call TNC in Bismark, ND at 701/222-8464.

North Dakota's state flower is the wild prairie rose, a prairie shrub. The state bird is the western meadowlark, one of the prairie's characteristic birds, which prefers dry grasslands. The state grass is the western wheatgrass, a tough prairie grass.

Adams County:
DOG TOWN WILDLIFE MANAGEMENT AREA: 37-acre prairie 11-miles north and 5-miles east of the junction of Hwy 8 and US 12 with a prairie dog town. Call the ND, Game and Fish Dept (NDGF) at 701/744-4320.

Benson County:
SULLYS HILL NATIONAL GAME PRESERVE: 1,674-acres containing a mixture of forest and native prairie ecosystems essential for its wildlife. It has a buffalo herd started from six animals managed at a population of 30-35 animals, along with an elk herd, a white-tailed deer population, and a prairie dog town.

Artifacts of historic and prehistoric origin were discovered, leading to the 1980 inclusion of this site in the National Register of Historic Places. The combination of the lake, woodlands, and prairie ecosystems provided a diverse group of resources for two prehistoric cultures. The earliest artifacts date to the Middle Woodland Culture, perhaps 1,800 years old, and suggest a focus on seasonal big game, primarily bison, hunting. An auto-tour route, picnic area, and nature trail are available to the public at no charge. The Preserve is located 1-mile east of Fort Totten, ND. Call the Sullys Hill manager at 701/766-4272.

Billings County:
THE LITTLE MISSOURI NATIONAL GRASSLANDS-MEDORA RANGER DISTRICT: 524,685-acres of National Grassland, (Federally owned land), intermingled with approximately 723,354-acres of private and state land. Rolling hills accented by woody draws, and scenic buttes are characteristic of the District. The Little Missouri River, a State Scenic River, meanders through the badlands, carving and exposing colorful geologic layers. Old homestead and Native American sites provide an abundance of archeological sites. "General" Custer marched through the District on his way to the Little Big Horn. The

south unit of Theodore Roosevelt National Park headquartered in Medora, ND is nearly in the center of the District. The Medora Ranger District has worked with Ducks Unlimited (DU) on several projects to provide habitat for waterfowl and other wetland species. An unusual burning Coal Vein is located in the grasslands (see Slope County). The grassland extends into Dunn, Golden Valley, McKinzie, and Slope Counties. The city of Medora, ND is centrally located for the Medora Unit and the southern unit of the Theodore Roosevelt National Park. Call the Medora Ranger District at 701/225-5151.

THEODORE ROOSEVELT NATIONAL PARK: 70,446.89-acres described in 1883 by Theodore Roosevelt as a "land of vast silent spaces" provide a glimpse of the dry and mixed prairie as he saw it. The bison herd carves trails, and the site supports elk, wild horse, prairie dog and badger plus long-horned cattle. The park was created to memorialize Theodore Roosevelt's contribution to public land management and conservation, and to preserve the environment of the Little Missouri Badlands. The Park is divided into two units, the North Unit located in McKenzie Co. and the Elkhorn Unit located in Billings Co. Each unit is associated with the Little Missouri National Grasslands. The North Unit is south of Watford, ND. The Elkorn Ranch Unit is north of Medora, ND. Call NPS North Unit at 701/842-2333. The South Unit can be reached at 701/623-4466.

Bowman County:
CEDAR RIDGE: 1,900-acres that lies at the eastern margin of the Big Gumbo, where a bedrock warp results in the largest exposure of "gumbo" shale in the state. It is also at the far northeastern edge of the extensive sagebrush plains of the western United States. Big Gumbo ranks among the state's most inhospitable blocks of land, and Cedar Ridge captures its character. Big Gumbo epitomizes a stark western beauty with resilient life forms that endure the harsh environment, with expanses of woody sage, barren eroding ridges and patches of buffalograss interspersed in a sparse mixed-grass prairie setting. The site is located 18-miles south of Marmarth, ND on west River Road. Call the BLM at Dickinsin, ND at 701/225-9148.

Burke County:
CROSBY WETLANDS MANAGEMENT DISTRICT: 17,000-acres of Waterfowl Production Areas (WPAs), including over 66,000-acres of wetlands under easement contracts and the 3,219-acre Lake Zahl National Wildlife Refuge (see Williams County below). One is encouraged to explore the prairie world of the WPA's. Please remember, all motorized vehicles are restricted to section line roads or trails. The WMD is also in Divide and Williams Counties. Most of the WMD is on privately owed land. Call the WMD in Crosby, ND at 701/965-6488.

DES LACS NATIONAL WILDLIFE REFUGE: 19,500-acres along the Des Lacs River from the Canadian border to a point 8-miles south of Kenmare, ND. A mix of natural lakes and managed wetlands in the valley provide a haven for migrating and nesting waterfowl and marsh birds. Autumn has brought as many as 500,000 snow geese to this refuge. Remnants of the vast native prairie are found on hillsides above the river. In summer, birdwatchers can glimpse grasshopper sparrow, Baird's, and other prairie sparrows, Sprague's pipit, and northern harrier. The NWR extends into Ward County. Call the NWR in Kenmare, ND at 701/385-4046.

LOSTWOOD NATIONAL WILDLIFE REFUGE: 26,747-acres of virgin prairie with numerous wetlands creates a feeling for our historical past. A few aspen groves and saline lakes add a sprinkle of diversity that is pleasing to the eye. This habitat diversity attracts a unique variety of native migrant and resident wildlife. Bird enthusiasts enjoy the abundant grasshopper sparrow, Baird's sparrow, and Sprague's pipit and the less common sedge wren, LeConte's and sharp-tailed sparrows. Different prairie species bloom about every other week, providing a continuous display of colors. As autumn approaches, the native grasses turn from greens to soft oranges, purples, pinks and tans. The Refuge extends into Mountrail County. The NWR is located 16-miles north of Stanley, ND, on Hwy 8. Call the NWR in Kenmore, ND at 701/848-2722.

Burleigh County:
LONG LAKE NATIONAL WILDLIFE REFUGE: 22,300-acres, of which 16,000-acres are lake bottom, with rolling prairie and cultivated uplands on the remaining 6,300-acres. About 500 upland acres are cultivated to provide food and nesting habitat for migratory and nesting birds and resident wildlife. The NWR extends into Kidder and Emmons Counties. The NWR is located near Moffit, ND. Call the NWR Manager in Moffit, ND at 701/387-4397.

MCKENZIE SLOUGH WILDLIFE MANAGEMENT AREA: 680-acres of grassland, cropland, and wetland. The WMA is located Sterling, ND. Call NDGF at 701/324-2211.

Cavalier County:
PEMBINA GORGE: 3,900-acres of mostly woods, interspersed with a mosaic of shrubland, prairie, and wetland types. The cobble-lined Pembina River threads a winding path through the valley floor. This broad spectrum of habitats and environmental extremes gives rise to some of the highest diversity of plant and animal life in the state. The Gorge is home to North Dakota's only naturally occurring herd of elk. The site has more than 75 species of breeding birds including 11 of the state's 14 breeding warblers and more than 480 species of plants,

which comprise a third of North Dakota's total flora. The Gorge is located west of Walhalla, ND and is very difficult to find. Call the NDGF, District Office, Devils Lake, ND at 701/662-3617.

Dickey County:
JOHNSON GULCH WILDLIFE MANAGEMENT AREA: 1,400-acres of native prairie dominate, but the ravines and wetlands support a variety of other species. The view eastward from the hilltops is of 12,000-acres of Drift Prairie that resemble the area when large herds of wild animals grazed on the plain below. One can see bison bones from Indian stampedes, which remain imbedded at the gulch bottom, and burial mounds and stone teepee rings. The WMA is located southeast of the intersection of Hwys 11 & 56. Call NDGF at 701/324-2211.

Divide County:
CROSBY WETLANDS MANAGEMENT DISTRICT: (See Burke County above).

Dunn County:
LAKE ILO NATIONAL WILDLIFE REFUGE: The refuge habitat is made up of native prairie, planted grasslands, and wetlands. Gently sloping hills and terraces with creeks and an occasional slough characterize the uplands. The average rainfall of 16.8 inches supports a prairie environment. This NWR's archeological finds date back 11,000 years. The Refuge is located near Dunn Center, ND. Call the NWR in Dunn Center, ND 701/548-8110.

THE LITTLE MISSOURI NATIONAL GRASSLANDS-MEDORA RANGER DISTRICT: (See Billings County above).

LITTLE MISSOURI STATE PARK: 6,000-acres of dry mixed-grass prairie home to mule deer, bobcat, prairie falcon and bald eagle. The park is located in a rugged area of jagged outcrops and barren slopes formed thousands of years ago, when the course of the Little Missouri River was permanently directed eastward by glaciers. The rerouted river boldly carved the soft sediments over which it flowed, resulting in a valley over 500 feet deep and created intricate scenery unparalleled in North Dakota. The }ark encompasses 5,900-acres of land in the deepest, most distinctive segment of the Little Missouri River Valley. Its physical beauty is both inspiring and imposing, as buttes, ravines, plateaus, and crevices blend to cast abstract landforms against the horizon. The Park is located northeast of Kildeer, ND. Call the North Dakota Parks and Recreation (NDPR) at 701/794-3731.

Eddy County:
LAKE WASHINGTON WILDLIFE MANAGEMENT AREA: 910-acres with about 150-acres of prairie located 6-miles south of Warwick, ND. Call NDGF at 701/324-2211.

Emmons County:
LONG LAKE NATIONAL WILDLIFE REFUGE: (See Burleigh County above).

Foster County:
(GEORGE) KARPEN MEMORIAL WILDLIFE MANAGEMENT AREA: 480-acre WMA with about 430 prairie acres located 6-miles west and 8-miles south of Carrington, ND. Call NDGF at 701/324-2211.

Golden Valley County:
THE LITTLE MISSOURI NATIONAL GRASSLANDS-MEDORA RANGER DISTRICT: (See Billings County above).

Grand Forks County:
FOREST RIVER BIOLOGY AREA: 160-acres encompassing the broad river valley of the Forest River, with approximately 120-acres of gallery forests and 40-acres of prairie and old fields. The south branch of the Forest River has cut through the beaches of glacial Lake Agassiz and carved a broad, densely wooded valley. The site is northwest of Inkster, ND. Call the Department of Biology, University of North Dakota (UND), Grand Forks, ND at 701/777-2621 or the general UND No at 800-CALL-UND.

KELLY'S SLOUGH NATIONAL WILDLIFE REFUGE: A 500 sq mile area of upland grasslands and wetland habitat has a prairie chicken re-introduction site. The NWR is located 8-miles west of Grand Forks, ND. For more information, call the NWR at 701/662-8611 ext 329.

OAKVILLE PRAIRIE: 800-acre remnant of the Red River Valley grasslands. The original grasslands of the Red River Valley, destroyed by sod-busting, persisted in a few sites as school sections set aside hayland for the benefit of the public schools of the state. One of these virgin prairie sites constitutes the main portion of an 800-acre field station of the University of North Dakota. The station is named Oakville Prairie because it is located in Oakville Township of Grand Forks County. Located on the relatively flat landscape of the Red River Valley, this prairie has developed on a thick and productive black soil representing nearly 10,000 years of decomposed vegetation since the departure of glacial Lake Agassiz. These soils support a colorful variety of prairie grasses and forbs. 236 species of vascular plants have been recorded from this site. Prairie animals here include 21 species of mammals, 40 species of nesting birds, 3 species of amphibians, 1 species of reptile (plains garter snake), and 23 species of ants. The Prairie is located southeast of Emerado, ND. Call the University of North Dakota Biology Department in Grand Forks at 701/777-2621.

TURTLE RIVER STATE PARK: 784-acres located on the Turtle River and north of Arvilla, ND on Hwy 2. Much of the area is wooded with mixed hardwood stands, timbered hills and lush river bottoms and an open prairie area with emerging native grasses, and wetland in the south section of the park. In spring and autumn, thousands of migratory waterfowl pass over and through the park. Call NDPR in Bismarck, ND at 701/328-5357.

Grant County:
CEDAR RIVER NATIONAL GRASSLAND: 6,700-public acres, with additional private acres in Sioux County (see below), of mixed-grass prairie supporting white tail and mule deer, pronghorn and grouse that mingle with introduced pheasant and cattle. The Grassland is situated along the North Dakota/South Dakota border in southwestern North Dakota. The land ownership is widely scattered and all but 400-acres lay within the Standing Rock Sioux Reservation boundary. This grassland abuts and is part of the Standing Rock Sioux Reservation and is south of Leith, ND. Call the managers of the Grassland at the Grand River Range Office in Lemmon, SD at 605/374-3592.

Kidder County:
DAWSON WILDLIFE MANAGEMENT AREA: 2,950-acres of grassland, former farmland, and trees. The WMA is south of Dawson, ND on Hwy 3. Call NDGF at 701/324-2211.

THE CHASE LAKE PRAIRIE PROJECT: (See Stutsman County below).

LONG LAKE NATIONAL WILDLIFE REFUGE: (See Burleigh County above).

Logan County:
MOLDENHAUER WATERFOWL PRODUCTION AREA: 600-acres of wetland and grassland. The area is located southeast of Gackle, ND. Call the USFWS at 701/647-2866.

McHenry County:
MCHENRY SCHOOL PRAIRIE: 130-acres of tallgrass prairie. The site is home to the Sprague's pipit. The Prairie is northeast of Towner, ND. Contact the North Dakota Natural Heritage Inventory Program at 701/224-4892.

(J. CLARK) SALYER NATIONAL WILDLIFE REFUGE: 59,000-acres of marshland, meadows, riverbottom hardwoods, sandhills, and associated uplands. The marshes were originally drained in the early 1900s and then restored and expanded in the '30s by constructing low earthen dikes across the valley floor. The 20,000-acres of shallow marshes represent some of the largest freshwater wetlands in the

United States. The Refuge here is mixed-grass prairie, which includes species from tallgrass and short-grass prairies. Two trails are open only in dry weather. A 22-mile auto tour route wanders through the lower one-third of the refuge. A 5-mile long grassland trail just east of the town of Newborn, ND is open in early spring until the end of September. The Refuge is located 2-miles north of Upham, ND. Call the NWR, in Upham, ND at 701/768-2548.

McKenzie County:
LITTLE MISSOURI NATIONAL GRASSLAND – North Unit-McKenzie Range District: 1.2-million-acres of dry mixed-grass prairie which has sharp-tailed grouse dancing areas, interspersed with private ranchlands. The public lands are leased for summer grazing to more than 190 ranching operations. The McKenzie District features four "low development" areas, totaling 35,000-acres: Long X, Horse Creek, Lone Butte, and Cottonwood Creek. These areas offer visitors open space, solitude and opportunities to hike, view wildlife and explore the badlands and mid-grass prairie. The Mckenzie Unit of the Little Missouri Grasslands is located south of Watford City, ND. Call USFS, McKenzie District Ranger in Watford City, ND at 701/842-2393.

THE MAAH DAAH HEY TRAIL: A 120-mile hiking, horseback and mountain bicycle trail that starts in the US Forest Service CCC Campground in McKenzie County, located 2-miles south of Watford City, ND off Highway 85. The trail ends at Sully Creek State Park, just south of Medora, ND in Billings County. The Trail passes through the Little Missouri National Grasslands, some state and private land and connects the North and South units of Theodore Roosevelt National Park. The trail name "Maah Daah Hey" is a Mandan Indians phrase for "grandfather" or "be here long," a fitting name for a trail that takes you through some of the most pristine wilderness many will ever experience. The trail is marked by posts inscribed with a turtle--honored by the Mandans because of its firm determination, steadfastness, patience, long life and fortitude. Once you have experienced the Maah Daah Hey Trail, you will get the connection. Contact the Maah Daah Hey Trail Association, Bismarck, ND at 701/628-2747.

McLean County:
AUDUBON NATIONAL WILDLIFE REFUGE: 14,735-acres with much of the refuge, 10,421-acres, being Lake Audubon itself. However, 3,020-grassland acres offer habitat for a variety of upland species. The 370-acres of wetlands offer habitat for shorebirds, gulls, terns, rails and cranes. Almost 100 islands dot Lake Audubon, enough for 450-acres of giant Canada goose and duck nesting habitat. The Refuge serves as an important feeding and resting area for waterfowl migrating in the Central Flyway. The NWR is north of Coleharbor, ND. Call

the Audubon NWR, Coleharbor, ND, at 701/442-5474.

FORT STEVENSON STATE PARK: 438-acre park with prairie on the north shore of giant Lake Sakakawea. The Park is 4-miles south of Garrison, ND. Call the Park at 701/337-5576.

KOEING WILDLIFE DEVELOPMENT AREA: 3,450-acres of native grassland and wetland. The site is southwest of Mercer, ND. Call the USFWS at 701/442-5474.

Mercer County:
THE KNIFE RIVER INDIAN VILLAGES NATIONAL HISTORIC SITE: 1,600-acres with 800-acres of native and mostly restored prairie with a 1½-mile self-guided walking tour and many archaeological sites suggest a possible 8,000 year span of habitation. In 1804 when Lewis and Clark arrived at Knife River, they found three Hidatsa villages and two Mandan towns. Sakakawea was living in one of the Hidatsa villages. The two tribes acted as middlemen or brokers between the Crow of the upper Yellowstone, the Cheyenne and Arapaho of the Plains to the southwest, and the Assiniboine, Cree and Dakota of the northeastern Plains.

The National Park Service operates the historic site, and preserves the ghosts of the three Hidatsa villages, namely: Awatixa Xi Village (Lower Hidatsa), Awatixa village (Sakakawea site) and Big Hidatsa village. The site features a museum, which has exhibits of Indian artifacts and crafts, an orientation film and a full-sized earth lodge. The site is located west of the Lewis and Clark Interpretive Center on ND Hwy 200A. Call the Historic Site at 701/745-3309.

LAKE NETTIE NATIONAL WILDLIFE REFUGE: 1,285-acres of native grassland and wetland that produces and supports waterfowl and other species of birds and mammals. This site's proximity to Lake Audubon (5-miles to the east) enhances the significance of both refuges' bird migrational rest areas. The NWR is northwest of Turtle Lake, ND. Call the NWR in Coleharbor, ND, at 701/442-5474.

(JOHN E.) WILLIAMS PRESERVE: 1,600-acres in a glaciated area known as the Missouri Couteau of mixed-grass upland (away from water and windswept) prairie and large alkali flats near Turtle Lake supporting the largest US breeding population of the federally endangered piping plover. A large bird blind permits views of prairie and a plover-nesting beach. Locals call this preserve the "Valley-of-the-Moon" because it appears as a barren landscape at first glance. Native prairie on the preserve is strewn with salt-tolerant plant species. In some areas adjacent to the lakes only the hardy salt grass can emerge through the hard gravelly substrate. The Preserve is located northeast of Turtle Lake, ND. Call TNC, ND at 701/222-8464.

Mountrail County:
LOSTWOOD NATIONAL WILDLIFE AREA: (See Burke County above).

SHELL LAKE NATIONAL WILDLIFE REFUGE: 530-acre permanent brackish to sub-saline lake that is surrounded by native grasses. The NWR is in the southwest corner of the county and west of Minot, ND. Today there is no public use of the refuge. Call the NWR at 701/848-2466.

Morton County:
FORT LINCOLN STATE PARK: 1,006-acres of mixed-grass prairie. The Park is 7-miles south of Mandan, ND on Hwy 1806. Call NDPR at 701/663-9571 or 701/328-5357.

MORTON COUNTY WILDLIFE MANAGEMENT AREA: 640-acres of mixed-grass prairie that support sharp-tailed grouse. The WMA is southeast of Mandan, ND. Call NDGF at 701/324-2211.

Oliver County:
CROSS RANCH NATURE PRESERVE: 6,000-acres of lush xeric or dry mixed-grass prairie described as "handsome high prairie" by Lewis and Clark on October 25, 1804. Today it is Cross Ranch Nature Preserve, which continues to have that pristine landscape and abundant natural diversity. The Preserve contains vast expanses of "handsome" native mixed grass prairie, one of the largest undisturbed tracts of Missouri River bottomland forest remaining in North Dakota, as well as upland woody draws and prairie potholes. Over 300 native plants have been identified, some out of their expected distribution ranges. Abundant wildlife is present here. The Preserve's objective is to protect and maintain the diversity of native plants and animals. The most important management tools are prescribed burning and bison grazing. A bison herd (not usually found in the area), will grow to a stable herd of 150 animals grazing 2,300 acres. The site is near Bismarck, ND and has over 100 archeological sites including Mandan-Hidatsa and Archaic periods (6000 BC to 1 AD). Call TNC, ND at 701/222-8464.

CROSS RANCH STATE PARK: 589-acre park that has been purposely left primitive to preserve the land's natural beauty. An extensive trail system can be explored either on foot or on cross-country skis during the winter months. During the summer, the trails allow access to a 5,000-acre dedicated nature preserve with mixed-grass prairie, river bottom forests and woody draws. The Park is located along 7-miles of the last free flowing, undeveloped stretches of the Missouri River and is 11-miles southeast of Hensler, ND. Call NDPR in Bismarck, ND at 701/328-5357.

Ramsey County:
ALICE LAKE NATIONAL WILDLIFE REFUGE: 12,179-acres of wetland and lake with some native grasslands in the uplands. The NWR is southeast of Maza, ND and extends into Towner County. Call the NWR at 701/662-8611.

Ransom County:
BROWN RANCH: 2,000-acre virgin tallgrass prairie with wetlands, supports fox, badger, coyotes and waterfowl and is adjacent to the Sheyenne National Grassland that holds rare oak savanna. Call TNC, ND at 701/222-8464.

ENGLEVALE WILDLIFE MANAGEMENT AREA: 160-acres of wetland that has grassland associated with it. The WMA is west of Englevale, ND off Hwy 27. Call NDGF at 701/324-2211.

FORT RANSOM STATE PARK: 900-acres that includes dry-mesic tallgrass prairie and a river valley supporting the pileated woodpecker. The Park is 2-miles north of Fort Ransom, ND and 20-miles northwest of Lisbon, ND. Call NDPR at 701/973-4331.

MIRROR POOL WILDLIFE MANAGEMENT AREA: 546-acres in three public tracts in the Sheyenne Sandhills, scattered along 4-miles of Sheyenne River. In this segment, the river receives its highest infusion of springwater, and shade from the stateliest of its forests. The stately basswood and elm forests, impenetrable thickets, beaver ponds, aspen groves and snaking oxbow pools are in the valley just below stunted oaks and grass-covered dunes, more closely resembling what we identify with northern Minnesota than with eastern North Dakota. A 2-mile prairie trail leads to the Mirror Pool WMA, which is southeast of Enderlin, ND. Call NDGF at 701/328-6300.

THE NORTHERN COUNTRY NATIONAL SCENIC TRAIL: (See Wells County below).

PIGEON POINT PRESERVE: 560-acres of tallgrass prairie and oak savanna. The Preserve contains wetlands, forest, prairie thickets, and numerous rare butterflies; the richest concentration of biodiversity in the state. The Preserve is northwest of the intersection of Hwys 18 & 27. Call TNC, ND at 701/222-8464.

SHEYENNE NATIONAL GRASSLAND: 70,268-acres of public land associated with 64,769 acres of privately owned land in the sandhills has abundant tall and short-grass and sand prairie. Wild turkey, white tail deer, greater prairie chicken, grouse, partridge, and butterflies share the landscape with cattle. The grassland is located southeast of Enderlin, ND. For information and trail maps, call the US Forest Service at 701/683-4342.

TEWAUKON WETLAND MANAGEMENT DISTRICT: (See Sargent County below).

Renville County:
UPPER SOURIS NATIONAL WILDLIFE REFUGE: 32,000-acres in the beautiful Souris River Valley of northwestern North Dakota and extends for nearly 30-miles along the River. The area is characterized by a narrow band of river bottom woodlands, fertile flood plains, native mixed-grass covered rolling hills and steep brush covered coulees. Opportunities for viewing and studying wildlife and plants, walking, photography, berry picking, and cross-country skiing are available along the 3½-mile Prairie-Marsh Scenic Drive, hiking trails, and other open public use areas. However, for your safety these activities are not permitted during the Refuge's rifle deer season. Serious birders will also be able to find Baird's, LeConte's, and sharp-tailed sparrows, as well as Sprague's pipit. The NWR is located north of Foxholm, ND. Call the NWR, Foxholm, ND, at 701/468-5467.

Richland County:
HARTLEBAN PRAIRIE: 1,000-acres of tallgrass prairie supporting Dakota skipper and other rare butterflies. The Prairie is northwest of Hankinson, ND. Call the US FWS at 701/724-3598.

MIRROR POOL WILDLIFE MANAGEMENT AREA: (See Ransom County above).

MUEHLER PRAIRIE: 80-acre privately owned prairie near Hankinson, ND has many grassland species. Call 701/474-5480 for permission to visit and directions to the site.

TEWAUKON NATIONAL WILDLIFE REFUGE: 97-acres of tallgrass prairie in Richland County of the 8,438-acres of the NWR (see Sargent County below). Call the USFWS at 701/724-3598.

Rolette County:
SHELL VALLEY PRAIRIE: 60-acres of natural fen community. The Prairie is located 10-miles north of Rolette, ND. This prairie is privately owned. Contact the North Dakota Natural Heritage Inventory Program at 701/224-4892.

Sargent County:
KRAFT SLOUGH: 1,310-acres of tallgrass prairie. The Slough is 5-miles southeast of Crete, ND. Contact the North Dakota Natural Heritage Inventory Program 701/224-4892.

TEWAUKON NATIONAL WILDLIFE REFUGE: 8,438 acres
&
TEWAUKON WETLAND MANAGEMENT DISTRICT: 11,893-acres of Waterfowl Production Areas (WPA's) and 32,000-acres of Waterfowl

Production Easements, located in scattered tracts in Sargent, Ransom and Richland counties. Small tracts of native prairie forbs and grasses (100-acres total) survived the plow and still exist on the refuge and on some WPAs and serve as important living museums of the wild prairie. The area around Lake Tewaukon (east of Co Rd 12) is open to hiking, photography and bird watching. The NWR is south of Cayuga, ND. Call the NWR and WMD in Cayuga, ND at 701/724-3598.

Sheridan County:
DAVIS RANCH NATURE PRESERVE (formerly called Sheridan Nature Preserve): 7,000-acres of mixed-grass prairie, prairie potholes and wetlands supporting sharp-tailed grouse, prairie songbirds and a host of shore birds. The Preserve is 14-miles north of Wing, ND. Call TNC, ND at 701/222-8464.

LONETREE STATE WILDLIFE MANAGEMENT AREA: 33,000-acres of mesic mixed-grass prairie and prairie potholes with a wildlife observation blind. 26.3-miles of trail were certified in Lonetree WMA in 1995. This means the route goes through tallgrass from one yellow trail marker to the next, but has no cut trail. Some sections of the trail follow long-abandoned roads that have been disked up and planted to prairie grass. The WMA is southwest of Harvey, ND. Call ND Game and Fish at 701/324-2211.

Sioux County:
CEDAR RIVER NATIONAL GRASSLANDS: (See Grant County above). This portion of the grassland is in the Standing Rock Sioux Reservation.

Slope County:
BURNING COAL VEIN: 384-acres of badlands landscape still in the making. The fire smoldering in the coal layer several feet underground was burning when viewed by the first white settlers in the area over a hundred years ago. Burning Coal Vein has since become part of a Little Missouri National Grasslands Natural Area (see Billings County above). The underground fire is less active in recent years, but local landscape features and columnar Rocky Mountain juniper (cedar) bear witness to it. The coal vein is southwest of Amidon, ND. Call the US FS at 701/225-5151.

THE LITTLE MISSOURI NATIONAL GRASSLANDS-MEDORA RANGER DISTRICT: (See Billings County above).

WHITE LAKE NATIONAL WILDLIFE REFUGE: The habitat in the refuge is made up of native prairie, tame grasses, a lake, and other wetlands. The NWR is east of Amidon, ND on US 83. Call the NWR at 701/442-5474.

Stanton County:

KNIFE RIVER INDIAN VILLAGES NATIONAL HISTORIC SITE: 1,758-acre site along the Knife and Missouri Rivers supports the remains of the Mandan and Minnetaree or Hidatsa villages, whose residents were so helpful to Lewis and Clark in 1804. The surrounding area has upland grasslands. Also found are archeological remains dating to 6000 BC. Call the Historic site at 701/745-3309 or 800/767-3555.

Stutsman County:

ALKALI LAKE SANCTUARY: 2,250-acres of lake, grassland and woods near Jamestown, ND. The Audubon Society of North Dakota is working to restore its native prairie. Audubon Dakota bought seed (including purple prairie clover, yellow cornflower, and big bluestem) to plant its 170-acres of former farmland. The Sanctuary is open to the public by appointment, and volunteers are needed for ongoing maintenance. For information, call Audubon Dakota at 701/298-3373.

ARROWWOOD NATIONAL WILDLIFE REFUGE: 15,934-acres made up of lakes, marshes, prairie grasslands, wooded coulees, and cultivated fields. A 5½-mile self-guided auto tour winds through both prairie grassland and marsh. Brochures are available at the tour entrance and an audiocassette for the tour is obtainable at the refuge headquarters. Dancing "sharp tailed grouse" can be observed on the refuge in April and early May from blinds that are open to the public by reservation. The Refuge is located northeast of Pingree, ND. Call the NWR in Pingree, ND at 701/285-3341.

CHASE LAKE NATIONAL WILDLIFE REFUGE: 4,385-acres located on the Missouri Coteau, a principle physiographic region of the Prairie Pothole Region, one of the most productive ecosystems on Earth. It supports grassland birds and more than 200 species of migratory birds and is known as the "duck factory" of North America. The lake itself comprises 2,503-acres with the remaining refuge acreage consisting of native and tame grasslands and small wetlands. The two islands in the lake are home to the refuge's primary attraction, its thousands of nesting white pelicans, gulls, and cormorants. The white pelican breeding colony at Chase Lake numbers between 10,000 and 12,000 birds, the largest in North America. The Refuge was established primarily to protect the native white pelican, which was threatened with extinction by uncontrolled shooting. This NWR was declared a wilderness area in 1975. The NWR is located northwest of Medina, ND. Contact the USFWS in Woodworth, ND at 701/752-4218.

THE CHASE LAKE PRAIRIE PROJECT: This project encompasses 5.5 million acres in 11 counties. 97% of this land is privately owned. The diversity and abundance of the wetlands as well as the native grasslands within the Chase Lake Prairie Project area support a wide variety of wildlife species. The Project area, which includes one of the largest blocks of native prairie left in North Dakota, surrounds the Chase Lake National Wildlife Refuge. Together, these areas provide some of the best breeding habitats in the Prairie Pothole Region and are home to nearly 120 nesting bird species. An additional 110 species stop here during their yearly migration flight. Most prairie birds build their nests in grassy cover, often near wetlands. Grazing cattle and harvesting grass for hay can destroy nests and remove protective cover, preventing these birds from raising young. CLPP programs provide farmers and ranchers with incentive to alter the timing of these practices to benefit nesting birds and improve the health of the grasslands. Programs include:

1. Rotational grazing systems that allow a rancher to move cows from pasture to pasture. This prevents the cows from feeding too long in any one section of land. Rotating the grazing areas allow the grasses to grow back, provides cover for nesting birds, and puts more weight on the cattle by grazing them on established grasslands.

2. Purchasing grassland easements from willing landowners. The easements perpetually protect the grasslands from being plowed. Cattle are allowed to graze and haying can be done after July 15th when most birds have finished nesting.

3. Restoring grasslands on private lands. Low-quality cropland is planted with native grass species and a rotational grazing system is developed.

The Core Area, 339 square-miles, includes parts of Stutsman and Kidder County. See the Chase Lake NWR above for contact information.

FRONTIER VILLAGE: 125-acres of woods and upland grassland with a buffalo herd. The site is at the south end of Jamestown, ND. Call the site at 701/252-6307.

Towner County:
ALICE LAKE NATIONAL WILDLIFE REFUGE: (See Ramsey County above).

Ward County:
DES LACS NATIONAL WILDLIFE REFUGE: (See Burke County above).

UPPER SOURIS NATIONAL WILDLIFE REFUGE: (See Renville County above).

Wells County:
(KARL T.) FREDERICK WILDLIFE MANAGEMENT AREA: 400-acres, with 40-acres of wetland and 360-acres of prairie located southwest of Hurdsfield, ND. Call NDGF at 701/324-2211.

LONETREE WILDLIFE MANAGEMENT AREA: 30,000-acres (7,240-acres in Wells Co) 70% of which will eventually be restored to prairie. A flock of prairie chicken resides here. The WMA is located ½-mile south of Harvey, ND. Call NDGF at 701/324-2211.

THE NORTHERN COUNTRY NATIONAL SCENIC TRAIL: A hiking trail that goes through 7 northern states. In North Dakota there are two rather long segments of certified trail—a 25-mile segment crossing the Sheyenne National Grassland near Lisbon, and a 32-mile segment crossing the Lonetree Wildlife Management Area near Harvey, ND. Both areas have native grasses and forbs and great flocks of geese, ducks and sandhill cranes migrate through the area. The trail through Lonetree WMA contains prairie as it was when the pioneers passed through and passes near booming grounds for prairie chicken and sharp-tailed grouse. During mating season, use extra caution to not disturb them. The headquarters for the Scenic Trail is in Madison, WI. Telephone number 608/441-5610.

WELLS COUNTY WILDLIFE MANAGEMENT AREA: 637-acres of mostly prairie. The WMA is located 7-miles north of Hurdsfield, ND. Call NDGF at 701/324-2211.

Williams County:

ALKALI LAKE: 320-acres of wetland and prairie northwest of Appam, ND. Call the BLM at 701/2259148.

CROSBY WETLANDS MANAGEMENT DISTRICT: (See Burke County above).

FORT UNION TRADING POST HISTORIC SITE: 462-acre historic site built in 1828 on the prairie near the confluence of the Yellowstone and Missouri Rivers by John Jacob Astor's powerful American Fur Company; it hosted John James Audubon, George Catlin, and Karl Bodmer and Prince Maximilean. Looking north from the fort, prairie can still be seen. (The site is also in Roosevelt County, Montana, see above). Call the Historic Site at 701/572-9083.

LAKE ZAHL NATIONAL WILDLIFE REFUGE: 1,250-acres of mostly prairie surrounding 2 large semi-permanent marshes. (See also Crosby Wetlands Management District in Burke County above). The NWR is southwest of Crosby, ND off US 85. Call the NWR in Crosby, ND at 701/965-6488.

LEWIS AND CLARK STATE PARK: 490-acres of grasslands, badlands, and woods northwest of Lunds Landing, ND off Hwy 1804 on Co Rd 15. Call the Park at 701/859-3071.

OHIO

"It may be surprising to learn that small patches of prairie occur throughout much of Ohio. These are not simply man-made meadows, but rather true prairie communities composed of essentially the same prairie plants as in the significantly larger western counterparts," notes an Ohio DNR publication. These "prairie openings" formed during the hot and dry Xerothermic Period that pushed western grassland east making Ohio a "battleground" for prairie and eastern forests. Ohio's prairies survived the early pioneer times because prairie soil was considered infertile and worthless, but they disappeared after the arrival of the plow. About 1,000 square miles supported Darby Plains, a tallgrass prairie wilderness dominated by big bluestem, which was sometimes wet and sometime powder dry, and interrupted by numerous groves of bur oak and hickory. Access was by way of Old Post Road (Hwy 161), originally an Indian trail. Contact the DNR at 614/265-6453 for a self-guiding auto tour of the Darby Plains and lists of state nature preserves open to the public.

Many ecologists subscribe to the opinion of Dr E Lucy Braun that the xeric or dry prairies moved in from the west long before the Wisconsin Glacier and even before the Illinoian Glacier of 125,000 years ago.

Below are some areas in Ohio where prairie and prairie plants can still be seen:

Adams County:
ADAMS LAKE PRAIRIE: 22.37-acres of cedar barren prairie located within Adams Lake State Park (see below). Visitors must not wander off the trails adjacent to the prairie. Call the Prairie at 513/544-9750 or DNR, OH at 614/265-6453.

ADAMS LAKE STATE PARK: 48-acres of land and the 47-acre Adams Lake. The park lies in an area rich in natural diversity with many unique plants and animals. Wedged between the foothills of the Appalachian Mountains to the east and the glaciated land to the north and west, no other area of Ohio boasts a richer abundance of plant species. Adams County holds scattered prairies and was once inhabited by prehistoric and mound building cultures, most notably the Adenas and Hopewell. The origin and purpose of the internationally renowned Serpent Mound, the hallmark of the Adena culture (1000 BC-100 AD) remains a mystery. The historical site can be found north of the park near Locust Grove, OH off Hwy 41. The shorter-lived Hopewell culture (100 BC-600 AD) created Tremper Mound, located along Hwy 104 in adjacent Scioto County. The park is located 1-mile north of West Union, Oh on Hwy 41. Call the Park at 740/544-3927.

CHAPARRAL PRAIRIE: 67.7-acres of prairie, forest and old field habitat growing on "till" left by glacial ice some 200,000 years ago during the Illinois Glaciation. Created by cumulative effects of past influences, its exact origin is not completely understood, but a state geologist described it in 1838 as "quite a paradise for the botanist." The prairie is located 3-miles northwest of West Union, OH. Call 513/544-9750 or 614/265-6453.

EDGE OF APPALACHIA PRESERVE: 12,000-acres of rugged woodland, mostly short-grass prairie openings, waterfalls, giant promontories and clear streams. The eminent ecologist E Lucy Braun originally studied the area in the late 1920s. She noted the significance of the remnant "prairie" communities persisting along cliff edges, narrow ridges, and forest openings on various calcareous substrates, particularly the Cedarville (Peebles) dolomite. The underlying bedrock is the key environmental factor related to the distribution of the plant communities.

The Nature Conservancy and Cincinnati Museum Center own and manage eleven contiguous preserves lying along a 12-mile stretch of Ohio Brush Creek. Three areas, Lynx Prairie, Buzzardroost Rock, and The Wilderness Preserve, are registered National Natural Landmarks and are open to the public for activities such as birdwatching, photography, and hiking. All visitors should use extraordinary care to protect natural features, plant and animal life. The route to Buzzardroost Rock Trail begins at a parking lot at the eastern end of Weaver Rd, which is reached from Hwy 125 just west of the town of Lynx, OH and crosses south over the highway and continues on with a round trip distance of 3-miles. The preserve also has a Wilderness Trail. Call the Wilderness Preserve Headquarters at 937/544-2188 for information and directions. Call TNC, OH at 614/717-2770 for general information about their preserves.

SERPENT MOUND: (See Adams State Park above).

STRAIT CREEK PRAIRIE BLUFF: 75-acres of summer-blooming prairie. This preserve is one of several remnant prairie communities persisting along cliff edges, narrow ridges, and forest openings on unglaciated Cedarville dolomite. These dry-adapted prairie communities are thought to predate white settlement and are considered climax communities, originating in the region during conditions that prevailed 6000-8000 years ago. The prairie is also in Pike County. Visitation is limited to work projects and staff-led field trips. Call TNC, OH at 614/717-2770.

Clark County:
HUFFMAN PRAIRIE: 109-acres making it one of the largest tallgrass prairie remnants in Ohio. This remnant of a once nearly two sq mile prairie is located on the Wright-Patterson Air Force Base owned by the US Department of Defense, and recognized by the Ohio DNR as an

Ohio Natural Landmark. A recent study of insect life revealed a large number of species of butterflies that were thought extinct, but were once abundant on our tallgrass prairie. The prairie is adjacent to the Dayton Aviation Heritage National Park. The Wright brothers made flight tests on both sites and a replica of the Wright Brothers 1905 Hangar is next to the prairie. A nearby garden of native prairie plants is used as a seed source to restore degraded portions of the prairie.

Huffman Prairie has two ecological goals:

1. To maximize plant diversity and to bring it back to a condition similar to what existed in the 1800s and

2. To maintain the diversity of nesting grassland birds and prairie lepidoptera.

These goals will be accomplished through prescribed burns (conducted by U.S. Air Force personnel), eradication of non-native plants, and reseeding with native plant seed (collected by volunteers and sown with assistance from Five Rivers Metropark personnel).

Visitors can access Huffman Prairie through volunteer work projects or by obtaining a visitor's pass at Wright-Patterson Air Force Base Visitor Center. For information, call the base at 937/255-3334. All visitors should use extraordinary care to protect natural features, plant and animal life. Through a broad-based agreement established in 1990 between TNC and the US Department of Defense, Huffman Prairie is currently managed through the cooperation of Wright-Patterson Air Force Base, TNC, and Five Rivers Metroparks. Call TNC, OH at 614/717-2770.

Drake County:
BALD KNOB PRESERVE: This preserve lies along a designated section of the Stillwater State Scenic River in western Ohio. The site is a series of three slump prairies located on the slope and crest of south-facing bluffs on a bend of the river. The name "slump prairie" refers to the periodic slumping of the bluff, which is located on a steep unstable slope composed of glacial clays, sand and gravel. The prairie openings owe their existence to the steepness of the bluffs and the unstable nature of the morainal drift. When the soils become thoroughly saturated, thick sheets of material occasionally slip downhill toward the eroding stream bank. This instability does not favor the establishment of trees, so prairie vegetation became established on the slump areas and along the dry, well-drained crest of the end moraine. Visitation is limited to work projects, staff-led field trips and special permit. All visitors should use extraordinary care to protect natural features, plant and animal life. Call TNC, OH at 614/717-2770.

Fulton County:
MAUMEE STATE FOREST: 3,100-acres of oak woodland, patches of

wet prairie, and planted pine forest characterize this forest; the only state forest in Ohio outside of the Appalachian plateau. The Dog Training Area, also known as the Muck Farm Wet Prairie, protects one of the finest wet prairie communities in the Oak Openings. The Forest is located at 3390 County Road D, Swanton, OH. For more information, contact the DNR, OH at 614/265-6453.

Greene County:
ZIMMERMAN PRAIRIE: 3.48-acre prairie. Call the DNR, OH at 614/265-6453.

Hardin County:
KILLDEER PLAINS WILDLIFE AREA: (See Wyandot County below).

Lawrence County:
COMPASS PLANT (O. E. ANDERSON) PRAIRIE: 15.5-acre prairie is located 1½-miles north of Aid, OH on the east side of Hwy 141. Call DNR, OH at 614/265-6453.

Lucas County:
(LOU) CAMPBELL STATE NATURE PRESERVE: 170-acre preserve is named after Northwest Ohio's most pre-eminent naturalist. This site protects a variety of Oak Openings habitats including oak savanna and mesic sand prairie. Hiking and nature study is allowed by permit only. For more information, contact DNR, OH at 614/265-6453.

IRWIN PRAIRIE: 223-acres lie within a sandy tract of land known as Oak Openings contain the state's best-preserved wet prairie remnant. Indians canoed through it in search of waterfowl, but most of the wet prairie disappeared after the 1859 initiation of an extensive network of drainage ditches for agriculture. The core of this preserve is a treeless, wet sedge meadow dominated by several species of sedges, rushes and wetland grasses, which is the finest in the state. The site also has tall-grass wet prairie communities, shrub swamp, grass meadow, and swamp forest. Among the rare animals reported from Irwin Prairie are sedge wrens, Bell's vireo, least bittern, golden-winged warbler, spotted and Blanding's turtles and the purplish copper butterfly. The Prairie is located 10-miles west of Toledo, OH. Call DNR, OH at 614/265-6453.

KITTY TODD PRESERVE: 600-acres of black oak savanna and wet prairie habitat. Black oak savanna is found on the dunes and ancient beach ridges. Growing under this light canopy of oaks is a mixture of grasses, sedges, wildflowers and shrubs. Its specialized animals include the rare lark sparrow, the elusive spotted turtle, badger, and several rare butterfly species. The Preserve is west of Toledo, OH at 10420 Old State Line Rd. Call TNC, OH at 614/717-2770.

MAUMEE BAY STATE PARK: 1,450-acres of lodge, cottages and golf course that are nestled among the scenic meadows, prairies, wet woods, and lush marshes teeming with wildlife. Shorebirds and ducks plus over 300 species of other birds have been recorded here. The Park is located at 1400 State Park Road, Oregon, OH. Call the Park at 419/836-7758

OAK OPENINGS PRESERVE METROPARK: 3,600-acres makes this the largest and best-known conservation area within the region. This site protects a variety of oak woodlands and savannas, remnant prairies and floodplain forest. Girdham Road dunes are the region's best example of open sand dunes and sand barren habitat. An extensive system of trails for biking, hiking and horseback riding is also available. An interpretive display on the Oak Openings region can be viewed at the Mallard Lake area. The Park is just northwest of Waterville, OH. This is a Metropark. For more information about Metroparks, call 419/535-3050, ext. 101.

SECOR METROPARK: 600-acre park located on the edge of the Oak Openings region protects an extensive swamp forest and a restored tallgrass prairie. The Nature Discovery Center has interpretive displays. The Park is 6-miles west of US 23 on W. Center Ave, Berkey, OH. For more information about Metroparks, call 419/535-3050, ext. 101.

UNIVERSITY/PARKS TRAIL: (See Wildwood Preserve below)

WILDWOOD PRESERVE METROPARK: 500-acre Metropark preserves tallgrass prairie, oak woodland, and floodplain habitats plus a Manor House, Visitor Center, restored one room schoolhouse, trails, and picnic shelters. The park is on W. Center Ave between Corey and Reynolds, OH. The park connects to the University/Parks Trail, which is a 6.3-mile paved all-purpose trail from King Road in Sylvania, OH to the University of Toledo campus. For more information about Metroparks, call 419/535-3050, ext. 101.

WABASH-CANNONBALL TRAIL: 18+ miles of both improved and unimproved bike, hiking and horse trails traverse the Oak Openings Region in two separate sections. For information, call NORTA at 800/951-4688 and the Toledo Metroparks at 419/535-3050. The Trail is owned and managed by Northwest Ohio Rails-to-Trails (NORTA), Toledo Metroparks and several others.

Madison County:
BIGELOW CEMETARY PRAIRIE: 0.5-acre prairie cemetery. "Like the weathered gravestones that are present-day reminders of a vanished way of life, the special community of plants at Bigelow Cemetery provides a glimpse of the beauty of a vanished landscape, the native Ohio prairie," notes a DNR pamphlet. This virgin tallgrass prairie, with

waist-high masses of flowers and 6-8 feet tall clumps of tall grasses is a remnant of Darby Plains. The Prairie is on Rosedale Rd, 1½-mile south of Hwy 161. Call DNR, OH at 614/265-6453.

SMITH CEMETERY PRAIRIE: 0.6-acre cemetery where the entire Smith family was buried. The prairie is a remnant of Darby Plains and its bur oaks are well over 200 years old. The Prairie is on Boyd Rd, which parallels Hwy 161 about 1-mile to the south. Call DNR, OH at 614/265-6463.

Marion County:
KILLDEER PLAINS WILDLIFE AREA: (See Wyandot County below).

Miami County:
(F L) BLANKENSHIP RIVERSIDE SANCTUARY: 5-acre site that includes native grassland. The Sanctuary is on Hwy 48, Covington, OH. Call the Miami County Park District at 513/667-1086 or 937/335-9547.

GOODE PRAIRIE: 28-acres of summer prairie wildflowers located on Union-Church Rd, Covington Oh. Call the Miami County Park District at 513/667-1086 or 937/335-9547.

STILLWATER PRAIRIE RESERVE: 217-acre park features a native prairie and includes 2-miles of trails, a fishing ponds, and a picnic area. The Prairie is located along the Stillwater River in Newberry Township. Call the Miami County Park District at 513/667-1086 or 937/335-9547.

Pike County:
STRAIT CREEK PRAIRIE BLUFF: (See Adams County above).

Scioto County:
TREMPER MOUND (See Adams State Park, Adams County above).

Union County:
MILFORD CENTER PRAIRIE: 7-acres of tallgrass prairie supporting the highest species diversity of any prairie remnant in the Darby Plains. The Prairie is located southwest of Milford Center, OH. Call DNR, OH at 614/265-6463.

Wyandot County:
KILLDEER PLAINS WILDLIFE AREA: 8,000-acres at the northern edge of an original 30,000-acres wet prairie that is "a living museum filled with remnants of its prairie history."Also in Marion and Hardin Counties. The WA is south of Harpster, OH. Call DNR, OH at 614/265-6463.

OKLAHOMA

The state's name derives from two Choctaw Indian words meaning "Land of the Red Men." Following its exploration by Spaniards Coronado and de Soto and a brief French rule, it was included in the 1803 Louisiana Purchase. 1867-Texas cattle drives passed through on the way to northern markets. In 1872 the Osage Indians began settling Osage County, followed in 1889 by the Boomers, the Sooners and other settlers. 1897 saw the first oil well production.

Originally spanning portions of 14 states and covering over 142 million acres, the tallgrass prairie was one of North America's major ecosystems. Today, less than 1% of the original tallgrass prairie remains. Large, unbroken tracts of tallgrass prairie only exist now in the Flint Hills of Oklahoma and Kansas. As a functioning ecosystem, the tallgrass prairie is extinct. Also present in Oklahoma are mixed-grass and short-grass prairie. These have fared better than tallgrass prairie.

Oklahoma participates in the "Prairie Passage" (US 35)(see Minnesota above) through the Oklahoma Department of Transportation (DOT, OK). However, DOT, OK emphasizes wildflowers over prairie grasses and although they do plant native prairie flowers, they also plant some non-native flowers. However, it is stressed that 90% of the plants are native. Moreover, the DOT, OK also plants another route, which includes US 44 and US 75 to the Kansas border, in order to grow prairie along roads that are close to the Tallgrass Prairie (see Osage County below). Oklahoma's mowing policy is not to mow before mid-July. For more information, call the DOT, OK at 405/521-4037.

Following are some prairies still viewable in Oklahoma:

Alfalfa County:

BYRON HATCHERY WATCHABLE WILDLIFE AREA: 40-acres with a self-guided ½-mile nature trail through three distinct habitats within a mixed-grass prairie. A diversity of songbirds, waterfowl, prairie grasses and wildflowers can be observed. The Hatchery is located southeast of Byron, OK. Call the Hatchery at 580/474-2663.

SALT PLAINS NATIONAL WILDLIFE REFUGE, STATE PARK AND LAKE: 32,324-acres of salt flats, marshes, open waters and uplands with native grasslands and forests. The NWR is north of Jet, OK on Hwy 38. Call the USFWS at 405/626-4731.

Beaver County:

BEAVER STATE PARK: 360-acres of sand dunes and sand-sage habitat.[1] The Park is 1-mile north of Beaver, OK on Hwy 270. Call the Oklahoma Tourism and Recreation Dept (OTRD) at 405/625-3373.

LAKE CHAMBERS: 80-acres of short-grass prairie where songbirds, raptors, and in migration, waterfowl can be seen. The lake is 18-miles west of Laverne, OK. Call the Oklahoma Dept of Wildlife Conservation

(ODWC) at 405/521-3851.

Caddo County:
FORT COBB WILDLIFE MANAGEMENT AREA AND STATE PARK: 8,020-acres with a 4,100-acre lake and a 1,872-acre State Park. The Area has native prairie and blackjack oak thickets. The WMA is 6-miles north of Fort Cobb, OK on Hwy 146. Call the Park at 405/643-2249.

RED ROCK STATE PARK: 310-acres of heavily wooded canyon with prairie at the rim area of the canyon and a small pond. Cheyenne Indians once roamed the area, using the canyons in winter as a refuge against the cold north wind. During the mid-1800s, the canyon was a favorite stop for wagon trains traveling from Arkansas to California. The Park is located ½-mile south of Hinton, OK. Call the Park at 405/542-6344.

Cherokee County:
(J T) NICKEL FAMILY NATURE AND WILDLIFE PRESERVE: 15,000-acres (formerly the J-5 Ranch). Adjoining the Illinois River in eastern Oklahoma, the ranch encompasses portions of four Ozark stream watersheds and protects the full spectrum of representative Ozark natural communities. The site includes significant areas of oak savanna and tallgrass prairie. Call TNC, OK in Oklahoma City, OK at 405/858-8557 or Tulsa, OK at 918/585-1117.

Cimarron County:
BLACK MESA NATURE PRESERVE: 1,600-acre nature preserve, which the TNC conveyed to the Oklahoma Tourism and Recreation Department (OTRD) with a management agreement. The Preserve protects about 60% of the mesa top in Oklahoma in addition to talus slopes and plains habitat. Here, the Rocky Mountains meet the short-grass prairie and it is unique in that it represents an area where many species are at the easternmost or westernmost portions of their range. The plains below the mesa support a short-grass prairie. The Preserve is a birder's paradise any time of the year. Black bear, bobcat, mountain lion, mule deer and antelope are some of the mammals that may be seen in the Mesa region. The Preserve is near Black Mesa State Park and southeast of Kenton, OK. Call TNC, OK at 405/858-8557 or 918/585-1117 or the OTRD at 405/521-3411.

KIOWA AND RITA BLANCA NATIONAL GRASSLAND: 229,327-acres of mostly short-grass prairie supporting black tailed prairie dogs, prairie chickens, bobcat, black bear, pronghorn, mule deer and red and gray fox. The grassland is also located in New Mexico, (See Colfax, Harding, Mora and Union Counties) and Texas (See Dallam County). The Grassland is southwest of Boise City, OK on US 64. Call the Grassland in Clayton, NM at 505/374-9652.

RITA BLANCA WILDLIFE MANAGEMENT AREA: 15,600-acres of short-grass prairie in scattered sites about 17-miles southwest of Boise City, OK. Call the ODWC at 405/521-3851.

Cleveland County:
LEXINGTON WILDLIFE MANAGEMENT AREA AND LAKE DAHLGREN: 9,440-acres of tallgrass prairie, crosstimbers forest and a 30-acre lake. The WMA is 5-miles south of Noble, OK. Call the ODWC at 405/521-3851.

Commanche County:
WICHITA MOUNTAINS WILDLIFE REFUGE: 59,020-acre refuge hosts a rare piece of the past, a remnant mixed-grass prairie. This refuge is an island where the natural carpet of grass escaped destruction because the rocks underfoot defeated the plow. The prairie community hums with life and provides habitat for large native grazing animals and Texas Longhorn cattle. Bison and prairie dogs are present along with a total of 50 mammal, 240 bird, 64 reptile and amphibian, 36 fish, and 806 plant species. The Refuge is located 25-miles northwest of Lawton, OK. Contact Sam Waldstein, Refuge Manager, at the Refuge in Indiahoma, OK at 580/429-3222.

Cotton County:
WAURIKA WILDLIFE MANAGEMENT AREA AND LAKE: (See Stephens County below).

Custer County:
WASHITA NATIONAL WILDLIFE REFUGE: 8,200-acres including: 2,000-acres of upper reservoir and river, 3,000 plus acres of mixed-grass prairie, and 1,200 of bottomland and forest along creeks. The NWR is located northwest of Clinton, OK. Call the NWR at 405/664-2205.

Dewey County:
CANTON WILDLIFE MANAGEMENT AREA: 16,775-acres of mixed-grass prairie, forest, and bottomland. The WMA is northwest of Canton on Hwy 58A. Call the USCE at 405/886-2989.

Ellis County:
ELLIS COUNTY WILDLIFE MANAGEMENT AREA AND LAKE VINCENT: 4,800-acres of shinnery oak-grassland[2] with woods and bottomland. Lesser prairie chicken can be seen here. The WMA is southeast of Arnett, OK on Hwy 46. Call the ODWC at 405/521-3851.

PACKSADDLE WILDLIFE MANAGEMENT AREA: 7,500-acres of rolling hills and canyons with short-grass prairie, sand-sage and shinnery oak. The WMA is south of Arnett, OK on Hwy 283. Call the ODWC at 405/521-3851.

Grady County:
LAKE BURTSCHI: 180-acres of tallgrass prairie and forest around the lake. The Lake is 10-miles southwest of Chickasha, OK on Hwy 92. Call the ODWC at 405/521-3851.

Greer County:
ALTUS-LUGERT WILDLIFE MANAGEMENT AREA AND ALTUS LAKE: 10,400-acres of mud flats along the lakeshore and upland prairie. The WMA is 2-miles east of Granite on Hwy 9 and is also in Kiowa County. Call the Bureau of Reclamation at 405/563-2238.

QUARTZ MOUNTAIN STATE PARK: (See Kiowa County below).

Harmon County:
LAKE HALL: 36-acre lake with shinnery oak, grassland and aquatic habitats. The Lake is 13-miles north of Hollis, OK. Call the ODWC at 405/521-3851.

Jefferson County:
LAKE JAP BEAVER: 65-acre lake with tallgrass prairie adjacent to it. The Lake is 4-miles northwest of Waurika, OK. Call the ODWC at 405/521-3851.

WAURIKA WILDLIFE MANAGEMENT AREA AND LAKE: (See Stephens County below).

Johnston County:
PONTOTOC RIDGE PRESERVE: (See Pontotoc County below).

TISHOMINGO NATIONAL FISH HATCHERY: 50 surface acres of production ponds with 181-acres of native grasses, shrubs, and trees. The Hatchery is northwest of Tishomingo, OK. Call the Hatchery at 405/384-5463.

Kay County:
KAW WILDLIFE MANAGEMENT AREA AND RESERVOIR: 49,754-acres of bottomland hardwoods and tallgrass prairie. The Reservoir and WMA is east of Ponca, OK on River Rd, and they are also in Osage County. Call the USCE at 405/762-5611.

Kingfisher County:
LAKE ELMER: 60-acres of tallgrass prairie and lake. The Lake is northwest of Kingfisher, OK. Call the ODWC at 405/521-3851.

Kiowa County:
ALTUS-LUGERT WILDLIFE MANAGEMENT AREA AND ALTUS LAKE: (See Greer County above).

QUARTZ MOUNTAIN STATE PARK: 4,200-acres of prairie shrub and woodland habitats plus granite buttes and peaks around Lake Altus.

The Park extends into Greer County. The Park is south of Lone Wolf, OK on Hwy 44. Call the Park at 580/563-2238.

Major County:
MAJOR COUNTY NATURE TRAIL: 46-acre tallgrass prairie and riparian hardwoods with a 1-mile trail. The Trail is 1.7-miles east of Fairview, OK on Hwy 58. Call the Major County Historical Society at 405/227-2265.

Murray County:
CHICKASAW NATIONAL RECREATION AREA: This area holds within its boundaries a vast diversity of natural resources. These unique flora, fauna, waters, and geological formations have withstood the external pressures of man-made and natural changes and combined to create an area unlike any in the surrounding territory. This site lies in a transition zone where the Eastern deciduous forest and the Western prairies meet and has flora and fauna from both environments, plus flora and fauna specific to such transition areas. The site is located just south of Sulphur, OK on Hwy 177. Call the site at 580/622-3165.

Muskogee County:
CHEROKEE AND GRUBER WILDLIFE MANAGEMENT AREAS: 62,733-acres of oak-hickory forest and tallgrass prairie. The WMAs are southeast of Fort Gibson, OK. Call the ODWC at 405/521-3851.

Noble County:
SOONER LAKE: 5,400-acre tallgrass prairie and aquatic habitats. The Lake is 15-miles north of Stillwater, OK at the intersection of Hwy 177 & 15E. Call the Oklahoma Gas & Electric Corp at 405/553-3000.

Oklahoma County:
OG&E PRAIRIE DOG VIEWING AREA: 10-acres where one can see prairie dogs in their natural habitat. This site is west of Oklahoma City, OK on Reno Ave. Call the Oklahoma Gas & Electric Corp at 405/553-3000.

Osage County:
(JOHN) DAHL WILDLIFE MANAGEMENT AREA: 480-acres of tallgrass prairie and agricultural fields. The WMA is 1-mile east of Foraker, OK. Call the ODWC at 405/521-3851.

HULAH WILDLIFE MANAGEMENT AREA & WAH-SHA-SHE STATE PARK: 20,676-acres of tallgrass prairie, oak uplands, wetlands, and bottomland hardwoods. The WMA and Park are northwest of Bartlesville, OK and also in Washington County. Call the USCE at 918/532-4627.

KAW WILDLIFE MANAGEMENT AREA AND RESERVOIR: (See Kay

County above).

SKIATOOK WILDLIFE MANAGEMENT AREA AND RESERVOIR: 19,049-acres of lake woodland and upland grasslands. The WMA is 5-miles west of Skiatook, OK on Hwy 20. Call the USCE at 918/288-6890.

TALLGRASS PRAIRIE PRESERVE: 37,000-acres of tallgrass prairie of which 32,000-acres was formerly the Barnard Ranch. Located in the Flint Hills landscape, it is maintained by fire and bison and supports much prairie life. TNC has an adopt-a-bison program here. The Preserve is located north of Pawhuska, OK. Call TNC Tallgrass Prairie Preserve at 918/287-4803.

WAH-SHA-SHE STATE PARK: (See Hulah Wildlife Management Area above).

WALNUT CREEK STATE PARK: 720-acres of tallgrass prairie and forests. The Park is east of Prue, OK. Call Oklahoma Parks at 800/654-8240.

Ponototoc County:
PONTOTOC RIDGE PRESERVE: 2,900-acres featuring rolling hills, limestone outcrops, high quality springs and streams, moist hardwood forests, both tallgrass and (on dry west-facing slopes) mixed-grass prairie, and an excellent example of crosstimbers. A 3-mile trail through both wooded and grassland areas features spring and summer wildflowers in an impressive vistas. The Preserve is south of Ada, OK and on the Pontotoc-Johnson County border and extends into Johnson County. Call the Preserve at 580/777-2224.

Rodgers County:
REDBUD VALLEY NATURE PRESERVE: 82-acres of upland prairie and wooded hillsides. The preserve is northeast of Tulsa, OK on 161st E. Ave. Call the TNC, Ok in Tulsa, OK at 918/585-1117.

Rogers Mills County:
BLACK KETTLE NATIONAL GRASSLAND: 31,576 scattered acres of tall and mid-grass prairie with 30,724-acres in Oklahoma. The grassland extends into Hemphill County, Texas. The Black Kettle National Grassland surrounds Cheyenne, OK. Call the Grassland in Cheyenne, OK at 580/497-2143.

Stephens County:
WAURIKA WILDLIFE MANAGEMENT AREA AND LAKE: 21,056-acres of lake with mixed-grass prairie and bottomland hardwoods around that lake. The lake is also in Cotton and Jefferson Counties. The WMA is 4-miles south of Corum, OK. Call the USCE at 405/963-2111.

Texas County:
GUYMAN GAME RESERVE AND SUNSET LAKE: 193-acres of grass-land and lake with a prairie dog town in the City of Guymon, OK. Call the City of Guymon at 405/338-3396.

SHULTZ WILDLIFE MANAGEMENT AREA: 340-acres of short-grass prairie with wooded stream corridors. The WMA is located southeast of Hardesty, OK. Call the ODWC at 405/521-3851.

OPTIMA WILDLIFE MANAGEMENT AREA: 13,249-acres of short-grass prairie and sand-sage upland that includes Optima NWR (see below). The WMA is northwest of Hardesty, OK. Call the ODWC at 405/521-3851 or the US Corp of Engineers at 405/888-4266.

OPTIMA NATIONAL WILDLIFE REFUGE: A small canyon sur-rounded by rolling prairie. Mixed-grass prairie grassland with sand sage, yucca and prickley pear cactus is the primary habitat type with a narrow band of mature cottonwood trees along the creek channel. The refuge was created to provide migration and wintering habitat for the short-grass prairie population of Canada geese and a high plains popu-lation of mallards. The NWR is 2-miles northwest of Hardesty, OK. Call the NWR at 405/664-2205.

Tulsa County:
BEAVER RIVER WILDLIFE MANAGEMENT AREA: 15,600-acres with 2 prairie dog towns. The WMA is 11 miles west of Beaver, OK. Call the ODWC at 405/521-3851.

KEYSTONE WILDLIFE MANAGEMENT AREA, STATE PARK AND LAKE: 49,313-acres of tallgrass prairie, bottomland hardwoods, and oak uplands. The Keystone Lake State Park has 720 land acres and the lake is 26,000-acres. The WMA is west of Sand Springs, OK on either Hwy 64 or 51. The Park is on Hwy 151. Call the USCE at 918/865-2621 or 4991.

Washington County:
COPAN WILDLIFE MANAGEMENT AREA AND RESERVOIR: 15,939-acres of tallgrass prairie, abandoned fields, wetlands and bot-tomland hardwoods. The WMA is west of Copan, OK. Call the USCE at 918/532-4334.

HULAH WILDLIFE MANAGEMENT AREA & WAH-SHA-SHE STATE PARK: (See Osage County above).

Washita County:
CROWDER LAKE STATE PARK: 158-acre lake with 10-acres of park that has native prairie and hardwoods in a canyon. The Park is 7-miles south of Weatherford, OK. Call the Park at 580/343-2443.

LAKE VANDERWORK: 135-acre lake and mixed-grass prairie. The Lake is north of Gotebo, OK off Hwy 54. Call the ODWC at 405/521-3851.

Woodward County:
FORT SUPPLY WILDLIFE MANAGEMENT AREA AND RESERVOIR: 5,418-acres of sand-sage grassland and bottomland forest around the lake. The WMA is 1-mile south of Fort Supply, OK. Call the USCE at 405/766-2701.

Note! Below are prairies owned or managed by TNC, OK that may not be open to the public. Call the TNC, OK at 918/585-1117.

(E C) SPRINGER PRAIRIE PRESERVE: 40-acres in the central mixed-grass prairie ecosystem in north central Oklahoma is a remnant of original prairie with big bluestem and switchgrass prairie grasses.

WHITE OAK PRAIRIE PRESERVE: In the southern tallgrass prairie ecosystem of northeast Oklahoma is an exemplary tallgrass prairie remnant that provides habitat for the prairie mole cricket. This is a private natural area managed by TNC for conservation purposes.

---

[1] Sand-sage habitats are dominated by many prairie species such as side oats grama and little bluestem.

[2] Shinnery oak-grassland is found in Texas, New Mexico, and western Oklahoma and along with shinnery oak is dominated by sand bluestem, little bluestem, Indiangrass, switchgrass, buffalo grass, sand dropseed, and sand sagebrush. 1,173 sq miles of Shinnery Oak - Grassland have been mapped in Oklahoma, principally in southwestern Woodward, central Ellis, western Roger Mills, Beckham and northern Harmon counties.

OREGON

Not a Great Plains or a Prairie State, but Oregon has areas that look like prairie and vegetation that is prairie vegetation or very similar to prairie vegetation. See below:

Marion County:
KINGSTON PRAIRIE PRESERVE: 152-acres near Stayton, OR protects one of the last remnants of native prairie in the Willamette Valley where more than 99% of the original prairie has been lost. Both wet and dry prairie habitats thrive including native grasses and rare wildflowers and nesting habitat for declining grassland birds, including the western meadowlark, the state bird. Call TNC, OR at 503/230-1221.

Wallowa County:
ZUMWALT PRAIRIE: (Formerly Camp Creek Ranch) 27,000-acres of the largest remaining expanse of native bunchgrass prairie. The preserve is on the western rim of Hells Canyon, where gently rolling grasslands drop off dramatically toward the Imnaha and Snake Rivers. TNC will manage this 42-square-mile preserve to safeguard critical habitats for native wildlife, fish and rare plants. This site was recently purchased. Call TNC, OR in Portland, OR at 503/230-1221.

PENNSYLVANIA

Not a prairie state, although at one time tallgrass prairie extended east as far as the "Prairie Peninsula" into extensive areas of Illinois, parts of western Indiana, isolated areas of central Ohio, and western Pennsylvania.

Butler County:

JENNINGS PRAIRIE: 310-acres with 7.5-miles of self-guiding trails meandering through what is believed to be a relict prairie left over from 7,000 years ago, before the climate changed. The prairie is located near Prospect, PA. Call Jennings Environmental Center/Western Pennsylvania Conservancy at 412/288-2777.

SOUTH DAKOTA
In South Dakota there are many Wetland Management Districts (WMD). The public lands of the WMD called Waterfowl Production Areas (WPAs) are a part of the National Wildlife Refuge System. WPA's are open year-round to many public activities. Visitors can expect to find a rich variety of plant and animal life. Native prairie grasses, wild-flowers, and other plants can be observed and studied at leisure in natural prairie settings. 95% of all WPAs in the United States are located in the Prairie Pothole Region of South Dakota. Waterfowl Production Areas (WPAs) are a part of the prairie wetlands region and provide nesting habitat for wild ducks. Management involves manipulation of habitats as wildlife managers strive to meet the needs of nesting ducks and other prairie wildlife. To stimulate the growth of native grasses at the expense of aggressive invaders, native grasslands are periodically grazed, hayed, and on occasion, burned. Grazing is most often used, as it stimulates the growth of grasses, returns nutrients to the soil, and breaks up litter that eventually may cause a grassland to stagnate. During migration, large numbers and diverse species of bird life make WPA's a bird watcher's paradise.

Glaciers repeatedly covered the state except for its southwest part. Sioux or Dacotah Indians roamed here. Pierre Gaultier de Varennes, Sieur de la Verendrye explored in 1738. The US acquired the southwest portion by the 1803 Louisiana Purchase and the northeast portion by 1818 treaty with Great Britain. In 1863, Dakota Territory opened for homesteading. Prairie covered over 90% of the state, but is now down to less than 15%.

Below are some prairies that can still be seen in South Dakota:

Beadle County:
THE HURON WETLAND MANAGEMENT DISTRICT: 11,000-acres of purchased waterfowl habitat in Beadle, Sanborn, Jerauld, Hand, Hyde, Hughes, Sully, and Buffalo counties. The District also administers 65,000-acres of wetlands protected from draining, burning, or filling through perpetual easements purchased from willing landowners. The District staff also administers 40,000-acres of perpetual easements protecting grassland habitat from being plowed or cropped, and 10,000-acres of conservation easements, protecting both grasslands and wetlands. Visitors can expect to find a rich variety of plant and animal life. Native prairie grasses, wildflowers, and other plants can be observed and studied at leisure in natural prairie settings along with birds and mammals native to the prairies. For more information, contact the Manager, Huron WMD, at 605/352-5894.

Bennett County:
LACREEK NATIONAL WILDLIFE REFUGE: It lies in the shallow Lake Creek Valley on the northern edge of the Nebraska Sandhills. The Refuge includes native sandhills, sub-irrigated meadows, impounded

fresh water marshes, and short-grass prairie uplands. This is the region where the transition of eastern and western flora and fauna occurs. Wildlife includes a wide variety of life forms from wetlands, aquatic and marsh dwelling species to short-grass prairie fauna. The Refuge is located south of Martin, SD. Call the NWR in Martin, SD at 605/685-6508.

Brookings County:
AURORA PRAIRIE: 30-acres of wet prairie and many showy wild flowers among 80 species of forbs, and a beaver dam. The Prairie is southeast of the Brookings Holiday Inn. Call TNC, SD at 605/331-0619.

Brown County:
CLOVIS PRAIRIE: 157-acres of tallgrass prairie and colorful wildflowers. The Prairie is northwest of Columbia, SD. Call TNC, SD at 605/331-0619.

SAND LAKE NATIONAL WILDLIFE REFUGE: 21,498-acres with a variety of habitats, which attract birds and many other animals. The Refuge has wetlands, woods and grasslands along with Mud and Sand Lakes, which cover half of the Refuge. Today the Refuge has replaced crops with a variety of grasses that provide much needed wildlife habitat. Forty miles of roads wind through marshes, trees, and prairie grasslands. The NWR is 27-miles northeast of Aberdeen, SD, and 8-miles north of Columbia, SD, in the heart of the Prairie-Pothole Region of North America. Call the NWR in Columbia, SD at 605/885-6320.

THE SAND LAKE WETLAND MANAGEMENT DISTRICT: This WMD is located in the north central counties of Brown, Campbell, Edmunds, Faulk, McPherson, Potter, Spink and Walworth. The District is administered out of Sand Lake NWR and includes Pocasse National Wildlife Refuge, (see Campbell County) Waterfowl Production Areas, and wetland and grassland easements. Call the Sand Lake NWR in Columbia, SD at 605/885-6320.

NOTE! Grassland easements protect important nesting habitat on privately owned grasslands. Landowners retain ownership of the grasslands and although they may not farm the land, they are allowed unrestricted grazing. To protect nesting birds the land cannot be hayed until after July 15 each year. Like wetland easements, grassland easements are purchased by the USDA and are perpetual.

Buffalo County:
THE HURON WETLAND MANAGEMENT DISTRICT: (See Beadle County above).

Campbell County:
HURON WETLAND MANAGEMENT DISTRICT: (See Beadle County

above).

POCASSE NATIONAL WILDLIFE REFUGE: 2,585-acre refuge under joint management of the USCE and USFWS, with more than half the Refuge open water/marsh habitat, and the remainder in grasslands. This region follows a band of rolling glacial hills and rugged river "breaks" located within 10-miles of the Missouri River and is composed of mixed and short-grass prairie and hosts birds indigenous to the prairie. The NWR is just north of Pollock, SD. Call the Sand Lake NWR in Columbia, SD at 605/885-6320.

THE SAND LAKE WETLAND MANAGEMENT DISTRICT: (See Brown County above).

Charles Mix County:
LAKE ANDES NATIONAL WILDLIFE REFUGE: A NWR that has a natural, shallow prairie lake whose water supply depends entirely on natural runoff. Lake levels periodically rise and fall, with the entire lake going dry about once every twenty years. The Sioux Indians knew this lake well, for they frequently made camp here during their pursuit of migrating herds of buffalo and flocks of waterfowl. Around the turn of the century, as white settlements were becoming firmly established, the lake became well known as a fine place to fish. Over 350-acres of cropland were re-seeded to native grass nesting cover. The area is now managed primarily for the production of waterfowl and various species of water birds. An educational interpretative area located at the north-west corner of the Owens Bay Unit is open during daylight hours year-round. A nature trail meanders along the wooded lakeshore, across marshlands in the prairie pond complex, and returns via native grass-land uplands. Early morning or late afternoon walks along the nature trail offer visitors views of the blue-winged teal or of bobolinks singing territorial songs as they cling to the swaying stems of grassy plants. Guided tours are available to organized groups; however, prior arrange-ment must be made with the Refuge Manager. An observation platform permits easy viewing of wildlife. The NWR is located just north of Lake Andes, SD. Call the NWR in Lake Andes, SD, at 605/487-7603.

LAKE ANDES WETLAND MANAGEMENT DISTRICT: 18,888-acres of purchased waterfowl habitat (WPAs) lie in this district. In addition, the District protects almost 54,716-acres of wetlands and grasslands through perpetual easements purchased from landowners. The District encompasses 13 counties in southeastern South Dakota. Call Lake Andes NWR at Lake Andes, SD, at 605/487-7603.

Clark County:
WAUBAY WETLAND MANAGEMENT DISTRICT: (See Day County below).

Clay County:
SPIRIT MOUND: 6-acre prairie remnant growing on the western slope of Spirit Mound located 6-miles north of Vermillion, SD on Hwy 19. It is a bedrock knob that was shaped by the last glacier 13,000 years ago. The rare regal fritillary butterfly resides here. Sioux, Omaha, and Ottoes believed spirits occupied the mound, when Lewis and Clark visited the site on August 25, 1804. Call Mark Wetmore st 605/624-3748.

VERMILLION PRAIRIE: 22-acres of hillside prairie. The Prairie is northwest of Vermillion, SD on Bluff Rd. Call TNC, SD at 605/331-0619.

Codington County:
WAUBAY WETLAND MANAGEMENT DISTRICT: (See Day County below).

Corson County:
GRAND RIVER NATIONAL GRASSLAND: 155,000-acres of mixed-grass prairie, (see Perkins County below), where raptors hunt prairie dogs. The grassland is near Lemmon, SD. Call the Grand River Ranger District, Lemmon, SD 605/374-3592.

Custer County:
BLACK HILLS NATIONAL FOREST: (See Lawrence County Below).

BUFFALO GAP NATIONAL GRASSLAND: (See Fall River County below).

CUSTER STATE PARK: 73,000-acres of rolling prairie in the black hills named for George A. Custer who led a scientific army expedition there in 1874. 1,500 bison roam and pronghorn bound across the Park's prairie, as well as prairie dogs, white tail and mule deer, howling coyotes (the state animal) and, at higher elevations, mountain goats. The Park is east of Custer, SD. Lodging, prairie trail and other information can be obtained at 605/255-4515.

WIND CAVE NATIONAL PARK: 28,295-acres of mixed-grass prairie, and one of the world's longest and most complex caves, ponderosa pine forest, and associated wildlife are the main features of the Park. The cave is well known for its outstanding display of boxwork, an unusual cave formation composed of thin calcite fins resembling honeycombs. The Park's mixed-grass prairie is one of the few remaining and is home to native wildlife such as bison, elk, pronghorn, mule deer, coyotes, and prairie dogs. The Park is south of Rapid City, SD and west of Bad Lands National Park and 7-miles north of Hot Springs, SD on Highway 385. Call the Park in Hot Springs, SD at 605/745-4600.

Day County:
HILLABRARD LAKE RESEARCH NATURAL AREA: (See the

240

Waubay NWR below).

WAUBAY NATIONAL WILDLIFE REFUGE: 4,650-acres of lakes, marshlands, grasslands, and bur oak woodlands, which support diverse and abundant wildlife and provide nesting habitats for over 100 species of waterfowl, passerines and upland game birds. Additionally 140 avian species have been seen during migrations. The Sioux Indian "Waubay" word means "a nesting place for birds," which aptly describes the Refuge. Artist George Catlin described this area as a "blue and boundless ocean of prairie." Home to 37 species of mammals and 11 species of reptiles and amphibians, "diversity" describes the site's habitat and wildlife. The Refuge includes the Hillebrand Lake Research Natural Area comprising 40-acres of bur oak and 35-acres of bluestem prairie cover types. The NWR is located north of Waubay, SD. Contact the NWR in Waubay, SD at 605/947-4521.

WAUBAY WETLAND MANAGEMENT DISTRICT: 40,000-acres of WPAs in Day, Clark, Codington, Grant, Roberts, and Marshall Counties in South Dakota. More than 100,000-acres of wetlands and 150,000-acres of uplands in the WMD are protected through agreements between the USFS and private landowners. The management goal is to restore grasslands and wetlands and protect and promote their long-term health for wildlife, plants, and people. Waubay WMD has a variety of wetland and upland habitats. There are 199 WPAs units, which range from 3-acres to over 1,325-acres. Waubay WMD is the site of the very first WPA. Purchased in 1959, the parcel is a 160-acre tract named for the previous owners, Arnold and Lydia McCarlson. The McCarlson WPA is a small, but integral part of the NWR system. Re-seeding cultivated fields to native grasses and filling ditches to restore natural wetlands have returned Waubay to a more natural state. Refuge management of the Refuge includes haying allowed only after July 15 when most grassland birds and waterfowl are done nesting. Contact the Waubay NWR in Waubay, SD at 605/947-4521.

Deuel County:
ALTAMONT PRAIRIE: 62-acres of hilly prairie with wetlands. The Prairie is east of Tunerville, SD. Call TNC, SD at 605/331-0619.

CRYSTAL SPRINGS PRAIRIE PRESERVE: 6,000-acres of tallgrass prairie and wetlands owned by Ducks Unlimited (DU) and managed by TNC. This site is rich in wetlands and prairie and provides habitat for many species of waterfowl, shorebirds, prairie plants and prairie endemic animals. The Preserve is northeast of Clear Lake, SD. Call TNC, SD in Sioux Falls, SD at 605/331-0619.

Edmunds County:
GOEBEL RANCH: 8,500-acres of mixed to tallgrass prairie that

extends into McPherson County. The Ranch is close to the Ordway Prairie (see McPherson County). Access is limited and permission from Ducks Unlimited (DU) must be obtained in advance. Call DU at 701/355-3500.

SANDS LAKE WETLAND MANAGEMENT DISTRICT: (See Brown County above).

Fall River County:
BLACK HILLS NATIONAL FOREST: (See Lawrence County Below).

BUFFALO GAP NATIONAL GRASSLAND: 591,000-acres of mixed and short-grass prairie intermingled with eroding badlands where Native Americans drove bison over a gap that provides an overwhelming sense of openness. At first glance, the space may seem "empty" but a close look brings an appreciation for the rich diversity of animal life that has adapted to this unusual and often harsh environment. Each animal has the right coloration and behavior patterns to survive in one or more of the site's habitats. One animal important to the survival of other prairie animals is the black-tailed prairie dog. Habitats found on this grassland include tallgrass prairie, mixed-grass prairie, short-grass prairie, woody draws, juniper breaks, wetlands, rivers and ponds, and badlands formations. Late spring and late summer produce the showiest displays of wildflowers throughout the grassland. A large expanse of native prairie can be experienced here. The "east half" of the Grasslands extends from Kadoka, SD on the east to the Cheyenne River on the west, north to US Hwy 14 and south to the Pine Ridge Indian Reservation. A corner of Badlands National Park (see Jackson County below) touches BGNG. Wind Cave National Park (see Custer County above) and Black Hills National Forest (see Lawrence County below) are nearby. This grassland abuts the Oglala National Grassland (see Nebraska). BGNG is also in Custer and Jackson Counties. The visitor center is in Wall, SD. Contact Wall Ranger District, Wall, SD at 605/279-2125 or the Buffalo Gap National Grassland, Hot Springs, SD at 605/745-4107.

GEORGE S MICKELSON TRAIL: (See Lawrence County below).

Faulk County:
SANDS LAKE WETLAND MANAGEMENT DISTRICT: (See Brown County above).

Grant County:
WAUBAY WETLAND MANAGEMENT DISTRICT: (See Day County above).

Hand County:
HURON WETLAND MANAGEMENT DISTRICT: (See Beadle County

above).

Hughes County:
HURON WETLAND MANAGEMENT DISTRICT: (See Beadle County above).

Hyde County:
HURON WETLAND MANAGEMENT DISTRICT: (See Beadle County above).

Jackson County:
BADLANDS NATIONAL PARK: 244,000-acres of sharply eroded buttes, pinnacles and spires blended with the largest protected mixed-grass prairie in the United States. The Badlands Wilderness Area (Sage Creek Wilderness) covers 64,250-acres and is the site of the re-introduction of the black-footed ferret, the most endangered land mammal in North America. The Stronghold Unit is co-managed with the Oglala Sioux Tribe and includes sites of the 1890s Ghost Dances. Over 11,000 years of human history pale to the ages old paleontological resources. This park contains the world's richest Oligocene epoch fossil beds, dating 23 to 35 million years old. The evolution of mammal species such as the horse, sheep, rhinoceros and pig can be studied in the Badlands formations.

The Park's seven short trails sufficiently penetrate the diverse terrain found within the Park. Easy loops through wooded prairie give way to steep hikes along precipitous Badland formations. The Fossil Exhibit Trail is a quarter-mile loop that allows visitors to see fossils dating from the late Eocene and Oligocene epochs, often referred to as the Age of Mammals.

It's hard to miss the 600 strong herd of massive 2,000-pound bison or American Buffalo, as they are popularly called, that graze on prairie grass in the Park, especially if you drive along Sage Creek Rim Road. In addition, you may catch a rare glimpse of the Park's 25–30 black-footed ferrets. The Park extends into Pennington County and is just north of Interior, SD. Call the Park at 605/433-5361.

BUFFALO GAP NATIONAL GRASSLAND: (See Fall River County above).

Jerauld County:
HURON WETLAND MANAGEMENT DISTRICT: (See Beadle County above).

Jones County:
FORT PIERRE NATIONAL GRASSLAND: (See Stanley County below).

Lake County:
MADISON WETLAND MANAGEMENT DISTRICT: Headquartered
in Madison, South Dakota, the District manages 31,000-acres of purchased wetland areas, Waterfowl Production Areas (WPAs) and 41,000-
acres of wetlands protected from drainage by easements with private
landowners. All remaining tracts of native prairie are protected and
made more attractive to nesting birds by periodic haying, grazing, and
prescribed burning. In spite of these efforts, native grasslands are
threatened by the invasion of non-native brome and blue grasses.
Wildlife observers will find a rich variety of animal and plant life and
during migration, large numbers of birds. For additional information,
call the Manager, Madison Wetlands Management District in Madison,
SD at 605/256-2974.

Lawrence County:
BLACK HILLS NATIONAL FOREST: The Black Hills cover an area
125-miles long and 69-miles wide in western South Dakota and eastern
Wyoming. They include rugged rock formations, canyons and gulches,
open grassland parks, tumbling streams, deep lakes, and caves. The
Black Hills represent an ecological crossroads, with wildlife and plant
species typical of habitats of the Rocky Mountains, Great Plains, northern boreal forests, and eastern deciduous forests.

For many people, from past and present, Native Americans to today's
visitors, the Black Hills is a special place for physical and spiritual
renewal. The Lakota Sioux phrase Paha Sapa, "hills that are black," is
a superficial translation. The true translation is "the heart of every-
thing that is."

The Forest Headquarters is located in Custer, SD, with offices also in
Rapid City and Spearfish, SD as well as Sundance, WY. A Visitor Center
is located at Pactola Reservoir. Mount Rushmore National Monument,
Devils Tower National Monument and Jewel Cave National Monument
are all found adjacent to or near the Black Hills National Forest.
Within the Forest is the George S. Mickelson Trail, (see below) and the
111-mile Centennial Hiking Trail. The lookout at Harney Peak provides visitors a bird's-eye view of the Forest and a panoramic view of
four states, South Dakota, Nebraska, Wyoming, and Montana. The forest is also in Custer, Fall River, Meade, and Pennington Counties. Call
the USFS in Custer, SD at 605/673-2251.

GEORGE S. MICKELSON TRAIL: 109-mile bicycle trail in the heart
of the beautiful Black Hills was completed in September of 1998. Its
gentle slopes and easy access allow people of all ages and abilities to
enjoy the beauty of the Black Hills, 100 converted railroad bridges and
4 hardrock tunnels. The Trail mostly passes through Black Hills
National Forest Land, but parts pass through privately owned land,

where trail use is restricted to the Trail only. The Trail starts in Deadwood, SD (Lawrence County) and ends in Edgemont, SD (Fall River County), with some 11 other trailheads in-between, and passes through forest and native prairie. Additional information can be obtained from the Black Hills Trail Office, Lead, SD at 605/584-3896.

Lincoln County:
WILSON SAVANNA: Prairie ridges interspersed among eastern deciduous forest species such as bur oak, hackberry and black walnut. Excellent birding opportunities on this preserve overlooking the Big Sioux River. Walk-in access is ½-mile north and 1-mile west of Hudson, SD. Call TNC, SD at 605/331-0619.

Lyman County:
FORT PIERRE NATIONAL GRASSLAND: (See Stanley County below).

Marshall County:
WAUBAY WETLAND MANAGEMENT DISTRICT: (See Day County above).

McPherson County:
GOEBEL RANCH: (See Edmunds County above).

SAND LAKE WETLAND MANAGEMENT DISTRICT: (See Brown County above).

SAMUEL H. ORDWAY, JR. MEMORIAL PRESERVE: 7,800-acre prairie with big bluestem and cordgrass towering 6-7' high from swales. Hillsides blaze with 300 plant species including wild flowers that bloom from late spring throughout summer. Several thousand pairs of waterfowl nest near the preserve's 400 potholes. Many types of shorebirds, the majestic ferruginous hawk and whitetailed deer, red fox, coyote, raccoons, badgers, tepee rings, homestead ruins, and buffalo can be seen from a self-guided nature trail. The Preserve is 8-miles west of Leola, SD on Hwy 10. Call TNC, SD at 605/331-0619.

Meade County:
BLACK HILL NATIONAL FOREST: (See Lawrence County above).

BEAR BUTTE STATE PARK: Mato Paha or "Bear Mountain" is the Lakota name for this unique formation at Bear Butte State Park, which is a lone mountain, not a flat-topped "butte" as its name implies. It is one of several intrusions of igneous rock that formed millions of years ago along the northern edge of the Black Hills and is sacred to many Native Americans. Thousands visit its ceremonial area each summer. Because of its natural and historical heritage, this park has been designated as a National Natural Landmark and a National Recreation Trail. Two hiking trails wind their way around the slopes of Bear Butte. The Ceremonial Trail is a 1-mile loop that branches into an additional 1-mile hike to the top of the mountain whose summit provides a breathtaking view of four states. The Park also serves as the northern trailhead for the 111-mile Centennial Trail.

To accommodate conflicts, which developed over using Bear Butte, one trail is provided for Native American spiritual ceremonial purposes and another trail is provided for recreational hiking. The Park is northeast of Sturgis, SD. Call the Park at 605/347-5240.

Moody County:
SIOUX PRAIRIE: 200-acres of hilly pothole country sheltering 200 grass and forb species and a variety of bird & animal life. To reach the Prairie travel west 1½-miles on Hwy 34 to Hwy 77 from the intersection of US 29 and Hwy 34 and then turn north and travel 3½-miles. The Prairie is on the east side of road. Call TNC, SD at 605/331-0619.

Minnehaha County:
MAKOCE WASHTE: 40-acres of big bluestem prairie, wild flowers and bird life. The prairie is northeast of the intersection of US 29 and Hwy 42 in Sioux Falls, SD. Call TNC, SD at 605/331-0619.

Pennington County:
BLACK HILLS NATIONAL FOREST: (See Lawrence County above).

Perkins County:
GRAND RIVER NATIONAL GRASSLANDS: 161,000-acres, (which includes the Cedar River National Grasslands), of public lands interspersed with approximately 46,000-acres of private lands in Grant and Sioux Counties, North Dakota, and in Perkins, Corson, and Zieback Counties, South Dakota. (See Cedar River National Grasslands, North Dakota, Grant County) The Grand River Ranger District of the Custer National Forest administers these National Grasslands from Lemmon, SD. The rolling hills, river breaks, and scattered badlands of the Grand River and Cedar River National Grasslands sprawl across the Missouri Plateau of the Great Plains. Mixed-grass prairies dominate the landscape, and a few wooded draws occur where ground water is near the surface. The Grand River and its tributaries bisect the southern portion of the Ranger District; the Cedar River flows through the northern portion. Both of these rivers flow eastward to the Missouri River. The Ranger District maintains 1,000-acres of prairie dog towns in scattered locations where raptors hunt prairie dogs, which provide homes for burrowing owls and rattlesnakes, while cattle graze instead of the former bison occupants.

Thanks to the partnership efforts of the Ducks Unlimited organization, the Grasslands also have some excellent waterfowl viewing and warmwater fishing opportunities. In cooperation with DU, the Ranger District has improved waterfowl habitat through the construction of reservoirs. Many colorful wildflowers bloom in the prairie. The Grassland is near Lemmon, SD. Call the Grand River Ranger District, Lemmon, SD at 605/374-3592.

Potter County:
SAND LAKE WETLAND MANAGEMENT DISTRICT: (See Brown County above).

Roberts County:
WAUBAY WETLAND MANAGEMENT DISTRICT: (See Day County above).

Sanborn County:
HURON WETLAND MANAGEMENT DISTRICT: (See Beadle County above).

Spink County:
SAND LAKE WETLAND MANAGEMENT DISTRICT: (See Brown County above).

Stanley County:
FORT PIERRE NATIONAL GRASSLAND: 116,000-acres of mixed grass prairie. The Grassland is intermingled with private rangeland and fields of wheat, sorghum, and occasionally, sunflowers. An average of 18 inches of annual precipitation allows the Grassland's rolling clay hills to produce mixed prairie grasses, which can provide tall, dense nesting cover for gamebirds. Greater prairie chicken, a species of grouse whose range across the continent has been reduced by 90%, is common on the Grassland as is a similar species, the sharp-tailed grouse. These birds nest on the prairie and feed on private cropland, which is especially important in winter. Productive cover potential, cropland interspersion and presence of prairie chickens combine to make this grassland nationally significant as grouse habitat. Eight percent of the Grassland is rested from livestock grazing to help provide habitat for nesting birds. Big-game animals also call the Grassland home. Prairie dog towns cover about 400-acres, providing habitat for many other species of wildlife. The Grassland's northern edge is 5-miles south of the state capital, Pierre, SD, and southeast of Fort Pierre, SD. Contact the Nebraska National Forest, Chadron, NE at 308/432-0300 or call 605/224-5517.

Sully County:
HURON WETLAND MANAGEMENT DISTRICT: (See Beadle County above).

(E.M & IDA) YOUNG PRAIRIE: 901-acres of prairie and wetlands in Sully County located 5-miles east of Agar, SD. Call TNC, SD at 605/331-0619.

Walworth County:
SAND LAKE WETLAND MANAGEMENT DISTRICT: (See Brown County above).

Zieback County:
GRAND RIVER NATIONAL GRASSLAND: (See Perkins County above).

Fig 15

Western Sunflower (with the sun). See Fig 2 for typical prairie plant root structure.

Illustration by Charlotte Adelman

TENNESSEE

Tennessee's prairie disappeared over a century ago but is being restored in some places. Prescribed burning is an essential management tool for the fire-dependent tallgrass prairie ecosystem, and helps promote native vegetation, states the Elk and Bison Prairie Fire Management Officer at Land between the Lakes. Because only a portion of the prairie is burned at one time, wild life is not threatened. Ridding the prairie of built-up leaves, needles and grasses, lessens the risk of an unplanned fire.

Montgomery County:
FORT CAMPBELL: (Also located in Stewart County, TN and Christian County, KY, see above).

Stewart County:
FORT CAMPBELL: (Also located in Montgomery County and Christian County in Kentucky, above.)

LAND BETWEEN THE LAKES: (See Lyon County in Kentucky, above).

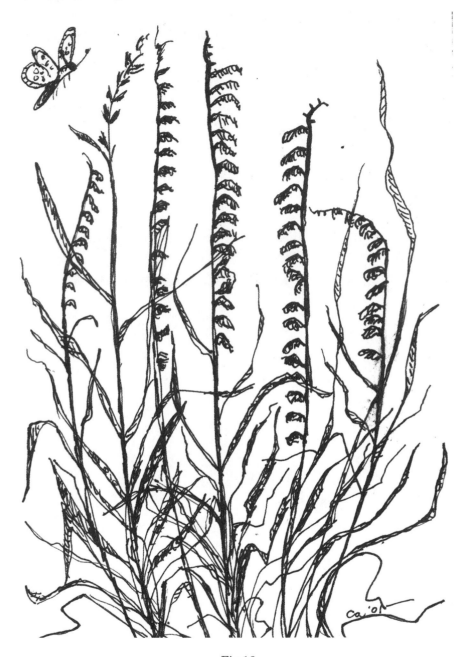

Fig 16
Sideoats Grama (with butterfly)-the state grass of Texas. See Fig 2 for root structure.

Illustration by Charlotte Adelman

TEXAS

Texas originally supported much prairie and savanna:

1. The Coastal Prairie Region covered approximately 500,000 acres along the coast, extending from Mexico to Louisiana with tallgrass prairie and post oak savanna.

2. The Blackland Prairies area intermingles with the Post Oak Savannah in the southeast and has divisions known as the San Antonio and Fayette Prairies. This rolling and well-dissected prairie represents the southern extension of the true prairie that occurs from Texas to Canada. Its dominant vegetation was tallgrass prairie.

3. The Post Oak Savannah lies just to the west of the Pineywoods and mixes considerably with the Blackland Prairies area in the south. This area includes the entire Claypan land resource area of Texas, which is part of the Southern Coastal Plains. The vegetation was tallgrass prairie and post oak and blackjack oak.

4. The Cross Timbers and Prairies area in North Central Texas includes the Cross Timbers, Grand Prairie, and North Central Prairies land resource areas. This area represents the southern extension of the Central Lowlands and the western extreme of the Coastal Plains.

5. The South Texas Plains lie south of a line from San Antonio to Del Rio. This area is the western extension of the Gulf Coastal Plains merging with the Mexico Plains on the west. The original vegetation was an open grassland or savannah-type along the coastal areas and brushy chaparral-grassland in the uplands.

6. The Edwards Plateau area includes 1.45 million acres known as the Granitic Central Basin in Llano and Mason Counties. The original vegetation was grassland, with some tallgrass prairie, and savanna.

7. The Rolling Plains area (24 million acres) coincides with the Rolling Plains land resource area of the southern Central Lowlands. The area is between the High Plains and the Cross Timbers and Prairies in the northern part of the state. The original vegetation was tall and mid-grass prairie.

8. The High Plains area is part of the Southern Great Plains. The original vegetation was short-grass prairie, mid-grass prairie and in isolated places tallgrass prairie.

9. The far west area of Texas (Trans-Pecos) contained dessert grassland and shrubs with mountainous areas with forest.

10. The Piney Woods Area in far eastern area of Texas was mostly forest with some savanna areas.

Much of this prairie no longer exists and only remnants remain. Although organizations are working to protect these areas, they need help.

The Texas Department of Transportation (TX DOT) plants many wildflowers and native plants along its roadways. Below is what it says about this effort:

1. TX DOT sows more than 47,000 pounds of wildflower seeds, including Bluebonnet, Buttercup and Indian paintbrushes; along the high-

ways each fall to ensure there are many spring flowers.

2. TX DOT has encouraged the establishment of wildflowers and other native vegetation for over 60 years.

3. Texas roadsides contribute substantially to the state's biological diversity. More than 800,000 acres of unpaved right of way is habitat to hundreds of species of animals and thousands of species of plants.

4. The Bluebonnet became the state flower in 1901.

5. All six species of Bluebonnets are considered the state flower of Texas.

5. Because Bluebonnets have deep root systems, the first Bluebonnet plantings were for erosion control rather than beauty.

6. Most Texas wildflowers are fall germinating.

7. Bluebonnets add nitrogen to the soil by fixating atmospheric nitrogen through root nodules.

8. Over 5,000 species of flowering plants are native to Texas.

9. Plantings of single species do not do well. Roadsides are most stable when planted in natural combinations of grasses, legumes and wildflowers. The varieties complement each other, form better ground cover, and are healthier, hardier and more drought resistant.

10. March, April and May are prime blooming months in Texas.

11 While spring hosts lavish wildflower displays, succeeding months offer their own spectacles. Brilliant yellow flowers thrive during summer's hottest months. In West Texas, colorful blossoms of cacti, succulents and other desert species may erupt following any rain.

12. While it is not illegal to pick Bluebonnets, it is illegal to trespass, damage, or destroy right of way or government property. So, do not go on private property, do not dig up clumps of flowers and do not drive over them. And remember because picked flowers cannot re-seed they will not return the next year.

13. In the spring, you can call TX DOT's toll-free travel information line, 800/452-9292, for automated information on the best locations for wildflowers along the Texas highway system.

In addition, Texas is in the "Prairie Passage" project to plant native prairie along the roadside of US 35 from the Oklahoma to the Mexican border. See Minnesota DOT in Minnesota, above, for more information.

The state grass is a short-grass prairie grass: Sideoats Grama.

Below are some areas where prairie, savanna and desert grasslands can still be seen.

NOTE! The mesquite prairie is unique to Texas.

Anderson County:
(GUS) ENGELING WILDLIFE MANAGEMENT AREA: 10,958-acres representative of the Post Oak Savannah Ecoregion which encompassed approximately 13,300 square miles of Texas reaching from Red River County in the northeast to Guadalupe County in the south. The area is gently rolling to hilly with a well-defined drainage system that

empties into Catfish Creek, which is a tributary of the Trinity River. Vegetation present in the uplands includes a dense overstory of oak, hickory, elm, and gum with a shade tolerant understory of flowering dogwood. Common grasses include little bluestem and broomsedge bluestem. Forbs include tickclover, wildbean, goldenrod, and doveweed. The WMA is 22- miles north of Palestine, TX, on US 287. Call the WMA in Tennessee Colony, TX at 903/928-2251.

RUSK AND PALASTINE STATE PARKS: 135.9-acres located in the area of transition from the Prairies, Cross Timbers, and the East Texas Forests. The Palestine Unit of the park is located 3-miles east of Palestine, TX on US Highway 84, adjacent to the Texas State Railroad State Historical Park Palestine depot in Anderson County. The Rusk Unit of the park is located in Cherokee County (see below). The Rusk Unit of the park is 3-miles west of Rusk, TX adjacent to the Texas State Railroad Rusk Depot off US 84 in Cherokee County. Call the Park in Rusk, TX at 903/683-5126.

Anahuac County:
ANAHUAC NATIONAL WILDLIFE REFUGE: 33,000-acres of mostly marsh. The Refuge is restoring its tallgrass and coastal wet prairie. Grassland birds nest here. The NWR is located southeast of Anahuac, TX. Call the Manager, Anahuac NWR, Anahuac, TX at 409/267-3337.

Aransas County:
ARANSAS NATIONAL WILDLIFE REFUGE: 70,504-acre refuge is made up of the Blackjack Peninsula, named for its scattered blackjack oaks. Grasslands, live oaks, and redbay thickets and some tallgrass prairie cover deep, sandy soils, ringed by tidal marshes and broken by long, narrow ponds, this NWR is home for cranes, alligators, deer, and many other species of wildlife including prairie species such as the prairie sparrow. This is where Cabeza de Vaca may have landed in the 1500s. The Refuge is also in Calhoun and Refugio Counties. (Also see Matagorda Island NWR, Calhoun County below). The NWR is northeast of Rockport, TX. Call the NWR Austwell, TX at 361/286-3559.

Armstrong County:
PALO DURO STATE PARK: (See Randall County below).

Bailey County:
MULESHOE NATIONAL WILDLIFE REFUGE: 5,809-acres of shortgrass rangeland (prairie) with scattered mesquite. Livestock are rotated among several pastures to keep grasslands in optimum condition for wildlife. The NWR is 20-miles south of Muleshoe, TX. Call the Refuge Manager, Muleshoe, TX at 806/946-3341.

Bandera County:
HILL COUNTRY STATE NATURAL AREA: 5,369.8-acre site has a

scenic mosaic of rocky hills, flowing springs, oak groves, grasslands, and canyons. This area is also in Medina County. The NA is southwest of Medina, TX. Call the NA at 830/796-4413.

LOST MAPLES STATE NATURAL AREA: 2,174.2-acres of outstanding examples of Edwards Plateau flora and fauna. It is a combination of steep, rugged limestone canyons, springs, plateau grasslands, wooded slopes, and clear streams. The preserve is also in Real County. The NA is located 5-miles north of Vanderpool on Ranch Road 187. Write to Lost Maples State Natural Area, HCR 1, Box 156, Vanderpool, TX 78885.

Brazoria County:
BRAZORIA NATIONAL WILDLIFE REFUGE: 43,388-acres consisting of saline and non-saline prairie, salt/mud flats, fresh and salt marsh, numerous potholes, several saltwater lakes, and two intermittent freshwater streams. Over 5,000-acres of native bluestem coastal prairie are also found here. The Western Hemisphere Shorebird Reserve Network has designated this NWR as an internationally significant shorebird site. Wading and shorebirds such as herons, ibis, gulls, terns, snipe, avocets, sandpipers, and stilts are common. Snow geese, along with smaller populations of Canada and white-fronted geese, usually reach peak numbers of 30,000 to 50,000 during December and January. Ducks winter at the Refuge and it supports other animals, such as alligators, snakes, turtles and amphibians. The upland prairies support sandhill cranes, quail, doves, hawks, and owls. Visitors can see abundant signs of coyotes, raccoons, bobcats, otters, and armadillos. The Refuge is southeast of Angleton, TX. Call the NWR Manager in Angleton, TX at 979/849-7771.

PEACH POINT WILDLIFE MANAGEMENT AREA: 11,190-acres in two units, one west of Freeport, TX off of Hwy 36, and the other unit is south of Freeport, TX on the Gulf Coast. Beyond the dense growth of trees is poorly drained coastal marsh and prairie. The public use areas adjacent to Hwy 36 are open from sunrise to sunset, 7 days a week. The remainder of the area is open to hunters or to organized groups for guided tours by special request. Call the WMA in Bay City, TX at 409/244-7697.

SAN BERNARD NATIONAL WILDLIFE REFUGE: (See Matagorda County below).

Brewster County:
BLACK GAP WILDLIFE MANAGEMENT AREA: 105,708-acres with some desert grassland east of the Big Bend National Park is the largest WMA in Texas and has some 10,000-13,000 acres of good desert grassland. The refuge also has a breeding population of Black Bear. Call the

WMA at Alpine, TX at 915/837-3251.

ELEPHANT MOUNTAIN WILDLIFE MANAGEMENT AREA: 23,147-acres of Chihuahuan Desert scrub to high desert grassland. The WMA is 25-miles south of Alpine, TX on Hwy 118. Call the WMA in Alpine, TX at 915/364-2228.

Brewster County:
BIG BEND RANCH STATE PARK: 280,280-acres of Chihuahuan Desert wilderness, extends along the Rio Grande from southeast of Presidio to near Lajitas, TX. Embracing some of the most remote and rugged terrain in the Southwest, it encompasses two mountain ranges containing ancient extinct volcanoes, precipitous canyons, desert grassland, and waterfalls. The park has a tremendous diversity of animal and plant species, including 14 species of bats, several species of hummingbirds, and mountain lions. A small herd of Texas Longhorn is a remnant of the property's ranching heritage. The Park is also in Presidio County. Call the Park at 915/229-3416.

Briscoe County:
CAPROCK CANYONS STATE PARK & TRAILWAY: 15,313.6-acres including the Trailway, a 64.25-mile Rail-to-Trail conversion that is open to the public from Estellene, TX to South Plains, TX. In addition 13 trails, (some still under construction), including 6 along the Trailway arc cach approximately 10-miles long and provide parking lots at each trailhead. Vegetation communities vary from sparse badlands, with their juniper, mesquite, and cacti, to abounding bottomlands with tall grasses, cottonwoods, plum thickets, and hackberries. The Park is alive with wildflowers.

A restoration project was started in 1980 on former cotton land adjacent to an approximately 250-acre area restored by the Soil Conservation Service's Great Plains Program in the 1960's. Diverse seeding and subsequent management have created a 600-acre mixed grassland that must be crossed to arrive at the Park headquarters. The 1983 introduction of black-tailed prairie dogs has gone on to produce today's well-established small colony. Several bison were added in 1985 and 10 pronghorn antelope were introduced later to the Park. Today this "natural" community is an important interpretive attraction at the Park helping visitors experience, on a small scale, the countryside, as it must have appeared before modern man modified the land. Caprock Canyons is home to the official Texas BisonHerd. The Park is 3½-miles north of Hwy 86 in Quitaque, TX on FM 1065. Call the Park at 806/455-1492.

Burleson County:
LAKE SOMERVILLE STATE PARK COMPLEX: Consists of four

units: Birch Creek, Nails Creek, Lake Somerville Trailway, and the Somerville Wildlife Management Area. This Complex extends into Lee County.

BIRCH CREEK is 2,365 acres in Burleson County on the north shore, and

NAILS CREEK consists of 3,155 acres in Lee County (see below) on the south shore near the West End of the lake. The two units are connected by a 13-mile trailway system. (See the Somerville WMA blow).

SOMERVILLE WILDLIFE MANAGEMENT AREA: 3,180-acres with the Yegua Creek Compartment in southwest Burleson County and the Nails Creek Compartment in northeast Lee County. The Texas Parks and Wildlife Department manage this WMA under a license agreement and in cooperation with the US Army Corps of Engineers. Objectives are to restore and maintain healthy populations of native fauna and flora in natural habitats and to provide for compatible public use. Beautiful prairie wildflowers can be found at both Birch Creek and Nails Creek and along the 13-mile trailway that connects the two areas. The trailway has one of the best spring wildflower displays in the Texas State Park System. For a scenic drive with abundant wildflowers take FM 180, FM 1697 and Scenic Highway 390. The best wildflower viewing is from March 15 to April 25. The Birch Creek Unit is located northwest of Somerville, TX. The Nails Creek Unit is east of Giddings, TX. Call the Birch Creek unit at Somerville, TX, at 979/535-7763. Call the Nails Creek unit in Ledbetter, TX at 979/289-2392.

Calhoun County:
ARANSAS NATIONAL WILDLIFE REFUGE: (See Aransas County above).

MATAGORDA ISLAND STATE PARK AND NATIONAL WILDLIFE REFUGE (Part of the Aransas NWR, see Aransas County above): 44,000-acres consisting of low lying coastal land and barrier islands, covered with prairie, woodlands, tidal marshes, and blackish ponds. An estimated 500-750 acres of barrier island-seacoast bluestem prairie are fenced to exclude grazing so that the tract can be managed as natural community, which is mostly gone in Texas. Matagorda Island is jointly managed by the US FWS and the Texas Parks and Wildlife Department (TPWD) and is accessible only by boat. Access is by ferry or private boat from Port O'Conner, TX. For passenger ferry information, contact the TPWD at 512/983-2215.
Note! Cabeza de Vaca ventured into this area, followed by Rene Robert Sueir de La Salle and Jean Lafitte.
Note also! This refuge and the immediate surrounding area serve as the wintering grounds for the whooping crane and provides excellent bird watching opportunities in fall, winter, and spring.

Cameron County:
LAGUNA ATASCOSA NATIONAL WILDLIFE REFUGE: 45,000-acres of a unique blend of temperate, subtropical, coastal, and desert habitats, including coastal prairie. Mexican plants and wildlife are at the northernmost edge of their range, and migrating waterfowl and sandhill cranes fly here from the north for the mild winters. When the Spanish explorer Alonzo Alvarez de Pineda arrived in the Rio Grande Valley in 1519, he found a landscape very different from what we see today. The area was abundant with wildlife, and 3 million acres were coastal prairies and brushlands. Doves darkened the sky, deer grew fat on grasslands, and ducks filled the bays near the coast. This NWR is one of the birdwatching "hot spots" in the United States with many species not found outside the lower Rio Grande Valley. Eighty percent of the North American population of redhead ducks winter here. Resident wildlife species include white-tailed deer, javelina, coyote, bobcat, alligator and armadillo. The Refuge is east of Rio Hondo, TX. Call the Refuge Manager in Rio Hondo, TX at 956/748-3607.

LOWER RIO GRAND NATIONAL WILDLIFE REFUGE: 90,000-acres expanding eventually to 132,000+ acres in scattered sites along the last 250-miles of the Rio Grande River. Habitat types include: chaparral, sub-tropical gallery forests, salt lakes, palm jungles, tidal flats, salt marshes, sand dunes (lomas), Bordas escarpment, and savannas. Considered one of the most biologically diverse NWRs on the continental United States, the NWR represents 11 distinct biotic communities that are host or home to 1,100 types of plants, 700 vertebrate species (including 484 bird species) and over 300 species of butterflies. The NWR extends into Hidalgo and Starr Counties. Call Santa Ana NWR in Alamo, TX at 956/787-3079.

Castro County:
PLAYA LAKES WILDLIFE MANAGEMENT AREA: 1,492-acre WMA in three units. The Armstrong and Dimmitt Units are located in the High Plains Ecological Area (originally short-grass prairie). The Armstrong Unit contains 480-acres leased for row crop agriculture, a 52-acre playa lake, and 108-acres of grassland surrounding the lake. The Dimmitt Unit contains a 77-acre playa lake and 345-acres of former farmland re-seeded with grass and forbs. These units are southwest of Dimmitt, TX off FM 1524 on Co Rd 503. The Dimmitt Unit is restricted to TPWD personnel. The Taylor Lakes Unit is part of the Rolling Plains Ecological Area and contains about 214-acres of former cropland being returned to grassland, 231-acres of pastureland and four lakes and wetlands consisting of 85-acres. This unit is southeast of Claredon, TX off US 287 in Donley County. All viewing here is restricted to the roads and all visitors are required to pre-register. Call the WMA in Paducah, TX at 806/492-3405.

Chambers County:
CANDY ABSHIER WILDLIFE MANAGEMENT AREA: 207-acres of coastal prairie, ponds and oak groves that is a very popular birding spot for hawks and migrants. The WMA is located at Galveston Bay on Smith Point. Call the WMA at 409/736-2551.

Cherokee County:
RUSK AND PALASTINE STATE PARKS: (see Anderson County)

Clay County:
LAKE ARROWHEAD STATE PARK: 524-acres of land surrounding the lake is generally semiarid, with gently rolling prairie, much of which has been covered by mesquite in recent decades. The park is home to a black-tailed prairie dog "town." Waterfowl and wading birds are common park visitors and residents. The Park is southeast of Wichita Falls, TX. Call the Park at 940/528-2211.

Collin County:
PARKHILL PRAIRIE PRESERVE & LAKE LAVON: 55-acre native prairie located within a 436-acre preserve approximately 50-miles northeast of Dallas. In addition to the native prairie, 15-20-acres of old-field on an adjacent northern site is being restored to prairie on which grazing has been eliminated. While no other restoration measures have been implemented, native grasses are flourishing. Native grasses are also returning to sites where grazing has been curtailed at Lake Lavon. According to Park Ranger Bob Wooley, little bluestem, big bluestem, and Indian grass are thriving on at least one "rested" site at Lavonia Park, located east of the lake dam. Lake Lavon is located southeast of McKinney, TX. Parkhill Prairie is located north of Farmersville, TX. Call the Collin County Open Space Program at the Collin County Administrative Office at 972/548-4603 or 972/548-4147.

HEARD NATURAL SCIENCE MUSEUM AND WILDLIFE SANCTU-ARY: 287-acre sanctuary, which include bottomland, woodland, prairie, and wetlands. The Sanctuary is a haven for more than 240 species of birds, mammals, reptiles and amphibians and nearly 150 species of wildflowers and other plants. A 50-acre wetlands features an outdoor learning center with an observation deck, a floating study laboratory and a boardwalk. The Heard Museum also has a Texas Native Plant Garden demonstrating how native plants, including prairie plants, can be used in an urban garden setting. The Museum is located southeast of McKinney, TX, 1-mile east of State Hwy 5 on FM 1378. Call the Museum at 972/562-5566.

Colorado County:
ATTWATER PRAIRIE CHICKEN NATIONAL WILDLIFE REFUGE: 10,000 plus acres of short-grass prairie supporting the Attwater prairie

chicken, a grouse, which is probably the most endangered bird in the United States. The Refuge is helping restore the Attwater's Prairie Chicken to a population goal of 5,000 birds. (Currently, there are 4 active captive propagation programs operating in Texas. These are: the Fossil Rim Wildlife Center, Glen Rose, Texas; the Houston Zoo, Houston, Texas; San Antonio Zoo, San Antonio, Texas; and the Small Upland-bird Research Facility (SURF) at Texas A&M University, College Station, Texas. All 4 of these locations have implemented captive-breeding programs for both Attwater's and greater prairie chickens. The greater prairie chicken often serves as a research surrogate due to the endangered state of the Attwater's.)

Much of the Refuge consists of virgin prairie, never plowed or converted to croplands. However, it also has formerly cultivated fields on their way to becoming prairie. In the fall the staff harvests native grass seeds from the virgin prairie and then distributes them in the old fields. Returning that field to a prairie takes years, but slowly the dedicated effort is paying off. During the day, one has a good chance of seeing bison. One might think the heavy hooves of bison, commonly known as American buffalo, pose an immediate threat to prairie chickens if they happen to be anywhere close by. Instead, the bison and cattle you may see on the Refuge are helping this bird with every mouthful they munch. Their grazing shapes the grassland into clumps with spaces between them that serve as pathways for young chicks. The NWR is located 7-miles northeast of Eagle Lake, TX off FM 3013. Call the NWR Manager in Eagle Lake, TX at 979/234-3021.

Comal County:
HONEY CREEK STATE NATURAL AREA: 2,293.7-acres of diverse habitat including ashe juniper, live oak, agarita, and Texas persimmon dominate the dry, rocky hills, and a few grasses such as little muhly and curly mesquite somehow find just enough soil in the cracks to persist. As the juniper and Baccharis are being removed from the upland flats, the stands of native grasses are increasing and Indiangrass, little bluestem, and switchgrass are reasserting their dominance. The NA is adjacent to Guadalupe River State Park and northeast of Boerne, TX. Call the NA in Spring Branch, TX at 830/438-2656.

Cooke County:
(RAY) ROBERTS PUBLIC HUNTING AREA: 40,920-acres dominated by the 29,000-acre Ray Roberts Lake with most of the land lying within the flood plain of the reservoir. The gently rolling landscape consists of post oak savanna, and the Grand Prairie Region to the west, which is covered principally with little bluestem on the uplands and mixed hardwoods in the bottomlands. The Area extends into Denton County. The Area office is northeast of Denton, TX off FM 3002. Call the Area

in Decatur, TX at 940/627-5475.

(RAY) ROBERTS LAKE STATE PARK: 5,848.8-acres located in the Eastern Cross Timbers area, a narrow strip of wooded terrain bordering the Blackland Prairies of north central Texas with prairie plants in evidence. The Park extends into Denton County. The Park is located southeast of Valley View, TX. Call the Park at 940/637-2294.

Cottle County:
MATADOR WILDLIFE MANAGEMENT AREA: 25,000-acres, with a plethora of grassland habitat, streams, a variety of soils, and the habitats associated with the Pease River riparian zone. The rich grasslands provide excellent cover for a plethora of life, and spring brings a tremendous wildflower display. The WMA is northwest of Paducah, TX off FM 3256. Call the WMA in Paducah, TX at 806/492-3405.

Culberson County:
MADERA CANYON PRESERVE: Desert scrubs such as creosotebush and tarbrush, desert grasslands, and pinyon-oak-juniper woodlands are present here. Call TNC, TX at San Antonia TX at 210/224-8774.

SIERRA DIABLO WILDLIFE MANAGEMENT AREA: 11,624-acres in 4 noncontiguous tracts. This WMA lies within the Chihuahuan Desert and has desert grasslands. The terrain is difficult and it may be impossible to gain access to public land over private land. Having your own drinking water is essential. Access is restricted and Texas Parks and Wildlife personnel must accompany visitors. The WMA is located in the Sierra Diablo Mountains north west of Van Horn, TX. Call the WMA at 915/364-2228.

Dallam County:
KIOWA AND RITA BLANCA NATIONAL GRASSLAND: 229,327-acres of mostly short-grass prairie supporting black-tailed prairie dogs, prairie chickens, bobcat, black bear, pronghorn, mule deer and red and gray fox. The Grassland extends into Colfax, Harding, Mora and Union Counties in New Mexico and Oklahoma. Call the US Forest Service at 505/374-9652.

Dallas County:
CEDAR HILL STATE PARK: 1,826-acre urban nature preserve located on the 7,500-acre Joe Pool Reservoir. Five native tallgrass prairie remnants are the park's most important natural resource. Cedar Hill is unique because it is where two climax eco-systems converge. The Park schedules off-trail walks on the prairie, with a discussion of the area's natural history and wildflowers. Bird watching is good and the Park has a mountain biking trail. The Park address is 1570 FM 1382, Cedar Hill, TX 75104. Call the Park at 972/291-3900.

CITY OF DALLAS: One can see pieces of prairie in and around Dallas, TX in places such as Reverchon Park, located at 3505 Maple Ave., Dallas, TX, phone 214/670-7720. Wildflower areas are located at White Rock Lake, 8300 Garland Road, Dallas, TX, phone 214-670-8242 and in the Dallas Nature Center, 7171 Mountain Creek Parkway, Dallas, TX, Telephone: 372/296-1955.

LAKEVIEW STATE PARK: Approximately 60-acres in four tracts are preserved as hay meadows consisting primarily of big bluestem-Indiangrass communities with abundant forbs. The best known is the 13-acre tract known as Penn Prairie, which is primarily big bluestem. The Park is located near Dallas, TX. Call the TPWD at 800/792-1112 or the Native Prairie Association of Texas (NPAT) at 512/339-0618.

PENN PRAIRIE: (See Lakeview State Park above)

Delta County:
COOPER LAKE STATE PARK, DOCTORS CREEK UNIT: (See Hopkins County for the South Sulphur Unit) 715.5-acres of post oak and various native grass species. Wildlife includes swamp rabbit, eastern cottontail, nine-banded armadillo, white-tailed deer, coyote, bobcat, waterfowl, bald eagle, beaver, raccoon, and wild hog. This unit of the Park is southeast of Cooper, TX. Call the Park at 903/395-3100.

Denton:
(RAY) ROBERTS PUBLIC HUNTING AREA: (see Cooke County above).

(RAY) ROBERTS LAKE STATE PARK: (see Cooke County above).

Dimmit County:
CHAPARRAL WILDLIFE MANAGEMENT AREA: (see LaSalle County below).

Donley County:
PLAYA LAKES WILDLIFE MANAGEMENT AREA: (see Castro County above).

El Paso County:
FRANKLIN MOUNTAINS STATE PARK: 24,247.56-acres, covering some 37 sq miles, all within the city limits of El Paso. Several thousand acres of desert grasslands are present on the park's eastern side, which are primarily composed of various species of grama grasses with a high percentage of stem and leaf succulents (desert plants). The Park's address is 1331 McKelligon Canyon Road, El Paso TX 79930. Call the Park at 915/566-6441.

Falls County:
LEONHARDT PRAIRIE PRESERVE: 40-acre preserve of unplowed Blackland Prairie. Access is restricted and allowed for research or vol-

unteer workdays. Call TNC, TX in Celeste, TX at 903/568-4139.

Fannin County:
BONHAM STATE PARK: 261-acre park including a 65-acre lake, rolling prairies, and woodlands. The Park is situated in the Blackland Prairie Region of Texas, and consists of terrain dominated by grassland interspersed by woodlands. Although the Park's grasslands are no longer pristine, they are recovering nicely and have small areas dominated by little bluestem and bushy bluestem. Numerous wildflowers and flowering shrubs cover the gently rolling prairie in the spring and stands of cedar and mixed hardwoods provide a panorama of multicolored leaves in the fall. The Park is southeast of Bonham, TX. Call the Park at 903/583-5022.

CADDO NATIONAL GRASSLAND: 17,785-acres in two units of open grasslands and post oak and blackjack oak savannas provide habitats for a variety of animal life, ranging from deer and opossums to bobwhite quail and mourning doves. One area of the Grassland is 11-miles north of Honey Grove, TX. The other section is south of Honey Grove, TX. Call the District Ranger, USFS in Decatur, TX, 940/627-5475.

HAGERMAN NATIONAL WILDLIFE REFUGE: 3,000-acres of marsh and water and 8,000-acres of upland and farmland, including restored prairie. Uplands are managed and restored by periodic burning, controlled grazing, and replanting of native grasses and forbs, which protect the soil and supply food and cover for many species of native and migrating wildlife. During the southern fall migration, many ducks and other birds frequent the NWR and wading birds are common throughout the warm months. The NWR is northwest of Sherman, TX. Call the Refuge Manager in Sherman, TX at 903/786-2826.

Fayette County:
KREISCHE BREWERY/MONUMENT HILL STATE PARK: 40.4-acres housing the old brewery and monument. This site contains about 10-acres of tallgrass prairie with big bluestem, Indiangrass and abundant forbs on a west-facing slope. This little known grassland occurs adjacent to post oak woodlands as well as communities akin to those as the Edwards Plateau. The site's unusual diversity is significant. A nature trail list of common plant and animal species and is available at the Park headquarters. The Park is 1-mile south of La Grange, TX. Call the Park at 979/968-5658.

Fort Bend County:
BRAZOS BEND STATE PARK: 4,897-acres in the Brazos River floodplains with areas of flat upland coastal prairies. 400-acres of fairly good Indian grass-little bluestem tall grass coastal prairie is managed through periodic prescribed burning and mowing. It is the best exam-

TEXAS

ple of coastal prairie on TPWD lands, and is an important aspect of the Park's interpretive program. Plans call for introduction of population of Attwater's Prairie Chicken, common here about 40 years ago. Nature lovers, birders, campers, and other outdoor enthusiasts will delight in an observation tower and platforms for wildlife observation/photography of more than 270 species of birds and other animals. The Park is 20-miles southeast of Richmond, TX on FM 762. Call the Park in Needville TX at 979/553-5101.

Freestone County:
RICHLAND CREEK WILDLIFE MANAGEMENT AREA: 13,796-acres in two units located where the Post Oak Savannah and the Blackland Prairie blend. The north unit plans to turn all open land into wetland by the year 2015. However, today both units hold numerous prairie flowers in the spring. The WMA is also in Navarro County. Both units are located south of Corsicana, TX off FM 488. Call the WMA in Streetman, TX at 903/389-7080.

Galveston County:
BOLIVAR FLATS SHOREBIRD SANCTUARY: 1,006-acres of coastal prairie and salt marsh managed to protect the productivity of large mud flats used by hundreds of thousands of birds. The Western Hemisphere Shorebird Reserve Network has declared this sanctuary a site of international importance. Call the Houston Audubon Society at 713/932-1639.

(LOUIS) SMITH/BOY SCOUT WOODS BIRD SANCTUARY: 50.8-acres of hackberry/oak motte and coastal prairie 1-mile from the Gulf of Mexico on High Island. This sanctuary is internationally famous for the large number of species of birds seen here in the spring. Call the Houston Audubon Society at 713/932-1639.

SMITH OAKS BIRD SANCTUARY: 122.2-acres on High Island which contain oak mottes with 100+ year old live oaks, ponds, wetlands and coastal prairie. This area is an important stopover habitat for migrating birds. Call the Houston Audubon Society at 713/932-1639.

TEXAS CITY PRAIRIE PRESERVE (formerly Galveston Bay Prairie Preserve): 2,263-acres feature rare coastal prairie habitat and is one of the last remaining sites that support wild Attwater's prairie chickens. At the turn of the century, approximately 1 million Attwater's prairie chickens lived along the Texas coast. However, loss of coastal prairie habitat over the years devastated the once-plentiful prairie chicken population. Restoration of the coastal prairie is one of the Preserve's primary stewardship activities. (See also Attwater Chicken Prairie National Wildlife Refuge in Anderson County above). In addition to habitat for the prairie chicken, the property provides a home for win-

263

tering and migrating grassland songbirds. The Preserve is situated on Galveston Bay in Texas City, approximately 40-miles south of Houston, TX. Call TNC, TX in San Antonio, TX at 210/224-8774.

Gillespie County:
ENCHANTED ROCK STATE NATURAL AREA: 1,643.5-acres of open oak woodland, mesquite grassland, floodplain, and a granite rock community. The park, also in Llano County, is on Big Sandy Creek, north of Fredericksburg, TX. Call the NA at 915/247-3903.

LYNDON B. JOHNSON STATE HISTORICAL PARK: 717.9-acres that is famous for its spring-blooming wildflower fields. Buffaloes, longhorns, and white-tailed deer are examples of the abundant wildlife of the Hill County. The Park is located 2-miles east of Stonewall, TX. Call the Park at 830/644-2252.

Gonzalas County:
(M O) NEASLONEY WILDLIFE MANAGEMENT AREA: 100-acres in the sandy post oak belt of Texas. An old field of about 40-acres remains treeless and contains some prairie plants. The WMA is south of Luling, TX on Hwy 80. Call the WMA in La Grange, TX at 979/968-6591.

Gray County:
MCCLELLAN CREEK NATIONAL GRASSLAND: 1,450-acres of short-grass prairie with over-wintering eagles and deer, quail and roadrunners. The grassland is northwest of McLean, TX on FR 2477. Call the USFS in Cheyenne, OK at 580/497-2143.

Grayson County:
EISENHOWER STATE PARK: 423.1-acres of grassy uplands, including rare remnants of the tallgrass prairie, terminate in rocky, shoreline bluffs and woodlands. A large variety of colorful wildflowers blooms throughout the growing season, March through November. Signs along the roadside in selected areas identify several wildflowers. A variety of mammals can be seen at the park as well as wintering bald eagles, pelicans, loons, and other waterfowl. Lake fossils are on display at the Park headquarters. The Park is northwest of Denison, TX on the shores of Lake Texoma. Call the Park at 903/465-1956.

Hardeman County:
COPPER BREAKS STATE PARK: 1,898.8-acres features rugged, scenic beauty with mixed grass/mesquite-covered mesas and juniper breaks with a restored prairie here. This is 120-acre project began in 1974 and has been re-seeded with initial mix of about 15 species. Today this area at the entrance to thePark looks like a natural prairie. North Texas wildlife abounds at the Park; wildlife and bird checklists are available at the park headquarters. The Park is 12-miles south of Quanah, TX. Call the Park at 940/839-4331.

Harrisson County:
CADDO LAKE STATE PARK & WILDLIFE MANAGEMENT AREA: 16,240-acres of diverse habitat among the grasses and trees of the area attracts small mammals, and a variety of birds. The Park and WMA is northeast of Marshall, TX. Call the WMA at 903/757-9572.

Hartley County:
LAKE RITA BLANCA STATE PARK: 1,668.4-acres, with Lake Rita Blanca itself covering 150-acres. This is the northernmost State Park in Texas and is located in the High Plains region of the Texas Panhandle. The vegetation is native short-grass. This prairie plant community provides a unique opportunity for education with the local schools and the general public. Each winter, thousands of ducks and geese come to Lake Rita Blanca, while during the year there is a variety of other wildlife. The Park is located just south of the City of Dalhart, TX off US 385/87 and FM 281. Call the Park in Canyon TX at 806/488-2227.

Hemphill County:
GENE HOWE WILDLIFE MANAGEMENT AREA: 6,714-acres in two units, the Main Unit and the 889-acre Murphy Unit. The Murphy Unit consists of old farm field and native short-grass prairie and is north of Glazier, TX off Hwy 305 in Limscomb County. The Main Unit is northeast of Canadian, TX off FM 2266 and has a 50-acre subirrigated meadow with switchgrass, prairie cordgrass, and eastern gamagrass with a prairie dog town. This tallgrass prairie remnant is subject to grazing and mowing. The WMA is open year round except during special permit hunts. Call the WMA in Canadian, TX at 806/323-8642 or TPW at 800/792-1112.

Hidalgo County:
LOWER RIO GRAND NATIONAL WILDLIFE REFUGE: (See Cameron County above).

Hill County:
AQUILLA WILDLIFE MANAGEMENT AREA: 9,826-acres located in the confluence of the Eastern Timbers and the Blackland Prairie regions consisting of open lands, which have areas of degraded prairies. Access to the WMA is by foot only. The WMA is southeast of Whitney, TX off FM 310. Call the WMA in Clinton, TX at 254/582-2719.

LAKE WHITNEY STATE PARK: 1,280.7-acre park located in the Grand Prairie subregion of the Black land Prairie natural region containing open disturbed tallgrass prairie remnants with scattered groves of live oak and a small area of post oak/blackjack oak woodland. In the spring, bluebonnets, Indian paintbrushes, and over 40 species of wildflowers cover the roadside and landscape. Many animals have been spotted here along with 194 species of birds, including wild turkeys and bald eagles. The Park is located southwest of Whitney, TX. Call the Park at 254/694-3793.

Hopkins County:
COOPER LAKE STATE PARK, SOUTH SULPHUR UNIT: (See Delta County above) 2,310.5 acres. This unit of the Park is northwest of Sulphur Springs, TX. Call the Park at 903/945-5256.

Howard County:
BIG SPRING STATE PARK: 381.99 acres located within the city limits of Big Spring, TX. To the north and east are the western Rolling Plains; to the south is the Edwards Plateau; and to the west are the southern High Plains (also known as the Llano Estacado or the Staked Plains). The mixing of ecological regions results in a variety of plant and animal life representative of each region. Prickly pear and other cacti are common on the rocky slops of the Park. A small prairie dog town lies in a little valley on the south side of the Park. Watch for wildlife near the ponds. A burrowing owl population can be observed at a nearby air-park. Comanches and earlier Indian groups frequently visited the park area in the past, probably attracted by the permanent source of spring water. Spaniards may have first visited the area as early as 1768. Call the Park in Big Spring TX at 915/263-4931.

Hudspeth County:
GYPSUM DUNES: 177-acres of dunes similar in community type to those found on deep sands elsewhere in the Trans-Pecos (See Monahans Sandhills State Park, Ward County). Significant dunes flora found on the dunes include sand bluestem, broom pea, rosemary mint, soaptree yucca, and gypgrama. Botanical diversity increases where the dune fields meet the surrounding grasslands and the less-saline quartzite sand areas. The Dunes are located near Del City, TX. Call TNC, TX in Del Rio, TX at 915/292-4351.

Hunt County:
CLYMER MEADOW PRESERVE: 1,000-acre virgin Blackland Prairie which is the Texas version of the tallgrass prairie that once stretched from near the Texas Coast to southern Manitoba. The prairie provides habitat for a great number of bird species whose presence changes according to the season. Wildflowers, such as rough-leaf rosinweed, Indian paintbrush, prairie clover and American basketflower are abundant. There is an effort to expand the Clymer preserve to more than 2,000-acres and in time protect more than 16,000 acres. In 2001, 30 bison were added to provide a more wild state in the Preserve. Access is limited and is by appointment. Call TNC, TX in Celeste, TX at 903/568-4139.

COUNTY LINE PRESERVE: 40-acres, 20 of which are virgin Blackland Prairie.Plant communities are similar to those found at Clymer Meadow. The preserve in located 3-miles west of Clymer Meadow (see above). Access is limited and allowed for research and volunteer workday purposes only. Call TNC, TX in Celeste, TX at 903/568-4139.

LAKE TAWAKONI STATE PARK: 376.3-acres of mostly upland regrowth and creek-bottom, post-oak woodlands, and a small tract of tallgrass prairie. The Park is north of Wills Point, TX. Call the Park at 903/425-2332.

TAWAKONI WILDLIFE MANAGEMENT AREA: 2,335-acres in three units. The land within the Tawakoni WMA is part of the Blackland Prairie and had been farmed for some 100 years, yet some prairie plants still survive here. The WMA's three units are south of Greenville, TX. Call the WMA in Sulphur Springs, TX at 903/945-3132.

Jeff Davis County:
DAVIS MOUNTAINS STATE PARK: 2,708.9 acres at extremes of altitude averaging 1-mile high produce both plains grasslands and pinyon juniper-oak woodlands. Montezuma quail, usually farther west, are regularly observed in the Park. During wet years, the Park abounds in wildflowers. The Park is northwest of Fort Davis, TX. Call the Park at 915/426-3337.

Jim Wells County:
LAKE CORPUS CHRISTI STATE PARK: (See San Patricio County below).

Kenedy County:
KENEDY RANCH: 400,099-acres of native prairies, coastal marshes, and brush country near Sarita, TX. Call the Kenedy Foundation Ranch Nature Tours at 800/757-4470.

Kerr County:
KERR WILDLIFE MANAGEMENT AREA: 6,493-acres of gently rolling rocky hills cut by small draws with limestone bedrock barely concealed beneath shallow soil. Grazing, prescribed burns and brush removal are being used to restore the area to its original habitat, savanna and prairie. This is a good birding spot. Visitors must register at the site before they enter. The WMA is east of Hunt, TX off FM 1340. Call the WMA in Hunt, TX at 830/238-4483.

Kimble County:
WALTER BUCK WILDLIFE MANAGEMENT AREA: 2,123-acres adjacent to South Llano River State Park. The WMA contains deep canyons and steep hills that have prairie grasses. The WMA is located south of

Junction, TX. Call the WMA in Junction, TX at 915/446-3994.

Lamar County:
(PAT) MAYSE WILDLIFE MANAGEMENT AREA: 8,925-acres in the Post Oak Savanna Region of Texas. The WMA contains 1,500-acres of lake surface, 2,500-acres of abandoned fields and pastures, and approximately 5,000-acres of hardwood timber. One can see prairie flowers and walk trails through open meadows, post oak savanna, and dense woodland. The WMA is located northwest of Paris, TX on FM 1499. Call the WMA in Paris, TX at 902/785-0482.

TRIDENS PRAIRIE PRESERVE: 97-acre prairie preserve possesses an abundance of wildflowers, which can be viewed from the road. Access within the prairie is by appointment. The Preserve is 8-miles west of Paris, TX. Call the TNC, TX in Celeste, TX at 903/568-4139.

LaSalle County:
CHAPARRAL WILDLIFE MANAGEMENT AREA: 15,200-acres of South Texas brush country. The WMA extends into Dimmit County. A 7-foot fence to facilitate scientific investigations encloses the Area. Sound wildlife management tools like prescribed burning, grazing, brush control, and hunting are used to demonstrate the results of proven practices to resource managers, landowners, and other interested groups or individuals. Thorny shrubs and cacti dominate the landscape. Grasses and forbs are fairly abundant, depending on seasonal rainfall patterns. Introduced perennial grasses (Lehmann lovegrass and buffalo grass) have become a nuisance. Overgrazing by former livestock has dramatically reduced native grasses. If rainfall and weather conditions come together, just right, spring and fall displays of wildflowers can be spectacular. The WMA is southwest of Cotulla, TX off FM 133. Call the WMA in Artesia Wells, TX at 830/676-3413.

Lee County:
LAKE SOMERVILLE STATE PARK COMPLEX: (See Burleson County above).

BIRCH CREEK: (See Burleson County above).

SOMERVILLE WILDLIFE MANAGEMENT AREA: (See Burleson County above).

Liberty County:
MARYSEE PRAIRIE: 10-acre coastal prairie remnant. Contact the Natural Area Preservation Association Inc, 4144 Cochran Chapel Rd, Dallas, TX 75209 or email napa@texas.net.

Lipscomb County:
GENE HOWE WILDLIFE MANAGEMENT AREA: (See Hemphill County above)

Limestone County:
FORT PARKER STATE PARK: 1,458.8-acres (758.8 land acres and a 700-acre lake). The Park planted a Native Prairie Demonstration Site near the dump station located across from historic Springfield Cemetery and about 0.3-miles down the Park road from the headquarters. It is planted with native grasses and wildflowers that grow in this particular region and soils. The Park is located, 7-miles south of Mexia, TX. Call the Park at 254/562-5751.

Live Oak County:
LAKE CORPUS CHRISTI STATE PARK: (See San Patricio County below).

Llano County:
ENCHANTED ROCK STATE NATURAL AREA: (See Gillespie County).

Lubbock County:
LUBBOCK LAKE LANDMARK STATE HISTORICAL PARK: 336.6-acre, day-use only, historic site, is an archaeological and nature preserve jointly operated by Texas Parks and Wildlife Department and Texas Tech University. This site encompasses most of the designated 300-acre National Historic Landmark, an archeology-rich area lying along Yellowhouse Draw, a dry tributary of the Brazos River. Lubbock Lake has also received designation as a State Archeological Landmark. It is one of very few sites in North America known to contain evidence of a complete sequence of human existence during the past 11,500 years: from the Paleoindian Clovis culture, through the Archaic, Ceramic, and Protohistoric cultures, to Historic times. The area has archeological digs and a bronze statute of a mother and baby mammoth. This site has been re-vegetated with native species. The Park is in northwest corner of Lubbock, TX. Call the Park at 806/765-0737.

Mason County:
MASON MOUNTAIN WILDLIFE MANAGEMENT AREA: 5,301-acres of mixed plant communities in a rugged landscape. The WMA is where plant communities from north, south, east and west blend including prairie grasses. Access is restricted to hunters with special permits and groups by appointment. The WMA is located north of Mason, TX off Old Mason Rd. Call the WMA in Mason, TX at 915/347-5037.

Matagorda County:
BIG BOGGY NATIONAL WILDLIFE REFUGE: 4,100-acres of coastal prairies and salt marshes, have three large saltwater lakes and three freshwater impoundment's. Its Dressing Point Island is a major rookery for colonial nesting birds on the Texas Gulf Coast. The Refuge is southeast of Wadsworth, TX. Call the NWR in Angleton, TX at 409/849-6062.

(CLIVE RUNNELS) MAD ISLAND MARSH PRESERVE: 7,048-acre preserve of wetlands, coastal prairies, tidal wetlands and crop fields. With the help of Ducks Unlimited, the preserve now has 120-acres of freshwater wetlands, 765-acres of resorted coastal prairie, 166-acres of freshwater wetlands, 2,522-acres of tidal wetlands, with 1,130-acres of native coastal prairies, and 1,450-acres of ricefield. The Preserve is next to the Mad Island Wildlife Management Area, which was turned over to the State by TNC, TX. The area is especially important to waterfowl and sandhill cranes and various wading birds. The Preserve is southeast of Collegeport, TX on West Matagorda Bay off FM 1095. Call TNC, TX in Collegeport, TX at 361/972-2559.

MAD ISLAND WILDLIFE MANAGEMENT AREA: 7,200-acres with half upland short to mid-grass prairie. The other half is marshes, lakes and ponds. (See Mad Island Marsh Preserve, above, for location of the WMA). Call the WMA in Bay City, TX at 409/244-7697.

SAN BERNARD NATIONAL WILDLIFE REFUGE: 27,414-acres of flat coastal prairie and salt marsh with numerous saltwater lakes, shallow freshwater lakes and marshes, an intermittent stream, and wooded areas. Natural elevations range from three feet below mean sea level at the bottom of Cow Trap Lake to nine feet above mean sea level on the upland prairies. The Refuge extends into Brazoria County (see above). Wading and shore birds are common. A rookery in the Cedar Lakes area provides nesting for more than 15 different species of colony nesting birds. Endangered eastern brown pelicans also use this area. The Refuge is southwest of Lake Jackson, TX. Call the NWR in Brazoria, Texas at 979/964-3639.

Medina County:
HILL COUNTRY STATE NATURAL AREA: (See Bandera County above).

Navarro County:
RICHLAND CREEK WILDLIFE MANAGEMENT AREA: (see Freestone County above).

Orange County:
(J D) MURPHREE WILDLIFE MANAGEMENT AREA: 24,498-acres in three units. The outstanding feature here is the extensive coastal prairie. The units are open to wildlife viewing whenever a hunt is not in progress. The WMA is located near Port Arthur, TX. Call the WMA in Port Arthur, TX at 409/736-2551.

Parker County:
LAKE MINERAL WELLS STATE PARK & TRAILWAY: 3,282.5 acres, encompassing Lake Mineral Wells. The peak blooming time for its won-

derful prairie wildflower display is from mid April to mid May. The best places to view the wildflowers are along the roadway and the Cross-Timbers Hike/Bike/Equestrian Trail, and the State Trailway, which is 20-miles in length and runs from Mineral Wells, TX to Weatherford, TX. The Park is located 4-miles east of Mineral Wells on US 180. Call the Park at 940/328-1171.

Pecos County:
DIAMOND Y SPRING PRESERVE: 1,502-acre preserve appears to be no more than a small pond and creek in the middle of desert grasslands. However, the rarity of the desert spring habitat and the organisms it sustains establishes the area as one of the most endangered and unique holes in the ground on the planet. The Preserve is 12-miles northwest of Fort Stockton, TX off Hwy 18. Public visits to the preserve are encouraged, but by appointment only. Call TNC, West Texas Office at Fort Davis, TX at 915/426-2390/1.

Randall County:
BUFFALO LAKE NATIONAL WILDLIFE REFUGE: 7,664-acres of short-grass prairie, marsh, woodland and cropland habitats. The Refuge contains some of the best remaining short-grass prairie in the United States, including 175-acres designated a National Natural Landmark. Short-grass prairie ecosystems were historically maintained by annual grazing of migrating American bison. With the bison gone, grazing cattle maintains this ecosystem. Over 300 Neotropical birds species have been recorded on the refuge. Resident species include mule and white-tailed deer, prairie dog, bobcat, coyote, wild turkey, pheasant, quail, and rabbit. The Refuge is near Umbarger, TX. Call the NWR Manager in Umbarger, TX at 806/499-3382.

PALO DURO STATE PARK: 16,402-acres located on the southern high plains, an area called El Llano Estacado or "staked plains." The Park is also in Armstrong County. The rim of the canyon is considered short-grass prairie while the elevated moisture of the canyon floor supports a greater diversity of plants including some medium and tallgrass species along with shrubs and trees. Abundant wildflowers bloom along the 16-miles of road inside the Park, the Paeso Del Rio Trail, the Sunflower Trail, and the Chinaberry day use area. The Park is located about 12-miles east of Canyon, TX on Hwy 217. Call the Park at 806/488-2227.

Real County:
LOST MAPLES STATE NATURAL AREA: (See Bandera County above).

Reeves County:
SANDIA SPRINGS: 240-acres of desert grassland. Access is limited.

271

Prairie Directory

Call TNC, TX in San Antonio, TX at 210/224-8774.

Refugio County:
ARANSAS NATIONAL WILDLIFE REFUGE: (See Aransas Co above).

San Patricio County:
LAKE CORPUS CHRISTI STATE PARK: 14,111.78-acre mixture of brushland, the sometimes marshy margins, and open waters of Lake Corpus Christi and the riparian woodlands along the Nueces River provide a diverse ecological area. This park extends into Jim Wells and Live Oak Counties. The State Park and nearby natural areas represents one of the few remaining stands of brushland in the area and provide an important landfall for neotropical bird migrants and play an even greater role in conserving plants and animals native to the mesquite grassland. The Park is located 4-miles southwest of Mathis, TX off State Highway 359. Call the Park at 361/547-2635.

(THE ROB & BESSIE) WELDER WILDLIFE FOUNDATION AND REFUGE: 7,800-acre in the Tamaulipan Biotic Province in a transitional area between the Gulf Prairies and Marshes and the Rio Grande Plains vegetation areas. 50% is degraded mixed-grass prairie and scrubland with some areas as big as 50-acres of prairie scattered throughout. The Refuge is located 8-miles northeast of Sinton, TX. Call the Refuge in Sinton, TX at 361/364-2643.

Smith County:
THE NATURE CENTER: 82-acres of prairie, pine forest, a constructed pond and wetland with a visitor center and nature trails. The Nature Center is south of Tyler, TX off FM 848. Call the Nature Center in Tyler, TX at 903/566-1626.

OLD SABINE BOTTOM WILDLIFE MANAGEMENT AREA: 5,158-acres of bottomland hardwoods, sloughs, small lakes, and remnants of old river channels. At the west end of the WMA is 221-acres of degraded prairie pastureland holding prairie plants within. The WMA is located 5-miles northeast of Lindale, TX and is bounded on the west by FM 1804 and meanders between the Old Sabine River Channel and the Sabine River. Call the WMA in Tyler, TX at 903/566-1626.

Starr County:
LOWER RIO GRAND NATIONAL WILDLIFE REFUGE: (See Cameron County above).

Taylor County:
ABILENE STATE PARK: 529.4-acres in a semi-arid region of short-grass prairie, brushland, and wooded stream valleys with wildflowers. The park has bluebonnets, black-eyed Susan, wild verbena, Indian blanket, dotted gayfeather, and Maximillian sunflower best seen from

272

the road into the park, the water tower, the Boy Scout Trail leading to Buffalo Wallow, the bank surrounding Buffalo Wallow, and the southern end of the Elm Creek nature trail. This is a good park for wildlife observation and photography. The Park is 16-miles southwest of Abilene, TX. Call the Park in Tuscola TX at 915/572-3204.

Tom Green County:
SAN ANGELO STATE PARK: 7,677-acres astride the junction of four ecological zones: the High Plains to the north, the Texas Hill Country to the south, the Rolling Plains to the east, and the arid Trans-Pecos to the west. Consequently, plant and animal life are highly diversified, including some 350 species of birds and about 50 species of mammals. An extreme drought situation over the past few years has deprived the Park of its normal flower blooms produced in wetter conditions. The Park is west of San Angelo, TX. Call the Park at 915/949-4757.

Travis County:
LADYBIRD JOHNSON WILDFLOWER CENTER: While the wildflower center has no preserves that it protects, it is a source for information on natural plantings and wildflower information. The Lady Bird Johnson Wildflower Center's Clearinghouse offers a wide variety of native plant information. Whether you are thinking of using native plants in your home garden, around your business, or at your local elementary school, the Clearinghouse has the information you need to get started.
The address is:
4801 La Crosse Avenue
Austin, Texas 78739-1702
512/292-4200.

TEXAS PARKS & WILDLIFE DEPARTMENT COMPLEX: 20-acres of the TPWD headquarters grounds, former cotton land, have been restored to resemble the region's natural Blackland Prairie community that once occurred here. The project was begun in 1976. The Complex is located at 4200 Smith School Road, Austin, TX 78744. Telephone: 800/792-1112 or 512/389-4800.

Tyler County:
BIG THICKET BOGS AND PINELANDS PRESERVE: 49-acre preserve contains two distinct forest communities: the dry upland pine community consisting primarily of shrubs, grasses, sedges, ferns, and pitcher plants and the wet pine savanna community. The Preserve is located near Warren, TX. Call TNC, TX in Texas City, TX at 409/945-4677.

Ward County:
MONAHANS SANDHILLS STATE PARK: 3,840-acres of sand dunes.

The Park features a very interesting tall grassland community within the Chihuahuan Desert related to those found on deep sands elsewhere in the Trans-Pecos (i.e. The Nature Conservancy's Gypsum Dunes Preserve-Hudspeth County) and eastward in deep sands throughout the Rolling Plains. However, few good undisturbed examples remain. The Park is located northeast of Monahans, TX and extends into Winkler County. Call the Park at 915/943-2092.

Wharton County:
(D R) WINTERMANN WILDLIFE MANAGEMENT AREA: 246-acres in the flat coastal plains area. Wetlands cover about 37-acres with most of the balance being fallow rice fields. Sedges and marsh elder cover the higher ground, and wet prairie areas support bluestem, switchgrass and Indian grass. Access is restricted to organized groups on specified dates when Texas Park and Wildlife personnel are present. The WMA is located about 15-miles northwest of Wharton, TX. Call the WMA in Warton, TX at 409/532-2170.

Williamson County:
GRANGER WILDLIFE MANAGEMENT AREA: 11,116-acres adjacent and around Granger Lake has 200 to 300-acres of remnant prairie. About 8,000-acres are being restored to tallgrass prairie. The WMA is generally open except during hunting season. The WMA is located southeast of Granger, TX. Call at 512/756-2945 or the WMA in Burnett, TX at 512/859-2668.

NATIVE PRAIRIE ASSOCIATION OF TEXAS: This association is another source of information on prairies and prairie plants, how to grow prairies, homegrown and small prairies; prairie burns and related information. Their address is P.O. Box 210, Georgetown, TX. Their website is located at www.texasprairie.org/. The president's phone is 512/339-0618.

Winkler County:
MONAHANS SANDHILLS STATE PARK: (See Ward County above).

Wise County:
LYNDON B JOHNSON NATIONAL GRASSLAND: 20,324-acres of open grassland. The Grassland is northwest of Decatur, TX. Call the District Ranger, USFS in Decatur, TX, 940/627-5475.

WISCONSIN

At one time, 2.1 million acres in Wisconsin were prairie and savanna. Today just a fraction of that amount still exists. However, Wisconsin Department of Natural Resources (DNR, WI) is restoring and protecting existing prairie and savanna. In the 1930s, the University of Wisconsin, under the direction of Aldo Leopold, initiated the first large-scale restoration of Midwest Prairie. It can be seen at the University of Wisconsin Arboretum (See Dane County). The Wisconsin chapter of The Nature Conservancy has launched a Tallgrass Prairie and Savanna Initiative to preserve representative samples. Contact the Wisconsin Bureau of Endangered Resources at 608/266-0394 or TNC, WI at 608/251-8140 or the Prairie Enthusiasts (TPE) at 608/375-5276.

Although Wisconsin is not a part of the "Prairie Passage," because US 35 does not pass through the State, the Wisconsin Department of Transportation (WDOT) does have a program of restoring prairies within its rights-of-way and is identifying remnant prairies and trying to restore them. Call the WDOT at 608/266-1017.

Below are some of the prairies that one can visit in Wisconsin:

Adams County:
QUINCY BLUFF AND WETLANDS PRESERVE: 3,298-acres of wide-open expanse, featuring wooded ridges, steep bluffs, open cliffs and wetlands. The pine-oak barren, and important natural community found at the preserve, is one of the rarest natural communities in the state. Barrens are sandy open areas of grasses and low shrubs that are sparsely timbered with pine and "scrub" oak. Natural fire, burning by Native Americans and fires following logging once maintained barrens communities. Beginning in 1993, TNC staff conducts controlled burns on small areas at Quincy Bluff to restore the pine-oak barrens. The preserve is northwest of White Creek, WI. Call TNC, WI at 608/251-8140 or the DNR, WI, West Central Regional Office in Eau Claire, WI at 715/839-3700.

Bayfield County:
MOQUAH BARRENS STATE NATURAL AREA: 640-acre NA with 90-acres of original Pine Barrens is set-aside as a research area to study natural succession in the absence of fire. The NA is located northwest of Ashland, WI. Call the USFS in Milwaukee, WI at 414/297-3600.

Brown County:
(L. H.) BARKHAUSEN WATERFOWL PRESERVE/FORT HOWARD PAPER FOUNDATION WILDLIFE AREA: 920-acres of marsh, shrub-lands, lowland woods and a tiny remnant of prairie are all that remains of a once vast wetland-prairie complex. The WA is northeast of Green Bay, WI and at the intersection of Co Hwys M & J. Call Brown County at 414/434-2824.

Buffalo County:
TIFFANY WILDLIFE AREA: (See Pepin County below).

Burnett County:
CREX MEADOWS WILDLIFE AREA: 30,000-acre landscape of sedge marshes and brush prairies or pine savannas supporting prairie grasses and flowers, sharp-tailed grouse, trumpeter swans and bobcats. The WA is located 1-mile northeast of Grantsburg, WI at Hwys D and F. Call the Grantsburg Ranger Station, in Grantsburg, WI at 715/463-2896.

DANBURY WILDLIFE AREA: 2,245-acres of sand barrens and forest. The WA is located 2½-miles southwest of Danbury, WI on Hwy F. Call the Grantsburg Ranger Station, in Grantsburg, WI at 715/463-2896.

KOHLER-PEET BARRENS AND CEDAR SWAMP STATE NATURAL AREA: 690-acres that features 340-acres of a nearly flat, sandy, open barrens, and an extensive swamp forest on the lower river terrace, and about 1-mile of wooded river terrace escarpment. Its very diverse barrens flora holds many species typical of prairie, barren, and bracken grassland[1]. The NA is northeast of Grantsburg, WI. Call the DNR, WI in Madison, WI at 608/266-0394.

NAMEKAGON BARRENS WILDLIFE AREA: 5,049-acres of shrub prairie habitat reminiscent of the rare Pine Barrens ecosystem, and upland forest. The WA is located 7-miles east of Hwy 35 on St Croix Trail, in the extreme northeast corner of Burnett County. Call the DNR, WI, 715/635-4091.

ST. CROIX WETLAND MANAGEMENT DISTRICT: 5,937-acre district encompasses 8 counties including Burnett County managing 38 Waterfowl Production Areas (WPA), and 19 conservation easements, (920-acres). A very active private lands program is heavily involved with wetland and grassland restoration. Roughly, half of the district was historically native prairie or savanna, with the rest wooded. The District includes the "Northwest Wisconsin Pothole Area," which is among the most important waterfowl breeding areas in Wisconsin. Gray wolves, trumpeter swans, and Karner Blue Butterflies all breed within the District. Development pressures from the Twin Cities of Minnesota are changing the character and land use of the District. Call the WMD at 715/246-7784.

---

[1] Bracken grassland is open upland areas, often on sandy soils, of the northern one-third of the state. Bracken fern, Penn sedge, Kalm's bromegrass, and Canada bluegrass dominate them. There may be a high cover of low shrubs. There is disagreement on whether bracken grassland should be considered a "natural community" in Wisconsin and elsewhere in the Upper Great Lakes region.

Calumet County:
LEDGEVIEW NATURE CENTER: 105-acres noted for its cave habitats and resident bats, encompasses forest, prairie and rocky ledges. The Nature Center is south of Chilton, WI off Co HWY G on Short Rd. Call Calumet County at 414/849-7094.

Chippewa County:
LAKE WISSOTA STATE PARK: The Park is on the northeast side of the 6,300-acre Lake Wissota. Scenic trails edge the shoreline and wind through woodland, prairie and marsh. The Park is northeast of Chippewa Falls, WI. Call the Park in Chippewa Falls, WI at 715/382-4574.

Columbia County:
AUDUBON GOOSE POND STATE NATURAL AREA: 174-acres with a 1-acre restored prairie. The site contains a prairie pothole lake that is used by exceptionally large numbers of birds, especially waterfowl and shorebirds. The pond is southeast of Arlington, WI. Permission of the resident managers is required for access, but birds can be observed from the south and east roads. Contact the Madison Audubon Society at 608/255-BIRD (2473).

MACKENZIE ENVIRONMENTAL EDUCATION CENTER: 280-acres of rolling fields, forestland, and restored tallgrass prairie being expanded through new plantings. See what a prairie looked like and see the bison that roamed the prairie. The Center is located at W7303 Hwy CS, Poynette, WI 53955. Call the DNR, WI at 608/635-8110.

ROCKY RUN OAK OPENING STATE NATURAL AREA: 315-acre site contains a large oak opening. The NA is located on a south-facing slope overlooking Rocky Run. Animal life is diverse due to the many microhabitats that can be found within short distances and over 100 species with prairie affinities have been recorded here. The NA is located south of Wyocena, WI. One can park in the Rocky Run Fishery Area parking lot. Call the DNR, WI, in Madison, WI at 608/266-0394.

Crawford County:
GIBRALTAR ROCK STATE NATURAL AREA: 35-acre site contains significant geological features with representative cliff and cedar glade. A major portion of the site is a dry-mesic forest dominated by red oak and basswood. Open cliff communities harbor several species of ferns, pale corydalis, columbine, and cliff goldenrod. The understory has a large component of dry prairie species. Migrating raptors catch thermals formed by the warm cliff face. The NA is southwest of Okee, WI. Call the DNR, WI, in Madison, WI at 608/266-0394.

THE HOGBACK: 962-acres with approximately 100-acres of dry prairie is one of the best remaining examples of dry prairie in

277

Wisconsin. To the south, the ridge widens out and the prairie grades into oak savanna and oak woodland. Smaller dry prairies exist on the surrounding bluffs. Volunteers collect native grass and wildflower seeds to use in future prairie restoration efforts and inventory the native plants and animals. The site is southwest of Steuben, WI. Call TNC, WI at 608/251-8140 for information or to volunteer.

MARIETTA UNIT- LOWER WI STATE RIVERWAY: 1,956-acres of upland hardwoods, fields, and steep bluff prairie. The Marietta Unit is located 2-miles east of Boscobel, WI on Hwy 60. Contact the Wilson Nursery, Richland Chamber of Commerce at 608/647-6205.

RUSH CREEK STATE NATURAL AREA: 1,137-acre site has several large dry prairie remnants and a continuum of three southern forest types. The prairie remnants are part of the most extensive series of "goat prairies" left in the state and host a nearly complete range of dry to dry-mesic prairie plant species. The NA is northwest Ferryville, WI. Call the DNR, WI, in Madison, WI at 608/266-0394.

Dane County:
ARBORETUM–UNIVERSITY OF WISCONSIN-MADISON: 1,260-acres of land bordering the southern half of Lake Wingra in Madison WI. It has two main vehicular entries: the northern most is at the intersection of McCaffery Dr, N Wingra Dr, and S Mills St. The southern most is north of the Beltline (Hwy 12) at the intersection of McCaffery Dr. and Seminole Hwy. Visit its Curtis Prairie (see below), Greene Prairie (50-acre native prairie restoration), Marion Dunn Prairie (a small prairie), the Carver Street Savanna and the Wingra Oak Savanna Restoration Projects. Call the Arboretum at 608/263-7888.

BADGER PRAIRIE PARK: 339-acres with some prairie. This site also provides access to Military Ridge State Trail and to a segment of the Ice Age National Trail. The Park entrance is at the intersection of Co Hwy PB and US 18 & 151 near Verona, WI. Call the Dane County Parks at 608/242-4576.

BELLEVILLE PRAIRIE: A remnant prairie along Hwy 69 north of Belleville, WI which runs for 1.65 miles from Co Hwy A south on the east side of the road, between the road and the railroad tracks. This is one of the prairies WDOT is restoring. Call the WDOT at 608/266-1017.

BETHEL HORIZONS NATURE CENTER: 460-acres of diverse plant and animal communities ideally situated adjacent to Governor Dodge State Park. Six well-made hiking trails allow people to experience the entire Center. The Old Prairie and Valley Nature Trails are self-guided. Guided tours and interpretive hikes examine general natural history, unique Driftless Area geology, spring and summer wildflowers, ferns, pond life, animal tracks, plant succession, and habitats of the woodland, meadow and prairie. The Center is located 7-miles north of Dodgeville, WI. All environmental education programs and special outdoor activities must be planned in advance. For information on tours and programming, contact Diane Holzman, Environmental Education Director, Bethel Horizons in Dodgeville, WI at 608/935-5885.

BLACK EARTH PRAIRIE STATE NATURAL AREA: 16-acres of a dry-mesic prairie on relatively level terrain, unusual for this natural division. This remnant harbors a rich flora of more than 80 native prairie species. The NA is located southwest of Black Earth, WI. Call TNC, WI in Madison, WI at 608/251-8140.

BLACK HAWK UNIT- LOWER WI STATE RIVERWAY: 800-acres of upland hardwoods, abandoned fields, prairie, and savanna. The unit of Tower Hill State Park is located 3-miles south of Sauk City on Hwy 78. Call the Park at 608/588-2116.

CHEROKEE MARSH: 4,000-acre marsh that is the most diverse of all nature study areas with a mosaic of wetlands, southern Wisconsin woodlots, old fields, restored prairie, oak savannah, two glacial drumlins and the Yahara River. Several thousand feet of boardwalks allow visitors to walk easily through the cattail marsh in the wetland formed from the former glacial Lake Mendota. The Yahara River boardwalk leads through a sedge meadow, over peat deposits and past a fen and is a distinctly different wetland from the cattail marsh. The Park contains two observation platforms for wildlife viewing and several belly boards that encourage the exploration of pond ecosystems. Fall tours frequently focus on fall plant communities, prairies, pond study, the values of wetlands, seasonal changes and Native American culture and lore. The area is intended as a study area for school children and the Cherokee Park staff gives educational tours. The Park is managed by the Madison Park System and is located only 7-miles from Madison, WI at the very northern end of Sherman Ave. Contact Pat Woicek at 608/249-4255 for access information and tour arrangements.

CROSS PLAINS PRAIRIE: 80-acres being restored by the WDOT. The Prairie is located between Cross Plains and Black Earth, WI on Hwy 14. Call the WDOT at 608/266-1017.

(JOHN T.) CURTISS PRAIRIE: 60-acres of tallgrass prairie in the 1,260-acre University of Wisconsin Arboretum in Madison, WI. Begun in 1934, this is the first restored grassland in the world, notes its director, Greg Armstrong. The John T Curtis Scientific Prairie Area aids research on prairie plants. The Arboretum's first director, Aldo Leopold, and the board were concerned about the recent dust bowl and forest clear cutting, so pursued the-then novel idea of restoring environmental health to an ecosystem. For the location, see the Arboretum-

University of WI above. Call the Arboretum at 608/263-7888.

GLACIAL DRUMLIN STATE TRAIL: Starting in Cottage Grove, WI the trail goes east for 52-miles where it ends in the Fox River Sanctuary in Waukesha. It traverses Jefferson and Waukesha Counties and in so doing passes wetlands, woods, farmland and restored prairie. Contact the Glacial Drumlin Trail – West, at 1213 S. Main St, Lake Mills, WI 53551 or call at 920/648-8774 or the Glacial Drumlin Trail – East, at W329 N846 Co Rd C, Delafield, WI 53018 or call at 262/646-3025.

GOVERNOR NELSON STATE PARK: Trails and restored prairie beckon nature enthusiasts. Five conical mounds and a large panther effigy mound represent two distinct periods of Native American mound building. The conical mounds are 1,500-1,900 years old, predating the effigy mounds, built 800-1,350 years ago. Remnants of an 18th century Winnebago village and cornfields were found nearby. The Park is located on Lake Mendota, within sight of the State Capitol, on Co Hwy M, in the town of Westport, WI. Call the Park at 608/831-3005.

HERITAGE PRAIRIE: 72-acre park with some prairie. The Park is one of the Madison Conservation Parks and is located at 802 Femrite Drive, Madison, WI. Call Madison City Parks at 608/266-4711.

HOOK LAKE WILDLIFE AND NATURAL AREA: 522-acres of bog lake, restored oak savannah, restored prairie, and cropland. The NA is located 2-miles east of Oregon, WI on Rutland-Dunn Rd. Call the DNR, WI South Central Office in Fitchburg, WI at 608/275-3266.

KNOLLWOOD CONSERVATION PARK: 14-acre park with a 2-acre sand prairie located at 5415 Queensbridge Rd, Madison, WI. Call Madison City Parks at 608/266-4711.

INDIAN LAKE PARK: 442-acres including a prairie. The main entrance to the Park is located on hwy 19 about 2-miles west of US 12. Call Dane County Parks at 608/242-4576.

LAKE FARM PARK: 328-acres with group camping areas, wildlife pond, overlook tower, and the Native American Archaeological Trail with informational markers describing the time from 10,000 BC to 300 AD when Native Americans lived in this area. The trail, used for cross-country skiing, follows ½-mile of wooded shoreline and then turns inward and winds through a restored prairie. The Park is reached by exiting US 12/18 south onto South Towne Dr and then left on Moorland Rd to Lake Farm Rd and left on Libby Rd. Call Dane County Parks at 608/242-4576.

LAKE KEGONSA STATE PARK: The White Oak Nature Trail's peculiar earthen structures are of mysterious origin. The woodlands, prairies and wetlands attract campers, hikers and skiers. The Park is located northwest of Stoughton, WI off US 51. Call the Park in Stoughton, WI at 608/873-9695.

LOWER WAUBESA WETLAND NATURAL AREA: 299-acres of marsh, woodlot, grassland, and prairie restoration. The NA is located 4-miles south of Monona, WI. Call the DNR, WI South Central Office in Fitchburg, WI at 608/275-3266.

MAZOMANIE OAK BARRENS: 120-acres of oak barrens located north of Black Earth, WI on Hwy 78. Call the DNR, WI, in Madison, WI at 608/266-0394.

MILITARY RIDGE STATE PARK TRAIL: Land around the Trail is largely agricultural, but also includes prairie, wetlands, woods, and small towns. Because this is not a loop trail, hikers who wish to hike the entire trail are advised to bring two vehicles. The Trail starts near Verona, WI (see Badger Prairie Park above) and ends in Dodgeville, WI (Iowa County). Call Blue Mound State Park, Blue Mounds, WI, at 608/437-7393.

OWEN CONSERVATION PARK: 93-acre park with about 35-acres of prairie. The Park is located at 6021 Old Sauk Rd, Madison WI. Call Madison City Parks at 608/255-4711.

PATRICK MARSH-DEANSVILLE WILDLIFE AREA: 270-acre restored wetland with an adjacent restored prairie and savanna community within current property boundaries. The 1,927-acre (1,687-owned, 240-leased) Deansville WA is nearby, and also has some prairie. The site is northeast of Sun Prairie, WI. Call the DNR, WI at 608/275-3242.

PLEASANT VALLEY CONSERVANCY: 200-acre site being restored by TPE to its original prairie, oak savanna, and open oak woodland. The site is 4-miles south of Black Earth, WI on Pleasant Valley Rd. Contact TPE at 608/375-5271 or 608/221-7065.

PRAIRIE MORAINE PARK: 160-acres with the Johnstown Moraine running through the northern portion of the site and is an important element of the Ice Age National Scenic Trail which runs along its narrow crest. This park is ideal for viewing the moraine and provides an excellent area for interpretation of Wisconsin's glacial history. There is also a beautiful oak savanna here. The entrance is 2-miles south of US 18/151 on Co Hwy PB. Call Dane County Parks at 608/242-4576.

PRAIRIE PIDGE CONSERVATION PARK: 48-acre park with about 40-acres of native and restored prairie. The Park is located at 2406 Berkley Dr, Madison, WI. Call Madison City Parks at 608/255-4711.

SCHUMACHER FARM: 40-acre outdoor museum representing local

farm life during the 1920s-30s, and features a 10-acre prairie restoration. This site is 6-miles north of Madison and 1-mile east of Waunakee, WI on Hwy 19. Contact the site at 608/849-4559.

SIX MILE/DORN CREEK BIKE TOUR: A 28-mile bike tour starting in the parking lot at the Governor Nelson State Park (See above) and looping past wetlands, restored prairie and towns in Dane County. Contact the Dane County Natural Heritage Foundation at 608/258-9797 or at their website: ww.dcnhf.org/indexrelatedsites.html.

STRICKER'S POND: 14-acre park with 2-acre prairie located at 1118 Middleton St Madison, WI. Call Madison City Parks at 608/255-4711.

SUGAR CREEK OAK SAVANNA: 10-acre private site being restored by agreement with Empire-Sauk Chap of TPE. Contact TPE at 608/845-7065 or 608/355-1987.

(EDNA) TAYLOR CONSERVATION PARK: The Park offers a variety of natural features, including woods, prairie, ponds, marsh, and a glacial drumlin. Seven Indian mounds are located on the crest and slope of the drumlin. The Park is in the southwest part of Madison, WI at 802 Femrite Rd. Call Madison City Parks at 608/255-4711.

THOMSON MEMORIAL PRAIRIE: 175-acres of dry prairie, surrounded on all sides by farmland, probably only survived because the limestone bedrock beneath the soil lies too close to the surface to permit cultivation. The Preserve is located on the border of Dane and Iowa Counties. A diverse natural community holds more than 68 species of plants and provides habitat for many grassland bird species. The Prairie is southwest of Blue Mounds, WI. Call TNC, WI at 608/251-8140.

TOKEN CREEK PARK: The Park is located on US 51 north of Madison, WI. Call Dane County Parks at 608/242-4576.

TURVILLE POINT CONSERVATION PARK: 65-acre park with 7-acre prairie located at Olin Turville CT, Madison, WI. Call Madison City Parks at 608/266-4711.

WALKING IRON PARK: 200-acre park offers miles of hiking and bridle trails winding through restored prairies, wooded areas and along Marsh Creek. The Park is on Hudson Rd north of US 14. Call Dane County Parks at 608/242-4576.

WAUBESA WETLANDS: 194-acres of wetlands including springs, sedge meadows, floating mats and a fen and a deep soil prairie and oak savanna restoration. The Wetlands is located southeast of Madison, WI on Lalor Rd. Call TNC, WI at 608/251-8140.

WHEELER ROAD FEN: A small but rich calcareous fen between the uplands to the east and the Yahara River to the west. The site is located off Wheeler Rd in Madison, WI and east of the Yahara River. Call the DNR, WI, in Madison, WI at 608/266-0394.

WESTPORT DRUMLIN PRAIRIE: This small remnant of the Empire Prairie occupies a ridge mantled with glacial till with more than 100 prairie species. 4-acres within the tract are considered dry prairie. This site is very sensitive and is not accessible by road. Call the DNR, WI, in Madison, WI at 608/266-0394.

YAHARA WET PRAIRIE: Located within the Cherokee Marsh Complex (see above).

Dodge County:
HORICON MARSH (HORICON NATIONAL WILDLIFE REFUGE AND HORICON WILDLIFE AREA): 32,000-acres represents the largest freshwater cattail marsh in the USA with some restored prairie in the area of the marsh. This is a very popular spot to view the spring and fall waterfowl migration including as many as 250,000 Canadian geese at peak times. The Marsh is just north of Horicon, WI and Hwy 33. Call the NWR at 414/387-2658 or the WA at 414/387-7860.

LEOPOLD WETLAND MANAGEMENT DISTRICT: 10,231-acres on 44 Waterfowl Production Areas (WPAs) in 16 southeastern Wisconsin counties, and with conservation easements in 33 eastern Wisconsin counties. The WPAs consist of marshland habitat surrounded by grassland and woodland communities, which are open to public hunting, trapping and fishing. The District covers one of the most important waterfowl areas of Wisconsin. The Leopold WMD Office is located at the Horicon National Wildlife Refuge. One of the management tools of the district is prairie restoration. This WMD was named in honor of Aldo Leopold (see the Leopold Memorial Reserve, Sauk County below). The Headquarters is located in Mayville, WI. Call the district at 920/387-0336.

WATERLOO FEN AND SPRINGS STATE NATURAL AREA: 78-acres of a raised fen, a moist meadow, and wet seepage slopes. The NA extends into Jefferson County. The NA is east of Waterloo, WI. Call the DNR, WI in Madison, WI at 608/266-0394.

Douglas County:
BUCKLEY CREEK AND BARRENS: Call the DNR, WI in Madison, WI at 608/266-0394.

SOLON SPRINGS SHARPTAIL BARRENS STATE NATURAL AREA: 240-acre site contains a large pine barrens that is representative of the vegetation that once covered much of northwestern Wisconsin. The site lies on rolling topography within northwestern Wisconsin's extensive area of outwash sands, part of an ancient glacial lakebed, from Burnett to Bayfield counties. Although the sandy podzolic soils are low in nutrients, a very diverse flora exists. The NA is southwest of Solon Springs, WI. Call the DNR, WI in Madison, WI at 608/266-0394.

Dunn County:
CARYVILLE SAVANNA STATE NATURAL AREA: 200-acre savanna is one of the biggest and best savannas in the state. Access is only by boat on the Chippewa River. The Savanna is west of Eau Claire, WI. Call the DNR, WI, in Madison, WI at 608/266-0394.

DEVILS PUNCH BOWL: A natural rock amphitheater located on a geological formation boundary contains 6 natural communities, including sand prairie. The site is west of Menomonie, WI. The Wisconsin Farmland Conservancy owns the site and can be reached in Menomonie, WI at 715/235-8850.

DUNNVILLE WILDLIFE AREA: 5,063-acres (3,673 owned and 1,388 leased) of marsh, river bottom, farmland, and planted prairie grass. The WA is located 5-miles south of Downsville, WI. Access is on Hwy Y. Call the DNR, WI, West Central Regional Office in Eau Claire, WI at 715/839-3700.

MUDDY CREEK WILDLIFE AREA: 4,351-acres, (3,185 owned, 1,166 leased) of marsh, woodlots, stream, and planted prairie grass. The WA is located 2-miles west of Elk Mound. It is 6-miles long and 2½-miles wide, intersected by Hwys 12, 29 and US 94. Call the DNR, WI, West Central Regional Office in Eau Claire, WI at 715/839-3700.

ROCK FALLS WILDLIFE AREA: 271-acres of stream bottom, marsh, and planted prairie grass. The WA is located 1-mile southwest of Rock Falls, WI. Call the DNR, WI, West Central Regional Office in Eau Claire, WI at 715/839-3700.

Eau Claire County:
BEAVER CREEK RESERVE: 360-acres of upland woods, roadside prairies and river bottom forests. A gently flowing river (Eau Claire), sandy beaches, rocky falls, clear cool streams, enhanced by a multitude of birds, wildlife, and native flowers. The Reserve is 4-miles north of Fall Creek, WI off Co Hwy K. Call Eau Claire County at 715/877-2212.

COON FORK BARRENS: Call the DNR, WI in Madison, WI at 608/266-0394.

SOUTH FORK BARRENS: Call the DNR, WI in Madison, WI at 608/266-0394.

Florence County:
SPREAD EAGLE BARRENS: Call the DNR, WI in Madison, WI at

608/266-0394.

Fond du Lac County:
(OWEN & ANNE) GROMME PRESERVE: (see Winnebago County below)

OAKFIELD RAILROAD PRAIRIE: Call the DNR, WI in Madison, WI at 608/266-0394.

Grant County:
BLUE RIVER BLUFF PRAIRIES AND SAVANNAS: Call the DNR, WI in Madison, WI at 608/266-0394.

BLUE RIVER SAND BARRENS STATE NATURAL AREA: 130-acre site contains the largest and best example of sand barrens in Wisconsin. The NA features a variety of xeric plant community types on Sparta loamy fine sand including sand blows, active dunes, flat sand barrens, and stabilized dunes forested with oaks. The dunes are bound together by an unusual plant community including prairie plants. The NA is located southwest of Muscoda, WI. Call the DNR, WI in Madison, WI at 608/266-0394.

BUSHCLOVER PRAIRIE: Small but very rich, dry-mesic prairie. The Prairie is northwest of Lancaster, WI on Badger Rd. The Prairie Enthusiasts, Southeast WI Chapter, own this prairie. Call TPE at 608/375-5271.

DEWEY HEIGHTS PRAIRIE STATE NATURAL AREA: 27-acres of dry lime prairie on a southwest-facing Mississippi River bluff holding a diversity of native grasses and prairie forbs. The NA is in Nelson Dewey State Park (see below) west of Cassville, WI. Call the DNR, WI at 608/725-5374.

(NELSON) DEWEY STATE PARK: 750-acres including a bluff prairie (see above) and a self-guided trail. Call the DNR, WI at 608/725-5374.

ELDRED RESTORATION: This is a 2nd year restoration being done by the TPE Southwest WI Chapter. The restoration is southeast of Boscobel, WI on Sleepy Hollow Trail. Call TPE, Southwest Chap at 608/375-5271.

HEATHER'S PRAIRIE: About 20-acre privately owned prairie managed by TPE Southwest WI Chapter. Call TPE, Southwest Chap at 608/375-5271.

HIGHWAY 133 (MUSCODA) PRAIRIE: 200-acre prairie being restored by the WDOT. The prairie is located between Boscobel and Muscoda, WI on Hwy 133. Call the WDOT at 608/266-1017.

IPSWICH PRAIRIE STATE NATURAL AREA: 20-acre site that

includes a deep-soil mesic prairie, the only remnant of the extensive prairie that once occurred in southwestern Wisconsin. The area is part of an abandoned railroad right-of-way. The NA extends into Lafayette County. The prairie supports numerous colonies of the prairie mound building ant, Formica Cinerea and more than 125 plant species. The prairie is southeast of Platteville, WI. Call the DNR, WI in Madison, WI at 608/266-0394.

WOODMAN LAKE SAND PRAIRIE & DEAD LAKE: 25-acres of sand prairie and dry lakebed located 8-miles west of Boscobel, WI just before Woodman, WI. Call the DNR, WI in Madison, WI at 608/266-0394.

MUSCODA UNIT- LOWER WI STATE RIVERWAY: 2,291-acres of river, slough, marsh, bottomland hardwoods, and prairie. Muscoda Unit is located 2-miles west of Muscoda, WI on W. Pine Rd. Contact Wilson Nursery, Richland Chamber of Commerce at 608/647-6205.

SEMRAD SLOUGH: 278-acres of mostly slough, with open marsh, and some prairie. The Slough is located 1-mile east of Woodman, WI on Hwy 133. Contact the Wilson Nursery, Richland Chamber of Commerce at 608/647-6205.

WYALUSING STATE PARK: 2,674-acre park including a restored prairie area, and also has good bird watching areas. The Park is located at the Mississippi River and is northeast of Bagley, WI. Call the Park in Bagley, WI at 608/996-2261.

Green County:
ABRAHAM'S WOODS: 63.5-acre remnant of a climax forest and dry prairie, that is an essential teaching research laboratory for the University of Wisconsin plant and forest scientists. The preserve is 35-miles south of Madison, WI. Call the Director, University of Wisconsin-Madison Arboretum at 608/262-2748.

MURALT BLUFF PRAIRIE: 62.4-acres contains dry prairie that occupies a long, sweeping ridge top in an area of older drift about midway between the recently glaciated lands to the east and the Driftless Area to the west. The sandstone bluff is capped with a thin rocky layer of limestone on which the dry prairie has developed. Such grassland species as bobolink and grasshopper sparrow are becoming more common as burning and brushing opens the area. The Prairie is west of Albany, WI. Call TPE, Prairie Bluff Chap at 608/368-0901.

Green Lake County:
FOUNTAIN CREEK WET PRAIRIE STATE NATURAL AREA: 50-acre site contains a large wet prairie, a very rare community in Wisconsin, and attracts large numbers of wetland birds. A former oak opening at the south end is now overgrown by brushy oak woods.

Because the area is adjacent to the Grand River Marsh Flowage, it attracts large numbers of geese, sandhill cranes, great blue herons, northern harriers, and bobolinks. The NA is southwest of Marquette, WI. Call the DNR, WI Wildlife Manager in Berlin, WI at 920/361-3149.

Iowa County:
ARENA PINES-SAND BARRENS: Call the DNR, WI in Madison, WI at 608/266-0394.

AVOCA UNIT- LOWER WI STATE RIVERWAY: 3,736-acres of marsh, potholes, forest, and prairie. The unit of Tower Hill State Park is located east and west of Avoca, WI off Hwy 133. Call the Park at 608/588-2116.

AVOCA PRAIRIE-SAVANNA STATE NATURAL AREA: 1,885-acre NA contains the largest native tallgrass prairie in Wisconsin and east of the Mississippi River. It spreads across approximately 970-acres. Scattered bur and black oak trees and groves dot the landscape. The moist prairie and wetland swales contain more than 200 species of vascular plants. This site is probably the only place east of the Mississippi River where, almost no matter where one stands, one sees only natural savanna features. The NA is northeast of Avoca, WI. Call the DNR, WI South Central Regional Office in Fitchburg WI at 608/275-3266.

BARNVELDE PRAIRIE: 85-acres of prairie remnants and more heavily grazed prairie pastures are surrounded by tilled agricultural fields, hay fields and pastures. The area consists of a system of north-south ridges. The prairies occur on the sides of these ridges. The Prairie and surrounding lands constitute a relatively treeless landscape, providing habitat for many grassland nesting birds. The Prairie is west of Barneveld, WI. Call TNC, WI at 608/251-8140.

UNDERWOOD PRAIRIE: 7-acres of prairie separated by a wooded draw. The Prairie is 5-miles south of Blue Mounds, WI. Call the Empire-Sauk Chapter of TPE at 608/845-7065.

Jackson County:
DIKE 17: 3,700-acres of marsh, wet prairie, upland, and brush. The area is 5-miles east of Black River Falls, WI off Hwy 54. Call the DNR, WI in Black River Falls, WI at 715/284-1400.

FAWN HALL PRAIRIE: A remnant prairie being restored by the WDOT off Hwy 27 south of Black River Falls, WI. The Prairie is on both sides of the road and runs from 7th Street-Castle Mound. Call the WDOT at 608/266-1017.

OSSEO PRAIRIE: A remnant prairie being restored by the WDOT is north of Hwy 10 and south of railroad tracks from county line (Co Hwy R) east of Osseo, WI to Shaky Ln. Call the WDOT at 608/266-1017.

Jefferson County:
BLUE SPRING OAK OPENING STATE NATURAL AREA: 19-acre site contains one of the least disturbed oak openings in the state with scattered open-grown bur and black oaks on a west-facing slope overlooking Blue Spring Lake with rich savanna flora under the oaks. More than 30 prairie species have been catalogued here. The NA is west of Palmyra, WI. Call the DNR, WI in Madison, WI at 608/266-0394.

FAVILLE PRAIRIE STATE NATURAL AREA: 60-acre prairie located 4-miles west of Lake Mills, WI at the end of Lang Rd off County G. The University of Wisconsin operates the prairie for research purposes and permission is required to enter. Call the University of Wisconsin-Madison Arboretum at 608-263-7888.

FAVILLE GROVE SANCTUARY: A 27-acre and a 12-acre prairie restoration, the large tract being adjacent to the Faville Prairie State Natural Area. These are highly successful prairie restorations on mesic and wet-mesic soils. The prairies are north of Lake Mills, WI. Call the Madison Audubon Society at 608/255-BIRD (2473).

GLACIAL DRUMLIN STATE TRAIL: (See Dane County above).

LAKE MILLS WILDLIFE AREA: 1,199-acres of open water marsh, oak savannah, woodlots, and grassland. The WA is located 1-mile southwest of Lake Mills on Hwy A. Call the DNR, WI in Madison, WI at 608/266-2621.

(CLIFFORD F.) MESSINGER, DRY PRAIRIE AND SAVANNA PRESERVE: 246-acres stretching across more than 20-miles of kettle moraine topography of kettle holes, interlobate moraine, and outwash plains in southeastern Wisconsin and extending into Walworth and Waukesha Counties. Its 5 units and 16 sites include some of the best remaining examples of dry prairie and oak opening found in southeastern Wisconsin. Each site has unique flora, which together characterize the pre-settlement flora of the region. However, the 2 below deserve special mention:

> 1. BALD BLUFF DRY PRAIRIE: The largest dry prairie of the group and the most diverse in terms of plant species. It also has historical significance: Abraham Lincoln visited it when he was in the U.S. Army and it is thought to be a Native American signal hill. Bald Bluff is 2-miles north of the intersection of Highways H and 12.

> 2. WHITEWATER OAK OPENING: 120-acres of rugged morainal topography is dominated by bur oak on the ridge tops and south and southwest facing slopes, by red oak on the north-facing slopes, and by white oak in other places. Like the few other remnant oak openings in the state, shrubs and

other woody growth have invaded it over the years, especially honeysuckle and prickly ash. However, a wildfire in the 1950's somewhat opened up the site. This natural fire is being mimicked by prescribed burning, reinstating this crucial process of the oak opening ecosystem.

Contact the DNR Parks & Recreation Manager, Superintendent, Southern Unit Kettle Moraine State Forest, S91 W39091 Hwy 59, Eagle, WI 53119.

SNAPPER MEMORIAL PRAIRIE: 28-acre low prairie remnant containing 20 never plowed acres. By mowing these acres for hay and burning them in the fall, the owner preserved many prairie plant species. The preserve is located north of Lake Mills, WI off Co Hwy G. Call TNC, WI at 608/251-8140.

WATERLOO FEN AND SPRINGS STATE NATURAL AREA: (see Dodge County above).

Juneau County:
CRANBERRY CREEK MOUND GROUP STATE NATURAL AREA: 243-acre site contains a diverse floodplain forest, and an old-growth northern dry forest and 43-acres of Bracken grassland.[1] The NA contains two distinct clusters having more than 180 conical and effigy mounds built by Indians of the Woodland Period. Plowing somewhat altered the northern cluster and it is now a pine plantation. The southern cluster is unaltered. The NA is northwest of Necedah, WI. Call the DNR, WI in Madison, WI at 608/266-0394.

NECEDAH NATIONAL WILDLIFE REFUGE: 43,696-acre NWR with the largest wetland-bog in the state, and large tracts of rare oak barrens habitat. The NWR is located 4-miles west of Necedah, WI, on Hwy 21. Call the NWR at 608/565-2551.

Kenosha County:
BONG STATE RECREATION AND WILDLIFE AREA: 4,500-acres of restored native plant communities. This flat expanse of land was intended as an Air Force Base in WWII, but was never built. The restored prairie grasses and flowers now provide habitat for grassland birds, such as bobolink, eastern meadowlark and sand hill cranes. The WA is located south of Union Grove, WI on Hwy 142. Call the DNR, WI at 414/878-5600 or 414/652-0377.

CHIWAUKEE PRAIRIE STATE NATURAL AREA: 354-acres made up of ridges and swales running nearly parallel to the Lake Michigan shoreline bounded on the east by the lake and on the west by the Toleston Terrace. Dunes are found a short distance inland, mostly in the northern portion. A fluctuating high water table combined with the ridge and swale topography created a diversity of vegetation (400+species) unequaled in the state. The rich prairie, along with its far southeastern location, provides habitat for several rare and geographically restricted amphibians, reptiles, and birds. This is the county's largest remaining unplowed prairie and considered an ecological jewel. Bird watchers find this wet or mesic lake prairie a haven for grassland and other migratory birds. Access the area, south of Kenosha, via State Hwy 32 at 91st Street to County Hwy T, 104th Street, 116th Street, or Tobin Rd. Call TNC, WI at 608/251-8140.

KENOSHA SAND DUNES: 56-acres of foredunes, backdunes, wet swales, and prairie. This site is located in the Village of Pleasant Prairie, WI just south of the City of Kenosha, WI. Call the DNR, WI in Madison, WI at 608/266-8916.

LaCrosse County:
LACROSSE RIVER MARSH AND HIXON FOREST: 1,100-acres nestled among Mississippi River Bluffs supports beautiful hardwood forests and native dry prairies alive with songbirds. The 6-mile Bicentennial Trail travels along a "goat" prairie, down through Hixon Forest, across the LaCrosse River Marsh to the banks of the Mississippi. The Hixon Nature Center is located off Hwy 16 and north of LaCrosse St. The City of LaCrosse owns the property, phone 608/789-7533 or the Hixon Forest, Telephone: 608/784-0303.

LACROSSE RIVER TRAIL PRAIRIE STATE NATURAL AREA: (see Monroe County below).

MIDWAY RAILROAD PRAIRIE STATE NATURAL AREA: 3-acre site contains a dry-mesic sand prairie remnant on a western-facing slope of a Mississippi River terrace that contains more than 70 species of prairie plants. The NA is north of Onalaska, WI. Call the DNR, WI in Madison, WI at 608/266-0394.

Lafayette County:
IPSWICH PRAIRIE STATE NATURAL AREA: (see Grant County above).

Marinette County:
DUNBAR BARRENS STATE NATURAL AREA: 240-acre site within Dunbar Wildlife Area is similar in composition to pre-settlement Pine Barrens, a rare community in northeastern Wisconsin, with unusual plants and animals. The dominant herbaceous vegetation on the barrens consists of strongly rhizomatous grasses and sedges. With broad sweeping vistas and a distinctive panorama, the general aspect is that of a prairie. The action of frost in low pockets contributes to the open situation. The NA is in the northwestern part of the county. Call the DNR, WI in Madison, WI at 608/266-0394.

Marquette County:
(MUIR'S) ENNIS LAKE - MUIR PARK STATE NATURAL AREA: 150-acre site includes a rich fen that lies along the outlet stream. The NA also contains sedge meadow, open bog, northern wet forest, southern dry forest, oak opening, and wet-mesic prairie. The NA lies within the John Muir Memorial Park located 11 miles north of Portage, WI. Call the DNR, WI in Madison, WI at 608/266-0394.

JOHN MUIR MEMORIAL PARK: (see Muir Park State Natural Area above). Call the DNR, WI in Madison, WI at 608/266-0394.

PAGE CREEK MARSH: 651-acres of wetland, sandy oak savanna, sedge meadow, prairie fens, tamarack swamps, and bogs. Natural fires and burning by Native Americans once maintained this type of barrens community. A portion of the overgrown canopy of pine and black oak is being removed so sunlight can benefit the many plants and animals living in the understory. TNC hopes to protect over 1,000-acres here. The marsh is southeast of Packwaukee, WI. Call TNC, WI at 608/251-8140 for information and to volunteer.

Milwaukee County:
WEHR NATURE CENTER: 220-acres of hardwood forest, lake, sedge meadow, marsh, oak savanna, and prairie as part of Whitnall Park. The Center is southeast of Hales Corner, WI on College Ave. Call the Milwaukee County Parks at 414/425-8550.

WHITNALL PARK: (See Wehr Nature Center above).

Monroe County:
LACROSSE RIVER TRAIL PRAIRIE STATE NATURAL AREA: 29-acre site contains dry to dry-mesic prairie along topographic and moisture gradients extending into LaCrosse County. Two stretches of dry-mesic to dry sand prairie are preserved along the LaCrosse River Trail, established on the abandoned Chicago and Northwestern Railroad right-of-way. The Monroe County segment contains excellent dry prairie. The LaCrosse County segment is more mesic and has different species. The NA is outside of Rockland, WI. Call the DNR, WI in Madison, WI at 608/266-0394.

Oconto County:
COPPER CULTURE STATE PARK: 48-acre park features an Indian burial ground from the Copper Culture of 2,000 years ago and a 15-acre short-grass prairie. The Park is located northeast of Green Bay, WI off Hwy 41. Call the Park in Green Bay, WI at 920/492-5836.

Pepin County:
20-acres of Brittle Prickley Pear. Contact TPE, West Central Chapter, at their website: http://www.prairie.pressenter.com/ or call at 715/246-

5975

9-MILE ISLAND STATE NATURAL AREA: 1,374-acres of river bottom, and prairie remnant. The NA is ½-miles northeast of Durand, WI on Hwy 85, and ½-miles north on Hwy M, access is by boat. Call the DNR, WI West Central Regional Office in Eau Claire, WI at 715/839-3700.

PEPIN COUNTY EXTENSIVE WILDLIFE HABITAT AREA: 293-acres of river bottom, forest, marsh, and planted prairie grass. The site is located 1-mile west of Durand, WI. Call the DNR, WI West Central Regional Office in Eau Claire, WI at 715/839-3700.

TIFFANY WILDLIFE AREA: 13,000-acre wildlife area extending into Buffalo County. The interior comprises a mixture of hardwoods and prairies rich with vegetation and animal life. The WA is northwest of Nelson, WI off Hwy 25. Call the DNR, WI, Alma, WI at 608/685-6222.

Pierce County:
MORGAN COULEE PRAIRIE STATE NATURAL AREA: 54-acre site contains the second largest dry prairie in the west central region and a small bur oak savanna. The prairie lies on a steep to moderately steep slope (with a southern exposure), which is entirely prairie coulee bottom to bluff top prairie. A southern dry Oak Forest tops the bluff. Between these communities is bur oak savanna, dominated by open-grown, gnarled bur oaks. The NA is northwest of Maiden Rock, WI. Call the DNR, WI in Madison, WI at 608/266-0394.

TRENTON BLUFF PRAIRIE STATE NATURAL AREA: 110-acre site containing a dry prairie on a southwest facing slope in the Mississippi River Valley, about 1-mile away from the river consisting of two units. The western portion consists of two prairies separated by a wooded draw. The eastern portion is much steeper; an open cliff grades quickly into shrubby oak woods. Fauna include such reptiles as milk snake, blue racer, and timber rattlesnake and nesting birds. The NA is north of Hager City, WI. Call the DNR, WI in Madison, WI at 608/266-0394.

Polk County:
STERLING BARRENS STATE NATURAL AREA: 168-acre site features a northern dry forest interspersed with barren openings containing dry prairie species situated on a gentle south slope. The NA is northwest of Cushing, WI. Call the DNR, WI in Madison, WI at 608/266-0394.

Portage County:
BUENA VISTA QUARRY PRAIRIE STATE NATURAL AREA: 40-acre site contains one of the least disturbed tracts in the Buena Vista Wildlife Area and supports the state-threatened prairie chicken. The

292

prairie is within the Buena Vista Marsh, formerly a sedge meadow and tamarack swamp. An oak knoll in the southeastern portion rises ten feet above the surrounding flat lands. Remnant dry and dry-mesic prairie species grow on this sandstone outcrop. The flat lands held gentle ridges that have lost their vegetation and organic matter due to agricultural practices, wind erosion, and peat fires, exposing the glacial sandy soil, but prairie species are gradually re-invading. The NA is southwest of Plover, WI. Call the DNR, WI in Madison, WI at 608/266-0394.

BUENA VISTA GRASSLAND: 12,000-acres scattered throughout southeast Portage County roughly 10-miles south of Stevens Point, WI off I-39. The grasslands surround the Buena Vista Quarry Prairie and although it is not native grassland, it holds areas of degraded prairie, mainly on ridges within the site. Managed primarily for Greater Prairie Chickens, this mix of farms and public lands has proven to be an excellent habitat for the them as well as many other grassland birds, and provide excellent birding year round. Call Jim Kier of the DNR, WI at 608/339-4819.

Racine County:
KARCHER SPRINGS STATE NATURAL AREA: 32-acre site contains a spring, fen, and stream complex. Calcareous fen habitat is found along the boggy banks. Near the parking lot is an area of recovering wet-mesic prairie. The NA is southwest of Burlington, WI. Call the DNR, WI in Madison, WI at 608/266-0394.

Richland County:
LONE ROCK PRAIRIE: 100-acres being restored to prairie by the WDOT. The Prairie is located 1½-miles west of Lone Rock, WI on Hwy 14. Call the WDOT at 608/266-1017.

KNAPP CREEK UNIT- LOWER WI STATE RIVERWAY: 5,001-acres, (2,998 owned and 2,003 in easements) of creek, brush, forest, prairie, and farmland. The site is located 5-miles east of Boscobel, WI on Hwy 60. Contact the Wilson Nursery, Richland Chamber of Commerce at 608/647-6205.

SMITH SLOUGH AND SAND PRAIRIE: Call the DNR, WI in Madison, WI at 608/266-0394.

GOTHAM JACK PINE BARRENS: Call the DNR, WI in Madison, WI at 608/266-0394.

Rock County:
NEWARK ROAD PRAIRIE: 33-acre wet prairie on Newark Rd near Beloit, WI owned and managed by Beloit College. Call Beloit College at 608/363-2000.

SWENSON WET PRAIRIE STATE NATURAL AREA: 40-acre site features an excellent example of a wet-mesic prairie. The NA features 10-acres of low prairie and sedge meadow near the confluence of Taylor Creek and the Sugar River. Some of the tract consists of low river bottom savanna and scrub interspersed with shallow, abandoned river channels. The remainder is savanna, formerly grazed and in various stages of being overgrown by shrubs. The NA is south of Brodhead, WI. Call the DNR, WI in Madison, WI at 608/266-0394.

YOUNG PRAIRIE: 53-acre prairie located 5-miles west of Whitewater, WI off Bluff Rd and ½-mile south of the County Line. Call the DNR, WI in Madison, WI at 608/266-0394.

Sauk County:
BADGER ARMY AMMUNITION PLANT: 7,350-acres of potential prairie. The plant is being closed and a coalition of organizations, led by the Aldo Leopold Foundation called the Community Conservation Coalition for the Sauk Prairie (CCCSP), is trying to save at least a portion of the area as the Sauk Prairie. Examples of mesic prairies can be seen along the east side of the Badger plant along Hwy 12 near the Baraboo Range Historic Marker. For more information about CCCSP and their vision of restoring the native landscape contact: CCCSP, P.O. Box 38, Prairie du Sac, WI 53578, or visit www.saukprairievision.org.

THE BLUFFLANDS RESTORATION PROJECT: The project is a joint venture between the Aldo Leopold Foundation and The Prairie Enthusiasts (TPE), a non-profit organization dedicated to preserving prairie and savanna remnants of the upper Midwest. In 1989, TPE volunteers began working with private landowners on a few prairie and savanna remnants in southern Sauk and northern Dane County, Wisconsin. The growing group of landowners and volunteers has logged over 900 volunteer hours and manage nearly 300-acres, mostly among the unglaciated bluffs and hills of the lower Wisconsin River Valley. They call themselves the Blufflands Restoration Project. Call the Aldo Leopold Foundation at 608/355-0279.

CASSELL PRAIRIE: 700-acre restoration project of prairie and savanna as a part of the Blufflands Restoration Project (see above). This project is about 10-miles west of Sauk City, WI on Cassell Rd off Hwy 60. Call the Aldo Leopold Foundation at 608/355-0279.

CASSELL PRAIRIE UNIT- LOWER WI STATE RIVERWAY: 400-acres of State owned prairie, floodplain forest and marsh. The unit of Tower Hill State Park is located 6-miles west of Sauk City, WI off Hwy 60. Call the Park at 608/588-2116.

DEVIL'S LAKE OAK FOREST STATE NATURAL AREA: 122-acre site features southern dry-mesic forest with an overstory of red oak and a nearly pure understory of red maple within Devil's Lake State Park. The forest is situated on top of the terminal moraine of the Cary Glacier, which blocked the ancient river channel. The bluff top holds areas of dry prairie. The Park and the NA are located 3-miles south of Baraboo, WI. Call the DNR, WI in Madison, WI at 608/266-0394.

DEVIL'S LAKE STATE PARK: (See above). A southeast bluff holds a prairie remnant. The Park is located 3-miles south of Baraboo, WI. Call the DNR, WI in Madison, WI at 608/266-0394.

GASSER PRAIRIE: A small remnant very dry prairie northwest of Sauk City, WI ½-mile south of Block Rd on Exchange Rd. For further information contact Michael Putnam, Department of Zoology, University of Wisconsin, 430 Lincoln Drive, Madison, Wisconsin 53706 Telephone: 608/262-6205.

HEMLOCK DRAW: 543-acres of abundant woods, a rocky canyon, a clear flowing stream, and an area of abandoned fields returning to native plant life. The preserve is north of Leland, WI on Reich Dr. Call TNC, WI at 608/251-8140.

HONEY CREEK STATE NATURAL AREA: 300-acre site contains several aquatic and terrestrial communities. The topography ranges from creek bottoms and boggy areas through steep slopes and rock escarpments to upland ridges, which includes dry prairie. Twenty-five distinct soil types lie within the NA boundaries. Given this range in topography and soils, it is no surprise that the site supports a varied and unusual fauna and flora, including more than 500 plant species. The site was originally protected as a bird sanctuary, and it supports over 80 nesting species. The NA is west of Prairie du Sac, WI. Call the DNR, WI in Madison, WI at 608/266-0394.

INTERNATIONAL CRANE FOUNDATION: Examples of wetland and restored prairie that Cranes depend on are found here. The Foundation is at E11376 Shady Lane Rd, Baraboo, WI. The telephone number is 608/356-9462.

LEOPOLD FAMILY FARM & LEOPOLD MEMORIAL RESERVE: 1,400-acre planted prairie, hardwoods and thousands of pines on its worn-out sand county farm. The Aldo Leopold Foundation actively practices restoration on the Leopold land and in collaboration with other landowners on and near the reserve. The LMF is an informal/formal agreement among six private landowners to manage their land in concert with each other. Situated along the Wisconsin River the LMF contains a diverse assemblage of plant and animal communities. Plant communities include floodplain forest, sedge meadow, prairie, savanna, oak woodland and agricultural fields. The reserve is located outside of Baraboo, WI. Reservations are required for public tours on Saturdays and last 1-1/2 to 2 hours, subject to weather conditions, and include the history and philosophy of Aldo Leopold, a visit to the Shack, and a walk through restored prairie and woods. Although there is no fee for tours, the Foundation recommends a contribution of $10/person to help support the continuing education and restoration programs. Call the Reserve at 608/355-0279. The email address is: rob@aldoleopold.org or visit the website: www.aldoleopold.org.

SCHLUCKEBIER SAND PRAIRIE: 23-acre short-grass prairie located northwest of Sauk City, WI on Co Hwy PF, west of Hwy 12. For further information contact Michael Putnam, Department of Zoology, University of Wisconsin, 430 Lincoln Drive, Madison, Wisconsin 53706 Telephone: 608/262-6205.

SPRING GREEN UNIT- LOWER WI STATE RIVERWAY: 600-acres of floodplain forest, and wet prairie. The Unit of Tower Hill State Park is located west and east of Spring Green, WI off Hwy 23. Call the Park at 608/588-2116.

SOUTHWEST WISCONSIN PRAIRIE POTHOLE INITIATIVE: Another Aldo Leopold Foundation project to protect and restore 5,834-acres of regional biodiversity within south-central Wisconsin, which historically was a glaciated mosaic of wetlands surrounded by tallgrass prairie and oak savanna, two habitat types among the state's most imperiled. This initiative emphasizes the acquisition and restoration of native prairie/savanna adjacent to or in close proximity to emergent wetlands. This initiative will help ground nesting migratory birds and protect rare and endangered plant and animal species. The project's partners include: the Aldo Leopold Foundation, U.S. Fish and Wildlife Service, DNR, WI, TNC, WI, Wisconsin Power and Light, Land Stewardship Trust, Ducks Unlimited, Wisconsin Waterfowl Association, Madison Audubon Society, Waterfowl USA, Pheasants Forever, Sand County Foundation, and several private landowners. Call the Aldo Leonard Foundation at 608/355-0279.

SPRING GREEN PRESERVE: 849-acres of one of the region's finest examples of dry sand prairie grading into dry lime prairie on steep dolomite cliffs where mixing occurs with southern mesic forest. Situated on an ancient terrace of the Wisconsin River that merges into the limey bluffs to the immediate north, the preserve is located in the driftless, or unglaciated, area of the state. The preserve resembles the desert land of the American West, a land of cacti and lizards, sand dunes and dry grasses and harbors some of Wisconsin's rarest plant communities, including sand prairie, dry bluff prairie, and black oak barrens. All of these communities, which once covered thousands of acres in the state, are now almost completely gone. What remains provide habitat for many rare and unusual plants and animals. One of the interesting mammals found at the preserve is the eastern pocket gopher. This solitary creature digs and forms tunnels about one foot below the surface of the soil, which also provides shelter for other animals. By mixing plant material and oxygen, the gopher's digging also enriches the soil. A 260-acre section of the preserve is a designated a State Natural Area. The Preserve is just north of Spring Green, WI. Call TNC, WI at 608/251-8140 or DNR, WI in Madison, WI at 608/266-0394.

St. Croix County:
WILLOW RIVER STATE PARK: 3,155-acres of rolling countryside. The Park includes two dams, two lakes, a trout stream, sand beach, hardwood forests, prairie remnants and a nature center. A finger of tallgrass prairie reaches into Wisconsin at this site. The Park is northeast of Hudson, WI. Call the State Park in Hudson, WI at 715/386-5931.

Trempealeau County:
BRADY'S BLUFF PRAIRIE STATE NATURAL AREA: 10-acre site is an outstanding undisturbed dry bluff prairie. The NA is a steep, southwest-facing dry prairie situated on a Mississippi River bluff that rises about 460 feet above the river. The prairie contains more than 100 plant species, many at their northeastern limit. Bull snake and milk snake are the prairies most common snakes. Timber rattlesnakes are found infrequently. The NA is in Perrot State Park, which is 1-mile west of Trempealeau, WI. Call TNC, WI at 608/251-8140.

DECORAH MOUNDS: 40-acre site that is a classic Mississippi River Bluff containing mixed hardwood forest and dry prairie. The Mounds are located 2-miles east of Galesville, WI. Call TNC, WI at 608/251-8140 for exact location and more information.

PERROT STATE PARK: (see Brady's Bluff Prairie above).

TREMPEALEAU LAKES FISHERY AREA: 164-acres of lakes, marsh, forest, and prairie. The area is located 1-mile southeast of Trempealeau, WI. Access to the area is from Hwy 35. Call the DNR, WI in Black River Falls, WI at 715/284-1400.

TREMPEALEAU NATIONAL WILDLIFE REFUGE: 5,754-acres adjoining both the Upper Mississippi River W&FR, and Perrot State Park. The core of the Refuge lands (4,778-acres) was a part of the former Delta Fish and Fur Farm. The NWR includes a 700-acre centrally located upland portion consisting of rolling sand prairies with scattered groves of oaks and pine plantations. A large shallow lake created by railroad dikes and diversion dikes built around the turn of the century surround this upland portion. The NWR is northwest of Trempealeau, WI. Call the NWR in Trempealeau, WI at 608/539-2311.

Vernon County:
BATTLE BLUFF PRAIRIE STATE NATURAL AREA: 31-acre site of one of the Black Hawk War battles contains a dry prairie with a diverse flora. The NA contains a 10-acre, south-facing dry prairie on a steep slope. The diverse prairie flora, which includes 80 species of native prairie plants, is interspersed with limestone boulders, sandstone outcrops, and a few stunted trees. The rapid warming of the steep, south-facing slope creates convective thermals used by migrating diurnal raptors. The NA is south of DeSoto, WI. Call TNC, WI at 608/251-8140.

Vilas County:
JOHNSON LAKE BARRENS STATE NATURAL AREA: 189-acre site contains most of the county's remaining communities of Pine Barrens and bracken grassland,[1] which were opened up by intensive cutting of aspen and small jack pine. The barrens are perched on a sandy outwash plain that slopes south, west, and north towards the streams, Johnson Lake, and the sedge meadows. The area has a wide range of animal life including smooth green snake, mink frog, hermit thrush, Connecticut warbler, spruce grouse, bobcat, and black bear. The NA is northeast of Boulder Junction, WI. Call the DNR, WI in Madison, WI at 608/266-0394.

Walworth County:
LULU LAKE STATE NATURAL AREA: 722-acre site contains excellent examples of a deep, hard, drainage lake, oak openings, and other communities that have been virtually eliminated from southeastern Wisconsin. The site includes a 3-acre dry prairie. Lulu Lake, a 95-acre, 40-foot deep, hardwater drainage lake, is situated at the base of glacial deposits in the abruptly rolling topography of the interlobate moraine of southeastern Wisconsin. The lake water is clear and supports excellent plant and animal communities. The NA is northwest of East Troy, WI. Access is limited to work parties or by permission. Call the DNR, WI in Madison, WI at 608/266-0394 or TNC, WI at 608/251-8140.

(CLIFFORD F.) MESSINGER, DRY PRAIRIE AND SAVANNA PRESERVE: (see Jefferson County above).

PICKEREL LAKE FEN: 46.5-acres that is mostly a wetland. The cessation of grazing and logging has produced the re-establishment of prairie along the northern oak-tree border. Access is only by special permission. Call the TNC, WI at 608/251-8140.

PRAIRIE VIEW ELEMETARY SCHOOL: The beginnings of a demonstration prairie located in East Troy, WI at the intersection of Co Hwy ES (Main Street) and Townline Rd.

Washington County:
RIVEREDGE NATURE CENTER: 350-acres adjacent to the

Milwaukee River and encompassing Riveredge Creek. The site contains a variety of wetlands, upland forest, and restored prairie and these attract numerous songbirds and amphibians. The Nature Center is northeast of Newburg, WI on Hawthorne Drive (Co Hwy Y). Call the Newburg Nature Center, Inc at 414/675-6888.

Waukesha County:
EAGLE OAK OPENING STATE NATURAL AREA: This 90-acre site was the first oak opening found in a statewide search and is an example of kettle hole-moraine topography. Its outstanding features are:
1. The abrupt morainal kettle hole topography typical of the Kettle Moraine State Forest,
2. The large numbers of open-grown white and bur oaks, some quite large, and
3. A prolific display of pasque flowers in the spring.
Most of the former oak opening has reverted to dry-mesic forest, but there are areas where some of these prairie species are still found. The NA is southwest of Eagle, WI. Call the DNR, WI in Madison, WI at 608/266-0394.

GLACIAL DRUMLIN STATE TRAIL: (See Dane County above).

HIGHWAY 59 PRAIRIE: 20-acres being restored to prairie by the WDOT located on Hwy 59 at the Jefferson-Waukesha County line, between the highway and the railroad tracks. Call the WDOT at 608/266-1017.

KETTLE MORAINE FEN AND LOW PRAIRIE STATE NATURAL AREA: 250-acre site contains a large part of the once extensive Scuppernong Prairie. The NA, part of a 3-mile-long low prairie and meadow in pre-settlement times, consists of several different communities. To the north of the access lane is a low area with gently undulating topography and standing water in low spots dominated by wet prairie and fen species. The area south of the access lane slopes gently toward the Scuppernong River covered with a rich wet-mesic prairie. Directly north of this prairie a degraded oak opening, invaded by brushy species sits on a small rise of about three feet and looks like a wooded island in a sea of prairie. Two other mounds, one to the north and one to the south are recovering from past disturbances and now contain dry-mesic prairie species. The NA is 2-miles north of Eagle, WI on Hwy 67. Call the DNR, WI in Madison, WI at 608/266-0394.

(CLIFFORD F.) MESSINGER, DRY PRAIRIE AND SAVANNA PRESERVE: (See Jefferson County above).

MUKWONAGO PARK: 222-acre park features a high ridge, formed during the last glacial period, which stretches nearly the length of the park. Its commanding view consists of the rolling terrain and farmlands typical of southeastern Wisconsin. The ridge contains an oak opening covered with pre-settlement vegetation including burr oak, shagbark hickory, and ground cover of prairie plants. The Park is located in the southwest quarter of Waukesha County on Co Hwy LO approximately 3-miles west of the Village of Mukwonago, WI. Contact Waukesha County Department of Parks & Land Use, Parks System Division at 262/548-7801.

NASHOTAH PARK: 450-acres offering nearly 7-miles of hiking trails taking visitors through eight distinct ecological environments, including two natural lakes, an oak forest, a rare oak savanna, a cedar glade, several varieties of wetlands and a meadow. The Park is located between the communities of Oconomowoc and Hartland, WI, ½-mile north of US 16 on the west side of Co Hwy C. Call the Waukesha County Department of Parks & Land Use, Parks System Division at 262/548-7801.

PAINT BRUSH PRAIRIE: 20-acre remnant lowland prairie in the Southern Kettle Moraine Forest. Call the DNR, WI in Madison, WI at 608/266-0394.

RETZER NATURE CENTER: 335-acres of restored prairies, a colorful butterfly garden, and an oak opening demonstration area greet visitors. The Center gives advise on land use and sells seeds and plants. The Center is northwest of Waukesha, WI. Contact Waukesha County Department of Parks & Land Use, Parks System Division at 262/548-7800 or 262/896-8007.

SCUPPERNONG PRAIRIE STATE NATURAL AREA: 185-acre site contains a 25-acre unit that was designated in 1952 and also consists of an intact wet-mesic prairie, a type that is very rare in Wisconsin, and southern sedge meadow. The NA is located in southwestern Waukesha County on the eastside of the 3,000-acre Scuppernong Marsh and includes characteristic low prairie plants. A low rise in the center of the area and along the east boundary holds scattered open-grown bur oaks, typical of this region in pre-settlement times. The Melendy's Prairie unit, on the westside of Co Hwy N, is a complex of sedge meadow, wet-mesic prairie, and degraded oak savanna. Its size and open nature provide excellent habitat for uncommon birds such as bobolink and upland sandpiper and uncommon animals including Franklin's ground squirrel, badger, and eastern hognose snake. The NA is northwest of Eagle, WI. The Scuppernong Prairie (25-acres) is 1½ miles northwest of Eagle, WI at the southwest corner of Co Hwys GN & Wilton Rd. Call the DNR, WI in Madison, WI at 608/266-0394.

Waupaca County:
MUD LAKE - RADLEY CREEK SAVANNA STATE NATURAL AREA: 100-acre site is a shallow, hard, drained lake in a wilderness setting. The surrounding undisturbed tamarack forest and the wild rice that covers nearly 90 percent of the lake form a system rarely found in the state. Mud Lake is a wilderness-type lake without access or man-made developments that covers nearly 11-acres and is only 3 feet deep. The major sources for clear, hard, and quite fertile water are seepage and springs. The lake has no inlet, but does have a short outlet to Radley Creek. Surrounding the lake is a forest of tamarack and poison sumac. To the north, the land rises into an open forest dominated by white and bur oaks, which has several groundlayer species that are more typical of prairie than woodland. The NA is southeast of Rural, WI. Call the DNR, WI in Madison, WI at 608/266-0394.

Winnebago County:
(OWEN & ANNE) GROMME PRESERVE: 608-acres of lakeshore, sedge meadows and uplands of Rush Lake. The changing water levels of the lake, combined with sedge meadow, prairie, and oak openings in the uplands, create and ideal environment for wildlife. The Preserve extends into Fond du Lac County. The Preserve is located north of Ripon, WI and surrounds Rush Lake. Call TNC, WI at 608/251-8140.

KORO PRAIRIE STATE NATURAL AREA: 3-acre site contains a high-quality mesic prairie remnant at the northeastern edge of Wisconsin's prairie-oak savanna region. The NA is northwest of Rush Lake, WI. Call the DNR, WI in Madison, WI at 608/266-0394.

OSHKOSH-LARSEN TRAIL PRAIRIES STATE NATURAL AREA: 7-acre site has a wet-mesic prairie, notable for its location at its north-eastern range limit. The NA is a series of three low prairie remnants within a 4-mile segment of the multi-purpose recreation trail from Oshkosh to Larsen, WI. Access to the prairies is along the Oshkosh-Larsen Trail that can be accessed at several points, one being off Hwy GG northwest of Oshkosh, WI. Call the DNR, WI in Madison, WI at 608/266-0394.

Wood County:
SANDHILL WILDLIFE AREA: 9,460-acres of which 9,150-acres are fenced. The purpose of the site is as an experimental and demonstration area. 400-acres are grassland/oak savanna of which 250-acres are fenced and support 15-20 American Bison. The 14-mile, self-guided Trumpeter Trail Auto Tour meanders through hardwood forests, sedge meadows, flowages, oak savannas, and dry prairies. The property head-quarters and visitor's entrance is 1-mile west of Babcock, WI on Co Hwy X. For more information call 715/884-2437 or the DNR, WI at 715/884-2437.

Fig 17

The bison (popularly known as the American Buffalo) is the State Animal of Kansas, Oklahoma, and Wyoming. This animal once roamed the Great Plains in the hundreds of millions, until the US Government decided to control the Indians by killing off their food supply (the buffalo). These animals were then taken to near extinction. When only a small group of animals survived, the policy was reversed.Today, Native American Tribes and conservationists are trying to rebuild the Buffalo population.

Picture provided by Zoological Society of Manitoba

WYOMING

Evidence reveals prehistoric human occupation in Wyoming. These groups include Clovis, 12,000 years ago, Folsom, 10,000 years ago, and Eden Valley, 8,000 years ago, notes "Taken from Wyoming Historical Facts," State of Wyoming.

"The name Wyoming is a contraction of the Native American word *mecheweamiing* ("at the big plains"), and was first used by the Delaware people as a name for the Wyoming Valley in northeastern Pennsylvania.

"Wyoming contains parts of four major natural regions, or physiographic provinces, of the United States: the Southern Rocky Mountains, the Wyoming Basins, the Middle Rocky Mountains, and the Great Plains. The Great Plains covered most of the eastern third of the state in a strip that broadens from south to north. It is an upland plateau, generally undulating, and in places broken by rough topography, low hills, and isolated buttes. The plant life of Wyoming includes about 2,200 species that form a variety of grasslands, desert shrublands, forests, mountain meadows, and alpine tundra. Several species of sagebrush are characteristic of much of the lowlands in Wyoming. The most common species, big sagebrush, forms extensive shrublands in the western two-thirds of the state. Western wheatgrass, blue grama, needleleaf sedge, Indian ricegrass, Junegrass, scarlet globemallow, fringed sagewort, phlox, milkvetch, rabbitbrush, and pricklypear cactus are also common. The grasslands in the eastern part of the state are dominated by the same species and others, but sagebrush is less common." The above was excerpted from "MSN's Encarta."

Some consider the Great Plains as limited to the short-grass prairie's former extent. Wyoming is an area that contains short-grass and mixed-grass prairies. The short-grass prairie has not disappeared to the same extent as tallgrass prairie because the soils are not suitable for farming and annual rainfall is not adequate to grow crops. Therefore, these areas are used for ranching, which protected much of the grasslands. However, much of the prairie grassland is in private hands or not accessible to the public. If one sees prairie in Wyoming, it will be short-grass or mixed-grass prairie.

The state animal is the bison (American Buffalo).

Below are some Wyoming sites where the Great Plains grassland is open to the public:

Albany County:

AMES MONUMENT: 7.5-acre monument, holding prairie dedicated to the Ames Brothers of Massachusetts, Oakes (1804-1873) and Oliver (1807-1877), whose wealth, influence, talent and work were key factors in the construction of the first coast to coast railroad in America. The Monument is 17-miles southeast of Laramie on Ames Rd. Call the Wyoming State Parks and Historical Sites at 307/777-6323.

BAMFORTH NATIONAL WILDLIFE REFUGE: 1,166 acres involving three separate parcels of land interspersed with private and state land, approximately 12-miles northwest of Laramie, WY. Except in extremely wet years, most of the lakebed is dry with a heavy salt crust. The remainder of the Refuge and the entire basin is a greasewood dominated upland, alkali flat with a limited amount of grassland. Call the Arapaho NWR, Walden, CO at 970/723-8202.

Campbell County:
THUNDER BASIN NATIONAL GRASSLANDS: 572,000-acres managed by the Douglas Ranger District of the Medicine Bow-Routt National Forest. The Grassland ranges in elevation from 3,600 feet to 5,200 feet, and the climate is semi-arid. Land patterns are very complex because of the intermingled federal, state and private lands. The Grasslands are also in Converse and Weston Counties. Call the USFS at 307/745-2300.

Carbon County:
FORT STEELE HISTORIC SITE: 145-acre site is characteristic of the Northern Rocky Mountain Basin. The variety of flora is limited, but prairie grasses, shrubs, grama and needle grass, sagebrush and saltweed bushes dominate the site. The Site is east of Sinclair, WY. Call Seminoe State Park at 307/320-3013.

LARAMIE PEAK WILDLIFE HABITAT MANAGEMENT AREA: 11,000-acres with a third covered by grassland. Isolated tracts of private lands remain in the area within the boundaries of the wildlife area. The site is 40-miles west of Wheatland, WY and 15-miles south of Laramie Peak, and is near the Medicine Bow National Forest. Call the Wyoming Game and Fish Dept (WGFD) at 307/777-4600.

MORGAN CREEK WILDLIFE HABITAT MANAGEMENT AREA: 4,125-acres of sagebrush grasslands, some conifers, aspen groves, and grassy meadows. The site is 30-miles north of Sinclair, WY. Call the Wyoming Game and Fish Dept at 307/777-4600.

SEMINOE STATE PARK: 16,970-acres with 4,870 land acres and the rest the reservoir. The Park is located on the west side of the reservoir and at the northern end of the reservoir near the dam and holds prairie. Patient visitors will see a variety of wildlife such as big horn sheep, elk, moose, mule deer, antelope, coyote, mountain lion, bobcat, fox, raccoon, skunk, jackrabbit and cottontail rabbit. Bird watchers may glimpse a Bald Eagle as well as several types of waterfowl. The Park is located 34-miles north of Sinclair, WY off US 80 via Co Rd 351. Call the Park at 307/320-3013.

Converse County:
FORT FETTERMAN: 62-acre historic site with prairie present. The

304

Fort is located 7-miles north of Douglas, WY on Hwy 93. Call the Historic Site at 307/358-2864.

THUNDER BASIN NATIONAL GRASSLANDS: (See Campbell County above).

Crook County:
DEVILS TOWER NATIONAL MONUMENT: 1,347 acres of rolling hills covered with pine forests, deciduous woodlands, and prairie grasslands supporting deer, prairie dogs, and other wildlife. Devils Tower rises 1,267 feet above the meandering Belle Fourche River. Known by several northern plains tribes as Bears Lodge it is a sacred site of worship for many Native Americans. The Monument is located north of US 94 off Hwy 24 and near the town of Devils Tower, WY. Call 307/467-5283.

KEYHOLE STATE PARK: 15,674-acre park with 6,256-acres of prairie land. The park is within sight of Devils Tower. The site is situated along the southeast shore of Keyhole Reservoir. The Park is southeast of Carlile, WY off Hwy 14. Call the park at 307/756-3596.

Fremont County:
BOYSEN STATE PARK: 39,545-acre park with 19,885-acres of land. There is prairie land here. The Park is located north of Shoshoni, WY on US 20. Call the park at 307/876-2796.

Goshen County:
HAWK SPRINGS RECREATIONAL AREA: 2,000-acres with 50-acres of land holding prairie. The sandstone bluffs, rolling hills and farmlands around the small town of Hawk Springs, WY resemble those of Nebraska, just a few miles away. The site is located 39-miles south of Torrington, WY off Hwy 85. Call Guernsey State Park at 307/836-2334.

RAWHIDE WILDLIFE HABITAT MANAGEMENT AREA: 740-acres of cottonwoods, willows along the riparian zones and short-grass prairie plants in the more upland areas. The Area is 2-miles south of Lingle, WY. Call the WGFD at 307/777-4600.

SPRINGER WILDLIFE HABITAT MANAGEMENT AREA: 1,911-acres of sagebrush grassland with a variety of native grasses, rubber rabbitbrush, sagebrush, and gray horsebrush. The Area is located 15-miles south of Torrington, WY. Call the WGFD at 307/777-4600.

Hot Springs County:
LEGEND ROCK PETROGLYPH SITE: 50-acre site with short-grass prairie. Some of the stone carvings at this site are estimated to be 2,000 years old. The Site is 27-miles west of Thermopolis, WY off Hwy 120. Call Hot Springs State Park at 307/864-2176.

Johnson County:
BUD LOVE WILDLIFE HABITAT MANAGEMENT AREA: 8,000-acres with some short-grass prairie. This area is habitat for big game species such as elk and mule deer. The MA is not far form Bighorn National Forest. The site is northwest of Buffalo, WY. Call the WGFD at 307/777-4600.

FORT PHIL KEARNY HISTORICAL SITE: 3.0-acre historic site, with some prairie present. Fetterman Fight and the Wagon Box Fight battlefield sites are located within a 5-mile radius of the Fort Phil Kearny Visitor Center. The Site is located 20-miles south of Sheridan, WY on US 90. Call the Historic Site at 307/684-7629.

FORT RENO: 14.7-acre historical site with prairie present. The Fort is located near the city of Kaycee, WY. Call the Wyoming State Parks and Historical Sites at 307/777-6323.

(ED O) TAYLOR WILDLIFE HABITAT MANAGEMENT AREA: 10,158-acres of mainly sagebrush, mountain shrubs, grasslands, conifers, wet meadows, and rock outcropping. This site is near the Bighorn National Forest and is 19-miles west of Kaycee, WY. Call the WGFD at 307/777-4600.

Laramie County:
CURT GOWDY STATE PARK: 1,960-acre park with 1,635-acres of land holding some prairie. The area is one of low-lying meadows, gently rolling hills and massive steep granite formations. The Park is located half way between Laramie and Cheyenne, WY off Hwy 210. Call the Park at 307/632-7946.

Natrona County:
INDEPENDENCE ROCK HISTORICAL SITE: 197-acre site on the Oregon Trail with some prairie. The Site is southwest of Alcova, WY off Hwy 220. Call the site at 307/577-5150.

PLATTE RIVER CROSSING HISTORICAL SITE: 12.5-acres with prairie. Call the Wyoming State Parks and Historical Sites at 307/777-6323.

Niobrara County:
WHITNEY PRESERVE: 4,600-acres and still growing. The Preserve is located in the southern Black Hills southwest of Hot Springs, SD. 2,000-acres of short-grass prairie grow on the tops of the canyons. The Preserve plans to open a birding loop in the fall of 2001. Otherwise, visitation is by permission only. Call the TNC, WY in Lander, WY at 307/332-2971 or the Preserve at 605/745-6990.

Park County:
BUFFALO BILL STATE PARK: 11,498-acre park with 4,338-acres of

land with some prairie. The Park is west of Cody, WY on US 20. Call the Park at 307/587-9227.

HEART MOUNTAIN RANCH: The preserve is north of Cody, WY. Call TNC, WY in Lander, WY at 307/332-2971.

Platte County:
GLENDO STATE PARK: 22,430-acre park with 9,930-acres of land containing some prairie. Although now mostly covered by water, evidence of two or more branches of the Oregon-Utah-California Trail that passed through the area can be seen upon close examination. The Park is near Glendo, WY off US 25. Call the Park at 307/735-4433.

GUERNSEY STATE PARK: 6,227-acres of land and 2,375 water surface acres. The park consists of high hills with generous stands of pine and juniper trees. The soil varies from large sandstone cliffs to sandy beaches. Depending on the soil, the grass ranges from the sparse to heavy stands of grass and sagebrush, and prairie. The scenic hills are part of the Hartville Uplift, forming one of the most attractive areas in the southeastern corner of Wyoming. The Park is located north of Guernsey, WY. Call the Park at 307/836-2334.

OREGON TRAIL RUTS HISTORICAL SITE: 320-acre site, holding some prairie, with ruts from the old Oregon Trail. The Site is south of Guernsey, WY. Call WSPHS at 307/777-6323.

REGISTER CLIFF HISTORICAL SITE: 0.16-acres near the Oregon Trail Ruts Historical Site holding some prairie. Call the WSPHS at 307/777-6323.

Sheridan County:
AMSDEN CREEK WILDLIFE HABITAT MANAGEMENT AREA: Windswept hills located on the foothills of the Bighorn Mountains supports grasses, shrubs and wildlife and are a good spot for bird watching. Vehicle access is limited, but access is available by foot. The Area is located west of Dayton, WY off Co Rd 92. Call the WGFD at 307/777-4600.

KERNS WILDLIFE HABITAT MANAGEMENT AREA: 4,995-acres consists of foothill benches and canyons with grasses covering the higher benches. Ponderosa and limber pine and some shrubs cover the lower areas. Kerns is 9-mile northwest of Parkman, WY and is near the Bighorn National Forest. Call the WGFD at 307/777-4600.

FETTERMAN BATTLEFIELD: 10.8-acre site of the massacre of Captain Fetterman and his men. High plains short-grass prairie is present here. Call the WSPHS at 307/777-6323.

Sweetwater County:
SWEETWATER RIVER PROJECT: The Project area includes 6-miles

of the free-flowing Sweetwater River, one of Wyoming's most extensive and intact river bottom areas anywhere in the western high desert. Dense stands of native willow along the river provide cover for numerous mammals and birds. Dry grasslands populated with big sagebrush extend for miles upland of the river. Call the TNC, WY in Lander, WY at 307/332-2971.

Weston County:
THUNDER BASIN NATIONAL GRASSLANDS: (See Campbell County above).

Section 2

CANADA'S PRAIRIES AND SAVANNAS

A vast expanse of grassland once stretched across the Canadian Prairie Provinces. Short-grass prairie, the most drought tolerant, was found in the rain shadow of the Rockies. In the moisture rich Red River Valley of Manitoba, a sea of grasses and wildflowers grew in the tallgrass prairie. Mixed-grass prairie lay between the two prairie types, blending elements of both short-grass and tall-grass prairie. Here, the wildflowers and grasses grew to knee height and huge herds of bison roamed the plains.

Mixed-grass prairie and many of its plants and animals have been and continue to be lost. As early as the 1860s, settlers were having dramatic, long-term effects on the prairies. By the 1880s, plains bison, plains wolves, and passenger pigeons had been eliminated and many other species were diminishing rapidly. The prairie itself was being lost as homesteaders broke the sod to grow crops. The introduction of exotic or weed species, such as leafy spurge and Canada thistle, encroachment by native shrubs and trees, and overgrazing by livestock have led to the degradation of thousands more hectares of Canada's approximately 24 million hectares (59 million acres) of mixed grass prairie. Less than one quarter remains, often in remnants intermingled with aspen stands or other grassland communities. However, in Manitoba only one tenth of one precent of mixed-grass prairie remains.

Fig 18

Switch Grass. See Fig 2 for root structure.

Illustration by Charlotte Adelmen

ALBERTA

Agriculture, industrial development and urbanization have transformed the majority of the native prairie landscape. 73% of Alberta's "at risk" wildlife species rely on prairie habitats. The 15% of the fescue grassland that remains in a "natural state," is mostly in small, fragmented parcels. Numerous prairie wetlands have been converted to agricultural use. Alberta's prairie birds, such as the Peregrine Falcon, Burrowing Owl, Ferruginous Hawk, Mountain Plover and Piping Plover are endangered. Alberta is, however, fortunate when compared to most North American jurisdictions, in terms of both the quantity and quality of its remaining native prairie landscapes. About 10-million acres (over 4-million hectares) of the original 23-million acres (9.7-million hectares) comprising the Grassland Natural Region, remain in a native state. Of this, 40% is deeded, with the rest in Crown ownership. The Special Areas, CFB Suffield and lands in southeastern Alberta hold extensive, contiguous tracts of native prairie, much of it without serious weed problems. The bad experiences of the 1980s drought years led to a great deal of land in the Dry Mixed-Grass sub-region being managed by rancher stewards under conservative stocking rates to retain cover, litter and moisture.

Much of the prairie in Alberta is in private hands. Areas that are ranched as opposed to farmed still have many native species, but are difficult to visit. Driving in those grazing areas gives one some idea of the original prairie.

Further, Alberta has a policy of planting some native grasses along its roadways and in other transportation related places. For further information, call the Alberta Transportation Department from within Alberta at 310-0000 and from outside Alberta at 780/427-2731.

Editors Note! The Canadian Government and some of the Provincial Governments (along with some western US States) have been slow to recognize the advantage of re-establishing degraded areas of prairie and restoring or planting prairie along their roadsides and in other places. Instead, these governmental units continue to re-seed these areas with alien grasses. Soon these alien species become a problem by migrating into otherwise pristine areas. Then these same governmental units spend money and time trying to control or eliminate these alien species, which is sometimes almost impossible to do.

Below are some areas in Alberta where the public can see prairie:

ALBERTA PRAIRIE RAILWAY EXCURSIONS: Round trip day excursions are offered on a vintage train powered by a steam locomotive. Experience the scenery, history, wildlife, and towns of the prairies. All trips depart from Stettler, AB and travel to selected destinations on 304-km (190-mile) route. Call the Prairie Railway Excursions at 403/742-2811.

ALKALI CREEK MORAINE/MAJOR LAKE PRAIRIE: This area comprises an extensive block of native mixed-grass prairie with low shrubbery and ephemeral ponds on strongly rolling to hummocky terrain. A number of small lakes dot this landscape and provide waterfowl staging and production areas. This area is in south central Alberta not far from the Saskatchewan border. Contact the Greatplains.org at http://www.greatplains.org

BEARHILLS LAKE: The shallow lake is located 13-km west of the town of Wetaskiwin in central Alberta. The site includes some grassland, shrubland and sandhill areas in the surrounding uplands and is one of Canada's important birding areas. Contact Bird Studies of Canada at 888/448-BIRD.

BEAVERHILL LAKE: The lake is located approximately 60-km southeast of Edmonton near the town of Tofield, AB. The site includes the waters of Beaverhill Lake (13,900-hectares) and the Beaverhill Natural Area (410-hectares, see below), which has flat to gently rolling open grasslands with a mix of aspen groves and willow stands. Outside of the NA, habitats are comprised primarily of rangeland with some cultivated areas. This is one of Canada's important birding areas. Contact Bird Studies of Canada at 888/448-BIRD.

BEAVERHILL NATURAL AREA: (See above) Contact Alberta's Community Development, Division of Parks and Special Places at 780/427-3582.

BOW VALLEY PROVINCIAL PARK: 7,923-acres of open meadows and forest. Trails in summer and winter provide examples of both mountain and prairie plants and animals. This is one of Alberta's Natural Heritage Sites. The Park is located east of Canmore, AB off Hwy 1X. Call the Park at 403/673-3663.

CAVENDISH RAIL LINE: 36-km long by 1-km wide strip of land along the Canadian Pacific Railway and Hwy 555 between the towns of Cavendish and Atlee, AB. The habitat consists of tall shrubs of mainly thorny buffaloberry interspersed among the exotic grasses of the right-of-way. Surrounding this strip of habitat is native mixed-grassland, interspersed with small amounts of cropland, and non-native plant pasturelands. This is one of Canada's important birding areas. Contact Bird Studies of Canada at 888/448-BIRD.

CHAIN, SPIERS AND FARRELL LAKES: A complex of shallow alkali lakes, some of which are ephemeral in nature. The surrounding landscape consists of grassy meadows (with some native grasses), aspen parkland, and alkali springs that feed small wetland areas. The Chain Lakes consists of a series of 8 small wetlands extending in a line northwest from the Dowling Lake IBA (See below). The lakes are northwest of Hanna, AB. This is one of Canada's important birding areas. Contact

Bird Studies of Canada at 888/448-BIRD.

CHAPPICE LAKE: A permanent saline lake, 2.1-sq km in size with a shoreline of 7.2-km, surrounded by native mixed grassland and a 1-km buffer of grasslands. The lake is northeast of Medicine Hat, AB and is one of Canada's important birding areas. Contact Bird Studies of Canada at 888/448-BIRD.

CYPRESS HILLS INTERPROVINCIAL PARK: 20,000-hectares (50,000-acres) in size with 11,700-hectares (29,900-acres) of forested land and 8,000 hectares (19,800-acres) of fescue grasslands. Elkwater Lake, Reesor Lake and Spruce Coulee Reservoir provide about 300-hectares (740-acres) of water surface in the Park. The majority of the Park's plateau area is defined as rough fescue grasslands. This ecosystem is unique to Western Canada and a small portion of northern Montana. The Park is southeast of Medicine Hat, AB off Hwy 41 and extends into Saskatchewan Province. Call the Park at 403/893-3777.

DILLBERRY LAKE PROVINCIAL PARK: 2,978-acres of stunted aspen growing on sand dunes combine with scattered lakes, grasslands and shrubland to create an intriguing landscape. Wildflowers abound, particularly brown-eyed Susans, crocuses, asters and western wood lilies. The park is south of Chauvin, AB on Hwy 17. Call the park in season at 403/858-3824, or off-season call Vermillion Provincial Park at 403/853-8159.

GRAND PRAIRIE: This is a modern city with a museum displaying prairie life. Call the Museum at 403/532-5482.

DINOSAUR PROVINCIAL PARK: 18,116-acres of forest and prairie grasslands, which dominate the landscape above the valley rim, and badlands where, after a century of excavation, over 150 complete dinosaur skeletons have been discovered as well as great-disorganized concentrations of bones called "bone beds." On rare occasions visitors witness the discovery of a dinosaur fossil. The Park is located east of Patricia, AB off Hwy 544. Call the Park at 403/378-4342.

DOWLING LAKE: Wetland complexes, consisting of ephemeral marshes, wet meadows (with native grasses) and alkali marshes surround this large, 30-sq km alkali lake northwest of Hanna, AB. This is one of Canada's important birding areas. Contact Bird Studies of Canada at 888/448-BIRD.

DRY ISLAND BUFFALO JUMP PROVINCIAL PARK: 3,949-acres where Aspen Parkland meets Prairie Grassland. The Park is so-named for an unusual land formation: a flat-topped mesa called a "dry island" rising 200 meters above the Red Deer River. In the distance, one sees the grassy cliff-top of an ancient buffalo jump where bison were hunted by stampeding them over the high cliffs. The Park is a mix of badlands and riparian forests where cacti and other plants typical of Alberta's Grasslands are found in proximity with species associated with the Boreal Forest. Prairie falcon nest on the Park's cliff faces. The Park is located northwest of Drumheller, AB on Hwy 585. Contact the Alberta Community Development-Division of Parks and Special Places at 780/427-4932 or 866/427-3582.

EAST PORCUPINE HILLS (CANDIDATE) NATURAL AREA: Characteristics of montane forest, sub-alpine forest, aspen parkland and prairie grassland are all found in this area. The potential NA is south of Furman, AB. Call Natural Resources Service, in Claresholm, AB at 403/625-1450.

EWING AND ERSKINE LAKES: The site is a series of discontinuous wetlands and adjacent parkland and native grassland within a largely cultivated landscape. The nearest town is Stettler, AB, which is approximately 10-km east of Erskine Lake and 20-km southwest of Ewing Lake. This is one of Canada's important birding areas. Contact Bird Studies of Canada at 888/448-BIRD.

FISH CREEK PROVINCIAL PARK: 2,938-acres of parkland, forest, and grassland found in an urban setting. The grassland is found on dry, south-facing slopes and wide areas of the valley, primarily at the east end of the park. The valley holds small patches of blue grama grass and spear grass but was mostly cultivated or used for pasture. Though the park has many prairie forbs the dominant grass now is awnless brome.[1] The Park is located in Calgary, AB at the south end of the town. Call the Park at 403/297-5293.

FRANK LAKE: A shallow lake bordered by marshes and low-lying meadows, although some of the shoreline is non-vegetated. Much of the surrounding landscape has been cultivated, but some native grassland remains. The lake is 6-miles east of the town of High River, AB. This is one of Canada's important birding areas. Contact Bird Studies of Canada at 888/448-BIRD.

GOOSEBERRY LAKE: Unlike most saline lakes in Alberta, this lake is permanent, although seasonal water level fluctuations result in extensive mudflats along the shore. Fescue-dominated grasslands, with scattered Trembling Aspen groves and areas of scrub vegetation characterize the surrounding landscape. The lake is about 12-km north of Consort, AB. This is one of Canada's important birding areas. Contact Bird Studies of Canada at 888/448-BIRD.

---

1 This is an invasive alien and in the authors' opinion should be aggressively controlled and eliminated if possible.

HAND HILLS ECOLOGICAL RESERVE: 5,508-acres (See Little Fish Lake below).

HEAD-SMASHED-IN BUFFALO JUMP: This is a World Heritage Site preserving a buffalo kill site and interpretive center portraying life on the prairies over thousands of years. The Park is located where the prairie meets the foothills of the Rocky Mountains southwest of Fort Mcleod, AB. Call the Park at 403/553-2731.

HIGH PRAIRIE & DISTRICT MUSEUM AND HISTORICAL SOCIETY: A historical museum located in the Centennial Library. Artifacts depict native and pioneer life of the area along with art and community displays, both early and modern. A regional archaeological collection dates back 9,000 years. Prairie does not grow here, but this site is still of interest to people interested in the history of the prairie, especially the influence of European settlers. The museum is located in High Prairie, AB at 53rd Ave and 49th St. Call the museum at 780/523-2601.

KINBROOK ISLAND PROVINCIAL PARK: (See Newell lake and Kitsim Reservoir below). Call the park at 403/362-2962.

LITTLE BOW PROVINCIAL PARK: 271-acres (See McGregor Lake below). The Park is east of Champion, AB on Hwy 529. Call the Park at 403/897-3933.

LITTLE FISH LAKE: This Important Birding Area (IBA, Canada) includes Little Fish Lake itself, the provincial park (see below) on the east side of the lake, and Hand Hills Ecological Reserve on its northwest. The Hand Hills area is an unusual feature in Alberta; they are a remnant Tertiary plateau that rises 146 meters above the surrounding area. Extensive areas of relatively undisturbed northern rough fescue grassland are found here. The IBA is southeast of Drumheller, AB. Contact Bird Studies of Canada at 888/448-BIRD.

LITTLE FISH LAKE PROVINCIAL PARK: 151-acre park oriented toward viewing waterfowl and other birds, and to experiencing a prairie landscape of rolling grassy hills in a near-natural state. The Park is located southeast of Drumheller, AB on Hwy 573. Call thePark at 403/823-1749.

MANITOU LAKE AREA: (See Saskatchewan Province below).

MCGREGOR LAKE: A large prairie reservoir surrounded by dry prairie uplands, badlands, eroding coulees, and native mixed grassland offer opportunities to observe marbled godwits and long-billed curlews. The lake is located southwest of Milo, AB. Call Natural Resources Service, Vulcan, AB at 403/485-6971. In addition, this IBA site includes Travers Reservoir. The IBA site also includes Little Bow Lake Reservoir and Little Bow Provincial Park (see above). Contact Bird

Studies of Canada at 888/448-BIRD.

NEWELL LAKE AND KITSIM RESERVOIR: The site includes Little Rolling Hills Reservoir, Kinbrook Island Provincial Park, some gently rolling uplands, and some native grassland. Lake Newell is a large, mildly eutrophic reservoir with extensive marsh habitat and a number of small to medium sized islands, most of which are included in Kinbrook Island Provincial Park. The site is significant for a population of Great Plains Toad (red-listed in Alberta). The area is south of Brooks, AB. This is one of Canada's important birding areas. Contact Bird Studies of Canada at 888/448-BIRD.

ONEFOUR HERITAGE RANGELAND NATURAL AREA: 27,589-acres of dry mixed grassland in three parcels along the Montana border. The area includes extensive grassland and ephemeral wetlands with minor badlands and riparian shrublands along streams. Uncommon birds found here include mountain plover, bobolink, Baird's sparrow, ferruginous hawk, burrowing owl, loggerhead shrike, and sage grouse. The area is important habitat for swift fox that has been re-introduced in the vicinity. Contact the Alberta Community Development-Division of Parks and Special Places at 780/427-3582.

PAKOWKI LAKE: This large lake is an intermittent (playa) freshwater lake and sand dune-wetland complex with extensive bulrush marshes and areas of open water. The surrounding uplands are predominantly mixed-grass prairie. The Lake is east-southeast of the town of Foremost, AB. This is one of Canada's important birding areas. Contact Bird Studies of Canada at 888/448-BIRD.

POLICE POINT PARK: 400-acre park with surrounding prairie habitat featuring cottonwood trees. Trees are rare on the prairies, therefore a river valley forest such as this attracts different wildlife and provides habitat for an abundance of birds and plant life. The Park is accessed only through the city of Medicine Hat, AB. The Park is in the northeast corner of the city off Parkview Dr. Call the Park at 403/529-6225.

PRAIRIE COULEES NATURAL AREA: 4,417-acres in the dry mixed-grass sub-region of the Grassland Natural Region. The site includes several ravines and coulees adjoining the South Saskatchewan River north of Medicine Hat, AB. Noteworthy is a number of springs and associated plant communities that are under represented in the protected areas system. Contact the Alberta Community Development-Division of Parks and Special Places at 780/427-3582.

RED ROCK COULEE NATURAL AREA: 801-acres of varying habitats ranging from prairie grasslands to evergreen forests and from scenic river valleys to semi-desert badlands. The NA is southeast of Medicine Hat, AB on Hwy 887. Call the Natural Resources Service, Medicine

Hat, AB at 403/529-3680.

ROSS LAKE NATURAL AREA: 4,800-acres includes the largest crown-owned area of Foothills Fescue. Portions of the area about 10-km north of the Montana border and south of Magrath, AB were unglaciated and as a result, the area includes a number of rare plants and insects. Contact the Alberta Community Development-Division of Parks and Special Places at 780/427-3582.

RUMSEY ECOLOGICAL AREA: 8,480-acres is adjacent to the RUMSEY NATURAL AREA: 36,872.24-acres of rolling aspen woodlands, wetlands and fescue grasslands. It is home to rare plant and animal species, such as Cooper's hawk and the prairie vole. These areas are south of Stettler, AB. Contact the Alberta Wilderness Association, in Calgary, AB at 403/283-2025.

SASKATOON LAKE BIRD SANCTUARY: 1,135-hectares, which includes Saskatoon Island Provincial Park. The vegetation on the island, which is actually a peninsula, consists of native and domestic grasses, forbs and an abundance of trees and shrubs. Most of the land surrounding Saskatoon and Little lakes is under cultivation. The sanctuary and park are northwest of Grande Prairie, AB. Contact Alberta Community Development-Division of Parks and Special Places at 780/427-4932 or 866/427-3582.

(HELEN) SCHULER COULEE CENTRE: 196-acre nature reserve surrounding the Center in the Oldman River Valley at the west side of Lethbridge, AB. There are patches of prairie vegetation on the coulee slopes in the reserve. Call the Centre at 403/329-7311.

SLACK SLOUGH: An extensive bulrush marsh is an exceptional area for viewing waterfowl, including a variety of diving and dabbling ducks, and a diversity of marsh birds. In addition, the area is replete with prairie wildflowers. The Slough is south of Red Deer, AB off Hwy 2. Call the Natural Resources Service, Red Deer, AB at 403/340-5142.

SOUNDING LAKE: Along with Greenlee Lake to the north (which is part of the site), these alkali lakes are dry in drought years. Habitat types include upland fescue and porcupine grass communities interspersed with aspen groves. There is no direct access to the lakes, which are located northeast of Consort, AB. This is one of Canada's important birding areas. Contact Bird Studies of Canada at 888/448-BIRD.

SPIERS LAKE NATIONAL WILDLIFE AREA: 64-hectares (60% grassland) which is planed to be ultimately 500-hectares. The area is one of the relatively few undisturbed sites of rough fescue grassland on hummocky disintegration moraine in the transition zone between aspen parkland and mixed-grass prairie. The uplands consist primarily of native fescue grassland with a variety of forbs interspersed with snowberry-rose and silverberry. Alkaline tolerant grasses, sedges and forbs dominate the associated wetland meadows. The area is northwest of Hanna, AB. Contact the Canadian Wildlife Service, Ottawa, ON at 819/997-1095.

TOLMAN BADLANDS HERITAGE RANGELAND NATURAL AREA: 9,143-acres of parkland and 5,436-acres of grassland. This NA preserves badlands and parts of the valley of the Red Deer River within the Central Parkland and Northern Fescue Grasslands north of Drumheller, AB. Small upland plateaus of fescue grassland are especially significant, as much of this landscape has been cultivated to produce cereal crops. In addition, prairie falcons nest on the badland cliffs. Contact the Alberta's Community Development-Division of Parks and Special Places at 780/427-3582.

TWIN RIVER HERITAGE RANGELAND NATURAL AREA: 19,000-hectares preserving an area of mixed-grass prairie. The NA supports dense nesting bird-of-prey populations, and is inhabited by rare yellow-bellied marmot and leopard frogs. The NA is located south of Warner, AB. Contact the Alberta's Community Development-Division of Parks Special Places at 780/427-3582.

WATERTON LAKES NATIONAL PARK: 203-square miles at the extreme southwestern point in Alberta, along the US border, where craggy mountains meet true prairie grassland. Buffalo once roamed this land many years ago. In this breathtaking part of the world, the majestic Rocky Mountains rise suddenly out of the rolling prairies. The vast grasslands support an abundance of wildlife, including roaming elk and mule deer. This rare phenomenon of wetlands, lakes and rivers, prairie, aspen parkland, montane and sub-alpine forests and alpine areas, offers a combination of terrain, which is found in no other National Park in Canada. The Park abuts Glacier National Park in the US. The Park is west of Cardston, AB on Hwy 5. Call the Park at 403/859-2224.

WATERTON PARK FRONT: 34,000-acres adjacent to the national park contain diverse foothills, parkland, and wetland habitat. The land is located within important spring and summer Grizzly and Black Bear habitat, and is the primary wintering area of a large Elk herd, as well as the core home range of the Belly River wolf pack. Contact TNC, Canada in Toronto, ON at 416/932-3202.

WILLOW CREEK PROVINCIAL PARK: 269-acres of rolling grasslands and tree-lined creek. The area is rich in aboriginal history, and has a teepee. The Park is west of Claresholm, AB. Call the Park at 403/549-2162.

WRITING-ON-STONE PROVINCIAL PARK: 4,245-acres making it the largest area of protected prairie in Alberta's parks network. It preserves significant coulee & prairie wildlife habitats. An archaeological preserve protects aboriginal rock art paintings and carvings, with an extensive collection of Plains Indian petroglyphs. A reconstructed Northwest Mounted Police outpost depicts the area's role in bringing law and order to the Canadian west. The Park is southeast of the city of Milk River, AB along the Milk River.

Note! Milk River Ridge encompasses a unique range of Plains communities. This is a landscape where mixed-grass prairie and foothills grasslands are traversed by low vegetated sand dunes, deeply incised ravines, unusual artesian-source wetlands, a spillway channel with remnant pre-glacial surface and two of Alberta's three unglaciated grasslands.

Call the Park at 877/877-3515 or 403/647-2364.

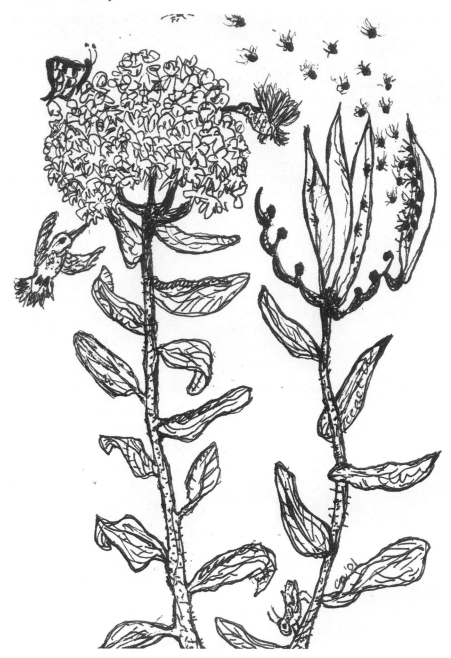

Fig 19
Butterfly Milkweed (with humming birds, a butterfly, and a cricket). See Fig
2 for typical prairie plant root structure.

Illustration by Charlotte Adelman

MANITOBA

The term Manitoba is generally believed of Cree or Ojibway Native origin meaning the manitou or spirit, a supernatural force, beating his drums. For information on the Manitoba Parks system, call the Manitoba Conservation Parks and Natural Areas at 800/214-6497.

Manitoba's Ministry of Transportation (MMOT) does plant some native grasses along some of their roadsides. For more information call MMOT at 204/945-3723.

Below are some areas of prairies viewable in Manitoba:

ALONSA WILDLIFE MANAGEMENT AREA: 10,917-hectares of aspen forest, with some native grassland. A hiking trail and Medicine Rock interpretive site were developed in cooperation with the Alonsa Conservation District. The WMA is northwest of Alonsa, MB and south of Hwy 235. Call the Manitoba Parks at 800/214-6497.

ASESSIPPI PROVINCIAL PARK: 5,757-acres where the Assiniboine and Shell Rivers meet. Present are meadows of mixed-grass prairie dotted with crocus and wild roses, and aspen forests and the waters of Lake of the Prairies, where once the Assiniboine, Cree and Anishinabe people lived. The Park is southwest of Dauphin, MB on PR 482. Call the Park at Manitoba Parks at 800/214-6497.

ASSINIBOINE CORRIDOR WILDLIFE MANAGEMENT AREA: 3,275-hectares made up of numerous parcels of land along the Assiniboine River, some units contain riparian forest as well as stabilized sand dunes dominated by little bluestem, and blue grama grasses. The WMA is South of CFB Shilo. Call Manitoba Parks at 800/214-6497.

BEAUDRY PROVINCIAL PARK: 2,320-acres along the Assiniboine River dedicated to protect and restore its tallgrass prairie remnants, supports owl, fox, beaver, muskrat and white-tailed deer. The Park is west of Winnipeg, MB on Roblin Blvd./PR 241. Call Manitoba Parks at 800/214-6497.

BERNICE WILDLIFE MANAGEMENT AREA: 65-hectares of mainly grassland. The endangered Baird's sparrow and other grassland birds nest in this WMA. The area was almost entirely cultivated at one time, but habitat was created for wildlife by planting trees and shrubs and seeding dense nesting cover. The WMA now consists mainly of grasslands, with a significant representation of native grass species. The WMA is west of Lauder, MB. Call Manitoba Parks at 800/214-6497.

BIG GRASS MARSH: The marsh is located just west of the town of Langruth in the Rural Municipalities of Lakeview and Westbourne, in south-central Manitoba, and includes Jackfish, Seagull and Chandler lakes and a variety of other habitats including remnants of tallgrass prairie, wooded areas, and willow scrub. The marsh was drained between 1909 and 1916 for agricultural purposes, but the area was found to be unsuitable for agriculture. In 1938, this is where Ducks Unlimited (DU) began its first Canadian restoration project. DU has managed the marsh since the early 1950's. This is one of Canada's important birding areas. Contact Bird Studies of Canada at 888/448-BIRD.

BIRDS HILL PROVINCIAL PARK: 8,673-acres of grassland that supports deer and hawks. The Park is north of Winnipeg, MB on Hwy 59. Call Manitoba Parks at 800/214-6497.

BRANDON HILLS WILDLIFE MANAGEMENT AREA: 722-hectares of rolling terrain, combined with dense aspen and bur oak forest interspersed with mixed-grass prairie openings, provides essential food and thermal cover for wildlife. Most of the land within the WMA was never cultivated and remains in a natural state. The WMA is south of Brandon, MB. Call Manitoba Parks at 800/214-6497.

BROOMHILL WILDLIFE MANAGEMENT AREA: 330-hectares originally established to protect grassland and wooded cover for wildlife such as sharp-tailed grouse. In recent years, its importance for the endangered Baird's sparrow and loggerhead shrike has been recognized. Portions of the WMA were cultivated before its acquisition, but mixed-grass prairie in varying degrees of quality continues to be found here. The WMA is northwest of Melita, MB. Call Manitoba Parks at 800/214-6497.

DEERWOOD WILDLIFE MANAGEMENT AREA: 262-hectares in 2 units, Deerwood and Miami, provide important habitat for deer and other wildlife. Both are primarily aspen-oak forest, with significant remnants of mixed-grass prairie. The WMA is northwest of Miami, MB off Hwy 23. Call Manitoba Parks at 800/214-6497.

DUCK MOUNTAIN PROVINCIAL PARK: 351,945-acres of rolling terrain, of woodland, wetlands and valley meadows, is home to a variety of wildlife including black bear, moose, white-tailed deer, lynx, coyote and wolves. Only the eerie, unmistakable bugling of a bull elk surpasses the calls of waterfowl and songbirds. The Park is northwest of Dauphin, MB on PR 366. Call Manitoba Parks at 800/214-6497.

EBOR WILDLIFE MANAGEMENT AREA: 62-hectares that contains mixed-grass prairie, aspen woodland and numerous small wetlands. The mixed-grass prairie on this WMA continues to be grazed, but has never been cultivated. The WMA is southwest of Virden, MB. Call Manitoba Parks at 800/214-6497.

HILBRE WILDLIFE MANAGEMENT AREA: 1,041-hectares of gently

rolling land with ridges dominated by bur oak and trembling aspen interspersed with native grasslands. The WMA is west of Hilbre, MB. Call Manitoba Parks at 800/214-6497.

THE FORKS NATIONAL HISTORIC SITE: This site in Winnipeg, MB is still home to several native plant species including big bluestem, prairie crocus, dropseed, and prairie sage. To maintain, protect and celebrate the site's natural heritage, the Site has planted a garden of native species near the Orientation Circle. Tall grasses mix with beautiful wildflowers in this living and breathing patch of history. A second re-planted prairie garden can be seen at The Forks along the Assiniboine River behind the Johnston Terminal. The Historic Site is located in the centre of Winnipeg, MB off Pioneer Blvd. Call the Historic Site at 888/748-2928.

LAKE FRANCIS WILDLIFE MANAGEMENT AREA: 6,782-hectares that includes wetlands, beach ridge, and tallgrass prairie habitats supporting Sprague's pipits and other grassland birds. An interpretive facility has been developed along Hwy 411 featuring the tallgrass prairie found in the WMA. The WMA is northeast of Winnipeg, MB at the southeast end of Lake Manitoba off Hwy 430 and Hwy 411. Call Manitoba Parks at 800/214-6497.

LITTLE SASKATCHEWAN WILDLIFE MANAGEMENT AREA: 323-hectares of terrain that is gently rolling on the uplands, with deep ravines leading down to the river lies in an important migration route for neo-tropical migrant birds. The vegetation is primarily aspen-oak forest, with some mixed-grass prairie openings. The WMA is north of Strathclair, MB. Call Manitoba Parks at 800/214-6497.

LIVING PRAIRIE MUSEUM: 30-acres of unploughed tallgrass prairie containing 160 native plant species. Set aside in 1968, as a City of Winnipeg nature park. This preserve is home to a great array of prairie wildlife, and it has an interpretive center where it sells prairie seeds. The museum is located at 2795 Ness Ave, Winnipeg, MB. Call the interpretive center at 204/832-0167.

MANTAGAO LAKE WILDLIFE MANAGEMENT AREA: 51,347-hectares of ridge-and-swale topography, eskers, beach ridges and end moraines produce varied vegetation among them coniferous forest and lakeshore marsh. Here, several prairie and eastern forest plant species reach their northern limits. The WMA is west of Ashern, MB north of Hwy 325. Call Manitoba Parks at 800/214-6497.

MAPLE LAKE WILDLIFE MANAGEMENT AREA: 65-hectares that includes a portion of the Maple Lake marsh and associated mixed-grass prairie uplands, providing habitat for waterfowl and grassland birds. The WMA is southeast of Pipestone, MB. Call Manitoba Parks at

800/214-6497.

MARSHY POINT: This area on the eastern shores of Lake Manitoba is situated just southwest of Lundar and northwest of Oak Point, MB. The terrain in this area is extremely flat, and Marshy Point is a maze of marshes and freshwater lakes that are connected by canals and extensive grassland meadows. Its rich diversity of habitats includes marshes and open water habitats, and an extensive expanse of prairie grassland that leads to aspen parkland. This is one of Canada's important birding areas. Contact Bird Studies of Canada at 888/448-BIRD.

MARS HILLS WILDLIFE MANAGEMENT AREA: 3,315-hectares dominated by aspen forest and extensive stands of jack pine. Wildflowers grow in profusion in open areas. A few grassland areas having tallgrass prairie species have been identified. The WMA is east of Libau, MB on Hwy 317. Call Manitoba Parks at 800/214-6497.

MIXED-GRASS PRAIRIE PRESERVE: Located southwest of Broomhill, MB, this preserve has been recently established. The extreme southwestern corner of Manitoba, containing the towns of Melita, Lyleton and Pierson, is the driest part of the province and is dominated by sandy soils, extensive rangeland and occasional tracts of mixed-grass prairie. Four small Wildlife Management Areas (WMAs) occur in the area. The Broomhill WMA (see above) is dominated by grassland and shrublands. Near Melita, MB, a wide variety of introduced and planted trees and shrubs have established at the Gerald Malaher WMA. Two widely spaced units of Pierson WMA are the Gainsborough Creek unit south of Melita containing native uplands, riparian forests and shrubland, and the Frank W Boyd unit near Pierson, MB dominated by native aspen parklands woods and willow shrubbery. This area of extreme southwest Manitoba is an important birding area. Contact Bird Studies of Canada at 888/448-BIRD.

NETLEY-LIBAU MARSH: An area on the south end of Lake Winnipeg holding several branches of the Red River, which empty into the lake. The area is very flat, and consists of many small bodies of water connected by channels and is interlaced with fingers of native grassland, trees and shrubs. This is one of Canada's important birding areas. Contact Bird Studies of Canada at 888/448-BIRD.

OAK HAMMOCK MARSH WILDLIFE MANAGEMENT AREA: 3,581-hectares providing a staging area for Canadian Geese. The Marsh is a remnant of the once vast St Andrews Bog set between the Stonewall ridge to the west and the lower Selkirk ridge to the east. Early drainage efforts all but eliminated the marsh, but it was restored through the construction of dykes and the creation of several impoundments. The Marsh is surrounded by remnants of tallgrass prairie and formerly cultivated areas that have been seeded to nesting cover. The WMA is north of Stony Mountain, MB off Hwy 67. Also this is an IBA site restored by Manitoba Natural Resources, Ducks Unlimited (DU), the federal government, volunteer conservation organizations and local landowners. The site is jointly managed by DU and the Province of Manitoba. Contact Bird Studies of Canada at 888/448-BIRD, Manitoba Parks at 800/214-6497 or DU in Canada at 800/665-DUCK (3825), or outside Canada at 204/467-3300.

PEMBINA VALLEY WILDLIFE MANAGEMENT AREA: 3,263-hectares in 13 units. The MARRINGHURST UNIT is aspen-oak forest and mixed-grass prairie along the valley slopes. A managed marsh unit with associated dense nesting cover was developed on the valley floor adjacent to the river. The RIVERDALE UNIT (northeast of Snowflake, MB) contains riparian woodland and some mixed-grass prairie. Call Manitoba Parks at 800/214-6497.

PIERSON WILDLIFE MANAGEMENT AREA: 264-hectares in two units. The GAINSBOROUGH CREEK UNIT (Southeast of Pierson, MB) contains remnant mixed-grass prairie and important riparian habitat along Gainsborough Creek. Call Manitoba Parks at 800/214-6497.

POPE NATIONAL WILDLIFE AREA: 31-hectares expanding to an ultimate 80-hectares. 22% of the area is grassland, which consists of a relatively narrow band of tame grass species around the reservoir and a mixture of tame and native grass species on the downstream channel. The area is northwest of Brandon, MB. Contact the Canadian Wildlife Service, Ottawa, ON at 819/997-1095.

PORTAGE SANDHILLS WILDLIFE MANAGEMENT AREA: 1,061-hectares consisting of sand dunes covered by aspen-oak forest and mixed-grass prairie. Vehicle use is restricted to protect this fragile ecosystem. The WMA is south of Portage la Prairie, MB on Hwy 240. This town goes back to Pierre Gaultier de Varnes Sieur de la Verendrye's days when it served as a portage resting area between the Assiniboine River and Lake Manitoba, and where in 1738, he built a nearby fort.

RIDING MOUNTAIN NATIONAL PARK: 1,145-sq miles of rolling hills and valleys with an expanse of boreal (northern) forest, a strip of eastern deciduous forest, huge meadows of rough fescue grasslands, and significant tracts of marsh and river-bottom wetland. The Park is south of Dauphin, MB, and is accessible off Hwy 10. Call the Park at 800/707-8480.

RIVERSIDE WILDLIFE MANAGEMENT AREA: 96-hectares located along the Souris River, provides habitat for grassland birds and white-tailed deer. It is primarily riparian woodland, with mixed-grass prairie in upland areas. The WMA is south of Brandon, MB and west of Hwy 10. Call Manitoba Parks at 800/214-6497.

SANDRIDGE WILDLIFE MANAGEMENT AREA: 1,251-hectares of limestone ridge covered by shallow sand and gravel deposits resulting in the widespread distribution of stunted aspen with native grasslands scattered throughout. The WMA is north of Inwood, MB on Hwy 17. Call Manitoba Parks at 800/214-6497.

SOURIS RIVER BEND WILDLIFE MANAGEMENT AREA: 2,196-hectares containing one of the most extensive areas of natural vegetation in southwestern Manitoba. The scenic landscape includes a significant tract of riparian woodlands and undisturbed mixed-grass prairie. Previously cultivated portions of the WMA were re-seeded to permanent cover or forage and some tree planting was undertaken. To protect sensitive habitats, vehicles are restricted to designated trails. There are excellent birding opportunities here. The WMA is southwest of Wawanesa, MB near Margaret, MB. Call Manitoba Parks at 800/214-6497.

SPRUCE WOODS PROVINCIAL PARK: 66,593-acres that includes mixed-grass prairie, sand dunes, a spruce forest, and a spring fed pond. In this park can be found the western hognose snake, two species of cacti (one is the pincushion cactus) and northern prairie skink, Manitoba's only lizard. The Park is south of Carberry, MB on Hwy 5. Call Manitoba Parks at 800/214-6497.

SPRUCE WOODS WILDLIFE MANAGEMENT AREA: 291-hectares situated on the ancient Assiniboine Delta. Its rolling sandhills have aspen-oak forest, stands of spruce, and native mixed-grass prairie, and provides habitat for elk, white-tailed deer, and upland game birds. The WMA is located on the southwest side of Spruce Woods Provincial Park (see above). Call Manitoba Parks at 800/214-6497.

STUARTBURN WILDLIFE MANAGEMENT AREA: 329-hectares is within the TALLGRASS PRAIRIE. (See below) The WMA is a combination of tallgrass prairie and aspen parkland, with several small sedge meadows. Neo-tropical migrant birds use the area as travel and breeding habitat. White-tailed deer, monarch butterflies, and several species of reptiles and amphibians are common. The WMA is north of Gardenton, MB on Hwy 209. Call Manitoba Parks at 800/214-6497.

TALLGRASS PRAIRIE: Over 5,000-acres (2,023-hectares) has been conserved by TNC, Canada to preserve a portion of tallgrass prairie that once dominated the area of southeastern Manitoba. The preserve is home to over 270 plant species, 155 bird species, 35 mammal species and a myriad of insect species, including 48 different types of butterflies. A self-guided trail is located 3.4-Km east of Tolstoi, MB on Hwy 209. Contact TNC, Canada in Toronto, ON at 416/932-3202 or the Critical Wildlife Habitat Program in Winnipeg, MB at 204/945-7775.

TIGER HILLS WILDLIFE MANAGEMENT AREA: 558-hectares in three units providing habitat for white-tailed deer, grouse and waterfowl. The Ninette Unit (North of Ninette, MB) is predominantly aspen-oak forest with interspersions of native grassland. Call Manitoba Parks at 800/214-6497.

TURTLE MOUNTAIN PROVINCIAL PARK: 45,886-acres of upland along with some 200 lakes. Moose, white-tailed deer, loons and grebes can be seen here. The Park itself is forest. However, the surrounding area has prairie. The Park is south of Brandon, MB on Hwy 10. Call Manitoba Parks at 800/214-6497.

UPPER ASSINIBOINE WILDLIFE MANAGEMENT AREA: 2,095-hectares in 12 units.
1.The BIRD TRAIL CREEK UNIT (North of Willen, MB) includes a deep ravine, mixed-grass prairie and aspen-oak forest.
2.The GAMBLER UNIT (Southwest of Binscarth, MB) has mixed-grass prairie and aspen-oak forest.
3.The MAYNE UNIT (North of Alexander, MB) has a large area seeded to tame forage and several shelterbelts have been established. It also includes native grasslands interspersed with aspen-oak bluffs.
4.The REEDER UNIT (Southwest of Miniota, MB) is characterized by flat uplands cut by steep ravines and Assiniboine valley slopes. Niso Creek runs through a portion of this unit. A Large portion of the unit was seeded to grass and alfalfa and several shelterbelts were planted. The remainder consists of some native grassland with aspen bluffs and oak on the valley slopes.
5.The RUTLEDGE UNIT (West of the town of Oak Lake, MB) has partially stabilized sand dunes underlying mixed-grass prairie, and aspen-oak forest. Several producing oil wells occur on this unit.
6.The RUNNYMEADE UNIT (Southeast of the town of Oak Lake, MB) is relatively flat with some stabilized sand dunes. The vegetation consists of aspen bluffs interspersed with native grasslands.
7.The TWO CREEKS UNIT (West of Village of Two Creeks, MB) features some native mixed-grass prairie and aspen bluffs. Formerly cultivated areas were seeded to grasses.
8.The WILLEN UNIT (South of Willen, MB) contains aspen bluffs, mixed-grass prairies and previously cultivated areas sown to grass.
9. A managed wetland was developed in cooperation with DU in the PLEASANT PLAINS UNIT (East of Routledge, MB) with dense nesting cover and shelterbelts. Call Manitoba Parks at 800/214-6497.

WATERHEN BAND WOOD BISON PROJECT: 9-square mile area features a wild herd of wood bison. The project is northeast of Waterhen, MB off Hwy 328. The admission is free and tours are available. Call the project at 204/628-3373.

WHITEMUD WATERSHED WILDLIFE MANAGEMENT UNIT: 5,682-hectares in 13 widely spaced units, which provide important habitat for deer, upland game birds, amphibians and other wildlife.
1.The EDINGTON, OAK LEAF, ROBINS RIDGE, GRASS RIVER, GLENELLA AND WALDGLEN UNITS (in the Gladstone-McCreary area) include aspen forest, mixed-grass prairie and formerly cultivated areas seeded to grasses or forage.
2.The EDRANS AND HUMMERSTON UNITS (Northeast of Carberry, MB) are characterized by sand dune formations, aspen-oak forest and native mixed-grass prairie.
3.The LOWER ASSINIBOINE UNIT (along the Assiniboine River) is made up of 10 parcels that include riparian forest and previously cultivated areas seeded to grasses and forage. Some parcels also have sand dune formations and native mixed-grass prairie.
Call Manitoba Parks at 800/214-6497.

YELLOW QUILL PRAIRIE: A rich and diverse native grassland, containing numerous grass and flowering plant species. It provides essential habitat for the rufous-sided (eastern) towhee, orange crowned warblers, elk and wolf. Contact TNC, Canada in Toronto, ON at 416/932-3202.

ONTARIO

Without the aid of fire to burn back the invading woody plants, the prairie would never have been able to maintain its tenuous foothold in the province of Ontario. In the end, neither the forest nor the prairie won the battle. The axe and the plough were the ultimate victors. Essex County, in extreme southern Ontario, retains less than 4% of its natural forest cover. Less than 0.5% of southwestern Ontario's original prairies and savanna remain. The largest surviving relicts are on lands that were controlled by native peoples, such as Walpole Island, and the Ojibway Prairie Complex, which are wedged between the developed urban portions of Windsor and LaSalle.

Tallgrass Ontario is a network of organizations and individuals working toward the shared goal of restoring savanna and prairie and related communities. To view its projects, visit its website at http://www.tallgrassontario.org/projects.htm.

Ontario is planting some of its roadside in native grasses. For more information, call the Ministry of Transportation at 800/268-4686.

BLACK OAK HERITAGE PARK: Of the areas that make up the Ojibway Prairie Complex this park is located closest to the Detroit River. The Park and surrounding lands have a rich cultural as well as natural heritage. Early explorers reported the presence of Huron Indian corn fields along this part of the river. By 1749, French settlers' fields replaced those of the Huron's. Industrial development threatened the site until 1989 when, as part of a larger land deal, the land was donated to the City of Windsor for parkland. Black Oak Heritage Park is made up of a variety of savanna and woodland species, including Black Oak woodland. It is the best local site to see American Chestnuts. (See the Ojibway Prairie Complex below).

CABOT HEAD: This area is located on the northeast side of the Upper Bruce Peninsula in south-central Ontario and extends into Georgian Bay. The area of significance includes the offshore waters and terrestrial habitats on the cape that are quite diverse and include some native grassland. This is one of Canada's important birding areas. Contact Bird Studies of Canada at 888/448-BIRD.

CARDEN PLAIN: This site is located in central Ontario to the east of Lake Simcoe. It is bordered to the north by the southern edge of the Canadian shield (extensive forests, lakes, and wetlands). To the south, much of the landscape is fragmented and utilized for agriculture. The plain consists of native grassland and alvar interspersed with scattered cropland, woodlots and some large wetlands. This is one of Canada's important birding areas. Contact Bird Studies of Canada at 888/448-BIRD.

EASTERN LAKE ST CLAIR: (See Walpole Island below).

THE ESC PRAIRIE/SAVANNA GARDEN: A restored prairie and savanna created by the Botany Dept at University of Toronto. Contact the University at 416/978-2011.

HIGH PARK: 398.5-acres including prairie/savanna, which is best represented locally in the degraded oak savanna, which is degraded because prior managers replaced the native prairie grasses with non-native grasses. High Park's original oak savanna is being restored by the City of Toronto, with the help of an active volunteer group. This will ensure both the re-generation of the open-grown black oaks that characterize the park and the protection of endangered species, such as the wild lupine. The restoration efforts includes using fire was in a small area of savanna at High Park in May 1997. The Park is located at 1873 Bloor St W, Toronto, ON. Call Toronto Parks and Recreation at 416/392-8186.

NAPANEE LIMSTONE PLAIN: This site is situated in eastern Ontario, with the town of Napanee at its centre. The site includes natural upland habitats between Belleville, ON and Kingston, ON north to Erinsville, ON and south to the Bay of Quinte. The area is a mosaic of shallow soil habitats such as savanna grasslands with scattered red cedar or hawthorn and small wood lots. Grassland habitats are in the early stages of succession, having been originally cleared for settlement. Four regionally rare snakes are present: Eastern ring-necked, Eastern milk, dekays and Eastern ribbon snake. This is one of Canada's important birding areas. Contact Bird Studies of Canada at 888/448-BIRD.

OJIBWAY PARK: 160-acre park with self-guiding nature trails on which visitors can discover and learn about the park's pin oak forest, savanna, ponds and tallgrass prairie (See Ojibway Prairie Complex below).

OJIBWAY PRAIRIE COMPLEX: A collection of five closely situated natural areas within a 10-minute drive from downtown Windsor, ON. Three of these areas: Ojibway Park, Tallgrass Prairie Heritage Park and Black Oak Heritage Park, for a total of approximately 127-hectares (315-acres) are administered by The Department of Parks & Recreation, call the Ojibway Nature Centre at 519/966-5852. Nearby Ontario Prairie Provincial Nature Reserve, owned by the Ontario Ministry of Natural Resources, adds more than 105-hectares (230-acres) of additional prairie and savanna. The City of Windsor and the Ministry of Natural Resources are continuing to acquire land. Rounding out the complex is the 117-hectare Spring Garden Area of Natural and Scientific Interest (ANSI). The Complex is located east of Detroit, MI in Windsor, ON off Hwy 18.

PELEE ISLAND NATURAL AREA: Pelee Island is the largest island in the Western Lake Erie archipelago. It has deciduous woods (temperate), savanna, freshwater marsh, coastal sand dunes & beaches, and abandoned & fallow farmland. Large areas of Chinquapin Oak alvar-savanna (a vegetation community of global significance) are located in many of the remaining natural areas. The NA including Point Pelee is a very significant birding area. Contact the Canadian Nature Federation at 613/562-3447.

THE PINERY PROVINCIAL PARK: 2,532-hectares of oak savanna, one of the largest oak savannas remaining in North America. The Park is near Grand Bend, ON. Call the Park at 519/243-2220.

RAINBOW TALLGRASS PRAIRIE RESTORATION: 20-acres of land being restored to Rice Lake Plains tallgrass prairie will be used by Sir Sandford Fleming College to teach students and firefighters how to conduct a prescribed burn and use the latest rural/agricultural fire control and suppression techniques. The restoration[1] is near Peterborough, ON and is adjacent to Rainbow Cottages Resort, on the Kenny Family Farm, in South Monaghan Township, on the north side of Rice Lake, and the west shore of the Otonabee River. Although privately owned, visitors are welcome. Contact Tony & Heather Kenny at 705/939-6995.

SPRING GARDEN ANSI: The City of Windsor announced a new program in December 1999 to acquire an additional 56-hectares of the Spring Garden Natural Area. The City will spend up to $2.2 million over a 5-year period to purchase private holdings in the 117-hectare site. In addition to being considered part of the Ojibway Prairie Remnants Area of Natural and Scientific Interest (ANSI) by the Ministry of Natural Resources, Spring Garden carries the designation of Environmentally Significant Area (ESA) by the Essex Region Conservation Authority. Spring Garden features dry prairie, buttonbush swamp and a wetland in the form of an old lagoon, plus oak savanna and woodland. An isolated population of the eastern Massasauga rattlesnake inhabits the wet prairie habitat of Spring Garden ANSI. In Canada, this snake can only be found in four regions, one of which is Windsor. (See the Ojibway Prairie Complex above).

TALLGRASS PRAIRIE HERITAGE PARK: This park is a part of the Ojibway Prairie Complex (See above.)

---

[1]The following are involved in the restoration project: Ontario Prairie and Savannah Association and the Tallgrass Communities of Southern Ontario Recovery Plan which are spearheaded by the Ministry of Natural Resources, the Natural Heritage Information Centre and the World Wildlife Fund.

TURKEY POINT PROVINCIAL PARK: 316-hectares of marshes, bluffs, and oak savanna near Turkey Point, ON. Call the Park at 519/426-3239.

WAPOLE ISLAND: A part of the Eastern St Clair Lake important birding areas of Canada. Lake St Clair, which forms part of the Great Lake system, is located in extreme southwestern Ontario to the north of the cities of Windsor, ON and Detroit, MI. Walpole Island, which is located within the St Clair delta, contains some of the most significant tallgrass prairie/oak savanna communities remaining in Canada. Contact Bird Studies of Canada at 888/448-BIRD.

Note! For more information on prairies and savannas in Ontario and on restoring degraded prairies and savannas email Mary and Peter at gartcar@kwic.com.

SASKATCHEWAN

" Within one human lifetime, the prairies have passed from wilderness to become the most altered habitat in this country and one of the most disturbed, ecologically simplified and over exploited regions in the world. The essence of what we risk losing when the grasslands are destroyed is not a species here or a species there, but a quality of life, the largeness and wildness that made this country remarkable." - Dr. Adrian Forsyth. An active settlement program in the 1800s left Saskatchewan with only about 20% of its original prairie, but the province is trying to maintain what is left. Call 800/667-7191 for Tourist Information.

Saskatchewan is also planting some prairie plants along some of their roadsides. For more information call the Department of Highways and Transportation at 306/787-4800.

Below are some Saskatchewan prairie areas:

ALKALI LAKE: The lake straddles the Montana-Saskatchewan border, and is about 18-km southeast of Gladmer, Sk and is located at the eastern edge of a hilly region called the Big Muddy Badlands. Much of the area immediately to the west of the lake was cultivated for agriculture, but some small areas of native grassland persist in areas to the north and east. This is one of Canada's important birding areas. Contact Bird Studies of Canada at 888/448-BIRD.

BARBER LAKE: The lake is in south-central Saskatchewan, near the small town of Wiseton, SK and is a fairly large lake with irregular water levels. Large tracts of native prairie remain, due to poor soils that preclude agriculture. This is one of Canada's important birding areas. Contact Bird Studies of Canada at 888/448-BIRD.

BIG MUDDY LAKE: A large saline lake in the semi-arid region of southern Saskatchewan. This region contains a wide variety of habitats that include undulating and rolling prairie uplands. The lake is located about 24-km south of the town of Bengough, SK and 12-km north of the Montana border. This is one of Canada's important birding areas. Contact Bird Studies of Canada at 888/448-BIRD.

BIGSTICK LAKE PLAIN: This semi-arid plain includes the large saline lakes, Bigstick (4,300-hectares), Crane (2,500-hectares) and Ingebright (390-hectares), as well as extensive grasslands, much of which is native mixed-grass prairie. DU has two projects in the area. One lies just to the northwest of Ingebright Lake. The other is on the west shore of Bigstick Lake, and consists of a restriction dam that was built in 1974 that produces a 100-200-hectare marsh. The closest towns are Fox Valley, SK to the northwest and Tompkins, SK to the southeast. This is one of Canada's important birding areas. Contact Bird Studies of Canada at 888/448-BIRD.

BLACKSTRAP COULEE: The coulee, which was carved by an ice age river, features a man-made, steep-sided reservoir (Blackstrap Lake), a large shallow-banked, marshy lake (Indi Lake) and wooded valley slopes. A mixed-grass prairie with wooded draws covers the west valley slopes. Blackstrap Lake contains a provincial park (see below), a ski hill, a summer camp and two town sites, Thode, SK and Shields, SK each with 20 or so year-round residences on the waters edge. The coulee is close to the town of Dundurn, SK and about 50-km south of Saskatoon, SK. This is one of Canada's important birding areas. Contact Bird Studies of Canada at 888/448-BIRD.

BLACKSTRAP LAKE PROVINCIAL PARK: 430-hectares of land not counting the lakes. (See Blackstrap Coulee above). Call the Park at 306/492-2276.

THE BLAINE LAKES: The lakes are located between the towns of Krydor, SK and Blaine Lake, SK in central Saskatchewan at the southern edge of the Aspen Parkland ecoregion. Most of the land surrounding the northern and western part of the Blaine Lakes remains in a mostly native condition (prairie). This is one of Canada's important birding areas. Contact Bird Studies of Canada at 888/448-BIRD.

BRADFORD NATIONAL WILDLIFE AREA: 123-hectares with a planned ultimate 250-hectares. The area is 33% native grassland and 36% tame grassland. The NWA is located in the mixed-grass prairie ecodistrict of central Saskatchewan. Wetlands consist of five inter-connected permanent basins, which receive run-off water from the surrounding undulating land surrounded by native grassland. This site is southeast of Saskatoon, SK and has a Ducks Unlimited (DU) cairn acknowledging donors who funded the project. Contact the Canadian Wildlife Service, Ottawa, ON at 819/997-1095.

THE BATTLEFORDS PROVINCIAL PARK: The inherent beauty of the prairies can be seen in The Battlefords Provincial Park. The Park is north of North Battlefords, SK on Hwy 4. Call the Park at 306/386-2212.

CABRI AREA: This area lies south of the South Saskatchewan River near the town of Cabri, SK. This area holds much prairie because the sandy soils limit agriculture. It provides a ideal habitat for grassland birds. This is one of Canada's important birding areas. Contact Bird Studies of Canada at 888/448-BIRD.

COLGATE AREA: This is an area located just west of the Village of Colgate, 25-km south of the city of Weyburn, in southeastern Saskatchewan. This expanse of mixed-grass prairie, surrounded by cropland, provides ample habitat for grassland birds and is one of

Canada's important birding areas. Contact Bird Studies of Canada at 888/448-BIRD.

COTEAU LAKES (EAST AND WEST COTEAU LAKES): These saline lakes are located just north of the Montana border about 11-km south of Minton, SK and are surrounded by a narrow band of native grassland. While the borders of the lakes are steep and undulating, the surrounding plateau is flat and mostly cultivated. This is one of Canada's important birding areas. Contact Bird Studies of Canada at 888/448-BIRD.

CROOKED LAKE PROVINCIAL PARK: The park is situated in a scenic portion of the Qu'Appelle Valley, featuring mixed-grass prairie, groves of trembling aspen and patches of American Elm. The Park is located southeast of Melville, SK on Hwy 247. Call the Park at 306/728-7480.

CYPRESS HILLS INTERPROVINCIAL PARK: (See Alberta Province, above).

DANIELSON PROVINCIAL PARK: 7,200-acre park located on Lake Diefenbaker and includes beaches, wetlands, forest and prairie. The native mixed-grass prairie is mixed with imported Siberian crested wheatgrass[1] and Siberian elm that the park is seeking to eliminate through burning and other management tools. The Trans-Canada Trail passes through the eastern portion. The Park is south of Saskatoon, SK off Hwy 219 and features panoramic views of Lake Diefenbaker, large coulees, native prairie vistas, wetlands, and strolls through wooded plantations. Call the Park at 306/857-2155.

DOUGLAS NATURAL ENVIRONMENTAL PROVINCIAL PARK: 16,347-acre park is a prairie oasis with access to natural sand beaches, large inland sand dunes, lush aspen forest, and native prairie on the shores of clean, clear Lake Diefenbaker. The Juniper Nature Trail is an interesting 2½-km walk through native prairie and sand dunes. The Park is south of Saskatoon, SK on Hwy 19. Call the Park at 306/854-2177.

DRYBORO/BURN LAKES: These lakes are located 5-km west of Ormiston, SK and are part of a larger complex of connected intermittent saline lakes surrounded by hilly terrain. This hummocky morainal terrain varies from gently to steeply sloping and supports communities of native vegetation typical of a semi-arid region. This is one of Canada's important birding areas. Contact Bird Studies of Canada at 888/448-BIRD.

---

1 Crested wheatgrass is not a native grass, but is in fact an invasive alien that was intentional ly imported from Siberia.

GRASSLANDS NATIONAL PARK: Two pockets of mixed-grass prairie on the Montana/Saskatchewan border, left relatively undisturbed, have been designated Grasslands National Park. The Park's size will increase as land becomes available for purchase from the ranchers until its full size of 900-sq km is reached. The Park features rolling terrain covered with tall and short varieties of grasses inhabited by prairie animals and birds. It also has miles of mixed-grass prairie supporting pronghorn, prairie rattlesnake, sage grouse, prairie falcon, burrowing owl, short-horned lizard and bobcat. Colonies of black-tailed prairie dogs live here surrounded by remnant tipi rings; vision quest sites and bison drive lanes. This is the first national park of Canada to preserve a portion of the mixed prairie grasslands. The Park plays a major role in promoting habitat restoration and species preservation and re-introduction. It also abounds with evidence of early human activity dating back thousands of years. Two land blocks comprise the Park. The Frenchman River Valley is the west block's dominant feature. Carved out by a glacial stream 10,000 years ago, the valley abounds in coulees, creeks, and buttes that rise as high as 100 meters above the valley floor. The eastern sector of the Park encompasses diverse natural features including deep wooded coulees in the north, extensive grasslands to the south, and the Killdeer Badlands in the east.

As long as 18 000 years ago, this was a prime buffalo hunting area for the migrant tribes that were the ancestors of the Assiniboine, the Cree and the Blackfoot. They followed the grassland herds, relying on the buffalo meat for food, its bones for tools, its skin for clothing and teepees and even the hooves for glue. The Park features teepee rings, examples of weapons, tools, pottery, and medicine wheels. By the 1600's, the Gros Ventre had arrived and in 1876, Chief Sitting Bull and his Sioux people found temporary refuge here after the battle of Little Bighorn. In 1870, the newly formed Canadian government began to lure thousands of European settlers to the area with the promise of free land purchased from the Hudson's Bay Company. The newly created Northwest Mounted Police enforced the appropriation of land to be distributed to the immigrants from the 170,000 existing Native Canadian and Metis. The wholesale slaughter of wildlife and the wide-scale plowing under of the grassland to satisfy the Dominion Lands Act which stipulated 10-acres be cultivated annually, destroyed habitats, disrupted interdependent ecosystems, and led to the extinction of entire species. The western portion of the Park is located southeast of Val Marie, SK on Hwy 4. The eastern portion of the Park is west of Killdeer, SK. Call the Park at 306/298-2257.

GREAT SANDHILLS: An area in the Chinook region of southwest Saskatchewan subject to strong winds where the sand dunes are moving to the east at a rate of about 4-meters a year. Here, native grass helps bind the sand together. Mule deer and sharp-tailed grouse live here along with antelope. For access to the Great Sandhills, turn south off Hwy 32 just west of the Village of Sceptre, or if traveling on Hwy 21 turn east at Liebenthal until arriving at an overhead ranch gate. Then turn north to travel through the hill to exit at Hwy 32 at Sceptre, SK.

GOVENLOCK-NASHLYN-BATTLE CREEK GRASSLANDS: This site is composed of large expanses of native grassland that are located in the southwestern corner of the province, close to the Montana border. The area extends approximately 35-km north into Saskatchewan. It is a huge region of prairie and sagebrush that is very sparsely populated. This area is important for several hundred fawning and wintering Pronghorn Antelope. This is one of Canada's important birding areas. Contact Bird Studies of Canada at 888/448-BIRD.

FIFE LAKE: The lake is a permanent prairie lake, located near the town of Rockglen, in south-central Saskatchewan. Although there are some eroded badlands in the vicinity, nearly all of the immediate sur- rounding area has been cultivated for agriculture though some native grassland survives. Rockin Beach Regional Park is located at the south end of the lake. This is one of Canada's important birding areas. Contact Bird Studies of Canada at 888/448-BIRD.

KINDERSLY-ELMA AREA: This large PFRA (Prairie Farm Rehabilitation Administration) pasture contains plentiful native grass- land habitat, including crested wheatgrass.[2] The area is located between the towns of Smiley and Kindersley, on the western side of Teo Lakes in southwestern Saskatchewan. This is one of Canada's impor- tant birding areas. Contact Bird Studies of Canada at 888/448-BIRD or PFRA in Regina, SK at 306/780-5150.
Note! PFRA implements and supports measures that protect Prairie lands, maintain biodiversity and ensure agricultural practices are sus- tainable. PFRA's avowed purpose is to restore prairie especially on marginal land.

KUTAWAGAN LAKE: This lake is located approximately 20-km north- east of Nokomis in south central Saskatchewan. The Lake is a saline prairie lake with an irregular shoreline that is divided into three basins. A large PFRA pasture encompasses much of the area around the lake. This is one of Canada's important birding areas. Contact Bird Studies of Canada at 888/448-BIRD.

---

2. As previously indicated, crested wheatgrass is not a native grass, but is in fact an invasive alien. Our source mistakenly indicated that crested wheatgrass was a native grass. Hopefully, native grasslands are actually present.

LAST MOUNTAIN LAKE: 314-acre (127-hectare) property supports approximately 260-acres of prairie habitat on one of the relatively few intact coulees that drain into Last Mountain Lake. Due to the variation in elevation, it supports a number of different plant communities such as mixed-grass prairie, aspen/shrub, marshlands, and a spring bog. Tepee rings and a sacred burial ground are located on the north side of the property. The Lake is north of Regina, SK. Contact TNC, Canada in Toronto, ON at 416/932-3202.

LAST MOUNTAIN LAKE NATIONAL WILDLIFE AREA: This is Canada's first cooperative wildlife area. From the original 1,025-hectares in 1887, more than 15,600-hectares are now protected. This area is part of a larger national system, established to protect important and unique habitats for migratory birds. Native grasslands cover 50% of the NWA. The remaining grasslands, 25% of the area, have been altered by agricultural activities but remain attractive to many wildlife species. The native mixed-grass prairie is dotted with groves of aspen and dense shrubbery whereas farmstead shelterbelts, pastures and crops characterize the areas modified by man. Last Mountain Lake has become one of Canada's few remaining oases of native mixed-grass prairie. Another project restores a portion of the NWA to its original mixed-grass prairie state. The NWA is north of Regina, SK and is managed by the Canadian Wildlife Service in cooperation with the Province of Saskatchewan. Cooperation with Ducks Unlimited, Canada has made possible the improvement of several basins where water control structures hold spring melt water for longer periods. Contact the Canadian Wildlife Service, Ottawa, ON at 819/997-1095. This is also an IBA, Canada. Contact Bird Studies of Canada at 888/448-BIRD.

MANITOU LAKE AREA: This area contains several lakes and sand hills situated mostly in west-central Saskatchewan, but also in adjacent Alberta. This hilly area includes the large, 8,000-hectare Manitou Lake as well as several smaller lakes including Freshwater, Wells, Reflex, Cipher and Colette (the last two being entirely within Alberta). The terrain between the lakes is characterized by sand hills that are covered by stunted aspen growth and native grassland. This is one of Canada's important birding areas. Contact Bird Studies of Canada at 888/448-BIRD.

MANTARIO HILLS: This site is located west of Mantario, SK along the Alberta border. It consists of a large PFRA pasture, a Wildlife Management Unit, and the surrounding lands and Cabri Lake. Sandy soils in this hilly region of southwestern Saskatchewan limit agricultural activity. Native grassland interspersed with some crested wheatgrass[1] covers the hills within the PFRA pasture. Outside of the PFRA, most of the land is cultivated and is interspersed with crested wheatgrass and native grassland pastures. This is one of Canada's important birding areas. Contact Bird Studies of Canada at 888/448-BIRD or PFRA in Regina, SK at 306/780-5150.

MAPLE CREEK GRASSLANDS: This site is located in southwestern Saskatchewan, north and west of Maple Creek along the Alberta border. This region has extensive areas of native mixed-grass prairie. The sandy soils limit agricultural activity in the area, so cattle grazing is the major land use. Bigstick Lake Prairie Farm Rehabilitation Administration site (8,151-hectares) covers a large portion of this area. This is one of Canada's important birding areas. Contact Bird Studies of Canada at 888/448-BIRD.

NICOLLE FLATS: This site is a marshy wetland that lies at the southeast end of Buffalo Pound Lake adjacent to the QuAppelle River. The Moose Jaw River flows into the QuAppelle River near the southeast end of the flats. The adjacent slopes associated with the valley contain native grasslands. The site is located 24-km northeast of Moose Jaw, SK. This is one of Canada's important birding areas. Contact Bird Studies of Canada at 888/448-BIRD.

PAYSEN, WILLIAMS, AND KETTLEHUT LAKES: These lakes in south central Saskatchewan form part of the Thunder Creek meltwater channel. This area consists of native grasslands, ponds, and marshes. This is one of Canada's important birding areas. Contact Bird Studies of Canada at 888/448-BIRD.

PORTER LAKE: This lake is located 20-km northeast of Saskatoon, SK. Except for the southern end, where native prairie still grows, cropland surrounds this shallow and ephemeral lake. This is one of Canada's important birding areas. Contact Bird Studies of Canada at 888/448-BIRD.

PORTICO PLACE: This site is a remnant native prairie in the moist mixed grassland ecoregion of Saskatchewan where less than 0.1% of the original native grasslands remain. The native grasses are interspersed with snowberry and silverberry providing diverse habitat for nesting passerine birds. Contact TNC, Canada at in Toronto, ON at 416/932-3202.

PRAIRIE NATIONAL WILDLIFE AREA: 2,933-hectares in 27 units with the ultimate planned size not yet determined. The 27 units are distributed throughout seven ecodistricts - mixed-wood forest, aspen and mixed-wood forest transition, aspen grove parkland, mixed-grass prairie, short-grass prairie, sandhill complex and Cypress Hills uplands. Each unit consists of one or more contiguous 30-to-65-hectare parcels. Approximately one quarter of the units have permanent and temporary wetlands and uplands with small to large areas of native vegetation. Most of the other units, with little to no wetlands, have upland habitat consisting of native grasses, shrubs and trees and tame grassland on previously cultivated lands. Contact the Canadian Wildlife Service, Ottawa, ON at 819/997-1095.

OLD MAN ON HIS BACK PRAIRIE AND HERITAGE CONSERVATION AREA: 13,100-acres of grassland on a high plateau. The area may well be the best intact expanse of short-grass prairie left in the province. It is a semi-arid region dominated by Junegrass, Northern Wheatgrass and Blue Grama. Contact TNC, Canada in Toronto, ON at 416/932-3202.

THE QUILL LAKES: The three lakes that makeup Quill lakes are located immediately north of the town of Wynard in east-central Saskatchewan. Native grasslands, aspen parkland, and numerous freshwater marshes surround the muddy and gravelly lakeshores. This is one of Canada's important birding areas. Contact Bird Studies of Canada at 888/448-BIRD.

RADISSON LAKE: This lake is located in central Saskatchewan, part way between Saskatoon and North Battleford, SK. Native grasslands surround most of the lake, with scattered groves of aspen and willow being located throughout the area. This is one of Canada's important birding areas. Contact Bird Studies of Canada at 888/448-BIRD.

REED LAKE: The lake is a shallow saline lake that lies parallel to the Trans-Canada highway. The towns of Herbert and Morse, SK are located on the north shore of the lake. The lake is surrounded by rangeland (which contains native grasses) and cultivated land. This is one of Canada's important birding areas. Contact Bird Studies of Canada at 888/448-BIRD.

ROCHIN BEACH REGIONAL PARK: (See Fife Lake above). Call the Park at 306/476-2464.

ST DENIS NATIONAL WILDLIFE AREA: 361-hectares located on strongly rolling land in the mixed-grass prairie ecodistrict. 16% of the NWA is native grassland, which along with native grassland, aspen bluffs with willow, serviceberry and chokecherry, are distributed throughout the NWA. The NWA is east of Saskatoon, SK. Contact the Canadian Wildlife Service, Ottawa, ON at 819/997-1095.

SASKATCHEWAN LANDING AND PROVINCIAL PARK: 13,830-acres of mixed-grass prairie supporting pronghorn, mule deer, burrowing owls, ferruginous hawks, bull snakes, golden eagles and prairie falcon. Steep rugged hills, razorback ridges, wooded coulees, and the expansive waters of Lake Diefenbaker await you at this historic river crossing in the Great Southwest. Breath-taking vistas, native grassland speckled with wildflowers and an abundance of wildlife are encountered throughout the South Saskatchewan River Valley as well as old Indian teepee rings can be found in the Park. In addition, the bison rubbing stone and remnants of the historic Battleford Trail are all located on the north side of the park. The Park is south of Kyle, SK on Hwy 4. Call the Park at 306/375-5525.

SOUTH SASKATCHEWAN RIVER: The stretch of the river running from the Alberta/Saskatchewan border eastward to the ferry crossing at Lancer, SK includes the forks where the Red Deer River joins the South Saskatchewan River. Forest dominates the riverbanks. However, most of the uplands, above the river valley are cultivated for agriculture, although some native prairie does exist. This is one of Canada's important birding areas. Contact Bird Studies of Canada at 888/448-BIRD.

STALWART NATIONAL WILDLIFE AREA: 1,525-hectares ultimately planned to be 1,909-hectares that lie in the mixed-grass prairie ecodistrict. 31% of the NWA is undulating to gently rolling native grasslands that surrounds the wetland complex, which is divided into three units (north, centre and south) by municipal roads. The NWA is northwest of Regina, SK. Contact the Canadian Wildlife Service, Ottawa, ON at 819/997-1095.

SUTHERLAND BIRD SANCTUARY: 130-hectares in the town of Saskatoon, SK. This site includes a park and zoo, known locally as the Forestry Farm Park, and a Canada Agriculture Research Station within the City limits of Saskatoon. Minimal natural vegetation exists within the Sanctuary, except for about 7-hectares of native grassland holding scattered clumps of aspen poplar and associated shrubs. Most of the Forestry Farm Park landscape consists of large expanses of lawn with exotic trees and shrubs. The Sanctuary is located at 113th St & Egbert Ave. Call the city's parks at 306/975-3300.

TWAY NATIONAL WILDLIFE AREA: 244-hectares that is planned to ultimately be 260-hectares is located on the perimeter of a depressional area in strongly rolling aspen parkland. Only 4% of the NWA is native grassland. The area is northeast of Wakaw, SK. Contact the Canadian Wildlife Service, Ottawa, ON at 819/997-1095.

WANUSKEWIN HERITAGE PARK: 300-acres devoted to Northern Plains culture including a bison kill site. On the edge of the prairie where Opimihaw Creek flows into the South Saskatchewan River, the First Peoples found peace in a place that has changed very little over thousands of years. Existing vegetation at this site is complex owing to the diversifying effects of topography and past land use. Numerous species of trees, shrubs, grasses, sedges and herbs have been identified and interpreted. The Park is located 5-miles north of Saskatoon, SK on Hwy 11: follow the buffalo signs. Call the Park at 306/931-6767.

WEBB NATIONAL WILDLIFE AREA: 427-hectares ultimately planned to be 451-hectares wetlands and uplands. Native grassland comprises 31% of the NWA. Moisture-conserving native grass species and three kinds of cactus exemplify the dryness of the upland. The NWA is west of Swift Current, SK. Contact the Canadian Wildlife Service, Ottawa, ON at 819/997-1095.

Note! American Bison are being raised on ranches in southwest Saskatchewan to provide low cholesterol meat. One of the ranches is Prairie Dawn Bison Ranch located 35-miles north of Maple Creek, SK on Hwy 21,which uses alternate grazing practices and has divided their ranch into sections for that purpose. Other ranches in the area also raise bison.

GLOSSARY

Alluvial: clay, silt, sand or gravel deposited by running water.

Alvar: thin soil layer over limestone.

Barrens: an extent of usually level land having an inferior growth of trees or little vegetation.

Bog: wet spongy ground; especially a poorly drained usually acid area rich in accumulated plant material, frequently surrounding a body of open water, and having a characteristic flora.

Bosque: a small wooded area.

Cairn:a memorial.

Choppies: areas of sparse vegetation in otherwise lush vegetation.

Coulee: a usually small or shallow ravine.

Driftless areas: landscapes that were not covered by Ice Age Glaciers

Drumlin: an elongated or oval hill of glacial drift.

Ecosystem: the complex of a community of organisms and its environment functioning as an ecological unit.

Ecotones: a transition area between two adjacent ecological communities.

Endemic: native to a particular field, area, or environment.

Erratics: occasional boulders deposited by glaciers.

Fauna: animals of a given region (ecosystem).

Fen: low land and plants covered wholly or partly with alkaline water.

Forbs: an herb (flowering plant) other than grass.

Flora: plants of a given region (ecosystem).

Glade: an open space surrounded by woods that usually refers to rocky openings surrounded by woodlands.

Goat Prairie: dry prairies on usually south facing hill tops.

Illinoian Glaciation: about 500,000 years ago, the third Ice Age Glacier extended south to a latitude of 37.5 degrees North in Illinois, setting a record.

Hectare: a land measurement equal to 2.471 acres.

Hogback: a ridge of land with a sharp summit and steeply sloping sides formed by the outcropping edges of steeply inclined strata.

Kame: a short ridge, hill, or mound of stratified drift deposited by glacial meltwater.

Kettleholes: an area formed by the melting of an isolated piece of ice broken off from a glacier as it retreats. (See potholes)

Local Ecotype: a subdivision of an ecospecies that survives as a distinct group through environmental selection and isolation.

Loess: an unstratified usually buff to yellowish brown loamy deposit found in North America, Europe, and Asia and believed to be chiefly deposited by the wind.

Marhly: loose soil containing calcium carbonate.

Mesic: characterized by, relating to, or requiring a moderate amount of moisture.

Moraine: an accumulation of earth and stones carried and finally deposited by a glacier.

Native: an original or indigenous inhabitant.

Petroglyphs: rock paintings by prehistoric peoples.

Playa: the flat-floored bottom of an undrained basin that becomes at times a shallow lake.

Pleistocene: relating to a period of geological time from about 2 million years ago and ending 10,000 years ago.

Potholes: a sizable rounded often water-filled depression in land.

Prairie: a tract of grassland that is mostly grass but contains a percentage of forbs.

Prairie Hammock: flatland with sand/organic soil over marl or limestone substrate.

Pre-settlement: the time before the first European settlements in North America.

Relict: a persistent remnant of an otherwise extinct flora or fauna.

Remnant: plant community that has survived on a site from a prior time to the present day.

Restore: to return something to a former or unimpaired state.

Savanna: a plant community that is a mix of forest, prairie and unique species. Tree species will often include oaks and hickories grown at a wide enough spacing not to make a canopy.

Scarp: a line of cliffs produced by faulting or erosion.

Shelterbelts: areas planted to shelter other areas from the weather in order to protect the flora and fauna.

Shinnery oak: a freely branched, clonal, thicket-forming shrub or small tree.

Slough: an area of soft muddy ground, swamp or swamp like region.

Swale: a low-lying often wet stretch of land.

Tamarack: a larch of northern North America that inhabits usually moist or wet areas.

Tipi: teepee

Transect: a small area that represents a larger area; a remnant prairie that represents the larger extinct prairie.

Wisconsin Glacier: The last glacier to cover northern North America was called the Wisconsin Glacier because Wisconsin has some of the best-preserved evidence of this glacier.

Xeric: adapted to a dry environment.

Bibliography

The Audubon Society Nature Guides GRASSLANDS by Loren Brown, Alfred A. Knopf, Inc 1989.

A Cajun Prairie Restoration Journal: 1988-1995, M. F. Vidrine, C. M. Allen and W. R. Fontenot.

A Sense of the American West by James E. Sherow 1998.

An Account of an Expedition from Pittsburgh to the Rocky Mountains (performed in the years 1819 and '20 by Order of the Hon. J. C. Calhoun, Secretary of War under the Command of Major Stephen H.Long) by Edwin James.- 2 volumes with Atlases.

Bones Boats & Bison – Archaeology and the First Colonization of Western North America by E. James Dixon, University of New Mexico Press 2001.

Boots and Saddles, or, Life in Dakota with General Custer. By Elizabeth B. Custer. 1885, University of Oklahoma Press 1961.

Central Plains Prehistory by Waldo Wedel 1968.

Cabeza de Vaca's Adventures in the Unknown Interior of America 1542, translated by Cyclone Covey. University of New Mexico Press 1998.

Climate – A Determining Factor in Locating Missouri's Prairie by Dr. Wayne L. Decker, Missouri Prairie Journal. Summer 1999 Vol. 20 No. 3.

Conservation Directory- issued by the National Wildlife Federation, 8925Leesburg Pike, Vienna, VA 22184. Phone: 410/516-6583

Contested Plains by Elliot West 1988.

Edible Wild Plants of the Prairie – An Ethnobotanical Guide. By Kelly Kindscher, University of Kansas Press. 1987.

Everyday Life of the North American Indian by Jon Manchip White. Indian Head Books. 1979.

Flora of Missouri, by Julian Steyermark, Iowa State University Press. 1963.

Hernando de Soto by David Ewing Duncan 1995.

Grasses of Louisiana, 1992, Charles Allen.

Grasses of the Texas Gulf Prairies and Marshes, Stepphan L. Hatch, Joseph L. Schuster and D. Lynne Drawe 1999.

Grassland-The History, Biology, Politics and Promise of the American Prairie, by Richard Manning. Penguin Books 1997.

The Great Ice Age by Louis L. Ray. U. S. Department of the Interior, U.S. Geological Survey.

The Journals of Lewis and Clark, 1803-05, Edited by Bernard DeVoto, Houghton Mifflin 1953.

LaSalle - Explorer of the North American Frontier, by Anka Mulstein. Arcade Publishing 1994.

Letters and Notes on the Manners, Customs, and Conditions of NORTH AMERICAN INDIANS, by George Catlin. 2 volumes. 1844, Dover Publications 1973.

Life in Prairieland by Eliza W. Farnham 1836.

Majestic Journey- Coronado's Inland Empire, by Stewart L Udall 1987.

My Life on the Plains, or Personal Experiences with Indians. By General George Armstrong Custer, 1872, University of Oklahoma Press. 1962.

Narrative Journal of Travels Through Northwestern Regions of the United States Extending from Detroit through the Great Chain of American Lakes to the Sources of the Mississippi River in the year 1820 by Henry Rowe Schoolcraft, 1821, Edited by Mentor E. Williams. Michigan State University Press 1992.

Native Americans - A Portrait - the Art & Travels of Charles Bird King, George Catlin, and Karl Bodner, by Robert J Moore Jr. Stewart, Tabore & Chang 1997.

Noah's Garden-restoring the ecology of our own backyards, by Sara Stein. Houghton Mifflin Co 1993.

The Oregon Trail By Francis Parkman 1849. Signet Classics 1978.

The Plains Indians, by Colin F. Taylor. Salamander Books 1994.

Pleistocene Extinctions by Paul S. Martin and Montgomery Slatkin 1967.

Prairie City-the story of an American Community, by Angie Debo, University of Oklahoma Press 1998.

Prairie Conservation- Preserving North America's Most Endangered Ecosystem, Edited by Fred Samson and Fritz Knopt 1996.

Prairie Establishment and Landscaping by William E. McClain. Division of Natural Heritage, Illinois Department of Natural Resources 1977.

The Prairie Garden-70 Native Plants You Can Grow in Town or Country. By Robert & Beatrice Smith. University of Wisconsin Press 1980.

The Prairie in 19th Century American Poetry, by Steven Olson. University of Oklahoma Press 1994.

The Prairie Logbooks – Dragoon Campaigns to the Pawnee Villages in 1844 and to the Rocky Mountain in 1845, by Lieutenant J. Henry Carleton, Edited by Louis Pelzer. University of Nebraska Press 1983.

Prairie Plants and Their Environment – A Fifty Year Study in the Midwest by J. E. Weaver, University of Nebraska Press 1968.

Prairie Plants of Illinois, by John W Voight & Robert H Mohlenbrock Illinois Department of Conservation.

Relics of the Past: Prairies by Roger Troutman, Guy L. Denny, Roger W. Bruckman. Ohio's Natural Heritage 1979.

Requiem for a Lawnmower and other essays on easy gardening with native plants, by Sally Wasowskii with Andy Wasowski. Taylor Press 1992.

Restoring the Tallgrass Prairie, An Illustrated Manual for Iowa and the Upper Midwest by Shirley Shirley. University of Iowa Press 1994.

Roadside Wildflowers of the Southern Great Plains, by Craig Freeman and Eileen Schofield, University of Kansas Press 1991.

The Santa Fe Trail, by R L Duffus, University of New Mexico Press 1999.

Sunlight and Storm- the Great American Plains, by Alexander B. Adams. G P Putnam 1977.

Tabeau's Narrative of Loisel's Expedition of the Upper Missouri.(1803-5), Edited by Annie Heloise Abel and translated from the French by Rose Abel Wright 1939.

Tallgrass Prairie, The Inland Sea by Patricia Duncan 1978.

Tallgrass Prairie Wildflowers-A Field Guide, by Doug Ladd. Falcon Press 1995.

Tallgrass Prairie, by John Madson, The Nature Conservancy/Falcon Press 1993.

The Tallgrass Restoration Handbook for Prairies, Savannas and Woodlands, Edited by Stephen Packard and Cornelia F. Mutel. Island Press 1997.

The Vegetation of Wisconsin- An Ordination of Plant Communities by John T. Curtis, University of Wisconsin Press 1959.

The West by Geoffrey C. Ward 1996.

The Westward Crossings by Jeanette Mirsky 1946.

Travels in the Interior of America in the years 1809, 1810 and 1811, by John Bradbury, Forward by Donald Jackson, University of Nebraska Press. 1986.

Travels in the Interior of North America 1751-1762 by Jean-Bernard Bossu, Translated and edited by Seymour Feiler 1962.

Where the Sky Began, by John Madson, Houghton Mifflin Co, 1982.

Wild Animals and Settlers on the Great Plains by Eugene D. Fleharty. University of Oklahoma Press 1995.

The Wildflower Gardener's Guide - Midwest, Great Plains, and Canadian Prairies, by Henry W Art. Story Communications Inc 1994.

Wildflowers of Houston, 1993, John & Gloria Tveten.

Wildflowers of Texas, 1994, Geyata Ajilvsgi.

Wildflowers of the Tallgrass Prairie-The Upper Midwest, by Sylvan T. Runkel and Dean M. Roosa, Iowa State University Press 1989.

Note: A great deal of information about various aspects of the prairie is available through numerous national and local environmental and prairie-specific organizations and state, local and federal agencies including Departments of Natural Resources and Transportation and also from many of the prairie preserves listed in this book. Contact these resources and libraries to obtain materials about the prairie's history, its flora and fauna, plant identification and how to grow and/or restore prairie.

INDEX

Pocket gopher, 79
Point Pelee, 331
Prairie
  Blackland Prairie, 260, 262
  bluff prairie, 286, 288, 292,
  295, 297, 298
  cemetery prairie, 43, 65, 81,
  82, 83, 85, 86, 95, 100, 104,
  107, 108, 225, 226
  coastal prairie, 257, 258, 270
  dry sand prairie, 291
  goat prairie, 106, 107, 145,
  157
  gravel prairie, 56
  Kansas Prairie, 197
  Konza Prairie, 123, 127
  loess hill prairie, 83, 113, 114
  mesic prairie, 76, 81
  nine-mile prairie, 192
  loess prairie, 38
  prairie pothole, 64, 144
  ripgut wet prairie, 164, 175,
  176
  sand prairie, 124, 286
  sand prairies, 56, 74
  sandhills prairie, 195
  Schwartz Prairie, 174
  slump prairie, 223
  upland prairie, 58
  wet prairie, 293
  wet-mesic prairie, 293, 294
Prairie chicken, 194
  Attwater's prairie chickens,
  259, 263
  greater prairie chicken, 36,
  78, 148, 163, 194
  lesser prairie chicken, 199
Prairie dogs
  black-tailed prairie dogs, 20,
  187, 242, 255, 260
  prairie dog town, 233, 247
Prairie grouse, 188
Prairie Passage, 98, 99, 141, 161,
  227, 252

Prairie pothole, 109, 113, 296
Prairie Spirit Trail, 120, 123
Prairie vole, 147
Pronghorn, 30, 125, 255, 260
R
Rattlesnake
  Massasauga rattlesnake, 171
  timber rattlesnake, 47
Roosevelt
  Theodore Roosevelt, 183, 207
S
Sagebrush grasslands, 177
Savanna, 170
  black oak savanna, 96
  dry oak savanna, 145
  dry sand savanna, 150
  oak savanna, 150, 153, 154,
  156, 291, 301
Sharp-tailed grouse, 183, 217,
  220, 322
Shinnery oak-grassland, 229
Sioux Quartzite
Slough, 317
T
Tallgrass Prairie National
  Preserve, 121
Tamarack, 94
Trails
  George S Mickelson Trail,
  242, 244
  Glacial Drumlin State Trail,
  288, 299
  Maah Daah Hey Trail, 212
Transect, 26
W
Walpole Island, 332
Weaver
  J E Weaver, 192
Western hognose snake, 79
Wolf, 328
Wright-Patterson Air Force Base,
  223

About the Authors

Charlotte Adelman and Bernard L. Schwartz spent their marriage practicing law and bird watching and enjoying nature. They took early retirements and transformed their backyard into an urban prairie. The success of this project inspired a more intense interest in the North American prairie. The results are this book and another book, which will examine the natural and human history of the prairie.

Photograph by L Sanford Blustin

Notes